# OUR PLACE IN THE SUN:
# CANADA AND CUBA IN THE CASTRO ERA

Penned during the transition of power from Fidel Castro to Raúl Castro, *Our Place in the Sun* explores the Canadian-Cuban relationship from 1959 to the present day. The essays in this volume reflect upon the past but also explore the internal issues and external forces that will continue to influence the Canada-Cuba association in the years to come.

Many of this volume's contributors draw upon newly declassified sources and original interviews, providing unique insight into the historical, economic, and political realities affecting the Canada-Cuba connection. Featuring eleven original essays by a variety of scholars, including the former Canadian Ambassador to Cuba, Mark Entwistle, this important interdisciplinary collection calls into question past understandings of the Canadian-Cuban relationship. It is a must-read for anyone interested in Canadian and Cuban history of the last half-century and the dynamics of North American politics more broadly.

ROBERT WRIGHT is an associate professor in the Department of History at Trent University.

LANA WYLIE is an assistant professor in the Department of Political Science at McMaster University.

EDITED BY ROBERT WRIGHT AND
LANA WYLIE

# Our Place in the Sun

## Canada and Cuba in the Castro Era

UNIVERSITY OF TORONTO PRESS
Toronto Buffalo London

© University of Toronto Press Incorporated 2009
Toronto Buffalo London
www.utppublishing.com
Printed in Canada

ISBN 978-0-8020-9970-9 (cloth)
ISBN 978-0-8020-9666-1 (paper)

Printed on acid-free, 100% post-consumer recycled paper with
vegetable-based inks.

---

**Library and Archives Canada Cataloguing in Publication**

Our place in the sun : Canada and Cuba in the Castro era / edited by
Robert Wright and Lana Wylie.

Includes bibliographical references and index.
ISBN 978-0-8020-9970-9 (bound). – ISBN 978-0-8020-9666-1 (pbk.)

1. Canada – Foreign relations – Cuba. 2. Cuba – Foreign relations –
Canada. 3. Canada – Relations – Cuba. 4. Cuba – Relations –
Canada – Foreign relations – 1945–. I. Wright, Robert A. (Robert
Anthony), 1960–. II. Wylie, Lana, 1968–. III. Title: Canada and
Cuba in the Castro era.

FC 251.C82O97 2009    327.7107291    C2009-902129-3

---

This book has been published with the help of a grant from the Canadian
Federation for the Humanities and Social Sciences, through the Aid to
Scholarly Publications Program, using funds provided by the Social Sciences
and Humanities Research Council of Canada.

University of Toronto Press acknowledges the financial assistance to its
publishing program of the Canada Council for the Arts and the Ontario
Arts Council.

University of Toronto Press acknowledges the financial support for its
publishing activities of the Government of Canada through the Book
Publishing Industry Development Program (BPIDP).

*For Helena, Anna, Michael, Duncan, and Chloe*

# Contents

# Contributors

**Greg Donaghy** is the head of the Historical Section of Foreign Affairs and International Trade Canada, and general editor of its series *Documents on Canadian External Relations*. He is the author of *Tolerant Allies: Canada and the United States, 1963–1968* (2002).

**Mark Entwistle** was Canada's ambassador to Cuba from 1993 to 1997 and is currently a leading private-sector specialist on Cuban affairs and business, director of several companies, and a fellow of the Canadian Defence and Foreign Affairs Institute.

**Mary Halloran** is a member of the Historical Section at Foreign Affairs and International Trade Canada. She is co-author, with John Hilliker and Greg Donaghy, of the third volume of the department's official history, which covers the years of the Trudeau government.

**John M. Kirk** is professor of Latin American studies at Dalhousie University. He is the author/co-editor of twelve books on Cuba, of which the most recent are *A Contemporary Cuba Reader: Reinventing the Revolution* (2008), *Sesenta años de relaciones bilaterales: Canadá y Cuba* (2007), and *Redefining Cuban Foreign Policy: The Impact of the Special Period* (2006).

**Hal Klepak** is professor of history and warfare studies at the Royal Military College of Canada.

**Peter McKenna** is an associate professor in the Department of Political Studies at the University of Prince Edward Island in Charlottetown. He is the co-author of *Fighting Words: Competing Voices from Revolutionary*

*Cuba* (forthcoming), the co-author of *Canada-Cuba Relations: The Other Good Neighbor Policy* (1997), and the author of *Canada and the OAS: From Dilettante to Full Partner* (1995).

**Dennis Molinaro** is a doctoral candidate in history at the University of Toronto. His research focuses on intelligence and international relations.

**Don Munton** is professor and founding chair of the International Studies Program at the University of Northern British Columbia. He taught previously at the University of British Columbia, the University of Toronto, and Dalhousie University, and is the co-author with David Welch of *The Cuban Missile Crisis: A Concise History* (2007).

**Archibald R.M. Ritter** was a professor in the Department of Economics and the Norman Paterson School of International Affairs at Carleton University, where since July 2008 he has been a Distinguished Research Professor Emeritus. His work has been in the area of development, with a focus on Africa and Latin America and especially Cuba. He has published numerous articles and authored or edited seven books on Cuba and Latin America.

**David Sheinin** is professor of history at Trent University and académico correspondiente in the Academia Nacional de la Historia de la República Argentina. His most recent book is *Argentina and the United States: An Alliance Contained* (2006).

**David Vogt** is an honours international studies graduate of the University of Northern British Columbia and has recently completed his master's degree at the Norman Paterson School at Carleton University.

**Cynthia Wright** teaches in the School of Women's Studies at York University. Her diverse research interests include Canada, Cuba, and the global 1960s as well as migration and the politics of no-borders movements.

**Robert Wright** teaches history at Trent University in Oshawa, Ontario. He is the author of four books, including *Three Nights in Havana: Pierre Trudeau, Fidel Castro and the Cold War World* (2007).

**Lana Wylie** is assistant professor of political science at McMaster University in Hamilton, Ontario. Her research focuses on Canadian and American foreign policy, the Caribbean, and international-relations theory. She is a co-editor of *Canadian Foreign Policy in Critical Perspective* (2009).

# Preface

This book was written and published during what most Western observers called a 'transitional' period in Cuba. For the Cuban people, however, it has been mostly business as usual.

Fidel Castro ceded power provisionally to his brother Raúl in July 2006 and on 18 February 2008 announced that he would not stand for re-election as president of the State Council and commander-in-chief. Less than a week later, the Cuban National Assembly voted Raúl Castro its new president. 'Fidel is irreplaceable,' Raúl said in his victory speech, 'and the people shall continue his work when he is no longer physically with us. His ideas will always be with us, the same ideas that have made it possible to build the beacon of dignity and justice our country represents.' As this book goes to press, Raúl Castro remains firmly at the helm in Cuba, and Fidel Castro is still in a state of almost-total seclusion, visible to Cubans and to the wider world only as the author of his 'Reflections' column in *Granma*. Political and economic reform is in the air in Cuba, but to date it has been piecemeal and cautious. And, despite Raúl Castro's public statement that he is open to normalizing diplomatic relations with the United States – 'on an equal plane,' as he puts it – the American embargo remains in force. Cuba's relations with Canada, meanwhile, remain cordial and correct, as they have for over half a century.

*Our Place in the Sun* takes a timely look back at the Cuban-Canadian relationship since Fidel Castro and his *barbudos* took power in January 1959. Though we, as editors, agreed from the outset that this book should be interdisciplinary and as wide-ranging as possible, readers will note that historians are disproportionately represented in its pages. Even the non-historians have kept their eyes keenly trained on the documentary record, eschewing fanciful prognostications – the stock-in-trade of so many Cuba-watchers in the press and elsewhere – in favour of careful consideration of the Canadian-Cuban reality as it has evolved since 1959. We are well aware that events in tumultuous times have a way of outpacing the scholarly writing that seeks to illuminate them. But we are confident that, whatever the post-Castro future holds for Cuba, and thus for Canadian-Cuban relations, *Our Place in the Sun* will have continuing relevance.

Our debts are many, and it gives us great pleasure to acknowledge them here. Our thanks go, first and foremost, to the contributors to *Our Place in the Sun*, with whom it has been a pleasure to work. Meaghan Willis, Lucy Draper-Chislett, Calum McNeil, A.J. Rowley, and Maegan Baird provided invaluable assistance at the research and manuscript-preparation phases of the project, for which we are indebted. We believe ourselves fortunate to have had as our editor at the University of Toronto Press Dan Quinlan, and as our copy editor Curtis Fahey. Len Husband of UTP also deserves a special word of thanks, for helping us shape this project its early days. We are indebted to our friends and colleagues in the Cuban-Canadian Working Group at the University of Havana, particularly Raúl Rodriguez and Jorge Mario Sanchez, and also to Beatriz Días, convener of the University of Havana's annual Conferencia de Estudios Canadienses. Lastly, for their assistance and hospitality over the years, we would like to thank our friends at the Canadian embassy in Havana, past and present – James Hyndman, Jean-Pierre Juneau, Alexandra Bugailiskis, Simon Cridland, Marc-Antoine Dumas, and especially Ram Kamineni.

OUR PLACE IN THE SUN:
CANADA AND CUBA IN THE CASTRO ERA

# Introduction: Worlds Apart

ROBERT WRIGHT AND LANA WYLIE

*Our Place in the Sun: Canada and Cuba in the Castro Era* is a collection of ten original essays by thirteen Canadian scholars; the conclusion takes the form of a short retrospective by a former Canadian ambassador to Cuba, Mark Entwistle. This book was inspired in part by Fidel Castro's unexpected cession of power to his brother Raúl in the summer of 2006, but it makes no claim to be the definitive treatment of Canada's fifty-year relationship with revolutionary Cuba. Rather, the essays in *Our Place in the Sun* are impressionistic, in the best sense of the term. They evince their authors' long experience of research and writing on Cuba, many of them drawing for the first time on newly declassified sources that call into question much of what we thought we knew about the Canadian-Cuban relationship. And yet they demonstrate how much remains beyond the reach of Canadian researchers, and how persistently the inner workings of the Cuban Revolution remain shrouded in mystery.

This Introduction is intended to afford some context for the essays that follow, first, by providing some historical background on Cuba's relationships with the United States and Canada, and second, by identifying some of the overarching themes that continue to colour these relationships.

## Cuba, Spain, the United States, and Canada

Even to the casual observer, Cuba seems a world away from Canada. In mid-winter, when most Canadian cities are iced in, Cuba's sand beaches, tropical climate, and balmy trade winds beckon like a siren song. Aboriginal peoples inhabited the island for approximately five millennia starting in 3500 BC, but it was Christopher Columbus who 'discovered' it in the fateful year 1492. Starting with Samuel de Champlain, who is thought to have visited Cuba in 1601 en route to founding New France, Canadians have been discovering it ever since.

As indelibly as Fidel Castro's Revolution has stamped contemporary Cuba, it is fair to say that the essential contours of Cuban life have for the last century been shaped by four elements over which neither the *Comandante* nor his predecessors have had much control: geography, climate, the legacy of Spanish colonialism, and the proximity of the United States.

In contrast with Canada, a vast and resource-rich land, climactically stable, with a long history of peaceful progress towards parliamentary democracy, Cuba is a poor island nation with an extremely violent history, a single-crop economy (sugar), and a climate that regularly delivers devastating hurricanes and ruinous drought. The areas of Cuba today visited by hundred of thousands of Canadian *turistas* annually – Old Havana and the exclusive beach-resort enclaves of Varadero and Holguin – are pockets of luxury far removed from the hardscrabble existence of most ordinary Cubans. But in the countryside, in the city side streets, and in casual conversation with Cubans, the day-to-day challenges of life on the island are impossible to ignore. Fidel Castro blames the U.S. embargo for his country's difficult economic conditions, but, as he also regularly tells visiting foreigners, Cuba is poor because most Caribbean and Latin American nations are poor. Thumbing through a Toronto or New York newspaper at virtually any point over the last century, one can't but help notice that the two items from Cuba that consistently made the headlines were the booms and busts of the island's staples-based economy and the casualty tolls from the autumn hurricane season. These are facts of life in Cuba that Castro inherited. They will outlive him.

To the surprise of no one, Cuba's Spanish colonizers proved every bit as unforgiving as its climate. Columbus's son, Diego, conquered the island mercilessly and established the first Spanish settlement at Santiago in 1511. The indigenous Arawak people were vanquished in the process, their leader Hatuey burned at the stake, their young people enslaved, their numbers reduced from 100,000 to 5,000 within one generation. Imperial rivalry led to a brief British occupation of Havana in 1762 but this would turn out to be the only hiatus in four centuries of unbroken Spanish rule. In the mid-sixteenth century, the enslavement of Africans began, providing the labour for Cuba's growing plantation economy and injecting into Cuban culture the many African traditions that continue to flavour the island's music, cuisine, and religion.

The American Revolution of 1776 turned out to be revolutionary for Cuba as well. It freed the Thirteen Colonies from British trade rules, opening up the United States as a vast market for Cuban sugar, the key ingredient in rum. By the mid-nineteenth century, the volume of Cuba's trade with the United States surpassed that of its trade with Spain. Four times the United States offered to purchase Cuba, annexation appearing to some Americans as the natural end point of the Cuban-American relationship and the sine qua non of Manifest Destiny. Within Cuba, resentment of Spanish rule inspired a revolutionary temperament that borrowed heavily from the idealism of the American Revolution and influenced generations of Cuban rebels including Fidel Castro. In 1868 the first war for Cuban independence, known locally as the Ten Years' War, was launched. After a decade of armed struggle against the Spanish, with upwards of 250,000 Cuban dead, the insurgents threw in the towel in exchange for a general amnesty. Most of the rebel leaders went to the United States. The result was the first of many Cuban exile movements to be based in the United States whose cause would be the liberation of their homeland.

This first generation of exiles planned and launched the second Cuban war of independence, also known as the Cuban Insurrection, in 1895. The leading figure in the independence movement – indeed, the leading figure in modern Cuban history prior to Fidel Castro – was the poet and nationalist José Martí. While in exile, Martí founded the Partido Revolucionarío, an umbrella organization for the many Cuban groups then organizing against the Spanish. In 1895 he returned to Cuba to fight in the revolutionary war he had inspired almost single-handed, dying in one of the first battles atop the white horse on which he was later to be immortalized by many a Cuban sculptor. The man to whom Fidel Castro believes he owes his greatest political debt is neither Marx nor Lenin but Martí. Seldom in his long career has the Comandante given a major speech to the Cuban people without quoting the almost-sacred words of 'the patriot.'

The war that took the life of Martí was as brutal as it was destructive. Employing guerilla tactics that Fidel Castro would later emulate, the Cuban rebels kept to the thinly populated mountains in the east and left the Spanish, whose army outnumbered them five to one, to hold the towns and cities. With each side incapable of defeating the other, the conflict became a war of attrition. By 1898, hundreds of thousands of

Cubans – one in six – lay dead of combat wounds or disease. Roughly two-thirds of the country's wealth lay vanquished in the war, most of its mines, mills, and farms reduced to rubble.

Watching from the sidelines with an increasingly lurid interest, owing to the tabloid journalism provided by newspaper mogul William Randolph Hearst, were the Americans. ('You furnish the pictures and I'll furnish the war,' Hearst reportedly told his illustrator in Cuba.) Washington took a cautious approach at first, refusing to recognize a rebel government and hoping that the Cuban stand-off would resolve itself without U.S. intervention. Then, on 15 February 1898, the U.S. battleship *Maine* exploded in Havana harbour, killing 260 American sailors. The best available evidence at the time suggested that an accident on the ship and not sabotage had caused the disaster. But the incident accelerated jingoist demands for war in the United States. 'Remember the *Maine*' became the vengeful rallying cry. In April 1898 President William McKinley, backed by the U.S. Congress, declared that the United States had no choice but to wage war against Spain in the name of 'humanity, civilization and American interests.' Eight months later, the Spanish-American War, as the conflict became known, ended in an easy victory for the United States. It was a 'splendid little war' for the Americans, as Secretary of State John Hay put it, because they enjoyed massive military superiority and an adversary exhausted by three years of brutal guerrilla warfare. In December 1898 Spain sued for peace. When Spanish and American representatives met in Paris to draft the treaty that ended Spain's 400-year role in Cuba, no Cubans were invited.

Prior to the Spanish-American War, the only Canadians who paid Cuba much notice were the handful of enterprising Halifax merchants trading with Havana via the British Empire's transatlantic shipping routes. In the nineteenth century and well into the twentieth, Canadian cod, potatoes, timber, and grain were exchanged for Cuban sugar, fruit, and rum. In the Castro era, Canadian and Cuban officials have occasionally boasted of their nations' uninterrupted trade relations dating back to the era of wood, wind, and water – a highly symbolic claim in light of the U.S. embargo. But the truth is that this trade was never anything more than modest, and certainly nothing to compare with either country's trade with the United States. By the late nineteenth century, for example, Canadians were importing roughly 2,000 tons of sugar from Cuba annually, a fraction of the 667,000 tons the island shipped every year to the United States.

The Spanish-American War brought Cuba into Canadian parlours for the first time. A handful of Canadian volunteers fought in the conflict, some alongside the Cuban insurgents and others within American combat units. Covered obsessively by the newspapers of the day, the heroes and villains of the Spanish-American War became household names in Canada, just as they did in the United States. Canadians' responses to the conflict were predictably mixed. A Toronto *Star* editorial published in April 1898 observed, for example, that although nobody in Canada wished to see a long and bloody war, the worry was that if the Americans beat Spain 'too quickly' they might get the idea to go after England as well. In such a scenario, 'the next conflict would be Canada.' All in all, concluded the *Star*, the 'average Canadian feels that he would like to see the United States get a lesson first and then wipe the Spaniards off the face of the earth.'[1]

At issue for Canadians, not only in 1898 but well into the twentieth century, was the Monroe Doctrine. Conceived in the early nineteenth century and constantly reinforced as a defining principle of U.S. foreign policy, this doctrine holds that European powers have no business in the western hemisphere. Its strategic logic dates from the American Revolution and the War of 1812, when the British used the Caribbean as a base for attacking the United States. Critics of the Monroe Doctrine have also pointed to its profound cultural and political legacy, however. They argue that it produced a tendency in the United States to think of the western hemisphere as an exclusively American sphere of influence. For the obvious reason that it challenged the right of the British Empire to defend its North American subjects, Canada's colonial leaders were openly contemptuous of the doctrine. Yet, even after Confederation in 1867, as the threat of an American invasion of Canada receded, Canadian prime ministers up to and including Pierre Trudeau continued to express anxiety about American claims to hemispheric dominance.

For four years after the Spanish-American War, Cuba was ruled by an American military government which oversaw the reconstruction of the devastated island. Early in 1901 the process of drafting a new Cuban constitution began, prompting widespread public debate in both Cuba and the United States. Cuban delegates to the constitutional conference naturally sought a fully independent republic. But in the end they were forced by the United States to accept what became known as the Platt Amendment – an arrogant imposition that would without question have appalled the Founding Fathers of the American republic. The amendment's infamous provisions included a clause giving the United States 'the right to intervene' in Cuban affairs in order to protect 'life, property and individual liberty.' Another prevented Cuba from 'enter[ing] into any treaty or other compact with any foreign power.' The most insulting of all obliged Cuba to lease to the U.S. government 'lands necessary for coaling or naval stations.' In accordance with the terms of this lease, construction of the U.S. naval base at Guantánamo began immediately. The Platt Amendment was abrogated in 1934 but, by the terms of the so-called Permanent Treaty that replaced it, the U.S. base at Guantánamo remained. To this day, 'Gitmo,' as it is commonly known in the United States, endures as the most enduring symbol of Cuba's historic subordination to American strategic interests.

### Fulgencio Batista and Fidel Castro

Fulgencio Batista Zaldívar's main claim to fame was that he went on to become Fidel Castro's nemesis, the torturer and murderer against whom the *Fidelista* rebels fought their guerrilla war, the corrupt dictator who conspired with American capitalists and gangsters to enrich himself and impoverish his own people. Even now, almost fifty years after fleeing the Cuban political stage, Batista's legacy is still invoked by Fidel and Raúl Castro as a powerful symbol legitimizing the Revolution.

Although he was always Washington's preferred strongman in Cuba, Batista was not always a tyrant. In 1940 an extraordinarily progressive Cuban constitution was hammered out by a multiparty assembly, emphasizing workers' rights, free elections, universal suffrage, and civil liberties. The same year, Batista won the first presidential election mandated by the new constitution. Four years later, however, he lost to his long-time rival Ramón Grau, the leader of the liberal Auténico Party, and retired to Daytona, Florida. Had Batista remained on the sidelines of Cuban politics from this point on, history would probably recall him as one of the heroic democrats from the ill-fated era of the constitution of 1940, and as a patriot.

The rise and fall of the Auténicos in the eight years between 1944 and 1952 proved fateful for Cuba, and especially for Cuban democracy. Grau had come to symbolize the enormous promise of the new Cuban constitution and, with it, the dream that a fully modern, democratic Cuba might now be built. His successor, Carlos Prío Socarrás, extended the Auténicos' reign with a victory in 1948 but then fell quickly into corruption and scandal – a betrayal not only of the Auténico promise of democracy but also of the hopes and dreams of the Cuban people. Prío, it was said, had disgraced not just himself but the nation. Cuban democrats who had enthusiastically rallied behind Grau in 1944 now openly questioned whether their compatriots were even capable of democracy. Many lost their faith in politics altogether.

Sensing that he could exploit this mood of defeatism, Batista declared himself a presidential candidate for the 1952 election. Polls showed that he did not have a hope of winning, and thus in March 1952, four months before the scheduled June election date, he took matters into his own hands. With the backing of the Cuban military and the U.S. government, he accomplished a non-violent coup d'état in exactly one hour and seventeen minutes – a feat about which he would later boast. Batista promised honesty and stability in government and agreed to hold elections within two years. But, to nobody's surprise, the 'elections' of 1954 were a sham. Rival political parties registered their objection to Batista's increasingly iron-fisted grip on power by refusing to run candidates. Unopposed, Batista 'won' with a 40 per cent voter turnout, confirming the view of young renegades like Fidel Castro that the only means of defeating him lay in armed struggle.

The United States not only gave the 1952 coup its blessing but showed indifference to Batista's dictatorial style, his heavy-handed suspension of civil liberties, and his use of informants and secret police to stifle dissent. From the American vantage point, of course, Batista's uncompromising anti-communism and his commitment to the protection of U.S. business interests in Cuba made him a great Cold War asset. But, from the Cuban point of view, the fact that the world's leading liberal democracy should arm and even train Batista's thugs was repugnant.

From the moment Fulgencio Batista moved into the presidential palace in 1952, Fidel Castro began fomenting revolution. Although he would later backdate his conversion to Marxism-Leninism to this period, at the time Castro spoke of restoring 'representative democracy' to Cuba. He chose as the first target of his revolution a military installation, the Moncada barracks in Santiago de Cuba. Between 23 and 25 July 1953, 130 Fidelistas travelled from the Havana area to Oriénte province on buses, trains, and rented cars. Most of the rebels were working-class supporters of the Ortodoxo Party, men (and two women) who believed they were fighting for social justice and Martí-styled nationalism. The now-famous attack on Moncada took place at dawn on 26 July 1953. Logistically, the campaign proved to be a comedy of errors, one rebel vehicle making a wrong turn approaching Santiago, another sidelined with a flat tire. Fidel Castro's own car stalled on approach to the barracks gate, and he and his seventy-nine-man unit got pinned down under heavy fire. In the end, sixty-nine Fidelistas died in the attack, eight in the actual fighting and sixty-one at the hands of their captors.

Fidel Castro remained at large until 1 August, when a military patrol surprised him and nine other sleeping Fidelistas and arrested them without bloodshed. Castro spent his jail time drafting a detailed apologetic for his raid on Moncada. With the eyes of the nation focused on him and his ragtag group of rebels, he knew that he had before him a once-in-a-lifetime opportunity to turn his defence into a full-fledged exposé of the Batista regime and its crimes. As highly anticipated as the trial had become, the revolutionary leader's performance exceeded everyone's expectations, cementing his status as one of the great orators of the twentieth century. Later, when he was serving out his prison sentence, he transcribed from memory the full text of his defence speech and then had it smuggled out for publication. The resulting document, roughly 26,000 words in length, became the gospel of the Cuban Revolution, immortalized by its brash concluding challenge to the court: 'Condemn me. It does not matter. History will absolve me.' Castro would later say that 'my Moncada speech was the seed of all things that were done later on.'[2] Much of the political program he laid out in that courtroom pointed not only towards revolution but also to radical economic and social reforms that included the confiscation of property and the redistribution of wealth.

Fidel Castro was sentenced to fifteen years in prison and was sent, along with twenty-four Fidelistas, to the Isle of Pines men's prison. In May 1955 he was released as the result of an amnesty issued by Batista. Within twenty-four hours of his release, Fidel Castro released to the Cuban press a 'Manifesto of the People of Cuba from Fidel Castro and the Combatants.' Calling this new phase of the struggle the 26th of July Movement, he plunged into the chaotic and violent Havana political scene, making speeches, publishing pamphlets, and haranguing Batista on the radio. By summer, there was so much heat on Castro from Batista's security forces that he fled to Mexico. There, he, the Argentinean doctor Ernesto 'Che' Guevara, and other exiled rebels dedicated themselves to training and equipping an army capable of launching a guerilla war against Batista. On 2 December, Fidel Castro and eighty-one of his comrades returned to Cuba. After a near-rout at the hands of Batista's army, he and the fifteen other surviving rebels disappeared into the rugged, largely inaccessible terrain of the Sierra Maestra mountains. Batista issued a $100,000 bounty for information on his whereabouts, but the peasants of the Sierra Maestra remained overwhelmingly loyal to Castro. His concern for the welfare of ordinary Cubans and his promise to make their problems a top priority of the Revolution became legendary. The Fidelistas' inclusive, egalitarian ethos greatly impressed the local people, drawing new recruits – men and women – to the rebel army practically daily.

On 17 January 1957 Fidel Castro had his first taste of military victory, taking a military outpost at La Plata by surprise and hauling its plentiful arms and munitions back into the mountains. After La Plata, Batista realized that the rebels presented a serious problem. He purchased sixteen B-26 bombers from the United States and deployed them against the Fidelistas' mountain camp to devastating effect. The three months after La Plata thus became, in Che's words, 'the bitter days, the most painful stage in the war.'[3] The 26th of July Movement suffered some of its worst losses, particularly among its clandestine operatives in Havana. Yet these were also the months in which the rebel army managed to consolidate its forces in the Sierra Maestra. The turning point came in June 1958 when a massive army assault against the vastly outnumbered rebels was beaten back. By December 1958, Batista knew that the end was near and began planning his own escape from Cuba. Over the week between Christmas and New Year's 1958, the rebels' successes came at a speed that surprised even themselves. Led by Che Guevara, the Fidelistas marched forcefully out of the Sierra Maestra westward to Havana. Santa Clara fell on 30 December, a decisive victory. During the early hours of the morning on New Year's Eve 1959, Batista and his family flew off to the Dominican Republic. A junta was proclaimed by one of Batista's generals in Havana but, using rebel radio to great effect, Castro told the Cuban people to oppose it. The junta collapsed within a day. Fidel Castro was victorious.

**The U.S. Response to the Cuban Revolution**

On 7 January 1959 the Eisenhower administration formally recognized the new Cuban government, despite harbouring serious reservations about Fidel Castro. Philip Bonsal, the American ambassador in Havana, was instructed by the State Department to be 'cool and distant' towards the new regime.[4] The revolutionaries' 1959 Agrarian Reform Act and especially Cuba's increasingly warm relations with the Soviet Union after 1960 were viewed with predictable Cold War enmity in Washington. In June 1960, at the urging of the United States government, the American petroleum companies Esso and Texaco refused a request from the new government to refine crude oil that had been imported to Cuba from the Soviet Union. Calling the subsidiaries' defiance a 'challenge to the sovereignty of the revolutionary government,' Castro seized U.S.-owned refineries in Santiago and threatened to nationalize every investment Americans had in Cuba, 'down to the nails in their shoes.'[5] On 7 July, Eisenhower called his bluff, announcing that he was slashing the 846,000-ton Cuban sugar quota, a $70-million hit on the Cuban economy. One month later, on 7 August, Castro retaliated by nationalizing virtually all major U.S.-owned industrial and agricultural firms in Cuba, estimated to be worth between $750 million and $1 billion; then, in mid-September, he had all American banks seized.

On 19 October 1960 the United States imposed an economic embargo on Cuba, restricting trade on all products excepting food and medicine. Calling the measure a 'program of economic denial' – in Cuba it is always called *el bloqueo* (the blockade), an act of war – Washington sought to increase the cost to the Soviet Union of maintaining Cuba as an ally, strangle Havana's capacity to export revolution, and demonstrate to the Cuban people that communism was not a desirable option for their country. The downward spiral of Cuban-American relations continued until January 1961, when the United States closed its embassy in Havana.

Between 1959 and 1962, approximately 250,000 Cubans emigrated to the United States. Some had always detested Fidel Castro. Others were appalled by the 'Orwellian' atmosphere that had accompanied his revolution – summary executions, arbitrary arrests, show trials, and the suspension of basic civil liberties.[6] As tensions escalated between Washington and Havana, the more militant of these Cuban émigrés launched a campaign of counter-revolution against the new government, which included bombing targets in Cuba from planes and boats based in Florida. Fidel Castro correctly charged that the Central Intelligence Agency (CIA) was complicit in this campaign, providing arms, supplies, and training to the exiles. The agency's efforts culminated in the Bay of Pigs débacle, in April 1961, when an invasion attempt by exile Brigade 2506 was routed by Cuban defenders. As the American people would discover in the mid-1970s, as a result of two congressional inquiries into U.S. intelligence, the CIA's clandestine campaign of harassment, sabotage, and attempted assassination in the Kennedy era was relentless.

In October 1962 American U2 overflights discovered that the Soviets were secretly building medium-range nuclear missile sites in

Cuba. The island quickly moved to centre stage in the most dramatic showdown of the Cold War. After thirteen harrowing days of back-channel diplomatic jockeying, President John F. Kennedy and Soviet General Secretary Nikita Khrushchev resolved the crisis – without any consultation with Fidel Castro. Khrushchev agreed to remove his missiles from Cuba in exchange for Kennedy's assurance that the United States would not invade Cuba. Castro was widely seen as 'the big loser' in the Cuban Missile Crisis.[7] Recently declassified State Department documents show that the CIA continued its harassment of Cuba without interruption during the stand-off; and once it was over, Congress tightened the embargo, preventing Americans from visiting Cuba and prohibiting all trade with the island.

The tough anti-Castro policies of the U.S. government did not stem the flow of Cuban emigrants to the United States. On the contrary, Washington ensured that Cuban émigrés received preferential treatment. The 1966 Cuban Adjustment Act automatically granted asylum to Cubans attempting to reach the United States, while generous federal aid – some of it provided by the CIA – subsidized Cuban businesses and assisted the families of exiles who were involved in anti-Castro activities.

In the mid-1970s, with the United States and the Soviet Union pursuing détente, it appeared as though change in U.S.-Cuban relations was imminent. Starting in June 1974 – when President Richard Nixon was still in the White House – Henry Kissinger embarked on a series of secret talks with Cuban officials, the goal of which was to end the embargo and normalize diplomatic relations. This dialogue would ultimately fail, early in 1976, for reasons known only to the Cubans. President Jimmy Carter resumed *el diálogo* in 1977, making several unprecedented concessions to Castro in an effort to warm the Cuban-American relationship. His administration halted reconnaissance flights over Cuba, negotiated new fishing and maritime agreements, and lifted the travel ban. In 1977 Cuba and the United States opened 'interests sections' in each other's capitals – de facto embassies, though they could not be called that since two countries had not officially restored diplomatic relations.

Mid-way through Carter's presidency, the promise of normalized Cuban-American relations began to sour. Cuban military involvement in Africa proved to be the decisive issue for the Carter administration, just as it was for the Canadian government in the same period. In February 1978 Carter followed Prime Minister Trudeau's example and suspended *el diálogo*.[8] Two years later – in what Castro himself called a deliberate 'act of defiance' against Carter – Cuban authorities opened the doors to emigration. Anyone who wanted to leave Cuba, Castro decreed, was free to go. This announcement set in motion the Mariel boatlift over the summer of 1980. With the help of 3,000 private boats from south Florida (dubbed the Freedom Flotilla), over 129,000 Cubans made their way to the United States. President Carter initially welcomed the refugees, praising their courage and allocating $10 million in emergency funding. But, when it was discovered that Fidel Castro had freed some of Cuba's worst criminal offenders from prison so he could dispose of them in the United States, the boatlift turned into a major political liability for the president.

Tensions between the two countries only intensified in the era of Ronald Reagan and George H.W. Bush. The Reagan White House approved the launch of Radio Martí, which began beaming its Spanish-language anti-Castro broadcasts into Cuba in 1985. In 1990 the Bush administration followed with TV Martí. Two years after that, when Cuba was reeling from the collapse of its economic benefactor, the Soviet Union, the U.S. Congress passed the Cuban Democracy Act (also known as the Torricelli Bill). This statute tightened the embargo by attempting to prevent subsidiaries of American companies from doing business with Cuba, prohibited ships that had stopped in Cuba from entering U.S. ports, and increased the disincentives for Americans to visit the island illegally. It also contained provisions to increase 'people-to-people' contact between Americans and Cubans, however, including the resumption of telephone and mail service with the island and an easing of the prohibition on the private delivery of medicine and food to Cuba.

During the 1992 presidential campaign, Bill Clinton pledged his support for the Torricelli Bill, and for the first couple of years after winning the White House he did nothing to dilute its punitive objectives. Before long, however, Clinton was confronted by an immigration crisis that threatened to become a second Mariel. Desperate Cuban *balseros* (rafters) began fleeing the economic privations of Cuba's 'Special Period'[9] en masse, some of them even hijacking boats owned by foreigners. Castro, frustrated by his inability to guarantee the safety of ships docked in Havana harbour – and by the apparent refusal of the United States to discourage the balseros – again opened Cuba's doors. As they had in 1980, thousands of Cubans immediately took to boats and rafts, and set out for Florida. The Clinton administration reacted to this mass exodus by amending the 1966 Cuban Adjustment Act. A new immigration accord was hammered out between the United States and Cuba, Castro agreeing to prevent Cubans from setting out for American shores in exchange for Clinton's guarantee that the United States would accept a minimum of 20,000 Cuban immigrants each year. A second agreement, signed in 1995, stipulated that henceforth the United States would return Cuban rafters intercepted at sea. Thus began the so-called 'wet foot, dry foot' policy.

Towards the end of his first term, Clinton began signalling that he might be interested in thawing relations with Cuba. He initially opposed the Cuban Liberty and Democratic Solidarity (*Libertad*) Act (also known as the Helms-Burton Bill), for example, which was making its way through Congress in 1995. The events of 24 February 1996 forced Clinton's hand, however. On that day, Cuban MIGs shot down two civilian Cessnas operated by the Miami-based exile organization Brothers to the Rescue, killing four Cuban Americans. In the face of massive public condemnation of the shoot-down – at the United Nations, among its allies, and especially within the United States – President Clinton announced that he had no choice but to support the Helms-Burton Bill. The controversial statute – which was also condemned almost universally by U.S. trading partners, and especially by Canada – was thus signed into law on 12 March 1996. It authorized new penalties on U.S. subsidiaries doing business in Cuba, allowed U.S. citizens to sue foreigners for attempting to profit from confiscated American assets, and even prohibited such foreigners from entering the United States.

President George W. Bush chilled Cuban-American relations even further. In 2001 Bush announced that his government would 'oppose any attempt to weaken sanctions against Cuba's government.' He increased U.S. support for human rights activists in Cuba and appointed several anti-Castro Cuban Americans to senior positions in his administration. Because Cuba is on the U.S. State Department's list of terrorist sponsors, the events of 11 September 2001 caused further acrimony in the Cuban-American relationship. In 2002 White House officials raised the possibility that Cuba was conducting biological-weapons research and providing American enemies with 'dual-use technology.' They also accused the Castro regime of supplying false information to the U.S. investigation into the terror threat, sending American officials on 'wild goose chases' and thus 'impeding our efforts to defeat the threat of terrorism.' These new animosities directly affected day-to-day diplomacy in Washington and Havana. In the spring of 2003, for example, the United States expelled fourteen Cuban diplomats for espionage.

American diplomats in Cuba were also instructed to assume a more confrontational tone. After Bush assumed power, the principal officer in Havana, Vicki Huddleston, began distributing books and shortwave radios programmed to receive Radio Martí. Her successor, James Cason, heightened diplomatic tensions even more by increasing contact between Cuban dissidents and officials at the U.S. Interests Section. The Cuban government reacted by severely limiting the movement of U.S. diplomats in Cuba. It also claimed that its March 2003 crackdown on dissidents, in which seventy-five Cubans were tried and jailed, was a reaction to this 'American offensive.'

In 2004 the first report of President Bush's Commission for Assistance to a Free Cuba was released; it was followed in 2006 with a second instalment. Both documents were premised on the imminent collapse of the Castro government and thus described, in minute detail, how the United States might assist the Cuban people in their transition towards liberal democracy. The second report was issued just weeks before Fidel Castro announced that he had to undergo intestinal surgery and was therefore ceding power 'provisionally' to his brother Raúl. Yet by the spring of 2007 the Comandante was back in full form, writing scathing attacks on U.S. policy from his hospital bed as he recuperated from his illness. Much to the chagrin of the Miami Cubans and many members of the Bush administration, this 'transition' period, capped in February 2008 by the permanent transfer of power to Raúl Castro, was handled smoothly by the Cuban government and life in Cuba went along as it had for decades.

**The Cuba Debate**

Fidel Castro has always inspired fierce debates on both sides of the 49th parallel but the end results have never been especially partisan. Every Republican and Democratic administration in the United States has enforced the embargo since 1960, and every Liberal and Tory government in Canada has refused to follow suit. Yet seldom has a month gone by in either country when Fidel Castro has not made the headlines and triggered a fiery public scrap.

In some important respects, Canadians' attitudes towards Cuba have been imported from the United States, where Castro has polarized public opinion and inspired antagonisms of almost inconceivable intensity. Anti-Castro hardliners in the United States believe that the Cuban leader betrayed his own Revolution after taking power and that he has ruled as a run-of-the-mill dictator ever since. They want nothing to do with Cuba until Castro is gone. Squaring off against the hardliners are American progressives who believe that isolating Cuba does little to check the worst abuses on the island and nothing to improve the lives of ordinary Cubans. The pro-business wing of the Republican Party, once adamant in its support of sanctions, increasingly views Cuba as a vast market from which American business has been sidelined long enough. But for the most part the battle lines are clearly drawn, and have been since the Kennedy era.

There are two aspects of the Cuba debate in the United States which distinguish it from the Canadian version, however. The first is that it influences American presidential politics directly, and with it U.S. foreign policy. There are today roughly 650,000 Cuban Americans in the Miami area alone, and, in tight presidential election races of the kind that Americans saw in 2000 and 2004, this constituency is crucial to carrying Florida, a so-called battleground state. In the 2000 presidential election, when Al Gore conceded the loss of Florida to George W. Bush, it was by only 537 votes. It is no exaggeration to say that Bush's successful courtship of the Cuban American constituency in that state made the difference between victory and defeat. Both parties know this. That is why, in 2004, both Bush and Democratic presidential candidate John Kerry spent a disproportionate amount of their time campaigning in Florida's émigré community. It is also why President Bill Clinton signed Helms-Burton in an election year.

The second aspect of the Cuba debate in the United States for which there is no Canadian equivalent follows from the first. Since both political parties believe the Miami exile vote to be crucial to their electoral successes, American political leaders have been reluctant to criticize some of the more extremist voices on its fringe. The late Jorge Mas Canosa, for example, co-founder of the anti-Castro Cuban American National Foundation (CANF) in 1981, was well known for his strong-arm political tactics, and also for consorting with suspected terrorists and other unsavoury characters. Yet he was a regular fixture of the Reagan White House, where he served both as an occasional adviser to the National Security Council and as the de facto gatekeeper for the Cuban American lobby.

Even more unnerving is evidence that, because of the prominence of Cuban Americans in the upper echelons of the Republican Party, that party's leaders are soft on the terrorism of Cuban exiles. Henry Kissinger has recalled, for example, that Richard Nixon was so heavily influenced by the anti-Castro politics of his close friend Charles 'Bebe' Rebozo that he vowed to go after the Cuban leader by virtually any means possible. ('I want a report on a crash basis,' Nixon told Kissinger in 1970, 'on what the CIA can do to support *any* kid of action which will irritate Castro.')[10] Similarly, just before leaving the U.S. presidency in 1993, George Bush, Sr, pardoned Orlando Bosch, a militant anti-Castro exile accused of blowing up an Air Cubana jetliner in 1976. The pardon caused a storm of controversy in the United States, since the president's own Justice Department had called Bosch 'a terrorist, unfettered by laws or human decency, threatening and inflicting violence without regard to the identity of his victims.'[11]

In contrast with the United States, where Fidel Castro has inspired the most passionate of emotions and distorted American politics at the highest levels, Canada's relationship with Cuba has been characterized by a remarkably high degree of detachment. This has had a great deal to do with the professionalism of the Canadian diplomatic corps, which has always understood the delicacy of Canada's position vis-à-vis both Cuba and the United States. But, even more fundamentally, Canadians have always known that their national interests are not at stake in Cuba. Having few vested interests there and even fewer axes to grind, they have had the luxury of viewing Cuba with an impartiality that Americans have not enjoyed since at least 1959. Debate about Cuba in Canada is just that – debate.

Yet debate matters. The open exchange of ideas is fundamental to defining who we are. It sets out the values and principles for which nations and individuals are willing to take a stand and, if necessary, make sacrifices. For this reason it is crucial to acknowledge two elements in the Cuba debate which are not in contention, even though it has been suggested otherwise on both sides of the 49th parallel. The first concerns the values of democracy and human rights. Most Canadians and Americans are in broad agreement on the fundamentals of civil society: the need for democracy and fair multiparty elections; the rule of law; respect for human rights, including the right to express political dissent; freedom of the press, of religion, and of association; and an open justice system. Most North Americans do not dispute that Cuban society has been illiberal in the Castro era, when judged against these principles.

The argument frequently made by opponents of Canada's policy of engagement with revolutionary Cuba is that it equivocates on these convictions. In fact, at no time since Fidel Castro took power in 1959 has this been true. For Canadians, the question is not whether the Cuban political system is in need of reform; the question is how best to promote reform without sabotaging the social benefits the Revolution has brought the Cuban people. Recognizing the state's achievements in providing for the health and education of its citizens, Canadians are leery of the one-sided rhetoric emanating from Washington. The United States has pursued a hardline policy of isolating Cuba as the most effective means of toppling Fidel Castro. That policy has patently failed. Canada has pursued a policy of engagement in the belief that dialogue will lead to political reforms in Cuba. That policy has also failed. Supporters of these policies continue to fight tooth-and-nail in defence of their views, each group attacking their opponents mercilessly, both oblivious to the practical irrelevance of the question. After fifty years, revolutionary Cuba remains by North American standards largely illiberal. That most Americans and Canadians would like to see reform of Cuban political life is not diminished by their disagreement over tactics.

The second area in which there is broad agreement might be called strategic. There has never been any question of the centrality of the Canadian-American alliance in Canadians' formulation of their foreign policy, even under the most ostensibly anti-American prime ministers, John Diefenbaker and Pierre Trudeau. Canada's *annual* trade with Cuba has never exceeded its *daily* trade with the United States. Canada is a founding member of NATO and of NORAD. Nothing in the Canadian-Cuban relationship has ever threatened the primacy of the Canadian-American alliance, nor have Canadian politicians ever allowed the appearance that it might. During the Cold War, there was no question of where Canada's strategic priorities lay. They lay with the Western alliance against the communist bloc. Thus, the Canadian insistence that its trade with Cuba was restricted to non-strategic materials was not mere hair-splitting. It was indicative of a clear commitment to the strategic priorities of the West.

Once the Cold War was over, of course, the idea of 'strategic superiority' as the moving force behind the Western alliance atrophied. In its place – especially where Cuba was concerned – a new agenda arose, that of human rights. But here, too, the Canadian case has always been clear. The idea that Canada is somehow 'soft on human rights' is as improbable today as the claim that it was 'soft on communism' during the Cold War. Yet this is precisely the charge that is levelled, even now, by critics of Canada's Cuba policy. The truth is that the debate about how best to expedite reform in Cuba – isolation versus engagement – has never undermined the liberal consensus in North America. Interestingly, ordinary North Americans appear to be far more pragmatic in their views than the political and media elites who have been stoking the Cuba debate for half a century. Polls show that roughly 70 per cent of citizens in both the United States and Canada today support an end to U.S. trade sanctions against Cuba.[12] They are puzzled by Washington's continuing hostility to the island, while it openly pursues links with China and Vietnam, one-party states with abysmal human rights records.

## Canada and Cuba in the Castro Era

Informed debate about the Canadian-Cuban relationship in the Castro era remains robust and exciting, as the essays in this book demonstrate. Adopting an interdisciplinary approach, the contributors to this volume make an original and much needed contribution to the literature on the Canadian-Cuban relationship during the Castro era. And they do so at an auspicious time, following on the heels of the first transfer of executive power in Cuba in nearly five decades, from Fidel Castro to his brother Raúl in February 2008.

There have been a number of books written on the Canadian-Cuban relationship but none of them examine the revolutionary period as a whole and none are multidisciplinary in their approach. *Our Place in the Sun* addresses Canada's relations with Cuba from the earliest days of the Revolution to the period marked by the ascendancy of Raúl Castro to the presidency. Two of the chapters (those by Don Munton and David Vogt, and by Dennis Molinaro), dealing with the early years of the Castro government, are based on newly declassified archival sources. Other chapters examine previously unexplored areas of the bilateral relationship. For example, Cynthia Wright recounts the forgotten story of the Fair Play for Cuba committees in Canada, arguing that, in both the United States and Canada, the committees were part of the difficult process of opening up political dissent in the era of McCarthyism and the Cold War consensus.

Still other chapters revisit the conventional narratives of Canada-Cuba relations. For instance, challenging the view that Canadian-Cuban diplomacy is somehow exceptional, Greg Donaghy and Mary Halloran place Prime Minister Trudeau's efforts to engage Cuba in the mid-1970s against the backdrop of his government's broader efforts to deepen Canadian relations within Latin America. Similarly, historian Robert Wright sees the differences in Canadian and American policies as largely superficial. He argues that Canadian and American Cuba policies in the 1990s shared the premise that liberal democracies in North America (and elsewhere) ought to be prodding the Cubans forcefully in the direction of liberal reforms.

Wide-ranging, rigorous, and original, *Our Place in the Sun* builds on established scholarship while breaking important new ground in the study of Canadian-Cuban relations in the revolutionary era.

NOTES

1 Editorial, Toronto *Star*, 16 April 1898, 4.
2 Fidel Castro, cited in Tad Szulc, *Fidel: A Critical Portrait* (New York: Post Road Press/Avon, 1986), 299.
3 Ernesto Che Guevara, cited in ibid., 415.
4 Philip Bonsal, cited in Morris H. Morley, *Imperial State and Revolution: The United States and Cuba, 1952–1986* (Cambridge: Cambridge University Press, 1987), 74.
5 Fidel Castro, cited in 'Expect Ike to Hit Cuba Early,' Toronto *Star*, 4 July 1960, 3.
6 Robert M. Levine, *Secret Missions to Cuba: Fidel Castro, Bernardo Benes and Cuban Miami* (New York: Palgrave Macmillan, 2001), 33.
7 Editorial, 'The Big Loser,' *Globe and Mail*, 30 October 1962, 6.
8 See Robert Wright, *Three Nights in Havana: Pierre Trudeau, Fidel Castro and the Cold War World* (Toronto: HarperCollins, 2007).
9 The 'Special Period in Peacetime' was a program of dramatic austerity measures introduced in 1991 after the collapse of the USSR and the termination of Soviet subsidies to Cuba.
10 Richard Nixon, cited in Henry Kissinger, *The White House Years* (New York: Little Brown, 1979), 642.
11 Joe D. Whitley, cited in Tim Weiner, 'Cuban Exile Could Test U.S. Definition of Terrorist,' New York *Times*, 9 May 2005, 1.
12 See Jane Perlez, 'Dispute Could Warm U.S.-Cuba Relations,' New York *Times*, 25 April 2000; and Beverly L. Campbell, 'Helms-Burton: Checkmate or Challenge for Canadian Firms Doing Business in Cuba?' in *Cuba in Transition* (Miami: Association for the Study of the Cuban Economy, 1996), http://lanic.utexas.edu/la/cb/cuba/asce/cuba6/58cambell.fm.pdf.

# 1 Canada, Cuba, and Latin America: A Paradoxical Relationship

HAL KLEPAK

This chapter argues that Cuba has acted as both a stimulus for the building of a closer relationship between Canada and the Latin American region and as a break on tendencies towards that end. Cuba is thus shown as having often kept Canadian decision makers wary of entanglements farther south than the United States *while* also having stimulated those same actors to engage further with the region.

I begin with a short overview of the Canadian relationship with Latin America before the Second World War when relations were established between Ottawa and several regional states including Cuba, and follow this with a look at the developments between the early 1940s and the historic decision to join the Organization of American States (OAS) in late 1989. This provides the background for an assessment of what has happened since in the relationship, always taking Cuba and its role in this process as the point of principle interest.

## Canada, Cuba, and Latin America before the Second World War

While Canada was, of course, part of the Americas long before it finally decided it was in the late 1980s, it is easy to exaggerate the impact of this on Canadians' view of themselves or where they fit into the international scene. Certainly, the long-standing French presence in northern North America tended to make at least some francophone Canadians comfortable with the idea of their actually belonging to their geographical space, but English-speaking Canadians were usually more comfortable with the thought of their being part of a vast and powerful British imperial system which could guarantee their cultural, political, social, and even economic future despite the asymmetries of North American political and military conditions.

As innumerable Canadian historians and political scientists have pointed out, Canada was able to hide behind British power, especially of the naval variety, and thereby ward off the expansionist designs of the United States as no other neighbour of that country was able to do, and thus develop as a nation without undue outside interference. Whereas Mexico lost roughly half of its national territory in its first half-century of independence, and Haiti, Nicaragua, the Dominican Republic, Panama, Costa Rica, El Salvador, Cuba, Honduras, and briefly even the British possessions of Bermuda and the Bahamas were the victims of official and 'filibustering' invasions by the United States on many occasions, British North America saw Canadian and imperial forces beat off numerous similar state and state-sponsored attempts to seize the country in the first hundred years of U.S. independence.[1]

Canadians watched with horror as other neighbours of the United States suffered that country's aggression while they themselves slowly built first a deterrent system against and then a modus vivendi with their huge rival and partner in North America.[2] Indeed, such was the success of these positive trends that the two countries were eventually to build one of the closest bilateral relationships in the world.[3]

This context meant that there was precious little desire at any time in Canada to see the model of U.S. relationships with Latin America also established to the north. Mutual respect, especially after the Washington Treaty of 1871, and even formal alliance in the First World War became the general, if not invariable, rule in the bilateral relationship, while, to the south, Washington behaved with a mixture of benign neglect and ferocious military intervention which would have made many more formal imperial powers blush.[4] Canadians remained steadfastly of the view that the United States should not be encouraged to regard its northern neighbour in the same light as their southern counterparts, and Ottawa was secretly pleased that, both in the Department of State and in the Department of Defense in Washington, Canada was squarely 'in' Europe and the British Empire and Commonwealth and not seen to be part of the rest of the Americas.

This did not mean that there was no Canadian relationship with Latin America before the Second World War. New France (1608–1759) had maintained reasonably close connections and trade with the French West Indies and, as the only part of the French empire with a reasonably large white population, often provided troops and resources for the defence of the French islands there.[5] British Canada after 1759, basking in the benefits of British naval power and imperial trade, was able to strengthen links with the south even further, although this was usually limited by Spanish mercantilist policies in its own empire. And, when the Reciprocity Treaty with the United States was clearly on its way to oblivion in 1866 after Britain and Canada's perceived backing of the South in the U.S. Civil War, the colonies founding the new Dominion the next year sent a trade mission to Latin America even before their status as a nation was formalized in order to try to find trading links that might reduce the impact of the treaty's demise.

This trade mission, however, found little that was encouraging on its trip. Mexico was in the throes of civil war and foreign invasion, Cuba was about to have its first war of independence and was simmering with discontent even though amazingly wealthy, Haiti was a disaster on all fronts, and generally the region appeared to the mission members to offer little potential to address the new Dominion's trade troubles.[6] And thus the long frustrating tradition of negligible trade with Latin America began for Ottawa. The figures are indeed depressing, normally in the range of 2 or 3 per cent of total international trade in peacetime, but they appear in a more positive light when set in the context of Canadian trade with the United States, which was so substantial as to have left, until recent decades, very little for the rest of the world at large.

What was more important and impressive was investment. Canadian expertise in many areas of development meant that the country was superbly placed, especially given its links to the mother country and British capital, to move into the investment field in Latin America. And move in it did, early and powerfully, by the late 1890s.[7] This trend continued up to the Great Depression of 1929 and started afresh after the Second World War.

Political connections were slower to develop. Under France, the Family Compact, the Bourbon alliance between the courts of Spain and France that endured for so much of the eighteenth century, ensured some linkages between French and Spanish colonies in the Americas. Indeed, the death of Canada's arguably finest general ever, Sieur Le Moyne d'Iberville, in Havana in 1706 was testimony to that connection.[8] But continued Spanish rule in most of the hemisphere meant that a British Canada was unlikely to have much political connection at all with 'Latin' America even though the ancient British alliance with Portugal entailed some stronger connections at times with Brazil.

Indeed, Cuban complications led to the undermining of the most potentially influential breakthrough of the British Empire in Latin America. Britain, having taken the western and most developed part of the island in 1762 as part of the extraordinary amphibious operations of the Seven Years' War that also delivered Canada itself into London's care, yielded it up at war's end in part at least because the British Empire – having already to absorb 70,000 French Catholics in the north – was in no position to easily do the same with almost a million more Spanish subjects of similar religion and loyalty in the south.[9] Cuba proved too large a pill to swallow even for the massively growing British American empire and it would be another half-century before other possibilities on this scale were to present themselves.[10]

When independence movements rocked Spanish America in the early years of the next century, there was little involvement by British North America save for attempts to share general British economic penetration of the area. British political penetration accompanied this process, of course, but direct Canadian involvement was small except when complications arising from Anglo-American rivalry there raised their heads, as they did, for example, in the diplomatic moves preceding the U.S.-Mexican War of 1846–8, various U.S. official and unofficial efforts to acquire Cuba from Spain throughout the century, and bilateral conflict in Central America.[11]

Anglo-American rivalry ensured that, long after acquiring Dominion status in 1867, Canada was not included in most multilateral political agendas in the hemisphere. This became especially true once the United States adopted Pan-American ideas in the late nineteenth century. Canada was excluded from the Pan-American movement, and by 1910 there was a view in Washington that the very weak Pan American Union (PAU) was merely a Trojan horse for of British power within the 'American family of nations.'[12] While Latin Americans increasingly tended to seek exactly such a horse in order to reduce U.S. power in the region, the United States was successful in barring its entry whenever the issue of Canada taking a greater role in hemispheric affairs arose.[13]

This situation was reinforced by the fact that, until the Statute of Westminster in 1932, Canada did not enjoy legislative autonomy or even have its own diplomatic representation abroad, although this began to change in 1927 with the opening of a legation in Washington.[14] The reluctance of Prime Minister Mackenzie King, head of government for the second time from 1935 until 1948, to broaden too quickly Canada's international linkages (and especially commitments) ensured that the Canadian political presence in Latin America remained small indeed and that, as British influence waned during and after the First World War, so did such Canadian influence as there was.

Cuba shared this context for Canada. Although Canadian investment in the country (including several schemes by the Van Horne railway and public-utility empire) became very large at century's end, in part stimulated by the formal independence of the island, the replacement of Spain by the United States as master of the island meant that hopes for a major place for Canada, and indeed Britain, in the country's economy were doomed.[15] Indeed, Cuba became the classic example of how U.S. political power could keep the British and Canadians, as well as other threatening real or potential rivals, out of play first in the Caribbean region and later farther south. And so, when official or business circles in Canada discussed the potential for progress in Latin America, Cuba was usually held up as the problem and not the solution.

## The Second World War

The Second World War was to change much of this but not necessarily for the better. While the war saw Canada and Cuba establish diplomatic relations as part of the former's growing place in the world, it also led to the final collapse of British power, with the result that Canada would henceforth deal with the United States in the region essentially alone. As during the First World War, Canadian trade with Latin America increased, from under 3 per cent to over 6 per cent of its total international trade. Unfortunately, this did not really reflect a permanent trend but rather the effects of distortions in normal hemispheric and world trade caused by the Royal Navy blockade of continental Europe and the German U-boat campaign against Britain and the Commonwealth. Be that as it may, Cuba and Latin America saw their trade with Canada grow strongly.

By 1942, the British minister in Havana was complaining to the prime minister and governor general in Ottawa that, since over half his business was Canadian, it might be a good idea for the Dominion to open its own diplomatic mission in Cuba. He argued that this made sense just in terms of the amount of work to be done but also the presence of two Commonwealth legations in Havana rather than one might help to lessen, at least to some degree, what he saw as the absolutely dominant position of the United States on the island and the difficulties this state of affairs posed to British and Canadian investment and trade prospects.[16]

The minister's suggestion, unlikely even to have been considered before the war, made some sense to Mackenzie King. The end of Canada's missions in The Hague, Paris, Rome, Tokyo, and Geneva as a result of the war and Nazi conquests had freed up a number of diplomats for reassignment. The costs of establishing relations with selected Latin American countries were thus reduced. When this was combined with what was hoped would be a permanent change in Canadian exports to the region, arguments for giving greater priority to Latin America began to carry more weight. Thus, by mid-war, missions were approved for Mexico, Argentina, Brazil, and Cuba and official relations with other Latin American countries were soon to follow.

Formally if indirectly, Cuba and Canada were now allies, as were most nations of Latin America. For, even before the United Nations arrangements for the war were fully in place, Cuba (like most other Latin American countries) was an ally of the United States in light both of its bilateral commitments with that country and of its engagements at the Rio Conference of February 1942, and Canada was in the same position. While this had been briefly the case in the First World War too, then it had had no real impact on public opinion or bilateral commitments and lacked even economic implications. In the Second World War, by contrast, Canada began to accept more fully that it was an 'American' nation and allied status moved this acceptance along even if the direct connections this arrangement involved were few.[17]

## The Post-War Relationship

The end of the war dashed the hopes of most of those wishing to see a rapidly developing Canada-Latin American relationship. Canada-Latin America trade eased back to its usual level, at nearly 3 per cent of total trade; Canadian investment, while still present, generally looked for easier pickings closer to home; and the United States rejected the possibility of Canadian membership in the PAU, an idea with which Mackenzie King had conducted a flirtation, albeit a lukewarm one, during the war. All of this spelled the end of the developments of 1939–45. Canadians had noticed that almost everyone but the United States had welcomed their interest in PAU membership, and the rebuff had pushed traditional Canadian thinking back to the fore: a Latin American link promised little gain for Canada and much potential difficulty for the bilateral relationship with its huge neighbour.

While Prime Minister John Diefenbaker early on in his government (1957–63) did again toy with the idea of a stronger connection with the region as part of his desire to diversify trade away from the United

States, this hope also flickered and died in the context of continuing trends in trading figures. Despite a visit to Mexico that seemed to herald new times, the wider initiative disappeared as did the inter-American elements of it.

In the Cold War the bedrock of Canadian foreign and defence policy had become alliance with the United States and membership in the North Atlantic Treaty Organization, which together permitted the 'muliteralization' of Canadian security and defence relations with the United States instead of the horrifying prospect of bilateral defence accords alone between the giant and the pygmy.[18] Nothing that threatened this comfort would long be considered by Canadian policy makers and too great a Latin American connection appeared on many occasions to do just that.

U.S. military interventions in Latin America had generally been unpopular with the Canadian public, and for obvious reasons, although it must be said that many Canadian investors joined their British colleagues in welcoming some U.S. interventions during the days of 'dollar diplomacy' prior to 1934 and the establishment of the Good Neighbour Policy by President Franklin Roosevelt. It was well known that Canadian public opinion would continue to decry such actions on the part of the United States and that Ottawa would then be walking a tightrope between remaining sensitive to domestic sentiment and keeping the favour of Washington when such events occurred. But this was largely a forgotten difficulty during the years 1934–54, when the new American policy not only eschewed intervention but harvested the benefits of such non-intervention in the form of exceptional Latin American support for the United States after it was attacked at Pearl Harbor in 1941.

By 1954, in the wake of the messy overthrow of the twice democratically elected, and very moderate leftist, Guatemalan government of Jacobo Arbenz, the Cold War had arrived in Latin America with a vengeance. Canadian interpretations of what was wrong with the region increasingly diverged from those of the United States, especially over the crucial question of whether one should welcome or resist moderate reformist movements. As one military intervention after another came upon the region, followed by the rise of military governments in the 1960s and 1970s, those divergences became even clearer.

When a less moderate reform movement assumed power under Fidel Castro in Cuba in January 1959, and then as· it moved steadily further to the left, Canada would not be cajoled by Washington and maintained relations with the island nation even when all of Latin

America save Mexico buckled under. Cuba came to be one of the most important thorns in the bilateral relationship with the United States at this time and yet the Canadian government would not bend to what were on occasion fairly ferocious blandishments. Even though Diefenbaker had little time for socialism and even less for communism, and despite the growing Cuban defence connection with the Soviet Union, he stood his ground on this issue, and the pundits who had been arguing that a too close relationship with Latin America was bound to bring much grief to the Canada-U.S. connection were proven right. But Diefenbaker and the more pro-United States Lester Pearson, who succeeded him in power in 1963, did not change their policies despite the cost.[19] And such a stance was nothing when compared with that of the next prime minister, Pierre Elliott Trudeau.

### The Trudeau Years, 1968–84

Soon after forming government, the Trudeau Liberals began a major study and then revision of Canadian foreign policy that was to have as a significant component yet another attempt at reversing one of the main trends in national trade in the twentieth century, the drift towards U.S. dominance. A 'Third Option' that called for diversification of trade as the key for national independence gave Latin America an important place in the Canadian government's strategic economic thinking.[20]

While rejecting full membership in the Organization of American States, Canada did become a formal observer in that body. And bilateral relations with a number of Latin American countries were strengthened. One of these was Cuba. Fidel Castro had long fascinated Pierre Trudeau and soon that feeling was mutual. Over the years, Trudeau visited the island on several occasions, and in the famous official visit of 1976 he made headlines by shouting 'Viva Cuba Libre' and 'Viva el Presidente Fidel Castro.'[21] This was the first visit of a head of government of a NATO nation to the country, and the attention it garnered was considerable, though not all positive, even at home. But acceptance of the Cuban revolutionary government had by then become something of a litmus test of an independent foreign policy for Canadian governments and the criticisms did not last long.[22] Instead, under Trudeau, the first waves of Canadian tourism to the island began and a host of bilateral agreements were signed.

U.S. (and domestic) negative reaction did nonetheless underscore the degree to which Cuba was both helpful and unhelpful for those in Canada promoting a more concerted drive southward. When rare discussions about joining the OAS occurred, for example, the perceived need to sign the Rio Pact (the 1947 collective-security accord formally known as the Inter-American Treaty for Reciprocal Assistance) was deemed a major obstacle since few Canadians were interested in joining an alliance totally dominated by the United States and particularly one seen as a tool used by that country to 'hold down' Latin America and 'prop up' its military dictators.[23] Indeed, many people saw the OAS as the likely instrument to be employed in toppling Fidel if that day came.

It was likewise felt that, if Ottawa did join the OAS, it would immediately bring Canada into conflict with the United States, for the two countries would then differ on one of the hottest issues facing the hemispheric organization – how to handle Cuba.[24] But, as Brian Stevenson argues convincingly, the Cuban question also focused Canadian attention on Latin America as nothing else had done, and even when Trudeau was annoyed by Havana, he remained close to it, its leader, and its problems.[25]

It was of course true that many Latin American countries in the OAS were revising their policies towards Cuba as the 1970s advanced. The expulsion of Cuba from the OAS at the Punta del Este conference in 1962, and that body's call for the governments of the Americas to break relations with the island, had fallen into abeyance. By 1975, many governments had already re-established relations with Cuba. The United States, seeing public defeat on the issue as inevitable, chose to quietly accept this state of affairs.[26] And, by the end of the decade, most countries in the OAS had re-established relations while new members of the Commonwealth Caribbean automatically opened missions on the island in response to Cuba's importance in the region. These countries, not surprisingly, looked to eventual Canadian membership as a boon in their drive to reopen the question of reversing Cuba's expulsion, a thorny issue for the United States, and this yet again raised concerns in Ottawa that the game was not worth the candle and that the Cuban question was one more reason not to join the hemispheric organization whatever the national love for multilateralism.

There were many reasons why Canada made no further moves to join the OAS after the decision in 1972 regarding observer status. Most were somehow connected to the overwhelming position of the United States both in the region and in the OAS itself. Certainly, Canada's Cuba policy was important factor in the discomfort felt by Ottawa about the prospect of moving towards full membership. When Ottawa opted a few years later to remove its observer from a permanent presence in Washington and return him to Ottawa, it caused hardly a ripple of public or press comment. A more forward policy towards Latin America brought simply too little gain and too many headaches to be palatable at the time. And Cuba was part and parcel of this equation.

## The Mulroney Government: Breakthrough of a Kind

When the Liberal government was replaced by a Conservative one in 1984, it came in the form of what many felt would be the most pro-United States prime minister in Canadian history. Brian Mulroney won the election promising that Canada's close relationship with the United States would be back as the number-one priority in the country's foreign policy.

In the face of trade trends that saw the United States account for some 80 per cent of total Canadian trade for the first time – clear evidence that a real North American market had been created, like it or not – Canada, like Mexico, abandoned schemes such as the Third Option and accepted that economic dependence on the United States was inevitable. Fearful of U.S. protectionism in this context, Mulroney abandoned the historic nationalist positions of his party and began negotiations for a free-trade arrangement with Washington.[27] The decision divided the country as rarely before, but by 1988 free trade with the United States was a fact.

The next year, Mulroney announced in Costa Rica that in January 1990 Canada would join the Organization of American States, which it duly did.[28] Many in Canada and Cuba saw this decision, and the general political stance that underlay it, as inevitably damaging to the bilateral relationship with Cuba. But such was the depth of the feeling in Canada about the correctness of the nation's Cuba policy that what argument there was about OAS membership, and there was astoundingly little for a move of such historic significance, suggested the role of Canadian membership in pressing the organization to readmit the island's government.

When Ambassador Paul Hubert, Canada's first permanent representative to the body, made his maiden speech, he caused something of a bombshell, although one very well received indeed among most Latin American ambassadors, by calling for Cuba's prompt return to the OAS. But the close relationship between Mulroney and President Ronald Reagan held as Washington, hardly pleased with the speech, kept its criticisms to a minimum in light of its pleasure at finally have Canada 'in.' U.S. policy towards Canadian membership in hemispheric bodies had changed a great deal in the last one hundred years but so had Canadian policy towards the United States and the Americas. The relative centrality of Cuba to the Canadian decision to move closer to the Americas had, of course, the welcome quality for the government of dampening the criticism of those who saw the OAS decision as currying favour in Washington and weakening the historic European connections that had kept Canada free.[29]

Indeed, some would argue that Cuba was particularly useful throughout the Mulroney years since it was difficult to accuse the prime minister of excessively pro-U.S. policies just as he was sending arguably the most successful Canadian ambassador ever posted to Havana, Mark Entwistle, to broaden the bilateral relationship with the island. For, by the late 1980s, the Soviet-Cuban 'alliance,' such as it was, was in deep trouble and the 'Special Period' was only around the corner.

## The Special Period, Canada, and Latin America

As President Mikhail Gorbachev's reforms in the USSR cut deeper through the mid- to late 1980s, Cuba felt more and more uncomfortable. At first, Fidel simply refrained from commenting on *perestroika* and *glasnost* but with time he could stand it no more and launched increasingly stinging attacks on these policies and even those who proposed them. Gorbachev responded in kind and the personal relationship between the two men rapidly became arguably even worse than that between Castro and Nikita Khruschev in the period after the Cuban Missile Crisis of 1962, until then generally agreed to have been the low point in bilateral relations between the two countries.[30]

Yet this paled beside what was to come. For the collapse of the Soviet empire in Eastern Europe during and after the autumn of 1989 was followed by a paring down of all Soviet commitments abroad and then by the disappearance of the 'mother country of socialism' altogether in 1991. The impact on Cuba was massive, as the trading arrangements that were the mainstay of the national economy disappeared and the island faced a crisis of unparalleled sweep and depth.[31] Cash and carry became the only way of buying goods from Havana's traditional Eastern European trading partners, and Cuba, lacking hard currency, was unable to obtain them.

Fidel was now obliged to act dramatically. Major reforms of the economy, and even some of the political system, were introduced.[32] The armed forces were ordered to move into the economy as never before, capitalist ideas of profit and loss and even of many management techniques were embraced if not eagerly at least strongly, and, perhaps most important, foreign investment was encouraged alongside a major campaign to find new foreign trading partners.[33] Canada, already a significant investor in Cuba, the leading or at least a major source of its largest tourist population, and one of its most significant trading partners, was well placed to take advantage of Cuba's needs. Bilateral exchanges grew quickly and Canada soon became much more important as an investor as well. Joint Cuban-Canadian ventures across a wide spectrum of economic activity were started, with the giant Sherritt mining company being merely the greatest of these.

Clouds were on the horizon, however. The new government of Jean Chrétien, in power from 1993, had no such close relationship with the United States as had Mulroney. Indeed, such relationship as there was soon was in trouble as one issue after another bedevilled the bilateral scene. Cuba was merely one such issue but it was certainly visible. While Washington initially seemed content to merely wait for yet another communist apple to ripen and fall, powerful Cuban-American influences, seeing no evidence that the Castro regime was about to collapse despite the massive economic crisis it was then confronting, became determined to use U.S. power to hasten the end.[34]

In 1991 the Torricelli Bill, or the Cuban Democracy Act, passed Congress and tightened enormously the embargo ('blockade' in Cuban parlance, not entirely without justification).[35] And five years later the Helms-Burton Bill formally codified the individual elements of that embargo and took away the president's ability to negotiate with Cuba without a series of impossible commitments on the Cuban side. U.S. pressure for its allies to comply with these new measures was formidable, but ire at what was seen as American unilateralism and the extraterritorial thrust of both the Torricelli and Helms-Burton bills ensured that just the opposite occurred.[36] Canada and Mexico passed blocking legislation to ensure that their firms did not toe the U.S. line and a trade crisis with the European Union was only narrowly averted by U.S. presidential guarantees that the bills would not fully be applied.[37]

Cuba's continued potential to disrupt the bilateral relationship between Canada and the United States was never clearer than in these years. When the 1990s ended with both foreign ministerial and prime ministerial visits to the island, the U.S. administration was livid and said so. Its views were echoed in the United States Senate and press, where attacks on Canada's policy were scathing. It is also true that these attacks struck a nerve more than in the past because the Chrétien government had unwisely predicted changes in the Cuban state at least in part as the result of Canadian pressure, a view that ignored the reality that few countries were as sensitive to foreign intervention in their domestic affairs as was Cuba. Instead, the Cuban-Canadian bilateral relationship went through a very rocky period, with Fidel disappointed by what he saw as Canadian amateurism in foreign policy and lack of understanding of Cuba's needs, and Chrétien feeling betrayed by Fidel on what the Canadian leader felt had been promises of political change. The opportunity was too great for the new (and, by Canadian standards, rightist) political formation based in Alberta, the Alliance Party. Breaking traditional Canadian solidarity on the subject of Cuba, the party, which had been highly critical of Helms-Burton only two years earlier, lashed out at what it saw as the prime minister's excessively pro-Fidel stance.

By now, however, the Latin American connection had a dynamic of its own and so did the Cuban. Despite Chrétien's call for putting some 'northern ice' into the bilateral relationship between Canada and Cuba, such moves as deciding that no further senior minister visits would occur and that some cooperation programs would be put on hold proved short-lived. Trade and investment precluded getting too close to the U.S. position; the nature and extent of the people-to-people connection in tourism, sport, education, and culture was simply too huge to stop; and the political relationship, while bumpy for a while, had too many favourable elements to it for Canada to allow for major changes in policy.

The Latin American relationship was still strongly touched by Cuba but not shaped by it. By the late 1990s, Canada had been a member of the OAS for almost a decade, had new embassies in the region (although some were much-criticized 'mini-embassies,' like those in Quito and Montevideo), and had seen its investment grow massively, especially in mining. In addition, tourism to Latin America had reached new heights. While trade remained at the usual disappointing level – 2 per cent of total international trade – it nonetheless was growing, in strict numerical terms, very fast indeed. Canada had become an active partner in many spheres of hemispheric affairs, even security and defence, which it had once avoided; it had extended its bilateral free-trade arrangement with the United States to Mexico; it had backed the idea of a Free Trade Area of the Americas forcefully; and it had signed a further free-trade accord with Chile.

But Cuba remained special. As what most Latin American saw as Washington's 'bullying' of Cuba gained momentum, Canada's long-time and officially correct if not particularly warm links with the island were widely and favourably commented upon in the region.[38] Though many Latin Americans occasionally complained loudly of Canada being too pro-United States in the OAS, Ottawa's legitimacy as an independent actor – in hemispheric free-trade talks, in defence matters, and even on issues such as drugs, access to markets, and illegal immigration – stood the test of time in large part because of its stance on Cuba. Respect, even on the Latin American right, for its position was widespread and earned Canada no end of kudos at a difficult time in its efforts to prove that it was not merely a stalking horse for the United States in the hemisphere. Thus, political integration into the Americas was in the end rather more eased than hindered in the 1990s by Canada's view of Cuba and its unwillingness to change course whatever the pressures from the south.

## Improvements in Cuba, Difficulties in the Hemisphere

By the turn of the century, things were improving for Cuba. The worst of the Special Period is generally regarded as 1994–5, and by 2000 much was better on the island and the government there felt less under siege but also less needful of reform. The economy was growing, although at debatable rates and from a very low point indeed. U.S. military and other security agencies appeared to appreciate Cuba's significant efforts against illegal immigration and the illegal international drug trade, while also downplaying its potential as a threat to the United States.[39] The worst of the crisis seemed over. 'Miami' influence in Washington had not brought down Fidel, and new movements in Latin America gave the Cuban government hope that the long period of loneliness was past. Hugo Chávez was firmly in power in Caracas, and his need of and affection for Fidel was clear as the Cuban leader set out to resolve the island's desperate fuel situation through special arrangements with Venezuela, paying for supplies of that country's oil with what Cuba had in most abundance – good doctors and nurses, excellent sports-training staff, and competent and dedicated teachers.[40] These were also what Venezuela most needed as the Chávez government pursued an ambitious agenda of social reform.

Relations were also good with a resurgent China, which, while not able to help on the scale Venezuela did, could still offer Cuba many products, especially much valued and needed electrical goods, under arrangements that were highly beneficial to Cuba and that took into consideration the Caribbean nation's lack of hard currency. So, even though economic reforms stalled or even went into reverse from a capitalist perspective, with the inevitable impact that was to have on trade and investment, Cuba still made progress in its recovery.

Also part of this context was a dramatically changed political landscape in Latin America. For Venezuela was not the only country that moved dramatically to the left in the late 1990s and the first decade of the twenty-first century. It was joined by the Bolivia of Evo Morales and the Ecuador of Rafael Correa. These two new governments share an admiration for Fidel Castro and the Cuban revolutionary experiment that is deep and sincere.[41] For them and others, the achievements of the Cuban Revolution in the areas of national independence, education, health care, and gender and racial equality, to name just a few, are much to be admired even if there is widespread unhappiness with the more repressive side of the Castro government. Indeed, the fact that those achievements came in the face of ferocious opposition from the United States – opposition that itself is seen by many as justifying Cuba's repressive political culture – makes them all the more remarkable and praiseworthy in the region. Alongside the populist and leftist governments that came to power in Caracas, La Paz, and Quito, and potentially in Managua, were new, more moderate, left-leaning governments in Argentina, Brazil, and Chile, and other countries, all democratically elected. Equally, quite radical populists were only very narrowly defeated in such key nations as Mexico and Peru. Thus, in most of Latin America, governments friendly to, or at least admiring of, Fidel came to rule at a time when the Washington consensus came unstuck.[42] And governments of the right and centre-right were often just as keen to show their independence of the United States by adopting policies towards Cuba which were much less critical of the island's government.

In these circumstances, Canada's historic position on the Castro experiment had even greater legitimacy. Far from being an outsider, as it had been in the 1960s and early 1970s, Ottawa found itself admired and cited as having a principles-based foreign policy and one visibly not at the call of Washington.[43] When buttressed by well-publicized decisions not only to abstain from supporting the United States and the United Kingdom in the invasion and occupation of Iraq (the first time in history that Canada failed to back a war effort in which both its principal partner and its mother country were involved) but also to opt out of the U.S. 'missile shield,' Canada's foreign policy began to bask in the light of Latin American respect.[44]

On the other hand, Canada was soon to wonder about the impact of these decisions. And, if this was true of the Chrétien government, it was doubly so of the minority Conservative government of Stephen Harper elected in January 2006. This was without doubt the most conservative and pro-U.S. government in Canadian history, one determined to strengthen relations with the United States and move to the right in all areas of Canadian life, internal and external.

The new government was generally quiet on the Cuban question, perhaps in recognition both of its minority status and of Cuba's status as a powerful litmus test of the independence of Canadian foreign policy. Still, Harper and his foreign minister were seen as forceful advocates of democracy, keen proponents of hemispheric free trade, strong supporters of U.S. leadership in the Americas and the world, and true believers in traditional liberal capitalism. Little wonder, then, that Havana and many other Latin American capitals were curious to see how the Harper government would view not only the island but also the arrival of so many leftist governments, some of them even speaking of the need for twenty-first-century socialism.

**Canada, Cuba, and Latin America Today and Tomorrow**

Canada is now a full member of the inter-American community after more than a century of holding aloof from it. It is active in the hemisphere's life in most of its institutional and other forms, ranging from health to education, culture to defence, trade liberalization to political consultation. While Asians may occasionally scoff at Canadian pretensions to be an Asia-Pacific nation, and Europeans may have forgotten the famous '100,000 graves' of Canadians who died so that the continent (and especially Britain and France) could live in freedom, and if Africans look to Europe and not to Ottawa for their future, Latin American and U.S. citizens accept Canada as a full-fledged American nation which is part and parcel of the hemisphere and which has a right to a say on all issues faced by the region.

Cuba and the Cuban question have played a part at every stage of the development of Canada's membership in the inter-American community since the first tentative moves in the 1940s towards a Latin American diplomatic presence on the part of the Canadian government. There were larger countries than Cuba in the region that might have logically had a better call on Canadian diplomatic resources, but none except Cuba received a diplomatic mission during the Second World War. This reflected the specific economic and political context that the island was passing through and that had resonance in Ottawa.

This special resonance has remained in the bilateral relationship in one way or another for most of the subsequent two-thirds of a century. Cuba is still small compared to many Latin American nations, but, to this day, its symbolic presence remains vastly greater than its size alone would warrant. And, if this is true on the world and Latin American stages, it is equally true on the Canadian. For Cuba has troubled Canadian diplomats and decision makers just as it has fascinated them, and this has been especially the case during most of the period after the amazing turn of events of early 1959.

At first, Cuba was merely a country with which we traded quite considerably and where the mother country was looking for some help in the face of a highly uneven playing field in terms foreign investment and trade. Fifteen years later, our diplomatic staff in Havana was fearful of what the Castro revolution meant for investment, while our commercial personnel thought that finally there was a chance of equal treatment at the hands of a Cuban government after six decades of absolute U.S. dominance of the nation's decision making on trade as on most other things. In the early years, our connection with revolutionary Cuba was pragmatic and non-ideological and followed the British tradition – long dear to Canadian diplomacy – that if a government controls its population and territory, and enjoys general support, it should be recognized whether one particularly likes it or not. At the time, this view complicated our desire to expand our relations with the Latin American region as a whole, but since then the opposite has generally been the case.

Thus, it can be concluded that, over many years, Cuba has played various roles for Canada in terms of its wider relationship with Latin America. It has variously been a stimulus to the development of such a relationship and an obstacle to it, or, somewhat curiously, both at the same time. This peculiarity of the Canadian relationship with Cuba is seen in many other countries' connection with the island as well. But, given Canada's growing desire to be a full part of the hemisphere, the very special nature of the Cuban link is nothing if not interesting.

NOTES

1 This often misunderstood evolution of North American bilateral defence is well discussed in Richard A. Preston, *The Defence of the Undefended Border: Planning for War in North America, 1867–1939* (Montreal and Kingston: McGill-Queen's University Press, 1977).

2 For a Latin American view of these years and events, see Juan A. Ortega y Molina, *Destino manifiesto: sus razones históricas y su raíz teológica* (Mexico City: Alianza Editorial Mexicana, 1989).

3 That relationship has stood the test of time and survived differing positions on many issues. See Martin Lipset Seymour, *Continental Divide: The Values and Institutions of the United States and Canada* (New York: Routledge, 1990).

4 For this evolution in relations, see Charles P. Stacey, *Canada and the Age of Conflict, 1867–1921* (Toronto: University of Toronto Press, 1977).

5 See Nellis M. Crouse, *The French Struggle for the West Indies, 1665–1713* (New York: Octagon, 1966); and George Nestler Tricoche, *Les milices françaises et anglaises au Canada 1627–1900* (Paris: Lavauzelle, n.d.).

6 See James Ogelsby, *Gringos from the Far North: Canadian-Latin American Relations 1866–1968* (Toronto: Macmillan, 1976), 10–14.

7 On this, see Christopher Armstrong and H.V. Nelles, *Southern Exposure: Canadian Promoters in Latin America and the Caribbean, 1896–1930* (Toronto: University of Toronto Press, 1998).

8 For the story of D'Iberville, see Martin Blumenson and James Stokesbury, *Masters of the Art of Command* (Boston: Houghton Mifflin, 1975), 197–204; and Nellis M. Crouse, *Lemoyne d'Iberville: Soldier of New France* (Toronto: Ryerson Press, 1954).

9 Guillermo Calleja Leal et al., *1762 La Habana: la toma de La Habana por los ingleses* (Madrid: Ediciones de Cultura Hispánica, 1999).

10 See Eduardo Torres-Cuevas and Oscar Loyola Vega, *Historia de Cuba, 1492–1898* (Havana: Editorial Pueblo y Educación, 2002), 120–3; David Syrett, ed., *The Siege and Capture of Havana 1762* (London: Navy Records Office, 1970).

11 For the Mexican dimension of this, see the excellent Josefina Zoraida Vázquez, *México frente a Estados Unidos: un ensayo histórico, 1776–1988* (Mexico City: Fondo de Cultura Económica, 1989). An interesting overview of Anglo-American rivalry and the place of the Americas in it is provided in William A. Dunning, *The British Empire and the United States: A Review of Their Relations during the Century following the Treaty of Ghent* (New York: Charles Scribner, 1914).

12  Pierre Queuille, *L'Amérique latine, la Doctrine Monroe et le panaméricanisme* (Paris: Payot, 1969), offers a good picture of the Pan-American context. And, for the British and Canadian features of this situation, see Rory Miller, *Britain and Latin America in the 19th and 20th Centuries* (London: Longman, 1993).

13  See the early chapters of Ogelsby, *Gringos from the Far North*, and Peter McKenna, *Canada and the OAS* (Toronto: University of Toronto Press, 1995).

14  Growing Canadian control of its national diplomacy is traced in John Hilliker, *Le Ministère des affaires extérieures du Canada, 1909–1946* (Quebec: Presses de l'Université Laval, 1990).

15  The most dramatic chapter of this story unfolds in Jorge Renato Ibarra Guitart, *El Tratado anglo-cubano de 1905* (Havana: Ciencias Sociales, 2006).

16  British minister in Havana to Mackenzie King, 25 April 1942, quoted in Ogelsby, *Gringos from the Far North*, 57.

17  For example, once Mexico entered the war in early 1942, Canada wished for a trilateral Permanent Joint Board of Defence to replace the bilateral one in place from 1938 to 1940. The United States rejected the idea, doubtless for reasons yet again related to Ottawa's links with London.

18  For an interesting treatment of this subject, see David Leyton-Brown, 'Managing Canada-United States Relations in the Context of Multilateral Alliances,' in Lauren Mckenzie and Kim Nossal, eds., *America's Alliances and Canada-United States Relations: North American Relations in a Changing World* (Toronto: Summerhill, 1988).

19  John Kirk and Peter McKenna, *Canada-Cuba Relations: The Other Good Neighbor Policy* (Gainesville: University Press of Florida, 1997), 42–9; and James Rochlin, *Discovering the Americas: The Evolution of Canadian Foreign Policy toward Latin America* (Vancouver: UBC Press, 1994), 51–3.

20  See Canada, *Foreign Policy for Canadians* (Ottawa: Queen's Printer, 1970); and Canada, Department of External Affairs, 'Canada and the World: A Policy Statement by the Prime Minister of Canada, the Right Honourable Pierre Elliott Trudeau, May 29, 1968,' *External Affairs*, 20, no. 71 (1968).

21  The most complete look at this visit, and its Canadian political context, is found in Robert Wright, *Three Days in Havana: Pierre Trudeau, Fidel Castro and the Cold War World* (Toronto: HarperCollins, 2007).

22  See Brian Stevenson, *Canada, Latin America and the New Internationalism: A Foreign Policy Analysis 1968–1990* (Montreal and Kingston: McGill-Queen's University Press, 2000), passim.

23  Horacio Veneroni, *Estados Unidos y las Fuerzas armadas de América Latina* (Buenos Aires: Periferia, 1973).

24  For the handling of the Cuban question in the OAS, see F.V. Garcia-Ama-

dor, *La cuestión cubana en la OEA y la crisis del sistema interamericano* (Miami: University of Miami Press, 1987).

25  See Stevenson, *Canada, Latin America, and the New Internationalism*, 171–2. Trudeau became particularly upset with what U.S. intelligence was painting as Cuban military intervention, at Soviet behest, in Africa. This even led Ottawa to suspend bilateral assistance. Recent scholarship has suggested that Trudeau may have been duped on the issue by Secretary of State Henry Kissinger. See Piero Gleijeses, *Misiones en conflicto: Habana, Washington y Africa* (Havana: Ciencias Sociales, 2002).

26  Ismael Moreno Pino, *Orígenes y evolución del sistema interamericano* (Mexico City: Secretaría de Relaciones Exteriores, 1977).

27  For context, see B.W. Muirhead, *The Development of Postwar Canadian Trade* (Montreal and Kingston: McGill-Queen's University Press, 1992); Richard Lipsey and Petricio Meller, eds., *Western Hemisphere Trade Integration* (London: Macmillan, 1997); and Teresa Gutiérrez-Haces, *Procesos de integración económica en México y Canadá* (Mexico City: Porrúa, 2002).

28  This did not entail, at least in theory, any security commitments since Ottawa formally eschewed the Rio Pact and did not join the Inter-American Defence Board, the Inter-American Defence College, the conferences of commanders of armies, navies, and air forces, or the rest of the accords and institutions of what is termed the Inter-American security system, from which Cuba had been progressively expelled in the early 1960s. See Rodolfo Garrié Faget, *Organismos militares interamericanos* (Buenos Aires: Lapalma, 1968). For a Canadian view, see the sections by Canadian diplomats and Jill Sinclair in my *Canada and Latin American Security* (Montreal: Meridien Press, 1993).

29  These subjects are all discussed in Stevenson, *Canada, Latin America and the New Internationalism*; Rochlin, *Discovering the Americas*; and McKenna, *Canada and the OAS* . See also my *What's In It for Us?* (Ottawa: Canadian Foundation for the Americas, 1995).

30  For the 1962 situation from a Cuban perspective, see Jose Lechuga, *Cuba and the Missile Crisis* (Melbourne: Ocean Press, 2001).

31  The breadth of the disaster is conveyed in Homero Campo and Orlando Pérez, *Cuba: los años duros* (Mexico City: Plaza y Janes, 1997), especially 14–15; and Luís Suárez Salazar, *El Siglo XXI: posibilidades y desafíos para la Revolución cubana* (Havana: Ciencias Sociales, 2000), passim.

32  These economic reforms are found in Carmelo Mesa-Lago, *Are Economic Reforms Propelling Cuba to the Market?* (Miami: North-South Center Press, 1994). The less well-known political reforms are examined (too optimistically, in this author's opinion) in Arnold August, *Cuban Democracy and the*

*1997–98 Elections* (Havana: Editorial Jose Martí, 1999). A more balanced view is that of Antoni Kapcia, 'Political Change in Cuba: Before and after the Exodus' (London: Institute of Latin American Studies, Occasional Paper no. 9, 1995).

33  See H. Michael Erisman and John Kirk, eds., *Cuba's Foreign Policy Confronts a New International Order* (Boulder, Colo.: Lynne Rienner, 1991).

34  Works putting these events in context include Thomas Paterson, *Contesting Castro: The United States and the Triumph of the Cuban Revolution* (New York: Oxford University Press, 1994); and Morris Morley and Chris McGillion, *Unfinished Business: America and Cuba after the Cold War, 1989–2001* (Cambridge: Cambridge University Press, 2002).

35  Cubans argue that a policy that is pursued by the greatest power in the history of the world and that restricts international shipping, impedes not only trade but investment by other countries, and blocks access to credit from international institutions and not just national U.S. ones is not really an embargo. It is in fact a blockade, especially when backed up by the largely unspoken military might of Washington. See Carlos A. Batista Odio, 'Bloqueo, no embargo,' in Carlos Batista Odio et al., eds., *El Conflicto Cuba-Estados Unidos* (Havana: Editorial Félix Varela, 1998), 38–48.

36  Joaquín Roy, *Cuba, the United States and the Helms-Burton Doctrine: International Reactions* (Gainesville: University Press of Florida, 2000).

37  John Kirk et al., 'Retorno a los negocios: cincuenta años de relaciones entre Canadá y Cuba,' *Cuadernos de nuestra América*, 12, no. 24 (1995): 142–59.

38  See Roy, *Cuba, the United States, and the Helms-Burton Doctrine*.

39  For Cuba's efforts on drugs and the U.S. reaction to it and to Cuba as a threat, see U.S. State Department, *International Narcotics Control Strategy Report* (Washington, 2005); Christopher Marquis, 'Pentagon Wants US Military to Work with Cuba,' Miami *Herald*, 21 February 1998; and Francisco Arias Fernández, *Cuba contra el narcotráfico: de víctimas a centinelas* (Havana: Editora Política, 2001).

40  The strength and breadth of the Caracas-Havana connection is well discussed, as are its limitations, in Richard Gott, *In the Shadow of the Liberator* (London: Verso, 2000).

41  For Venezuela, see Rosa Miriam Elizalde and Luís Báez, *El Encuentro* (Havana: Oficina de Publicaciones del Consejo de Estado, 2005). It is interesting to note that, in the present confrontation between Washington and La Paz on the Cuban issue, Cuba's military influence in Bolivia is very limited indeed despite the two countries' mutual affection and their cooperation on many social and economic fronts. See Sonia Alda Mejías, 'La Participación de las Fuerzas Armadas en la revolución democrática del MAS:

el proyecto de Evo Morales,' in Isidro Sepúlveda, ed., *Seguridad humana y nuevas políticas de defense en Iberoamérica* (Madrid: Instituto Universitario General Gutiérrez Mellado, 2007), 445–71, especially 468–70.

42  The Washington consensus was roughly that body of elite views across the region that called for fiscal responsibility (and thus reduced social services and state employment), U.S. leadership in the drive for hemispheric free trade, and liberal economies and democracy on the United States model.

43  This is mentioned several times in Sahadeo Basdeo and Heather Nicol, eds., *Canada, the United States and Cuba: An Evolving Relationship* (Miami: North-South Center Press, 2002).

44  Here again, this was of course not the case in Washington and the negative context produced was highly troubling to Canadian political leaders, who had to make what were among the most difficult strategic decisions in the country's history. See Claude Denis, 'Conclusiones: mirando hacia el futuro,' in Athanasios Hristoulas et al., eds., *Canadá: política y gobierno en el siglo XXI* (Mexico City: Porrúa, 2005), 287–96, especially 292–4.

# 2 Inside Castro's Cuba: The Revolution and Canada's Embassy in Havana

DON MUNTON AND DAVID VOGT

Canada's relationship with Cuba in the 1950s was mostly trade-oriented, largely uncontroversial, and thoroughly laid back. The coming to power of Fidel Castro and the 26th of July Movement brought dramatic changes. Relations with revolutionary Cuba became highly political, extraordinarily controversial, and more than difficult for those involved.

Canada maintained both economic and diplomatic relations with the island nation through the politics, controversies, and challenges of the early 1960s, and continues to do so today. The United States did not and does not. During a period of rising tensions and then outright hostilities, Castro accused the United States of interference and outright aggression, took over American oil companies, and eventually nationalized all American-owned firms and property, proposing a compensation scheme unacceptable to American interests. Washington, for its part, began planning covert operations, cut off Cuba's main export to the United States, erected a trade embargo, and then severed diplomatic relations and ultimately supported an unsuccessful invasion of Cuba in April 1961.[1]

As Cuban-American relations declined precipitously through the early 1960s, the Canadian government found itself in an increasingly awkward international triangle. It attempted to maintain ties and trade with Cuba, for reasons of principle more than profit, and to demonstrate an independent foreign policy, while trying to avoid Cuba becoming a major problem and a painful public dispute in Canadian-American relations. These objectives were not easily reconciled.[2]

Canada's long-standing relationship with Castro's Cuba is the subject of the present volume and a growing literature. However, the roots of this unusual relationship, dating back to 1959 and beyond, have not been as well explored or documented. The aim of this chapter is to examine those roots from a particular vantage point – that of the Canadian embassy in Havana – and a particular time period – the six years preceding Fidel Castro's coming to power and the three years following it.

In part, the time period here is what is manageable in a short chapter. Yet 1961 is arguably a suitable end point of sorts. The Bay of Pigs invasion in April of that year simultaneously diminished the serious external threat to Cuba and consolidated the new regime domestically. Fidel Castro acknowledged the Cuban Revolution as socialist and then proclaimed his devotion to Marxist-Leninism at the end of 1961. The essence of Cuba's relationships not only with the United States and the USSR but also with Canada was then basically cast for the coming decades.

The present chapter is not an exhaustive history of Canadian-Cuban relations in the early Castro years, and such a detailed account remains to be done.[3] While the chapter provides a glimpse into Canadian and Cuban policies during this time, and returns to these policies in the conclusion, they are not the focus here. The spotlight is on Cuba itself, as seen by resident Canadian diplomats, sent abroad not (as the old saying goes) to lie for their country but rather to observe for it. The views highlighted are those of the Canadian ambassadors: Harry Scott (1951–6); Hector Allard (1957–9); Allan Anderson (1959–61); and George Kidd (1961–4).

Focusing on the Havana embassy during this era entails both limitations and benefits. The risks of such a restricted perspective, in terms both of narrow viewpoint and of short time frame, are obvious. Taking a Havana perspective also runs counter to the Ottawa-centric focus of much writing on Canadian foreign policy. To offset these limitations, we will make some reference to the observations of others, including government officials in Ottawa and Washington, other diplomatic missions in Cuba, and writers on the early years of the Castro era. The view here, however, is largely that of Canadian diplomats reporting from Havana. The major benefits of this focus are immediacy, in terms of proximity to the events unfolding in Cuba, and impact, at least in Ottawa. While diplomatic reporting has recently become less valued as a resource and a skill, it was governments' most important window on events abroad in the 1960s and earlier.[4]

One existing survey of Canada-Cuba relations criticizes Canadian diplomatic reporting from Havana in general for being inaccurate and prone to personal judgments.[5] Our analysis is rather more positive. To be sure, biases existed and mistakes were made, usually in the press of time. Given the circumstances, however, the reporting overall was balanced, accurate, and perceptive – on occasion, remarkably so.[6]

Three themes dominated the reports from Havana (and international discussions about Cuba) during this period. They were: the fate of the government of President Fulgencio Batista Zaldívar, in power since 1952, and the prospects for Fidel Castro's 26th of July Movement; the viability of the Castro government after coming to power in 1959; and the extent to which Castro and his government were, or were becoming, communist.

### Ousting Batista: Castro's Rise to Power

The Canadian embassy in Havana exhibited a markedly ambivalent attitude towards the Batista regime that ruled Cuba for most of the 1950s. In mid-decade, for example, the Canadian ambassador, Harry Scott, found a 'cautious hope' among the Cuban populace that Batista's government would offer progress and stability to the nation. Nevertheless, the ambassador noted, Cubans would 'not forgive him for the way in which he subverted their constitutional government.' As a result, Batista 'is unpopular with the Cubans, is becoming more so very day, and knows it.'[7] One positive mark was that, if not explicitly 'anticommunist,' Batista was at least not 'pro-communist.'[8]

Fidel Castro first came to the attention of Canadian diplomats with his famous, ill-fated 26 July 1953 attack on the Moncada barracks in Oriénte province. The embassy noted that the 'brief but bloody' assault led by 'Dr Fidel Castro' had failed spectacularly and that the Batista government was able to weather the storm with ease.[9]

The year 1953 marked not only the birth of Castro's 26th of July Movement but also an extraordinary meeting in a most unlikely place. Representatives of two major Cuban political parties opposing Batista met in June at the Ritz Carlton Hotel in Montreal. Prevented or discouraged from getting together in the United States, Mexico, and Guatemala, they had opted to gather in Canada. They issued a declaration, the so-called Charter of Montreal, calling for a provisional government to oversee elections free of violence. While aimed at restoring constitutional government to Cuba, the declaration did not reject revolutionary activity. The Batista government believed that the plotters were trying to buy weapons in Canada and ship them to Cuba, destined for the hands of anti-government revolutionaries.

The Montreal gathering displayed an unusual, albeit limited, unity of purpose and not surprisingly received considerable media and diplomatic attention. The Canadian government was both caught by surprise and slightly concerned. The publicity given to Montreal and Canada was unwelcome, and official Ottawa fretted that the meeting implicated Canada in a foreign conspiracy and thus violated the international norm of non-intervention, with possibly damaging effects on relations with the existing government in Cuba.

The embassy was more sanguine. While 'Montreal and Canada have temporarily become household words here,' Ambassador Scott reported, 'there has been no public criticism of the Canadian government for not preventing the meeting.' The Cuban government, certainly, 'is taking it all very seriously and would, in my opinion, regard it as an unfriendly act if the Canadian Government were to permit a similar meeting ... again.'[10] On the other hand, 'many Cubans are sympathetic to the aims of the leaders who met in Montreal' and 'it is conceivable that Canada has gained some prestige in certain quarters here.'[11]

These events are of interest, parenthetically, for at least three reasons. First, the Ritz Carlton meeting and the Castro group's attack on 26 July may be directly connected. Certainly, Batista claimed that such a link existed (though he is a suspect source) and at the time the Canadian government took seriously reports of arms shipments from Canada to rebel groups.[12] Secondly, the meeting puts Castro's efforts to overthrow Batista in a broader perspective, one missed in much of the literature on the Cuban Revolution that, understandably, focuses on Fidel. For all his prominence after 1958, Castro was, in the early 1950s, but a part of a broader opposition effort. Thirdly, the plotting of the anti-Batista groups highlights the fact that other Cuban opposition groups had used many of the techniques Castro later adopted – the covert organization of rebel movements, acquisition abroad of arms, secret landings on the shores of Cuba, and so on. Compared with other similar efforts, Castro's revolution was thus not particularly original in its beginnings but was ultimately much more successful in its execution.

The Canadian embassy continued to track Fidel Castro through the 1950s, from his confession and trial for the 1953 Moncada attack to his incarceration on the Isle of Pines and later release from prison, his departure for the United States and Mexico and the warrant for his arrest (for receiving funds from the Ortodoxo Party, the Communist Party, and 'other revolutionary organizations'), the discovery of his illegal training camp and arms cache in Mexico, and his ultimate return to Cuba.[13]

Castro came back, as he had promised, landing in easternmost Oriénte province on 2 December 1956. While the embassy's report on the almost disastrous landing was based largely on government information, it correctly estimated the size of Castro's forces and noted that they were surviving, though in much reduced numbers, 'in the difficult and virtually deserted country between Niquero and the Sierra Madre.' It also concluded, however, that the numbers killed or captured 'should reduce the effectiveness of the force to a negligible quantity.'[14] Additionally, the embassy suggested that student demonstrations begun a few days earlier, on the occasion of Memorial Day for the student martyrs of 1871, in Santiago de Cuba, Camagüey, and Holguin were related to the invasion. The demonstrations 'were taken over and carried forward with more determination by well-armed groups of young Santiagueros dressed in khaki or olive drab and wearing armbands of the 26th of July Movement' who attacked and damaged some government buildings. The embassy cited reports from Mexico that 4,000 Cuban exiles were heading for the island and other reports in Cuba that Fidel himself was dead, but it emphasized that these were unconfirmed. 'Nothing is known,' it said, 'of [the] whereabouts of Fidel Castro.'[15] With their leader unaccounted for and the remnants of Castro's forces taking refuge in the distant Sierra Maestra, they dropped off the Havana embassy's radar screen for awhile.

The Canadian diplomats trying to make sense of all this felt the drama unfolding. 'It was impossible,' they told their Ottawa-bound colleagues, 'even for those determined to remain objective, to escape the effects of tension, rumour and excitement.'[16] After the apparent disaster of the invasion, the embassy was too quick to write off the 26th of July movement and dismiss its leader. Castro clearly harboured 'deadly intention' but was 'not a military genius.' Either he was 'mad' or was let down by expected supporters and was possibly suffering from 'megalomania.' Perhaps the Canadians' most serious misjudgment was that Fidel would likely 'fizzle as a political leader' if he chose to leave his refuge in the mountains.[17] 'Fidel Castro the militant idealist cannot become Fidel Castro, President of Cuba,' argued Hector Allard, the new ambassador. If he did, a Castro government 'would be worse than the present one.' President Batista thus offered 'the best hope for the future.' He could promise 'the stability demanded by foreign investors,' was overseeing 'the diversification of the economy of Cuba,' and had far more governing experience than the youthful Fidel.[18] A stable Cuba with a diversified economy, of course, was a Cuba that could trade more with Canada and have more business for the Canadian banks (Royal Bank of Canada and Bank of Nova Scotia) located there.

Here Allard was reflecting both Canadian national interests and a preference, which diplomats and their home governments often share, for stability abroad and leaders who can and do provide it. The Canadians in Havana soon changed their tune, however, on Batista and on Castro.

The ambassador initially argued that Fidel was a serious *problem* to the Batista government but not really a serious *threat*. While 'the strength in the situation seems to remain with Batista,' Allard did suggest that 'it will be more than difficult for the Government to exterminate the guerrillas of the Sierra Maestra.'[19] Within months the embassy was reporting that the government had indeed been unable to quell the movement. [20] Although relatively inactive at first, the rebels definitely survived in the mountains. They soon controlled 'substantial areas' and were 'more than just a thorn in [the government's] side.'[21] Indeed, they now 'cast a shadow over the country.'[22] At year's end, Allard would proclaim 1957 in Cuba 'the year of Fidel Castro.'[23]

Allard nevertheless dismissed Castro's call for a general strike in April 1958; the rebel leader 'did not have the support of the working masses on which he was counting.'[24] After the strike faltered, the ambassador suggested that Fidel 'had shot his bolt.'[25] Yet, by July, the embassy was also branding as a failure Batista's repeated and extensive efforts to defeat the rebel forces. The discrepancy between peaceful Havana and the unstable Oriénte province was 'startling,' the ambassador concluded. As long as the 26th of July Movement was able to continue operations, he added, 'the long-range chances for rebel success appear to expand.'[26] Waging a classic guerrilla campaign, they began with night raids on isolated outposts and moved steadily to attacking larger centres. By the end of August, the embassy was reporting that the rebels controlled most of Oriénte and key areas of next-door Camagüey province. To his credit, Allard voluntarily retracted the 'shot his bolt' comment; to the contrary, he said, the rebel leader had clearly recovered.[27] The Canadians were not alone in reversing themselves; American diplomats also interpreted the failed general strike as a sign of Castro's decline, before doing a volte-face and concluding that it was the Batista regime that was 'expiring.'[28]

By the fall of 1958, the embassy was reporting that fighting had spread to four of Cuba's six provinces – even though the government had still not acknowledged that the rebels had moved beyond Oriénte.[29] The

November elections did nothing to attract support to the government. Castro had rejected the process. In November, Ambassador Allard reported 'scattered armed clashes' in the capital.[30] In mid-December, fighting was moving westward towards Havana. Although the *guerrilleros* still fully controlled only eastern Cuba, Allard said that 'the final crisis appears to be drawing near.'[31]

Throughout 1957 and 1958, the embassy's sources of information about affairs outside Havana and its immediate surroundings were strictly limited. Consequently, its assessments of the regime's stability often took on an urban-centric flavour; in November 1958, for example, it reported that, 'while the masses may not be pro-Batista, they have not yet reached the stage where they will take to the streets to rid the country of him in favour of Fidel Castro.'[32] Embassies, of course, are located in capital cities. The opportunities for staff forays into the countryside were few, and news from Oriénte province, especially news unfavourable to Batista, frequently faded behind a cloud of censorship. From time to time, the Canadians did receive updates on what was happening in Oriénte from the British and American embassies, both of which had consulates in Santiago de Cuba.[33] However, Canada's embassy was often left with 'more rumours than news,' and it sometimes had to rely upon American news reports received via New York and Washington.[34]

Castro's forces not only gained strength militarily through 1957 and 1958 but also broadened their political base. Opposition to Batista coalesced to a certain degree with formation of the Council of Cuban Liberation in November 1957 in Miami (which included Felipe Pazos, who was thought to be representing Castro).[35] The Canadian ambassador noted that the movement 'had begun making the transition into a political as well as a military force.' Although Castro severed ties with the council a few months later, the apparent rift was patched up in Caracas in July 1958 and subsequently the anti-Batista groups once more presented 'a more or less united front.'[36] While the so-called Caracas Pact was not made public, Allard discovered that its signatories were wide-ranging – including Castro; José Miro Cardona, former head of the Havana Bar Association; former president Prío Socarras; the Ortodoxo Party; participants in the 1956 officers' coup; the Students' Revolutionary Directorate; the University Students' Federation; and labour unions. The pact, however, merely papered over a serious split, between moderates who wanted to get rid of Batista and restore democracy and those of a more radical view who, like Castro, wanted to achieve a social revolution.

The diplomats in Havana did not overlook the repressive side of the Batista government, nor refrain from criticizing what they saw. The president repeatedly suspended constitutional guarantees for periods (of forty-five days each) through 1957 and 1958 – a sure reflection, the embassy noted, of the seriousness with which he regarded the uprising. Batista also fired judges, imposed press censorship when there was too much coverage of the rebels, and twice assumed virtually complete powers in 1958 under declarations of a national emergency. 'While prosperous as never before,' one Canadian declared, Cuba 'is a police state.'[37] Batista had amply demonstrated that the constitution of 1940, however democratic and republican in principle, 'allowed for military despotism.'[38] His army often inflicted harsh and violent treatment on the local populations where rebel forces were active. By mid-1958, embassy reports noted, Batista's forces were being regularly accused in Cuba of 'brutality, graft, blackmail, and less avowable activities.'[39] His secret police were particularly notorious.[40]

The Canadians also observed Batista's popular support trickle away. Even before Castro and his small band landed in Oriénte, there were conspiracies against the president. In 1957 the embassy reported that the military and the police were 'harbouring plotters against the Government'[41] and commented on a violent uprising from within the navy.[42] As the rebels continued to win battles in the provinces, units of Batista's army in the east began surrendering.[43] The government responded by arresting senior army officers and threatening court-martials for cowardice and conspiracy. Batista was clearly losing the crucial support of the armed services. As early as April 1958, Ambassador Allard concluded that the regime persisted largely because of peoples' fear of the secret police. By 'spreading terror,' however, they were 'at the same time increasing the ranks of those who believe ... that Batista and particularly his henchmen should sooner or later go.'[44]

And go they did.[45] On New Year's Eve 1958, Batista and many senior officials suddenly took flight – some, the embassy noted, also took with them 'all the public funds they could.'[46] Although such an event was not entirely unexpected, the embassy had no advance warning, and it sent a hastily prepared telegram advising Ottawa of the collapse early on New Year's Day.[47] Watching the events, the Canadians expressed the hope 'that the crisis would bring hardship to as few people as possible and that order might arise quickly from the inevitable chaos in Cuba marking Batista's fall.'[48]

Fidel Castro's coming to power was in many respects an extraordinary event, and was so partly because this first phase of the Cuban Revolution ended without any sort of culminating military triumph. There was no Battle of Diên Biên Phu or even a storming of the Winter Palace. The Batista regime, challenged but not yet soundly defeated, simply melted away. In contemporary parlance, the existing Cuban state failed.

While the Canadian diplomats in Havana refrained from joining the 26th of July Movement's victory celebrations, they certainly did not lament the passing of the Batista regime. The embassy placed the responsibility for much of the success of Castro's movement upon hostility towards Batista's own authoritarian tendencies, a view shared by much of the subsequent literature, rather than several competing explanations advanced at the time, including communist infiltration of opposition movements and long-standing resentment of poverty, particularly in rural areas.[49] Ultimately the diplomats were surprised not by the regime's demise but only by the speed of its collapse, and they were not the only ones. Fidel himself was still in distant Oriénte province when the Batista gang fled.

## Prevailing in Power: The Revolution Consolidated

From Santiago de Cuba, Castro announced that he would be proceeding to Havana and proclaimed Manuel Urrutía Lleo as provisional president. Canada recognized the new government of Cuba a week later, not with any reluctance born of misgivings but with some uncertainty, given the confusion and suddenness of Batista's demise. The Canadian decision came shortly after the United States, United Kingdom, and France, as well as various Latin American states, had all extended recognition.[50]

Almost immediately the Canadian diplomats in Havana began reflecting on the nature and viability of the new government. They correctly saw major challenges on three fronts: the domestic-political, the economic, and the diplomatic.[51] The third, Cuba's international political challenges, centred principally on Cuba's relations with the United States, at least initially. Growing hostility led to Washington's decision to break off relations in early 1961 and the abortive Bay of Pigs invasion in April of that year, and culminated in Cuba's steady movement into an alliance with the USSR. Space constraints here will not allow a detailed discussion of these now well-covered events. The focus, instead, will be on the political and economic challenges in Cuba itself.

Domestically, the politics of the early Castro years were never bor-

ing. The embassy was thoroughly unpersuaded by Urrutía's appointment as president. Ambassador Allard suspected that the former judge
would be a figurehead,[52] referring on one occasion to his 'puppet' government.[53] When Castro's forces swiftly began organizing a large public demonstration in Havana, Allard somewhat sarcastically described
its purpose as being to prove that he, Castro, was 'lord and master
in Cuba.' The Canadians were thus less than shocked when interim
prime minister Cardona resigned suddenly on 13 February and Castro replaced him.[54] Regarding the new government, the ambassador
expressed hope that 'the well-disciplined *barbudos*' would successfully
restore 'more normal conditions.'[55] Their young leader, he noted, 'may
not yet be aware that he is going to be busy not only for months but for
years to come' creating order out of the chaos.[56]

Castro and his colleagues opted to place reform ahead of order, and
ahead of promised elections. In April 1959 Allard reported the new
government's publicly stated view that elections were not feasible until
underlying problems in health care, land ownership, education, and
national sovereignty had been addressed.[57] 'Those who talk of elections,' Fidel soon proclaimed, 'are enemies of the revolution [because]
the Cuban democratic procedure does not require elections.'[58]

As the speed of reform accelerated, and the new government's commitment became clearer, Cardona's resignation was soon followed by
others. Some of those leaving had been stalwarts of the 26th of July
Movement. The most notable departure, though, was that of Castro himself, who announced his own resignation abruptly on 17 July.
An External Affairs memorandum to Canadian Prime Minister John
Diefenbaker the same day, based on reporting from the Havana embassy, attributed the move to 'growing opposition to [Castro's] recently
proclaimed agrarian reform' but expressed 'little doubt that Castro will
remain the effective head of the Cuban Government.'[59] Much as expected, Fidel re-emerged as prime minister after a 'huge demonstration
of public support.' His resignation had 'strengthened' his hand but also
forced the departure of President Urrutía.[60]

Two particularly controversial government legislative initiatives, according to the embassy, were the far-reaching Agrarian Reform Law,
capping land ownership and providing for expropriation above certain limits, and a Fiscal Reform Law, introducing luxury taxes on such
products as automobiles. The former was popular in the rural areas and
welcomed by the *campesinos* but opposed by landowners and investors. 'Rent reductions, restrictions on new building construction, and

new taxes on vacant lots ... administered several body blows to the proprietary and property-owning classes.'[61] Some of the reforms particularly affected American investments in Cuba and raised substantial concern in Washington, especially when U.S. properties were nationalized without what was deemed to be adequate compensation. Disquiet about reform measures also 'widened and strengthened' opposition to the government within the Cuban public,[62] an opposition that was growing 'in volume and intensity.'[63] Facing public protest, the government did withdraw a proposed tax on newspapers.

The Canadian observers, as well as many Cubans, found troubling the public 'revolutionary trials' of Batista government and military officials. The trials 'continue[d] to grow in number' 'rather than drawing to a close.'[64] The embassy found it particularly unsettling when Castro intervened in one trial, 'order[ing] the appeal tribunal to sentence the defendants to long prison terms.'[65]

In April 1959 Allard suggested that decreasing turnouts at labour and political rallies were evidence of growing passive resistance to implementation of the revolution. Indeed, he indicated that 'Castro's star seems to be on the wane ... With each new government decree ... there are fewer and fewer Cubans with a desire to celebrate.'[66] By June, what had been 'scattered murmurs of dissent' were now 'a steady growl of disagreement.' The occasional bombing or 'armed outburst' prompted 'mass arrests.'[67] 'Fidel Castro and his government have faced one crisis after another,' chargé d'affaires R.W. Clark noted. 'The Cuban situation today is still far from normal.'[68] Somewhat in contrast, the new U.S. ambassador, Philip Bonsal, had initially believed that Castro 'would have a difficult time holding his government together,' but he soon changed his mind, concluding that Castro had the support of a 'large majority' of the public even as the 'propertied' and middle classes gradually fell away.[69]

Revolutionary Cuba also faced economic and financial problems. A new Canadian ambassador, Allan Anderson, used his first monthly report in October 1959 to note a break from the procession of 'regular political crises' that had so far dominated the year. He reported, however, that Cuban reserves 'are dwindling dangerously,' which spelled problems for international trade. The government imposed currency restrictions and announced a 'temporary import tax' on imported items.[70] At year's end, the embassy regarded the Cuban Banco Nacional as essentially insolvent and suggested that the government might be addressing its problems by seeking further Soviet aid.[71]

A few months later, Anderson opined that 'the number of people who are disenchanted with the present government appears to be growing continually.'[72] The opposition to the government became 'much bolder, more articulate, more determined and apparently stronger' over the course of 1960. (The true extent of anti-government military activity, Anderson complained, was now more difficult to assess; the Batista government had at least permitted newspapers to 'print reports regarding casualties inflicted by the army.')[73] Despite the mounting opposition, the likelihood of 'a successful counter-revolution' was 'still remote.'[74] The ambassador estimated that, overall, Castro 'probably still has a majority,' owing more to rural than urban support.[75]

Departures of disaffected Cubans became an exodus and included numerous defectors from within the government and the military as well as from the managerial and professional groups of society. The ambassador emphasized the harm done to the country but the exodus simultaneously and substantially weakened the opposition ranks within Cuba. The Catholic Church was now the only organized opposition, and it was not going to lead a counter-revolution. The opposition, Anderson predicted, could not overthrow Castro without 'outside help.'

No event showed the dynamics of the Cuban Revolution, and the quality of Canadian diplomatic reporting from Havana, better than what became the Bay of Pigs invasion by Cuban exiles. By the time it eventually occurred, the invasion was fully anticipated. So too was its failure.

As early as January 1960, the embassy reported rumours of anti-Castro invasion forces training in Central America, backed by the Central Intelligence Agency (CIA). While repeated false alarms of an attack on Cuba during 1960 led Ambassador Anderson to suggest that some of the alarms represented government attempts to distract attention from growing domestic opposition,[76] he soon took the threat seriously. This was the case despite a sense of disbelief, reflected in the despatches, that the government of the United States would not only mount such an effort but think it had a genuine chance of success. In January 1961 Anderson noted that the invasion rumours had reached a fever pitch. Havana was a 'lunatic scene' with 'guns being transported in all directions.'[77] Press reports in the United States itself pointed to preparations in Guatemala for an invasion. By March, Anderson sensed a difference from previous alerts: 'There is enough extra emphasis, enough people believing, enough increased tension quite obviously in the air.'[78] Days before the actual attack in April 1961, the ambassador warned Ottawa: 'Something is going to happen' and soon.[79]

Through 1960 the embassy had reported increased internal opposition to the Castro government and fighting in eastern Cuba. Then, in the months preceding the invasion, Anderson indicated that the government was mounting a major military effort and successfully challenging the rebels in the Escambray Mountains. He predicted, correctly, that the anti-Castro forces would be largely eliminated. The embassy also noted that the Castro administration was rounding up thousands of suspected anti-government individuals. It could now be overthrown 'only with the greatest of difficulty and in all probability not at all.'[80] The ambassador renewed warnings that nothing short of a massive invasion could succeed under present conditions.[81]

The Canadians were thus perhaps only slightly more surprised by the CIA-sponsored attack in mid-April 1961 than Cuba's government, which had infiltrated the exile movement. Nor were they surprised by the attack's failure. The Canadian ambassador and his British counterpart conducted their own post-mortem on the invasion and agreed that 'the Castro Government knew of the time and the place of the attack before it occurred.'[82] The British ambassador, Herbert Marchant, in his report to London, quipped that 'this Government of inexperienced young men has managed to win a three-day war, throw a minimum of 30 000 ... citizens into prison and come up smiling broadly, if a little strained.'[83]

In the months leading up to the Bay of Pigs invasion, American government officials had been far from unanimous in their support of the operation. A December 1960 U.S. intelligence estimate had found 'no significant likelihood that the Castro regime will fall of its own weight.' In CIA eyes, this view provided further justification for covert action to tip the scales.[84] The State Department and officials from the Havana embassy were never fully convinced of the prospects for the invasion. The Department of Defense's position was not clear; while it had endorsed the invasion, it did so under the code name BUMPY ROAD. CIA analysts, consistently more prone to see vulnerabilities in the Castro regime, argued just prior to the invasion that the Cuban people were 'los[ing] their fear of the government' and the army would 'not fight in the event of a showdown.'[85] Only after the failed invasion did agencies agree on the strength of Cuba's new security apparatus.[86]

The Canadian assessment of the Bay of Pigs was much different. In the view of the Canadian embassy, the invasion had the opposite effect to that intended by the United States; rather than overthrowing Castro, it had actually strengthened his government. For Cubans, Anderson would later write, the attack seemed to validate claims that Cuba must be defended 'against the onslaught of revanchist United States imperialism,' the truth of which many people had until then been 'unconvinced.' It also eliminated 'the possibility of a return to friendly relations with the United States' and confirmed Cuba's turn into the 'Sino-Soviet orbit.'[87]

Anderson's successor shared his opinion of the invasion's impact. Reflecting back on 1961, George Kidd told Ottawa that the invasion had bolstered Castro's political power and his prestige with Cubans at a time when his popularity had begun to falter. There was now no serious opposition.[88] And, as it turned out, there would be none.

### Going Communist: Fidel and Cuba

Almost three years before the overthrow of Batista, the Canadian embassy had noted evidence suggesting communist influence in the 26th of July Movement.[89] At the time, the focus was largely on two close and trusted advisers, Fidel's brother Raúl, a long-standing member of the Communist Party in Cuba, and Ernesto 'Che' Guevara, the Argentine revolutionary who had left Guatemala in 1954 after its government had been overthrown in a CIA-sponsored coup.[90] In early 1958 Allard reported rumours that 'Castro had sold out to the Communists' and they were now paying his bills.[91] Two months after his first report, the ambassador stated that Castro's new funding appeared in fact to come from 'a number of Cuban businessman,' some with the Bacardi Rum company. Later the embassy passed on another claim – that the rebellion 'was very largely financed by the USSR Embassy in Mexico.'[92]

The embassy monitored Cuba's inexorable movement towards becoming a socialist state and Soviet ally in terms of both people and policies. The people-watching involved both departures and arrivals of personnel. The policy-watching covered both domestic measures and external ties.

On the 'departures level,' the Canadian diplomats watched as various prominent figures followed Cardona out of the government and military. These included Cuban air force chief Major Pedro Díaz Lanz and army major Hubert Matos, both of whom tendered resignations, criticizing growing communist influence in the military. Another prominent figure, Colonel Ramón Barquín, accepted a foreign posting rather than stay in Cuba. (Air force officer José Castiñeiras approached Canadian embassy officials about emigrating to join his Canadian-born wife.) When Treasury Minister Rufo Lopez Fresquet resigned in March 1960, Ambassador Anderson characterized him as 'the last of the conservatives.' He bluntly warned Ottawa that the remaining non-communist officials in the government were 'sitting ducks.'[93]

On the 'arrivals level,' the embassy's observations came early and often. Beyond Raúl and Che, the appointment of known or suspected communists, such as Carlos Rafael Rodriguez, Nuñez Jiménez of the Instituto Nacional de Reforma Agraria (INRA), and Carlos Franqui, the editor of *Revolución*, to key official or advisory positions became the norm.[94] Within weeks of Batista's ouster, the new government legalized the Popular Socialist Party (PSP – the Cuban Communist Party) and returned to public circulation the communist daily *Hoy*.[95] The embassy also observed the government's silencing of the remaining media (such as *Diario de la Marina*) and its gaining of effective control over the remaining independent papers.[96] While the PSP itself 'remained in the relative background ... individual communists were assuming more power.'[97] There were occasional reversals, such as editorials in *Revolución* that attacked the communists for making 'unnecessary demands' on the revolution, but they were short-lived.

One central question proved elusive – was Fidel Castro himself a communist? Initially, and for a lengthy period, the Canadians in Havana thought not.[98] Fidel's links with communism were too numerous to overlook, including various activities during his time as a student, but for years these links offered no conclusive proof. Ambassador Allard, who was more suspicious than his successor, Anderson, noted in March 1959 that communist elements were infiltrating the government and that 'Castro is fast becoming victim of his own verbosity and also a tool of Communist elements surrounding him.' Nevertheless, Allard still did not believe that Fidel himself was, at least yet, a true communist, and confidential sources agreed.[99] Even in late 1961 Ambassador Kidd was unconvinced about Castro.[100]

The embassy also kept its eye on government policies. Despatches generally tracked an increasing level of intervention in what had been a substantial private sector in Cuba, wide-scale nationalization of businesses, American-controlled and others, and expanding control of the economy and foreign trade by the Cuban government. A report prepared by the embassy's commercial secretary in December 1959 summarized the extent of the intervention.[101] 'If there is no communist influence,' Ambassador Anderson concluded in 1960, 'some of the measures taken by the government are incomprehensible ... There seems to be enough circumstantial evidence to indicate at least a substantial amount of communist influence.'[102] Che Guevara had, for example, publicly acknowledged that his economic policy had 'a Marxist tinge.'[103]

Allard was especially prone to viewing the regime's growing hostility to the Roman Catholic Church as an indicator of communist influence in Cuba. While the rebels had been 'extremely correct in ... relations with the Roman Catholic hierarchy' during their days in the Sierra Maestra,[104] the government was now less so. He noted, for instance, that Havana now sported anti-religious graffiti; two pro-revolutionary papers, *Revolución* and *Bohemia*, had both attacked Catholic officials; and the education minister had barred Catholic teachers from certain positions within his department.[105]

Given the concerns about Cuba's international orientation, the embassy reported on the visits not only of such high-level figures as Soviet deputy prime minister Anastas Mikoyan, who came in 1960 after some delay, but even of minor officials to and from 'the bloc' (Bulgaria, Poland, North Korea, and China as well as the USSR).[106] It noted an increasing presence of Soviet technical assistance and the flourishing of bloc diplomatic representation in Cuba (new missions from Czechoslovakia, Poland, Hungary, Bulgaria, Romania, East Germany, China, North Korea, and North Vietnam).[107] Cuban officials may initially have given 'evasive' answers to questions on whether Cuba was moving towards the communist bloc,[108] but the embassy was more persuaded by the deeds.

By late 1960, Anderson concluded that Cuba was in essence a communist state. Officials in Ottawa subsequently agreed. He summarized and concurred with the view from Washington: 'We do not know whether Castro is a Communist or not. That is to say, we do not know whether ... he follows the orthodox Marxist ideology. But we believe that he is closely entangled with Communists, here and abroad. If we are right, the precise label on Castro as a person makes no difference. Castro as an executive of the State acts like a full Communist.'[109]

Arriving in Cuba in February 1961, chargé d'affaires M.N. Bow (later to return as ambassador) argued that the country had become 'a dictatorship pure and simple,' backed by 'happy ... young rebels' full of *'joie de vivre.'* 'Cuba,' he wrote, 'has gone much farther along the road to communism than is generally realized outside the island,' with striking social and economic reforms pushed forward 'under the guise of Cuban nationalism.'[110] Whether or not the new regime was explicitly communist was increasingly irrelevant: 'The ideological label that should be affixed to Castro's Cuba may still be somewhat obscure but the nature of his regime is not difficult to discern: it is [a] ruthless dictatorship ... [that] is establishing a highly nationalized and planned economy on the basis of the experiences of the Sino-Soviet bloc nations; [and] it is pursuing a dynamic and aggressive foreign policy which is closely synchronized with that of the Sino-Soviet bloc. By whatever name they may be called, these are unmistakably the characteristics common to communist countries.'[111]

The last doubts about the direction of the country were soon settled at the Bay of Pigs. Castro himself announced during the April invasion that 'this is a socialist revolution.' His government furthermore proclaimed that 'Cuba was now the first Socialist Republic in Latin America' and hoped that 'it should not be the last.'[112]

In September, Ambassador Kidd reported 'a gradual but detectable evolution of political organization in Cuba towards a single party system on Communist lines,' much as Castro had forecast in a July speech. The governing party, the Organizaciones Revolucionarias Integrados (ORI), showed 'overt Communist penetration.' Kidd stated that 'the present Communist Party of Cuba will be the basis of the new Party and ... its political doctrines would be those of Marxism-Leninism.'[113]

The embassy highlighted Fidel Castro's decisive statement on 1 December 1961 proclaiming himself a Marxist-Leninist and acknowledging that the Cuban Revolution constituted 'a Marxist-Leninist program adjusted to the precise objective conditions of our country.' Kidd nevertheless dismissed Castro's 'public profession of faith in the Marxist creed' as an appeal 'to his new communist friends, both Cuban and Soviet,' suggesting that Fidel was merely 'putting the seal of his approval on what had already been announced by others.'[114]

After the fact, Castro himself insisted that he had always been a communist, at least from his student days. Some observers make that case.[115] Others argue that he did not begin as a communist but that his thinking evolved and he ultimately became one through the influence of events and people around him (especially his brother, Raúl, and Che Guevara).[116] A third group argues that Castro was not and has never really been a doctrinaire communist but found it necessary or politically expedient to cast his lot with Cuban and Russian communism in order to ensure the implementation of desired reforms.[117] Some of the Canadians in Havana would concur with the third of these camps.

This view was initially shared as well by many in the U.S. embassy, although the CIA's Havana station found 'definite Communist overtones' in his movement even before 1959.[118] The American ambassador, too, hoped that Castro could be held back by 'mature moderates,' though, when most of these departed over the course of 1959, he requested a 'qualified Communist expert' for his staff.[119] A government that fell 'under Communist influence' in 1959 accepted communist 'guidance' in the summer of 1960 and was under the 'effective control' of communists by November.[120] The United States had placed greater faith in the influence of Cuban moderates than Canada, and had mistakenly seen the second president of revolutionary Cuba, Osvaldo Dorticós Torrado, as one such moderate; when this influence proved extremely limited, it much more readily saw communist influence and control in Cuba.

## Conclusion

In hindsight, and particularly from the vantage point of the twenty-first century, developments in Cuba in the late 1950s and early 1960s follow an almost natural course. It is essential to realize, however, that events seemed much less predictable at the time. As Ambassador Anderson confessed in October 1959, 'I still dare not attempt to predict what will happen here.' There was, he said, an atmosphere of 'profound uncertainty, tinged with apprehension.'[121]

One part of Anderson's 'Letter of Instructions' in September 1959 encapsulates a key problem facing contemporary observers of Castro's Cuba. There was a chance, External Affairs suggested, that 'the revolution ... is not ... a mere change of guard at the top ... [but] a deeply popular revolution.' Changes of guard at the top had long been a pattern in Latin American politics. Deeply popular revolutions had not. It is always more difficult to comprehend the unusual than explain a well-established pattern. As we have suggested, the Castro revolution was never a 'sure thing.'

There were accordingly major constraints on what could be expected of mortals caught in a maelstrom. That being said, the diplomatic reporting from the Canadian embassy in Havana provides not only a fascinating inside look at revolutionary Cuba but also a historically insightful and useful one. The Canadians covered the sudden downfall of the Batista regime, the extraordinary challenges of the new government, and the movement of Cuba towards a socialist or communist state, and reported on them with considerable objectivity and accuracy. The embassy in 1958 pointed to the success of the rebels and later was particularly prescient about what became the Bay of Pigs invasion. Canadian reporting was certainly better than that of some contemporary press coverage in Cuba.[122] A review by the Department of External Affairs concluded that political reporting from Havana in 1958 had been generally 'very good,' indeed 'remarkable' given extenuating circumstances.[123] We concur, and our view of the Canadian reporting over the longer term thus differs from earlier, more critical accounts. Despite some significant exceptions, such as the timing of Batista's fall, the Canadian embassy reported events in Cuba reasonably accurately with considerably less resources than those possessed by the embassies of the British or, until their withdrawal in 1961, the Americans.

To be sure, the despatches from Havana reveal definite biases and some weaknesses. The most obvious bias is the preference for stability evident in the 1950s reporting on Cuba's turmoil. One weakness was Ambassador Anderson's occasional tendency to report others' ideas about the nature of the Cuban revolutionary government, and to do so often rather uncritically. Based on a conversation with the French ambassador, Anderson suggested, for example, that Castro might be a Soviet 'decoy' intended to draw the United States military into Cuba and 'ruin' U.S. 'relations with the rest of Latin America.'[124]At the very least, these comments were at variance with what was well known about Fidel's personality. Anderson had lived in and was familiar with the 'old Cuba, but he was not a career diplomat and did not posses the analytical skills particularly evident in his successor, George Kidd.

Another weakness, arguably, was a degree of denial, on the part of both the Canadians in Havana and External Affairs, that Castro and his government had more than communist leanings. It is possible that maintaining this claim was not merely a failure of perceptions. It perhaps served a functional purpose – making it easier, for awhile, for the government of Canada to justify maintaining economic and diplomatic relations with Cuba. Acknowledging that Cuba was a communist state would likely not have forced Canada's hand, since it had relations with most communist countries (though not with the Peoples' Republic of China). Doing so would, however, have made defending Canadian policy more difficult in Washington. The spiralling conflict between revolutionary Cuba and the United States was one from which there was no easy escape for Canada. As one ambassador noted, 'we have to walk delicately.' Canada must 'maintain friendly relations with the Cuban Government,' and 'encourage the sale of Canadian goods,' but also bear in mind that 'the Castro Government is not only pro-communist but communist-controlled.' Canadians, surely, did not want to become known as 'friends of the Castro-Khrushchev-Guevara-Mikoyan syndicate.'[125]

These considerations underscore another point. Perceptions, reporting, and policies were related, although not always directly. In a short overview such as the present chapter, it is not possible to trace with certainty the impact of the despatches from Havana. It is clear, however, that the embassy's reporting influenced some views in official Ottawa and thus perhaps the foreign policies being pursued – for example, with respect to the nature of the Castro government and its to-be-or-not-to-be embrace of socialism. Consequently, the reporting from the Havana embassy provides a valuable glimpse into the early years of revolutionary Cuba as well as representing an important contribution to understanding Canadian policy towards Cuba during that period.

NOTES

The research herein was funded by a research grant from the Social Sciences and Humanities Research Council of Canada and by the University of Northern British Columbia. We are grateful to Jillian Merrick, Stephanie Campbell, and Kylee Ronning for their research assistance, and to Suzanne LeBlanc for comments.

1  Existing studies of the Castro revolution and of U.S.-Cuban relations include Aleksandr Fursenko and Timothy Naftali, 'One Hell of a Gamble': Khrushchev, Castro, and Kennedy, 1958–1964 (New York: W.W. Norton, 1997); Gladys Marel García-Pérez, Insurrection and Revolution: Armed Struggle in Cuba, 1952–1959, trans. Juan Ortega (Boulder, Colo.: Lynne Rienner, 1998); Thomas M. Leonard, Castro and the Cuban Revolution (Westport, Conn.: Greenwood, 1999); Thomas G. Paterson, Contesting Castro: The United States and the Triumph of the Cuban Revolution (New York: Oxford University Press, 1994); and Richard E. Welch, Jr, Response to Revolution: The United States and the Cuban Revolution, 1959–1961 (Chapel Hill: University of North Carolina Press, 1985).
2  At a National Security Council meeting in July 1960, U.S. officials expressed their frustration at Canadians' apparent rejection of 'any view

of Cuban developments except the view that it was simply an internal revolution.' This reticence was blamed in part on naiveté and in part on Canada's desire to protect financial interests in Cuba: Mark Falcoff, ed., *The Cuban Revolution and the United States: A History in Documents, 1958–1960* (Washington, D.C.: U.S. Cuba Press, 2001), 9.7.

3   John Kirk and Peter McKenna's *Canada-Cuba Relations: The Other Good Neighbor Policy* (Gainesville, Fl.: University Press of Florida, 1997) provides a broad history of Canada-Cuba relations through the twentieth century, with an emphasis on more recent decades.

4   The bulk of this chapter is based on 'despatches' from the Canadian embassy in Havana during the 1950s and early 1960s. These documents were written by embassy officials, often but not always by the ambassador himself. The common term 'despatches' covers telegrams and letters as well as actual despatches. For short, urgent messages, the embassy used (enciphered) telegrams. Despatches (for longer, more general analyses) and letters (for shorter, more specific ones) were sent to Ottawa from Havana, as elsewhere, by secure diplomatic bag, carried by an External Affairs courier. These documents, mainly originating with the Department of External Affairs, are not systematically organized but rather located across various files. The documents cited herein are located at Library and Archives Canada (LAC), except where otherwise noted, and are from the External Affairs RG 25 series, unless otherwise noted. LAC declassified many of the relevant files at the request of the senior author of this chapter; however, a few files and individual documents remain closed under Canada's Access to Information legislation, despite the fact they are more than four decades old. Some potentially relevant documents also appear to be missing. The embassy used a sequential numbering system for both despatches and letters (within a given year) and there are gaps in both series.

5   Kirk and McKenna, *Canada-Cuba Relations*, 57–9.

6   We would argue that balance was sought and achieved even though, after 1961, many if not most of the embassy's reports were passed to the United States government, including the Central Intelligence Agency – as embassy staff in Havana themselves were well aware. In short, the Canadians aimed to 'speak truth to power' rather than tell the Americans what they may have wanted to hear.

7   Despatch D-28, 'Annual Review of Events in Cuba for 1953,' 26 January 1954, vol. 8326, file 10224–40, pt. 3.2; and Despatch D-176, 'Activities of Ex-President Prio Socarras,' 20 June 1953, RG 25, vol. 8326, file 4568-40, pt. 3.1.

8   Despatch D-257, 'Communism in Cuba,' 15 September 1953, vol. 8326, file 4568–40, pt. 3.2. Overall, 'communist strength' in Cuba was said to be low.

9  Despatch D-28, 'Annual Review of Events in Cuba for 1953,' 26 January 1954, vol. 8326, file 4568-40, pt. 3.2

10 Despatch D-176, 'Activities of Ex-President Prio Socarras,' 20 June 1953, vol. 8326, file 4568-40, pt. 3.1

11 Despatch D-160, 'Activities of Ex-President Prio Socarras,' 5 June 1953, vol. 8326, file 4568-40, pt. 3.1

12 'Ammunition labelled "Montreal" Reported Used in Cuban Uprising,' Montreal *Gazette*, 28 July 1953. See also: Department of External Affairs, American Division, Memorandum, 'Revolutionary Movement in Cuba,' 28 July 1953, vol. 8326, file 10224–40, pt. 3.1.

13 On these events, see, respectively: Despatch D-357, 'General Developments in Cuba during October and November, 1953,' 18 December 1953, vol. 8326, file 10224–40, pt. 3.2; Despatch D-61, 'Current Events in Cuba for the Month of February 1956,' 3 March 1956, vol. 7059, file 7590-N-40, pt. 3.1; Canadian Embassy, Mexico City, Despatch 303, 'Report for June 26, 1956 to July 23, 1956,' 23 July 1956, vol. 8326, file 4568–40, pt. 3.2; Telegram, 'Disturbances in Santiago,' 2 December 1956, vol. 7257, file 10224–40, pt. 4.1; Despatch D-332, 'Current Events in Cuba, November 1-December 8, 1956,' 9 December 1956, vol. 7059, file 7590-N-40, pt. 3.2; Telegram, 'Disturbances in Santiago,' 8 December 1956, vol. 7257, file 10224–40, pt. 4.

14 Despatch, D-332, 'Current Events in Cuba, November 1–December 8, 1956,' 9 December 1956, vol. 7059, file 1590-N-40, pt. 3.2. The New York *Times* correspondent in Havana, R. Hart Phillips, was similarly dismissive of Castro's action, regarding it as 'another hare-brained scheme, like the suicidal attack on Moncada.' See his *Cuba, Island of Paradox* (New York: McDowell, 1959), 291.

15 Telegram, 'Disturbances in Santiago,' 8 December 1956, vol. 7257, file 10224–40, pt. 4.

16 Despatch D-332, 'Current Events in Cuba, November 1-December 8, 1956,' 9 December 1956, vol. 7059, file 7590-N-40, pt. 3.2.

17 Despatch D-283, 'Political Situation in Cuba,' 29 July 1957, vol. 7257, file 10224–40, pt. 4.

18 Despatch D-87, 'Political Situation in Cuba,' 26 March 1957, vol. 7257, file 10224–40, pt. 4. British representatives in Cuba expressed similar views.

19 Despatch D-87, 'Political Situation in Cuba,' 26 March 1956, vol. 7257, file 10224–40, pt. 4. A State Department official told the Canadian embassy in Washington the same month that Castro 'is considered by the Cuban people as a living spirit of resistance to oppression' and suggested that Batista 'might well find himself in a dangerous situation' (Canadian embassy, Washington, D.C., telegram, 'Political Situation in Cuba,' 12 June 1957, vol.

7257, file 10224–40, pt. 4.1). A few months later, the British ambassador in Havana termed Castro the 'main threat' to the Batista regime.

20  Despatch D-248, 'Political Situation in Cuba,' 29 June 1957, vol. 7257, file 10224–40, pt. 4.

21  Despatch D-9, 'Annual Review of Events in Cuba – 1957,' 14 January 1958, vol. 2494, file 10463-AH-40, pt. 1.

22  Despatch D-283, 'Political Situation in Cuba,' 29 July 1957, vol. 7257, file 10224–40, pt. 4.

23  Despatch D-9, 'Annual Review of Events in Cuba – 1957,' 14 January 1958, vol. 2494, file 10463-AH-40, pt. 1.

24  Despatch D-21, 'Annual Review of Events in Cuba – 1958,' 20 January 1959, vol. 2444, file 10463-AH-40, pt. 1.

25  Despatch D-172, 'Internal Situation of Cuba,' 9 May 1958, vol. 7257, file 10224–40, pt. 4.

26  Despatch D-237, 'Situation in Oriente Province,' 4 July 1958, vol. 7257, file 10224–40, pt. 4.2; and Letter L-277, 'Cuban Internal Situation,' 1 August 1958, pt. 5.1.

27  Despatch D-327, 'Cuban Internal Situation,' 29 August 1958, vol. 7257, file 10224–40, pt. 5

28  Paterson, *Contesting Castro*, 147; and Falcoff, *The Cuban Revolution and the United States*, 1.23.

29  Despatch D-368, 'Cuban Internal Situation,' 25 September 1958, vol. 7257, file 10224–40, pt. 5.1

30  Despatch D-447, 'Cuban Internal Situation,' 20 November 1958, vol. 7257, file 10224–40, pt. 5.1.

31  Despatch D-497, 'Cuban Internal Situation,' 18 December 1958, vol. 7257, file 10224–40, pt. 5.2.

32  Despatch D-447, 'Cuban Internal Situation,' 20 November 1958, vol. 7257, file 10224–40, pt. 5.1.

33  Despatch D-237, 'Situation in Oriente Province,' 4 July 1958, RG 25, vol. 7257, file 10224–40, pt. 4.2.

34  Telegram, 2 August 1957, vol. 7257, file 10224–40, pt. 4; see also Despatch D-473, 'Effects on Cuba of the Continuing Crisis,' 4 December 1958, vol. 7257, file 10224–40, pt. 5.1.

35  Despatch D-429, 'Political Situation in Cuba,' 21 November 1957, vol. 7257, file 10224–40, pt. 4.1.

36  Despatch D-21, 'Annual Review of Events in Cuba – 1958,' 20 January 1959, vol. 2444, file 10463-AH-40, pt. 1. Allard speculated that this could mean that Castro would 'once more have access to Prío's stolen millions' (Despatch D-296, 'Castro Relations with the Cuban Liberation Board,' 13

August 1958, vol. 7257, file 10224–40, pt. 5.1; and Despatch D-322, 'Fidel Castro and the "Caracas Pact,"' 28 August 1958, pt. 5).

37  Despatch D-320, 'Political Situation in Cuba,' 27 August 1957, vol. 7257, file 10224–40, pt. 4.

38  Despatch D-367, 'Cuban Elections,' 25 September 1958, vol. 7257, file 10224–40, pt. 5.

39  Letter L-277, 'Cuban Internal Situation,' 1 August 1958, vol. 7257, file 10224–40, pt. 5.1.

40  Telegram, 'Cuban Internal Situation,' 23 April 1958, vol. 7257, file 10224–40, pt. 4.2.

41  Despatch D-381, 'Cuban Political Situation,' 23 October 1957, vol. 7257, file 10224–40, pt. 4.

42  Despatch D-332, 'Current Events in Cuba, November 1-December 8, 1956,' 9 December 1956, vol. 7059, file 7590-N-40, pt. 3.2; and Despatch D-9, 'Annual Review of Events in Cuba – 1957,' 14 January 1958, vol. 2494, file 10463-AH-40, pt. 1.

43  Letter L-62, 'Recent Events in Cuba.' 5 February 1959, vol. 7257, file 10224–40, pt. 5.2.

44  Telegram, 'Cuban Internal Situation,' 23 April 1958, vol. 7257, file 10224–40, pt. 4.2.

45  Telegram, 'Batista's Resignation,' 1 January 1959, vol. 7257, file 10224–40, pt. 5.1. The embassy's use of telegrams here rather than the slower despatches and letters reflects the urgency and rapidity of events.

46  Despatch D-31, 'Cuban Internal Situation,' 22 January 1959, vol. 7257, file 10224–40, pt. 5.2.

47  Telegram, 'Batista's Resignation,' 1 January 1959, RG 25, vol. 7257, file 10224–40, pt. 5.1. By contrast, the American State Department and the Central Intelligence Agency had reached the conclusion that Batista's downfall was imminent by early December, when an unofficial envoy was sent to attempt (unsuccessfully) to persuade Batista to turn over power to a military junta, and the intelligence agency hastily activated several poorly conceived contingency plans to prepare for a post-Batista Cuba. Perhaps because of his sympathy for Batista, Ambassador Earl Smith was not officially informed of the envoy sent to Batista and was called back to Washington for consultations: Philip W. Bonsal, *Cuba, Castro, and the United States* (Pittsburgh: University of Pittsburgh Press, 1971), 22–3; Falcoff, *The Cuban Revolution and the United States*, 1.40; Paterson, *Contesting Castro*, 16, 220; and Jack Pfeiffer, *The Bay of Pigs Operation, III: Evolution of CIA's Anti-Castro Policies, 1950-January 1961* (Central Intelligence Agency, 1970s), http://www14.homepage.villanova.edu/david.barrett/bop.html, 18.

48  Despatch D-21, 'Annual Review of Events in Cuba – 1958,' 20 January 1959, vol. 2444, file 10463-AH-40, pt. 1; see also telegram, 'Batista Resignation,' 1 January 1959, vol. 7257, file 10224–40, pt. 5.1.

49  See, for example, Leonard, *Castro and the Cuban Revolution*, 6–8; and Paterson, *Contesting Castro*, 29. Some of Castro's early supporters argued instead that desperate poverty in rural Cuba provoked the revolution: e.g., Leo Huberman and Paul Marlor Sweezy, *Cuba: Anatomy of a Revolution* (New York: Monthly Review Press, 1960). Several of his opponents claimed that this poverty had deliberately been manipulated by communist elements: e.g., Mario Lazo, *Dagger in the Heart* (New York: Funk and Wagnalls, 1968), 83, 152.

50  Department of External Affairs, Sidney Smith, Memorandum for the Prime Minister, 'Recognition of New Cuban Government,' 8 January 1959; and Department of External Affairs, telegram to Canadian embassy, Wellington, New Zealand, 'Recognition of Cuban Government,' 12 January 1959, both in vol. 7257, file 10224–40, pt. 5.1.

51  Despatch D-305, 'Opposition to Fidel Castro,' 22 June 1959, vol. 7257, file 10224–40, pt. 6.1.

52  Telegram, 21 January 1959, vol. 7257, file 10224–40, pt. 5.2. As Allard may have known when writing his report, his colleague in Havana, the United Kingdom ambassador, had earlier come to the same conclusion. Their beliefs were essentially confirmed by subsequent accounts of the early Castro regime by Urrutía himself (*Fidel Castro and Company, Inc.* [New York: Praeger, 1964]) and by one of his ministers, Rufo López-Fresquet (*My Fourteen Months with Castro* [Cleveland: World, 1966]).

53  Telegram, 27 January 1959, vol. 7257, file 10224–40, pt. 5.2.

54  Despatch D-87, 'Prime Minister's Resignation,' 18 February 1959, vol. 7257, file 10224–40, pt. 5.2.

55  Despatch D-31, 'Cuban Internal Situation,' 22 January 1959, vol. 7257, file 10224–40, pt. 5.2.

56  Telegram, 27 January 1959, vol. 7257, file 10224–40, pt. 5.2.

57  Despatch D-175, 'The Elusive Cuban Elections,' 15 April 1959, vol. 7257, file 10224–40, pt. 6.

58  Letter L-295, 'Annual May Day Celebrations,' 3 May 1960, vol. 5351, file 10224–40, pt. 8.

59  Canadian Department of External Affairs, Memorandum for the Prime Minister, 'Resignation of Fidel Castro,' 17 July 1959, vol. 7257, file 10224–40, pt. 6.1.

60  Osvaldo Dorticós Torrado replaced Urrutía (Despatch D-386, 'Cuban Internal Situation to July 31, 1959,' 4 August 1959, vol. 7059, file 7590-N-40, pt. 3.2). The embassy noted that Dorticós was 'reputed to have been one of the

hardest working members of Castro's Cabinet and … one of the more left-ist-inclined' and thus more amenable to the reforms than his predecessor, the moderate 'troublesome little president,' Urrutía (Despatch D-362, 'Castro's Resignation,' 22 July 1959, vol. 7257, file 10224–40, pt. 6; Letter L-361, 'Appointment of New President,' 21 July 1959, vol. 7257, file 10224–40, pt. 6). The American State Department, by contrast, initially thought Dorticós a 'moderate' (Canadian embassy, Washington, D.C., telegram, 'Situation in Cuba,' 21 July 1959, vol. 7257, file 10224–40, pt. 6).

61  Despatch D-151, 'Cuban Internal Situation to March 31,' 1 April 1959, vol. 7257, file 10224–40, pt. 6.
62  Despatch D-342, 'Cuban Internal Situation to June 30,' 8 July 1959, vol. 7059, file 7590-N-40, pt. 3.2.
63  Despatch D-280, 'Cuban Agrarian Reform Law,' 11 June 1959, vol. 7257, file 10224–40, pt. 6; and same author, Despatch D-281, 'Cuban Fiscal Reform Law,' 11 June 1959, vol. 7257, file 10224–40, pt. 6.1.
64  Despatch D-151, 'Cuban Internal Situation to March 31,' 1 April 1959,' vol. 7257, file 10224–40, pt. 6.
65  Despatch D-128, 'Trial of Cuban Airmen,' 18 March 1959, vol. 7257, file 10224–40, pt. 5.2; Despatch D-61, 'Cuban Internal Situation to January 31,' 5 February 1959, vol. 7257, file 10224-40, pt. 5.2
66  Despatch D-151, 'Cuban Internal Situation to March 31,' 1 April 1959, vol. 7257, file 10224–40, pt. 6.
67  Despatch D-305, 'Opposition to Fidel Castro,' 22 June 1959, vol. 7257, file 10224–40, pt. 6.1.
68  Despatch D-342, 'Cuban Internal Situation to June 30,' 8 July 1959, vol. 7059, file 7590-N-40, pt. 3.2.
69  Pfeiffer, *The Bay of Pigs Operation*, 18; and Falcoff, *The Cuban Revolution and the United States*, 4.5, 6.1.
70  Despatch D-480, 'Cuban Internal Situation to September 30, 1959,' 1 October 1959, vol. 7258, file 10224-40, pt. 7.
71  Despatch D-88, 'Annual Review,' 26 January 1961, vol. 2494, file 10463-AH-40, pt. 1.
72  Letter L-122, 'Castro's Cuba by Robert Taber,' 19 February 1960, vol. 7258, file 10224–40, pt. 7.2.
73  Letter L-669, 'Counter-Revolutionary Activities in Cuba,' 26 September 1960, vol. 5351, file 10224–40, pt. 9.
74  Letter L-122, 'Castro's Cuba by Robert Taber,' 19 February 1960, vol. 7258, file 10224–40, pt. 7.2.
75  Despatch D-88, 'Annual Review,' 26 January 1961, vol. 2494, file 10463-AH-40, pt. 1.

76 Ibid.

77 Militia troops were also on the move: 'Fifty girl [sic] *militianas* have been billeted in the San Vicente monastery; this possibly presents problems for the monks' (Letter L-21, 'Cuba – Political: More Impressions,' 5 January 1961, vol. 5351, file 10224–40, pt. 10).

78 Despatch D-260, 'Cuba: Political: Impressions,' 22 March 1961, vol. 5352, file 10224–40, pt. 11.

79 Despatch D-303, 'Cuba: Political: The First of May,' 11 April 1961, vol. 5352, file 10224–40, pt. 11.

80 Despatch D-260, 'Cuba: Political: Impressions,' 22 March 1961, vol. 5352, file 10224–40, pt. 11.

81 Despatch D-24, 'Annual Review of Events in Cuba: 1959,' 13 January 1960, vol. 2494, file 10463-AH-40, pt. 1; and Despatch D-303, 'Cuba: Political: The First of May,' 11 April 1961, vol. 5352, file 10224–40, pt. 11.

82 Letter L-336, 'Cuban Conflict – Military Implications,' 10 May 1961, vol. 5352, file 10224–40, pt. 11.

83 United Kingdom embassy, Havana, Marchant to Lord Home, 'May Day in Cuba and the Socialist Revolution,' 23 May 1961, vol. 5352, file 10224–40, pt. 11.

84 Department of State, *Foreign Relations of the United States, 1961–1963: Volume X: Cuba, 1961–1962* (Washington, D.C.: Government Printing Office, 1997), no. 46: Paper drafted by Bissell, 17 February 1961.

85 Department of State, *FRUS 1961–1963*, no. 75, Memorandum from Chester Bowles to Dean Rusk, 31 March 1961; Pfeiffer, *The Bay of Pigs Operation*, 19; and Central Intelligence Agency, Information Report, 'Signs of Discontent among the Cuban Populace; Activities of the Government to Strengthen the Regime,' 6 April 1961, http://www.gwu.edu/~nsarchiv/bayofpigs.

86 Department of State, *FRUS 1961–1963*, no. 194, Paper by Combined Working Group of BNE [Bureau of Northern Europe] and INR [Bureau of Intelligence and Research], 2 May 1961.

87 Despatch D-397, 'Cuba – Final Impressions,' 15 June 1961, vol. 5352, file 10224–40, pt. 11.

88 Despatch D-643, 'Opposition to the Castro Regime,' 1 January 1962, vol. 5352, file 10224–40, pt. 12.1.

89 Despatch D-193, 'Current Events in Cuba,' 20 July 1956, vol. 7059, file 7590-N-40, pt. 3.2. The British ambassador, A.S. Fordham, wrote in 1957 that Castro's objective was 'to overthrow Batista, then to abolish all the existing political parties ... and finally to set up a government of enlightened, forward-looking patriots.' 'I cannot help feeling,' he added, 'that any revolution engineered by him would result either in chaos or else in

something closely resembling Communism' (United Kingdom embassy, Havana, Fordham to Selwyn Lloyd, AK 1015/28, 'The Opposition to President Batista,' 8 July 1957, RG 25, vol. 7257, file 10224–40, pt. 4.1).

90  The overthrow of Arbenz is described in Nick Cullather, *Secret History: The CIA's Classified Account of Its Operations in Guatemala, 1952–1954* (Stanford, Calif.: Stanford University Press, 1999).

91  Despatch D-14, 'Cuban Political Situation and Progress towards Elections,' 15 January 1958, vol. 7257, file 10224–40, pt. 4; and Despatch D-119, 'Cuban Internal Situation,' 31 March 1958, vol. 7257, file 10224–40, pt. 4.2. Most observers conclude that the Cuban Communist Party supported Castro only in the dying days of the Batista regime.

92  Letter L-576, 'Cuba Political: Communism and Castro,' 20 November 1959, vol. 7258, file 10224–40, pt. 7.

93  For these reports, see respectively: Telegram, 'Resignation of Air Force Chief,' 30 June 1959, vol. 7257, file 10224–40, pt. 6.1; Letter L-215, 'Cuban Interest in Munitions Factories,' 29 April 1959, vol. 7257, file 10224–40, pt. 6; Letter L-95, 'Defection of Cuban Air Force Officer,' 11 February 1960, vol. 7258, file 10224–4+0, pt. 1.2; Letter L-191, 'The Last of the Conservatives,' 21 March 1960, vol. 7258, file 10224–40; and Letter L-104, 'Cuba Political: Impressions,' 15 February 1960, vol. 7258, file 10224–40, pt. 1.2. In early 1960 the Washington embassy reported a State Department official's comment that nearly all the moderate elements in the Cuban government had been 'booted out or muffled': Letter L-81, 'Situation in Cuba,' 18 January 1960, vol. 7258, file 10224–40, pt. 7.

94  Letter L-555, 'Communists in the 26th of July Movement,' 22 August 1960, vol. 5351, file 10224–40, pt. 9.

95  Despatch D-31, 'Cuban Internal Situation,' 22 January 1959, vol. 7257, file 10224–40, pt. 5.2.

96  Despatch D-88, 'Annual Review,' 26 January 1961, vol. 2494, file 10463-AH-40, pt. 1.

97  Letter L-130, 'Annexex "A" and "C" to Annual Review,' 7 February 1961, vol. 2494, file 10463-AH-40, pt. 1.

98  See, for example, Telegram, 'Castro's Visit,' 24 April 1959, vol. 7257, file 10224–40, pt. 6. The British ambassador concurred (United Kingdom embassy, Havana, Fordham to Selwyn Lloyd, 'Reflections on the Revolution and Its Aftermath,' 9 March 1959, LAC, RG 25, vol. 7257, file 10224–40, pt. 6.1).

99  Telegram, 'Fidel Castro,' 16 March 1959, box 7665, file 11562–116–40, vol. 1; Letter L-95, 'Defection of Cuban Air Force Officer,' 11 February 1960, vol. 7258, file 10224–40, pt. 1.2. In one report, Allard cited rumours that Castro

was taking 'massive doses of barbiturates' and sleeping only one hour a day, which put him in a vulnerable position. If he collapsed, 'his brother and his chief adviser Guevara, both known for their Communist affiliations, would seek to take over power for themselves' (Despatch D-154, 'Fidel Castro,' 2 April 1959, vol. 7257, file 10224–40, pt. 6).

100  Letter L-625, 'Castro and Communism,' 15 December 1961, vol. 5352, file 10224–40, pt. 12.1; see also Letter L-589, 'Revolutionary Cadres,' 16 November 1961, vol. 5352, file 10224–40, pt. 11.

101  'Cuba: State Intervention in Production and Trade, December 23, 1959,' attached to Letter L-14, 'State Intervention in Production and Trade,' 6 January 1960, vol. 7258, file 10224–40, pt. 7.

102  Despatch D-24, 'Annual Review of Events in Cuba: 1959,' 13 January 1960, vol. 2494, file 10463-AH-40, pt. 1.

103  Che's announcement came in an address to the Congress of Latin American Youth on 26 July 1960: 'Indications of "Che" Guevara's Philosophy,' 23 August 1960, vol. 5351, file 10224–40, pt. 9.

104  Despatch D-252, 'The Church and Fidel Castro,' 28 May 1959, vol. 7257, file 10224–40, pt. 6. Allard acknowledged that 'most Catholics ... were not so pro-Castro as anti-Batista' so, as the new regime established itself, the support that such moves garnered began to falter.

105  Despatch D-218, 'The Church and Fidel Castro,' 30 April 1959, vol. 7257, file 10224–40, pt. 6.1.

106  Despatch D-862, 'International Situation to October 31, 1960,' 12 November 1960, vol. 5351, file 10224–40, pt. 10; and same author, Despatch D-973, 'Cuban Internal Situation to November 30, 1960,' 22 December 1960, vol. 5351, file 10224–40, pt. 10.

107  The Soviet Union had had an ambassador in Havana since August 1960. Letter L-429, 'Communist Bloc Representation in Cuba,' 27 July 1961, vol. 5352, file 10224–40, pt. 11.

108  Despatch D-66, 'Cuba: Foreign Policy,' 29 January 1960, vol. 7258, file 10224–40, pt. 7.

109  Letter L-68, 'Cuba – Political,' 24 January 1961, vol. 5351, file 10224–40, pt. 10.

110  M.N. Bow, 'Cuba – First Impressions,' 14 February 1961, vol. 5351, file 10224–40, pt. 10.

111  Letter L-304, '"Castro's Cuba" – Article in March Issue of *Encounter* Magazine,' 11 April 1961, vol. 5352, file 10224–40, pt. 11.

112  United Kingdom embassy, Havana, Marchant to Lord Home, 'May Day in Cuba and the Socialist Revolution,' 23 May 1961, vol. 5352, file 10224–40, pt. 11.

113  Letter L-509, 'Recent Developments in Party Organization in Cuba,' 23 September 1961, vol. 5352, file 10224–40, pt. 11.

114  Letter L-625, 'Castro and Communism,' 15 December 1961, vol. 5352, file 10224–40, pt. 12.1.

115  Julie Marie Bunck, *Fidel Castro and the Quest for a Revolutionary Culture in Cuba* (University Park, Penn.: Pennsylvania State University Press, 1994), 9; and Salvador Díaz-Versón, 'When Castro Became a Communist: The Impact on U.S.-Cuba Policy,' Institute for U.S.-Cuba Relations, Occasional Paper Series 1:1, November 1997, http://www.latinamericanstudies.org/diaz-verson.htm (accessed 30 June 2005).

116  Paterson, *Contesting Castro*, 186; Robert E. Quirk, *Fidel Castro* (New York: W.W. Norton, 1993), 247; and Fursenko and Naftali, *'One Hell of a Gamble,'* 20–1.

117  Theodore Draper, *Castro's Revolution: Myths and Realities* (New York: Praeger, 1962), 26, 90–1; Leonard, *Castro and the Cuban Revolution*, xv, 14–15; Louis A. Pérez, *Cuba: Between Reform and Revolution* (New York: Oxford University Press, 1988), 323–8; and Wayne S. Smith, *Castro's Cuba: Soviet Partner or Nonaligned?* (Washington, D.C.: Woodrow Wilson International Center for Scholars, 1984).

118  Falcoff, *The Cuban Revolution and the United States*, 1.25, 2.7; and Pfeiffer, *The Bay of Pigs Operation*, 24–6. Setting himself apart from his diplomatic colleagues, Ambassador Earl E.T. Smith insisted for some time that Castro's own communist sympathies were being deliberately overlooked by liberals in Havana and Washington. Smith, who had been a close friend of Batista, was replaced by Philip Bonsal almost immediately after Castro came to power: see, for example, Falcoff, *The Cuban Revolution and the United States*, 1.25. The CIA chief of station, for his part, remained convinced of Castro's communist ties, and, when Castro visited the United States in April 1959, urged his colleagues in the agency to plant 'embarrassing questions' at press conferences: Pfeiffer, *The Bay of Pigs Operation*, 20.

119  Falcoff, *The Cuban Revolution and the United States*, 3.10; and Pfeiffer, *The Bay of Pigs Operation*, 26.

120  Falcoff, *The Cuban Revolution and the United States*, 7.3, 8.2, and 10.5.

121  Despatch D-525, 'Fidel Castro: Second and Third Impressions,' 26 October 1959, vol. 7258, file 10224–40, pt. 7.

122  See, for example, Richard Beeston, 'Moscow's Grip on Cuba Closes: Soviet-trained Communists in "Take-Over from Dr Castro,"' *Sunday Telegraph*, 4 March 1962.

123  Canadian Department of External Affairs, American Division, C. Hardy,

'Political Reporting from Cuba,' 19 January 1959, vol. 7257, file 10224–40, pt. 5.2. The circumstances included Ambassador Allard's illness and the rapidity of the Batista government's collapse.

124 Despatch D-536, 'Cuba: Political,' 29 October 1959, vol. 7258, file 10224–40, pt. 7. Anderson later passed on a version of this idea as his own: Despatch D-24, 'Annual Review of Events in Cuba: 1959,' 13 January 1960, vol. 2494, file 10463-AH-40, pt. 1.

125 Letter L-837, 'Canadian Position in Cuba,' 14 November 1960, vol. 5074, file 4568–40, pt. 2; and Letter L-846, 'Albert A. Shea,' 16 November 1960, vol. 5074, file 4568–40, pt. 2.

# 3 'Calculated Diplomacy': John Diefenbaker and the Origins of Canada's Cuba Policy

DENNIS MOLINARO

Canada's working relationship with revolutionary Cuba is commonly viewed as having originated with Prime Minister John G. Diefenbaker. In *Three Nights in Havana: Pierre Trudeau, Fidel Castro and the Cold War World*, Robert Wright states that Pierre Trudeau 'inherited' the Cuban policy from Diefenbaker.[1] Two other authors, John Kirk and Peter McKenna, argue in *Canada-Cuba Relations: The Other Good Neighbor Policy* that Diefenbaker's decision not to follow the U.S. embargo against Cuba was based on his refusal to be 'pushed around by Washington' and on his 'moral support' for Cuba. Diefenbaker's personal distaste for President Kennedy, they write, unlike President Eisenhower, whom Diefenbaker viewed as a close friend, played a major role in the shaping of Canada's Cuba policy.[2] Both interpretations are problematic in that they accept Diefenbaker's account of his relationship with Eisenhower and Kennedy more or less at face value. A critical reappraisal of Diefenbaker's acquaintance with Eisenhower and Kennedy is warranted not only to discern what effect (if any) these relationships had on Canada's Cuba policy but to understand one of Canada's most celebrated foreign-policy biases.

This chapter will revisit the Diefenbaker era and the origins of the Canadian Cuba policy. Relying on recently declassified documents, it shows a prime minister who had little choice but to respond to U.S. pressure on Cuba, whether this meant maintaining trade relations under Dwight Eisenhower or ignoring John F. Kennedy's strong-arm tactics to join the U.S. embargo. Both Eisenhower and Kennedy shaped Canada's Cuba policy. Even as a Canadian nationalist, Diefenbaker's Cuba policy was influenced and in many ways constrained by the United States. With Eisenhower in power in the White House, Diefenbaker could preserve his staunchly nationalist stance so long as it did not interfere with the U.S.-Canadian strategic partnership. During the late 1950s, Canada's position on Cuba closely followed the American lead. Once Kennedy entered the White House in the 1960s, Diefenbaker quickly discovered that Kennedy cared little for Canadian nationalist sentiments and expected Canada to follow the U.S. hard line on Cuba. It was a position that Diefenbaker had little choice but to rally against lest Canada be viewed as an American satellite. Canada's Cuba policy derived initially from the idea of an allied North American front against the Soviets. But by the 1960s it became a symbol of Canada's independence in foreign policy. Revisiting the nationalist myth of Diefenbaker shows Canada's Cuba policy to be more dynamic, evolving, and self-serving than previously thought.

The American position on revolutionary Cuba fit perfectly into Eisenhower's conception of the world and the communist threat facing North America. Diefenbaker saw himself as a close friend of Eisenhower and Canada as a full-fledged partner in hemispheric defence. But both of these ideas would turn out to be largely illusory. Even so, the facade of a friendship and partnership with the United States was politically important to Diefenbaker. The U.S.-Canadian partnership projected an image to the world of a strong, allied North American consensus during the Cold War; perhaps ironically, this partnership ensured the survival of Canadian nationalism despite the concessions Canada made and continued to make at the behest of its southern neighbour. Diefenbaker maintained this partnership with Eisenhower in his dealings with Cuba, which were never at odds with the U.S. policy on the island nation. President Kennedy's government would later come to threaten Diefenbaker's conception of Canada in the world. For Diefenbaker, Kennedy openly flaunted the North American partnership (facade or not), and when Kennedy's government attempted to force Diefenbaker's and Canada's hand in joining the U.S.-led embargo against Cuba, Diefenbaker had no choice but to oppose Kennedy or publicly surrender Canada's sovereignty. At this moment, Canada's Cuba policy entered into the realm of the country's nationalist discourse. It, like John Diefenbaker, became a symbol of resistance to American hegemony.

### 'He Is Your Nassar?'

When Eisenhower took office the Cold War was being fought across the globe, openly and covertly. Historians now acknowledge the active and influential role Eisenhower played in the secret wars of the Central Agency Agency (CIA) during the Cold War. He epitomized the doctrine of 'plausible deniability' and relied upon covert operations in the place of conventional armed forces.[3] Also during Eisenhower's term, the Third World became the new focal point for the Soviet-U.S stand-off,[4] with Latin America a primary focus for the Eisenhower administration because of its proximity to the United States and its lack of economic development. The United States would have to counter the threat of the 'communist menace' through a combined political and economic plan. To achieve this, Eisenhower supported strong free-trade links, foreign investment, and aid.[5] In January 1956 the Soviets expanded their own trading arrangements and investment in Latin American nations. Eisenhower sought to combat this 'economic offensive' by shoring up trade deals such as the Cuban Sugar Act of 1956, which gave Cuba preferential treatment in the U.S. sugar market.[6]

As the Soviets began offering more lucrative financial offers to newly independent nations elsewhere in the world, such as Egypt and India, Eisenhower was not willing to rule out using other means to combat communist influence in the developing world.[7] In his diaries Eisenhower outlined the U.S. attitude towards national independence movements across the globe. On 6 January 1953 he wrote: 'Nationalism is on the march and world communism is taking advantage of that spirit of nationalism to cause dissension in the free world. Moscow leads many misguided people to believe that they can count on communist help to achieve and sustain nationalistic ambitions. Actually what is going on is that the communists are hoping to take advantage of the confusion resulting from destruction of existing relationships and in the difficulties and uncertainties of disrupted trade, security, and understandings ... in some instances immediate independence would result in suffering for people and even anarchy.'[8] Eisenhower saw the rush to independence by Third World nations as an opportunity for international communism to take advantage of a chaotic situation, thus increasing the Kremlin's march towards world domination. A 'slower and more orderly' advance to independence seemed to Eisenhower more 'healthy and sound.'[9]

In the case of Latin America, the Eisenhower administration insisted that 'any other political, economic, or military action deemed appropriate' would be necessary if Soviet penetration of a Latin American nation endangered U.S. interests.[10] Nationalist movements, particularly those that accelerated quickly, were to be scrutinized closely for fear of Soviet influence.

Enter Fidel Castro, who in 1952 began his attempt to overthrow the corrupt government of Fulgencio Batista. Venturing to the United States in an effort to shore up support for a rebellion that would take place in 1956, Castro believed that Batista's government was fuelled by corruption and gambling and sustained through extensive U.S. aid and investment.[11] In 1956 Castro retreated to the Sierra Maestra, and by mid-1958, as he and his rebels began to make steady advances, the United States started to seriously entertain the idea that Batista's government was in jeopardy. Military aid was sent to Batista's army because, as Thomas Paterson states in *Confronting Castro: The United States and the Triumph of the Cuban Revolution*, 'a stable, orderly Cuba that quelled insurrectionists and communists would better serve the U.S. goals of hegemony and Cold War victory.'[12] The United States helped train Cuban infantry and American weapons were used in the fight against the rebels. Castro also endeared himself to U.S. media to bring to light his struggle against Batista and to expose American intervention in the struggle.[13] This pressure coupled with Batista's authoritarian rule began to embarrass the United States and increase Cuban anti-Americanism. By 1958, the United States sought, as Paterson states, a more moderate 'third alternative' to Castro and Batista.[14]

The Eisenhower administration never found a 'third' option in Cuba that was to its liking, and thus it was forced to deal with a victorious Castro in January 1959. Despite offering official recognition on 8 January 1959, the Eisenhower White House viewed Castro with apprehension.[15] Reports to Eisenhower by CIA Director Allen Dulles claimed that the Cuban situation was 'far from stable.' The State Department viewed Castro's young group as 'inexperience[d]' and the group's ability to remain aligned with the West as uncertain.[16] By the time Castro began his agrarian-reform and nationalization projects, the Eisenhower administration had begun to fear communist influence in Cuba and the export of revolution from that country to others in the region. Prominent figures in Castro's government, including Ernesto 'Che' Guevara and Raúl Castro, were Marxist-Leninists. By early 1960, the United States was 'not able to tolerate the Castro regime in Cuba,' as Allen Dulles put it.[17]

As Castro began his nationalization projects, Eisenhower upped the ante by undercutting the Cubans' ability to sell sugar to the United States. After approving the Emergency Sugar Act, Eisenhower wrote in his diary that Castro was a radical, unpredictable tyrant and thus susceptible to communist influence. He wrote on 6 July 1960 that everyone should be on alert because when 'dealing with a little Hitler anything can happen.'[18] With interventions in nations such as Guatemala and Iran in mind, Eisenhower believed that a similar intervention in Cuba would prove just as successful.[19] Plans were drawn up for a proxy invasion of Cuba.[20] In letters to British Prime Minister Harold Macmillan in July 1960, Eisenhower suggested that Castro needed to be removed. In addition to the secret plans for invasion, Eisenhower continued to take 'economic measures' to demonstrate to the Cuban people the price of supporting Castro's descent into communism. Eisenhower stated that he hoped that these measures would not prove to be 'irreversible' or 'so drastic' as to 'permanently impair' the interests of Cubans and Americans.[21] Macmillan shared Eisenhower's views, describing Fidel Castro as 'the very Devil. He is your Nassar.'[22] Yet, although Macmillan was able to offer his support in not sending weapons to Castro and limiting trade, there seemed to be little else he could do. He supported the 'unseating of Castro' but was not clear how Eisenhower planned to achieve this.[23] Eisenhower appeared to value Macmillan's views and expressed his thanks for whatever help the British prime minister felt he could offer, but he did not push the issue much further.[24]

In sum, towards the end of his presidency, Cuba was becoming a Cold War nightmare for Eisenhower, and he began taking any and all steps to end it short of invasion by U.S. forces. Even after the Cuban Missile Crisis of 1962, Eisenhower expressed his reservations to President Kennedy about his deal with the Soviets that ruled out invading Cuba in the future.[25] Yet never did he pressure his allies publicly into agreeing with or following U.S. policy. The U.S. policy of isolating Cuba economically originated as a Cold War measure designed to curb what was perceived to be a newly minted communist regime. It was created and maintained through a Cold War lens.

## Appearances Mattered

John Diefenbaker became prime minister during Eisenhower's second term, in 1957. Like Eisenhower, Diefenbaker was staunchly anti-communist. He agreed with the Cold War conviction of Churchill and Eisenhower that the Kremlin was struggling to achieve world domination.[26]

In terms of Canada's dealings with the United States, Diefenbaker's memoirs indicate that he felt that the previous Liberal government had pursued 'economic continentalism' too vigorously. He believed that his

Conservative government could borrow from Sir John A. Macdonald's legacy and engage in 'nation building.'[27] Once elected, Diefenbaker's government sought to rectify certain inequalities he thought existed between the United States and Canada. Besides advocating a 15 per cent shift in trade from the United States to Great Britain,[28] Diefenbaker sought to end the unfair grain-storage practices of the Americans, which hurt Canadian business. 'The Chief,' as he came to be known, also sought to have China recognized officially by Canada. It was the one issue where Diefenbaker felt Eisenhower would not listen to him.[29] Diefenbaker believed that, during Eisenhower's term, there was U.S. and Canadian 'cooperation' and that Canadian 'subservience' was not essential to this cooperation.[30] Diefenbaker also worked towards a partnership with the United States on North American defence. He signed the North American Air Defence Agreeement (NORAD), sought a U.S. market for Canadian fighters, and tried to acquire nuclear weapons for Canada.

Reminiscing about Eisenhower's visit to Canada in 1958, Diefenbaker referred to 'Ike' and himself as the 'best of friends' in his memoirs.[31] H. Basil Robinson, liaison between the prime minister and Foreign Affairs, recounts that 'Diefenbaker believed he had a source of information on the global game which would never be matched' in his friendship with Eisenhower.[32] Robinson recalled how, during Eisenhower's 1958 visit, Diefenbaker desired the meeting to be 'informal' in an effort to 'reinforce the personal links' which had already developed between the two men.[33] Diefenbaker's memoirs reveal a high level of admiration for the former U.S. war general. He took pride in the fact that he and the president were on a first-name basis; in one of his last letters to Eisenhower on 26 February 1961, Diefenbaker told Eisenhower how he 'felt' the two of them were 'friends.'[34]

The U.S.-Canadian relationship was not a true Cold War partnership, if by that term equality is implied. At this time, the United States and Canada were allies but not partners (in the sense that the United States and the United Kingdom still were). Diefenbaker's attempts to limit U.S. intrusion into the Canadian economy never amounted to much. Indeed, the continental pressures turned out to be much too strong even for Diefenbaker to resist.[35] Diefenbaker gave his 'tentative approval' to NORAD (whose main operations were to be based in the United States) after only two weeks in office and without any extensive explanation regarding the agreement.[36] Nor was the Canadian government able to procure a U.S. market for the CF-105 'Arrow,' a project that Diefenbaker eventually concluded was too costly to pursue given that ballistic missiles would replace the expensive and soon to be outdated fighter.[37] Canada never received nuclear weapons either. An agreement could not be reached with the United States, as the *Globe and Mail* reported on 5 July 1960. Unable to broker a deal, Canada 'looked to be dragging its feet,' hoping that 'disarmament talks' would make a deal unnecessary.[38] On the one issue where Eisenhower would not listen at all to Diefenbaker, the recognition of 'Red' China, it was Diefenbaker who capitulated and refused to recognize China. In the meeting that took place between Eisenhower, Secretary of State John Foster Dulles, Secretary of State for External Affairs Sidney Smith, and the prime minister during Eisenhower's 1958 Canadian visit, Smith made a quasi-joke about Canada recognizing China. Upon hearing this, Eisenhower slammed his fist on the table and exclaimed that the day Canada recognized the Chinese government would be the day he would 'kick the United Nations out of the United States.' The Canadians present at the meeting agreed not to pursue the issue.[39] But, in a letter dated 26 January 1964, Diefenbaker's brother Elmer remarked that in regard to Chinese recognition 'you [John] were so right when you withheld – you & Eisenhower were right.'[40] Elmer had somehow got the impression that the withholding of recognition to China was a policy that both Diefenbaker and Eisenhower agreed on, which it was not.

The historical record also does not seem to bear out Diefenbaker's claim that he and Ike were 'the best of friends.' Despite Diefenbaker's inclusion of a letter from Eisenhower in his memoirs, which he uses as a means of demonstrating his friendship with Ike, Eisenhower's personal diaries contain no mention of John Diefenbaker. Nor was Eisenhower any less or more formal with other heads of state within the NATO alliance such as Harold Macmillan. Yet Diefenbaker frequently recalls in his memoirs the informality of his meetings with Ike and their being on a first-name basis as evidence of their close friendship. This was an exaggeration. An examination of documents now declassified regarding Eisenhower's visit to Canada in 1958 (his only trip to Canada with Diefenbaker in power) makes it apparent that the informal and casual nature of the trip was, to put it bluntly, staged.

U.S. Ambassador Livingston Merchant notified Canadian officials that, because of the health concerns of the president, the Canadian visit would be set up to appear informal and no major announcements were to be expected. This message was relayed by the under-secretary of state for external affairs, Jules Leger, to Sidney Smith, [41] who in turn advised the prime minister that, owing to the time and content restrictions being placed on the Canadians, important discussions should be held and agreements made beforehand.[42] A number of Canadian officials, recalling Eisenhower's previous visit with Prime Minister St Laurent, which was also perceived as a 'show visit' rather then a productive one, were not pleased. J.H. Cleveland of External Affairs dubbed this second Eisenhower visit 'a weak tea party' in which Canada would play the role of 'a forty ninth state composed of mounted police, Eskimos and summer vacations.'[43]

Through June and early July 1958, Merchant coordinated with Canadian officials on the topics for the meetings that would take place during the visit and the answers that could be expected.[44] The announcement that was made regarding the Ministerial Committee on Defense Matters was prearranged and made during Ike's visit in order to give the press something to take out of the meeting.[45] Canadian officials correctly recognized, as Jules Léger observed, that Eisenhower 'charm' and informality were 'calculated diplomatic tactic[s].'[46] Diefenbaker was well aware that Eisenhower's visit was to be a staged showing of Americana in Canada. He went along with the plan. Eisenhower and Diefenbaker's friendship was never intended to extend beyond the symbolic. The Eisenhower 'charm' was yet another tool in the president's political arsenal, and Diefenbaker knew it.

The question remains: Why did Diefenbaker believe he and Eisenhower were such close comrades? Whether he admitted it to himself or not, Diefenbaker never publicly wavered in his belief that his friendship was sincere. He not only greatly respected Eisenhower on account of his achievements in the Second World War but believed him to be genuinely concerned about Canada.[47] Their friendship made Canada appear to be a bigger player on the world stage as well, while allowing Canada some semblance of autonomy in the bilateral relationship. In this light, any disputes between Canada and the United States were not serious schisms but merely strains in a 'friendship.' Diefenbaker was always a staunch Canadian nationalist, but he knew that nationalism could not be allowed to risk fracturing the Cold War alliance. Eisenhower recognized the importance of maintaining the image of a bilateral friendship; the 'Chief' recognized that Ike made the effort at least to pretend to care about Canada. Finally, Eisenhower knew the importance of putting on a good face when it came to appeasing his allies. He could not let the growing Canadian frustration with the U.S. partnership fester. Indeed, as Phillip Deane of the *Globe and Mail* reported on 8 July 1958, Ike was not about to let another highly public display of anti-Americanism, such as the one that occurred during Richard Nixon's South American trip, take place north of the border.[48] Appearances mattered.

## 'Combat Planes' and Communists

In addition to being anti-communist, Diefenbaker also shared Eisenhower's ideas about identifying and dealing with the enemies of freedom in the Cold War. Fidel Castro appeared to be one of those enemies. Yet the Canadian position on Castro's Cuba was increasingly diverging from that of the United States as U.S.-Cuba tensions rose. In his memoirs Diefenbaker reiterated his government's reasons for not following the American embargo of Cuba. He argued that Canada had always enjoyed 'cordial relations' with Cuba, even before Castro; that normal relations should have been continued with Cuba despite the philosophical differences between that country's communist regime and the West; and that the 'Monroe doctrine' did not apply in Canada and that Canada should hardly be required to tighten its trade restrictions above and beyond those of other Latin American nations.[49] In all of these beliefs, which were in line with Canadian public opinion, Diefenbaker was correct, but it would be misleading to suggest that the Canadian policy on Cuba was much different in its beginnings from the American one.

In defending his Cuba policy in retrospect, Diefenbaker stated that Canadian relations with Cuba were amicable even before Castro but that Canada's general policy 'was that of refraining from exporting military or strategic material to any area of tension in the world ... we would not have exported them to the Batista government, let alone the Castro government.'[50] This claim is not consistent with the historical record.

Canada's arms shipments to Cuba (including military parts and supplies) dated back to at least 1949.[51] Primarily dealing in small arms, aircraft, and aircraft supplies, the Canadian government continued this practice until late 1958, throughout Batista's war against the Castro rebels. With Canadian companies receiving frequent requests from the Cubans for munitions and other weapons in 1957, government officials expressed concern that the weapons would be used against the Castro rebels and thus that Canadian sales would be in conflict with Canada's non-intervention stance. The Canadian embassy in Washington notified External Affairs in October 1957 that the Cuban military was using American-sold weapons against Castro and that it would likely direct its requests to Canada because the United States had denied the Cubans sales of arms.[52] The problem was, as Jules Léger pointed out in a memo to Sidney Smith on 15 November 1957, that Canada did 'not normally ... release items likely to be used in internal conflicts.' Léger also outlined how Washington was embarrassed by its recent military assistance to the Cuban government and was now seeking to delay shipping military supplies to Cuba.[53] The goal, then, was for the Canadians to continue selling goods to the Cubans without being seen as taking sides in an internal conflict or violating the desires of Washington.

This concern frequently presented itself in internal memos between Canadian officials. On 22 October 1957 de Havilland (a Canadian aircraft manufacturer) requested an export permit for three DHC-2 Beaver landplanes. Jules Léger wrote to Sidney Smith that the Cuban air force was requesting these 'civil' aircraft, adding that the U.S. State Department had told him that the normally 'civil' planes 'might well be useful for spotting and reconnaissance purposes, if as is likely, the rebel units lack anti-aircraft equipment.' Léger also noted that Washington was not opposed to selling these planes to Cuba and so the Canadian company was at risk of losing the deal to an American firm. He therefore recommended that the order be approved.[54] Smith's memo to the prime minister reiterated Léger's points and the prime minister concurred.[55] On 27 December 1957 the Canadian embassy in Washington notified External Affairs that several DHC-2 Beavers were being used by Batista's forces against the rebels and that the planes were ideal in the conflict because of their 'high maneuverability.' External Affairs was also notified that the rebels had shot down one of these 'combat planes.'[56] For its part, External Affairs notified its personnel in Washington that the planes were not 'combat planes' and they had been sold precisely because they were civilian planes. It also requested that the State Department not be told that it was the fear of losing the order to an American firm that ultimately influenced the Canadian decision.[57]

As orders continued to come in from Batista for military supplies, the extent of Canada's involvement in the conflict continued to be an issue of concern for Canadian officials. The government continually stalled Cuban requests for munitions and weapons. Yet, despite the Canadians' concerns, and despite the previous experience with the Beaver aircraft shipment in 1957, three more DHC-2 Beavers were approved for shipment to the Cuban air force in May 1958. The memos between Léger and Smith in 1958 were identical to those of 1957 in terms of the rationale for approving the sale. By the spring 1958, however, the

Canadians believed that Castro's insurrection had failed.[58] After learning that this was not true, and that Beavers were again being used in the fighting, shipments that were potentially military in nature were to be stopped. In August 1958 both Sidney Smith and the prime minister agreed that there were to be no further shipment of 'arms,' including Beaver aircraft, to Cuba.[59]

On 4 September 1958 the Toronto *Star* reported that Ottawa had approved the sale of 100 fighter aircraft to two men in Dewitt, New York. The purchasers, Defuria and Ritts, were keeping their final destination for the craft a secret from reporters, but when asked if the planes would go to the rebels in Cuba, they stated in no uncertain terms that they most certainly would not.[60] In a telegram to the Canadian embassy in Washington, External Affairs concluded that the planes may have been intended for the Cuban government but that no export permit was needed for an order going to the United States. The Canadians later discovered the press story to be inaccurate; only thirty-eight Mustangs were sold. They also discovered that Defuria was a suburb of Syracuse.[61]

One month after the last aircraft sale, 96,000 pounds of automotive truck parts for '2 ½ ton Staghounds (a lightly armored vehicle)' was approved for export to 'Cuartel Maestre General Ejercito' of the Cuban army. It was approved by Sidney Smith and seen by Prime Minister Diefenbaker. The rationale for approving this order was that it offered 'no new combat potential' to Batista's forces.[62] When another order involving munitions for Batista's army was placed in November, Canadian officials again decided to stall it until U.S. intentions were known.[63]

One final note on arms exports to Cuba. Files recently obtained through an Access to Information request reveal that Castro was also seeking military supplies from Canada in 1959. None of the orders were approved, but one order in particular deserves closer scrutiny. A Beaver aircraft (the same model sold to Batista) was requested by the Cubans for agricultural and Castro's personal use. The order was placed on 22 October 1959.[64] External Affairs believed that the 'unstable political situation' in the Caribbean and the possibility of the plane being used for combat purposes warranted a refusal. The Canadians, however, were aware that the United States had approved the export of fifty-four similar civilian planes to Cuba (four of which were for Cuba's defence department and nineteen for other governmental departments).[65] In a memo from External Affairs to the Canadian embassy in Havana, Canadian officials also conceded that there was 'truth' in the Cubans claims for this order.[66] Yet, despite these admissions, and even though

Cuba's internal conflict was officially over, Canadian officials refused to fill the order.

In short, notwithstanding the official Canadian position of non-intervention in Cuba, the government had approved the sale of Canadian military equipment to Batista's army. Officials knew that the shipments were going to be used against the rebels, but they decided to follow the American lead on arms shipments. According to this logic, if the Americans had no qualms about a sale, then the Canadians would sell the product, such as the Beaver aircraft, lest the sale go to an American competitor. When it became clear that Castro's revolt had not been defeated, the Canadians sold planes to buyers in the United States in the knowledge that they likely would go to the Cuban government. Even after the complete ban on military supplies was put in place, the Canadians approved the sale of military supplies to Batista's generals, as late as November 1958. Afterwards, despite the official end of Cuba's internal conflict, military sales were denied to Castro's government. The dissembling of the Canadian position is quite clear. So, too, is the importance the Diefenbaker government placed on trading with Cuba even if such trade involved Canada in Cuba's internal struggle. The Canadian position on Cuba accorded perfectly with that of the United States at this point.

Politically, Diefenbaker's government viewed Castro's new government with just as much apprehension as the White House. In his memoirs Diefenbaker states that he approved 'immediate formal recognition' of Cuba on the recommendation of Sidney Smith.[67] This, too, was a half-truth. Recognition of Cuba came quickly but not because the Canadians desired it. Sidney Smith's memo on the matter is worth citing at length: 'I am not fully satisfied that the new Cuban government fulfills the usual conditions for recognition and that it is in full control of all national territory; it seems, however, to enjoy popular support to a reasonable degree and has undertaken to respect its international obligations. In the circumstances, in order not to lag behind the other governments who have already extended recognition, I am inclined to recommend that we should do likewise without delay, although I feel that the action taken by the other governments may have been somewhat precipitate ... as Canada has a large investment in Cuba, it is highly desirable that Canada not lag in recognizing the new government.'[68] The Canadian decision to recognize Castro's government, then, was based on the value that the Diefenbaker government attached to following the lead of its allies, even though those allies, in Smith's view, had acted too rashly in extending diplomatic recognition.

As Castro's revolutionary government began instituting its agrarian reforms and its 'trials' of Batista's former cronies, Canadian officials became increasingly worried. The Canadian embassy in Havana, in reporting to the under-secretary of state on 19 March 1959, mentioned that there existed a 'strong possibility' that Castro's government would 'exhibit communist tendencies.' The embassy noted, however, that the situation in Cuba 'does not appear to have unduly alarmed the Cuban on the street, who does not fully understand what is happening.'[69] Castro's anti-Americanism also raised the suspicions of Canadian embassy officials in Washington. On 27 January 1960 an embassy telegram to the under-secretary of state asserted that the United States was 'leaning over backwards' for the 'inexperienced' and 'garrulous' Cuban leader.[70] Canadian officials were clearly apprehensive about the influence of communists in Castro's new government. As for Diefenbaker himself, as historian Robert Wright claims, he had 'no love for Fidel Castro.'[71] He would later remark that 'Castroism was at worst a symptom and the most radical manifestation of the social and economic tensions existing in Latin America.'[72]

Cuba was not the only newly communist country that posed dilemmas for Canadian foreign policy. 'Red' China was another. In 1958 pressure on the Canadian Ford Motor company, a subsidiary of the American parent firm, resulted in the cancelling of a vehicle shipment to China. The issue was a hotly contested one in Canada and was mentioned during Eisenhower's 1958 visit.[73] The Canadians felt that the United States was interfering in Canadian trade. Canada's economy relied heavily on foreign trade and Eisenhower recognized this. After his 1958 meeting in Canada, Eisenhower's government moved to allow permits to be granted to U.S. parent companies which would enable their Canadian subsidiaries to ship to China.[74] But, even after this agreement, the Americans still influenced Canadian companies trading with China, such as Alcan, which refused a million-dollar aluminum shipment to China for fear of losing U.S. business.[75]

For Diefenbaker, trade with communist nations, such as China and Cuba, offered Canada a means of confronting international communism while strengthening Canada's economy. Accordingly, into the 1960s, Diefenbaker and his minister of external affairs, Howard Green, believed that a hard-line prohibition on trade with Cuba could drive Castro further into the Soviet camp.[76] China was a similar case, for, in their view, isolating it from international trade would only have the effect of entrenching its communist regime. This view of the world was not a new one for Diefenbaker's government. When Eisenhower visited Canada in 1958, Diefenbaker made it clear in a speech to the House of Commons that he, like Eisenhower, believed that the USSR posed a serious threat, economic and military, to the West. Yet Diefenbaker also remarked that 'joint efforts are needed to expand world trade to increase the financial base of liquid reserves necessary for such expansion and to end it where it prevails, and to help in raising the standards of peoples in underdeveloped countries.'[77]

Eisenhower understood all of this but the issue of Canadian trade with 'Red' nations remained a delicate one, especially after Washington's decision to implement an embargo.[78] When Diefenbaker commented on Cuba in 1960, he expressed sympathy for the U.S. position. On 24 December 1960 the *Globe and Mail* quoted Diefenbaker as stating that the U.S 'embargo was necessary' for the 'arbitrary, illegal and discriminatory measures' that were taken against the United States. Yet he added that, if Canada were to invoke trade controls with a communist nation that it had no quarrel with, namely Cuba, it 'may be under pressure' to invoke trade controls 'elsewhere.' Canada could simply 'not afford' to do that. Diefenbaker also gave his assurances that his government had no plans for an increase in Cuban trade, even in 'peacetime.'[79] The United States understood the Canadian position and never requested that Canada abide by American trade restrictions towards Cuba or China. Indeed, the United States preferred that Canada maintain normal relations with Cuba so that Canada could, as Wright suggests, help to gather intelligence.[80]

In short, Diefenbaker's government supported the sale of military supplies to Batista, just as the United States did. It was also in agreement with the United States immediately after Castro's victory in Cuba. Canadians, like Americans, were hesitant in recognizing Castro, fearful of his communist sympathies. While Canada maintained trade with Castro, this was no different from other American-supported trading relationships, such as Canada's trade with 'Red' China. In short, Canada could agree with the U.S. policy on Cuba without participating in the American-led embargo. Tactics might differ but principles still mattered. The allied front against communism was maintained by Diefenbaker in his dealings with Cuba.

**The War of 1812 Revisited**

The question that must be answered, therefore, is why Canadian and U.S. policies on Cuba diverged after 1960. Seen in retrospect, the crucial differences between the U.S. and Canadian policies began to develop after John F. Kennedy entered the White House. It was no secret that Diefenbaker and Kennedy did not get along. Diefenbaker's memoirs contain numerous jabs at Kennedy but all contained a similar theme. Diefenbaker recalled after their first meeting, 'I became increasingly aware that President Kennedy had no knowledge of Canada whatsoever. More important, he was activated by the belief that Canada owed so great a debt to the United States that nothing but continuing subservience could repay it.'[81] Diefenbaker realized in his talks with Kennedy that the 'youthful' and 'proud' new president did not care much for the Canada-U.S. partnership.[82]

Almost immediately after the U.S. presidential election of 1960, the American government sought Canadian cooperation on Cuba, specifically, backing for the embargo. In December 1960 an editorial in the *Globe and Mail* reported statements made by the U.S. ambassador to the United Nations, Adlai Stevenson, while he was in Toronto, namely, that Canada should be 'harmonizing' its Cuba policy with the United States.[83] In response to such statements, Canada frequently reiterated its stance on Cuba, a stance that was identical to the one Diefenbaker cited in his memoirs. On 28 January 1962 Arthur M. Schlesinger, adviser to President Kennedy, publicly criticized Canada's Cuba policy while he was in Canada, stating that 'anything that supports Castro threatens the prospects of democratic success in Latin America.'[84] Howard Green quickly voiced his displeasure.[85] The tactics of Kennedy officials reinforced Diefenbaker's belief that the president did not appreciate the Canadian position on Cuba. The events of the Cuban Missile Crisis bore this out. Diefenbaker's main sticking point about Kennedy's actions during the crisis was that Canada had not been consulted about the Americans' intended actions. In a phone conversation with Kennedy, Diefenbaker later recalled, he asked the president, 'When were we consulted?' Kennedy replied, 'You weren't.'[86]

For the Kennedy administration, Diefenbaker's argument that other NATO countries did not follow the U.S. embargo (hence neither should Canada) did not hold weight. Cuba was a hemispheric issue, and the Canadians were partners in continental defence.[87] But Diefenbaker despised Kennedy's attitude towards Canada. Unlike Eisenhower, who felt that cooperation did not mean 'subservience,' Diefenbaker believed that only Canadian 'subservience' would satisfy Kennedy. The president was indifferent to Canadian nationalism – he did not even pretend to sympathize with it. And so, in Diefenbaker's eyes, Kennedy had undermined the delicate balance he and Eisenhower had established, that of a Canada-U.S. partnership during the Cold War which maintained at least some semblance of Canadian autonomy. Since Kennedy cared little for such appearances, Diefenbaker felt that all bets were now off. Canada would not budge on its Cuba policy despite repeated U.S. calls to do so. Kennedy gave Diefenbaker no option but to refuse because of his strong-arm tactics.[88] If Diefenbaker had yielded to American pressure to join the embargo, Canada might well have been viewed as nothing more than, as Howard Green put it, 'vassals' of the Americans.[89] For Diefenbaker, the policy on Cuba became an issue of Canadian nationalism because Kennedy, not Diefenbaker, had made it one.

Canada's Cuba policy, then, became a cause célèbre of Canadian nationalism only after John F. Kennedy entered the White House. At that point, the United States hardened its position towards Cuba, and, because of the White House's diplomatic tactics, Diefenbaker would not allow himself to be pressured into following the American lead. Just as President Eisenhower was an influence in Diefenbaker's policy decisions, so was President Kennedy. Diefenbaker's about-face on Cuba was based on his conviction that Canada *had* to resist Kennedy's strong-arm tactics. It had little to do with Castro or the interests of the Cuban people.

While 'what ifs' make for bad history, it is worth pondering the question of whether a Republican president would have made a difference in Diefenbaker's Cuba policy after 1961. In retrospect, it seems highly significant that Diefenbaker considered Canadian membership in the Organization of American States (OAS) under Eisenhower but refused such membership under Kennedy. His reasoning on this point is interesting. Under Eisenhower, Diefenbaker felt that OAS membership would be considered as long as it would not conflict with Canada's Commonwealth status. Under Kennedy, Diefenbaker believed that OAS membership would endanger Canada's image and autonomy in Latin America.[90]

## Conclusion

During Castro's war against Batista, the United States began structuring its Cuba policy around the goal of removing the rebel leader, whom U.S. officials believed to be too radical. In doing so, the United States failed to honour the first law of unintended consequences. Castro's Cuba became Eisenhower's worst communist nightmare turned reality – a direct result of his policy of isolating the island and eliminating Fidel Castro. Despite his hope for backing from his allies, Eisenhower never demanded compliance with the U.S. embargo. He sought support and non-interference where he could, but he did not demand publicly that America's allies fall in line. His hard-line Cuba policy was one that Eisenhower hoped would not be in place for so long as to jeopardize U.S. and Cuban interests.

Diefenbaker believed himself to be in a partnership with the United States and Eisenhower. Regardless of whether the partnership was real or imagined, it allowed for the appearance of a united North America during the Cold War, which did not conflict with the nationalist idea of an autonomous Canada. Whether it took the form of sending military supplies to Batista or delaying recognition, fearing Castro's descent into communism, or trading with just another 'Red' country, the Canadian position under Diefenbaker differed little from that of Washington while Eisenhower was in the White House. Neither nation publicly opposed the other's strategies. Once John F. Kennedy came into power, however, Diefenbaker had to adapt quickly to the fact that Kennedy had no appreciation for Canada's nationalist dilemma. If Kennedy was willing to treat Canada as anything other than a full partner, Diefenbaker, too, was willing to ignore the partnership. Canada's Cuba policy became one means of doing this.

If the genesis of Canada's Cuba policy could be described in one word, it would be this: optics. Whatever its main objective, be it contributing to the united front against communism or presenting the illusion of a unique foreign policy, Canada's Cuba policy was the product of Cold War pressures writ large. Cuban interests never took centre stage. From the day Diefenbaker became prime minister, continentalizing forces were already much too strong to be stopped. He had no choice but to manage them as best he could, his powerful nationalist yearnings notwithstanding. Far from being exempt from U.S. influence, the Canadian strategy on Cuba was originally influenced and shaped by Washington – a historical reality that has had implications for Cuban-Canada relations up to the present.

NOTES

1  Robert Wright, *Three Nights in Havana: Pierre Trudeau, Fidel Castro and the Cold War World* (Toronto: HarperCollins, 2007), 52.

2  John Kirk and Peter McKenna, *Canada-Cuba Relations: The Other Good Neighbor Policy* (Gainesville: University Press of Florida, 1997), 33–8.

3  John Prados, *Safe for Democracy: The Secret Wars of the CIA* (Chicago: Ivan R. Dee, 2006), 147–8.

4  Stephen G. Rabe, *Eisenhower and Latin America: The Foreign Policy of Anti-communism* (Chapel Hill: University of North Carolina Press, 1988), 2.

5  Ibid., 64–5.

6  Ibid., 90.

7  Ibid., 90.

8  Robert H. Ferrell, ed., *The Eisenhower Diaries*, 6 January 1953 (New York: W.W Norton, 1981), 223.

9  Ibid.

10  Rabe, *Eisenhower and Latin America*, 91.

11  Thomas G. Paterson, *Contesting Castro: The United States and the Triumph of the Cuban Revolution* (New York: Oxford University Press, 1994), 20–1.

12  Ibid., 60.

13  Ibid., 78.

14  Ibid., 102–12.

15  Prados, *Safe for Democracy*, 206.

16  Ibid., 206–7.

17  Ibid., 209.

18  Ferrell, ed., *The Eisenhower Diaries*, 6 July 1960, 379.

19  Zachary Karabell, *Architects of Intervention: The United States, the Third World, and the Cold War, 1946–1962* (Louisiana: Louisiana State University Press, 1999), 177.

20  Prados, *Safe for Democracy*, 212–13.

21  Eisenhower to Macmillan, 11 July 1960, in E. Bruce Geelhoed and Anthony O. Edmonds, eds., *The Macmillan-Eisenhower Correspondence, 1957–1969* (New York: Palgrave Macmillan, 2005), 358.

22  Macmillan to Eisenhower, 22 July 1960, ibid., 365.

23  Macmillan to Eisenhower, 25 July 1960, ibid., 369.

24  Eisenhower to Macmillan, 8 August 1960, ibid., 375.

25  Ferrell, ed., *The Eisenhower Diaries*, 29 October 1962, 391.

26  Wright, *Three Nights in Havana*, 64.

27  John G. Diefenbaker, *One Canada: Memoirs of the Right Honourable John G. Diefenbaker: The Years of Achievement 1956–1962* (Scarborough, Ont.: Macmillan-NAL Publishing, 1976), 13.

28  Bruce Muirhead, 'From Dreams to Reality: The Evolution of Anglo-Canadian Trade during the Diefenbaker Era,' *Canadian Historical Association Journal*, 9 (1998): 243–5.

29  Diefenbaker, *The Years of Achievement*, 125.
30  Ibid., 129.
31  Ibid., 125.
32  H. Basil Robinson, *Diefenbaker's World: A Populist in Foreign Affairs* (Toronto: University of Toronto Press, 1999), 167.
33  Ibid., 51.
34  Diefenbaker, *The Years of Achievement*, 129; Robinson, *Diefenbaker's World*, 168.
35  Muirhead, 'From Dreams to Reality,' 243–5.
36  Robinson, *Diefenbaker's World*, 18.
37  John G. Diefenbaker, *One Canada: Memoirs of the Right Honourable John G. Diefenbaker: The Tumultuous Years 1962–1967* (Scarborough, Ont.: Macmillan-NAL Publishing, 1977), 29–36.
38  'Canada-U.S Atom Pact Still in Air,' *Globe and Mail*, 5 July 1960, 1.
39  Robinson, *Diefenbaker's World*, 51.
40  Elmer to John Diefenbaker, 26 January 1964, in Thad McIlroy, ed., *Personal Letters of a Public Man: The Family Letters of John G. Diefenbaker* (Toronto: Doubleday Canada, 1985), 202.
41  Jules Léger, 'Memorandum for the Minister: The Press and President Eisenhower's Visit,' 27 June 1958, Library and Archives Canada (LAC), RG 25, file 1415-E-40, pt. 1, 1.
42  Sidney Smith, 'Memorandum for the Prime Minister: Proposed Visit of President Eisenhower July 8–10, 1958,' 23 May 1958, LAC, RG 25, file 1415-E-40, pt. 1, 1.
43  J.H. Cleveland, 'From American Division to Department of External Affairs,' telegram, Ottawa, 21 May 1958, LAC, RG 25, file 1415-E-40, pt. 1, 1.
44  Douglas Le Pan, 'Memorandum for Mr. Tremblay,' Ottawa, 4 July 1958, LAC, RG 25, file 1415-E-40, pt. 1, 1–2.
45  Smith, 'Memorandum,' pt. 1, 2.
46  Jules Léger, 'Memorandum for the Minister: Proposed Visit of President Eisenhower,' 26 May 1958, LAC, RG 25, file 1415-E-40, pt. 1, 1.
47  Canada, 'Remarks by the Prime Minister, the Right Honourable John G. Diefenbaker, in the House of Commons, on the Occasion of the Visit by the President of the United States, Dwight D. Eisenhower,' Ottawa, 9 July 1958, LAC, RG 25, file 1415-E-40, pt. 1, 1–4. See also Diefenbaker, *The Years of Achievement*, 129.
48  Philip Deane, 'Sympathy, Promises All Canada Will Gain from Talks, It Is Believed,' *Globe and Mail*, 8 July 1958. 1.
49  Diefenbaker, *The Years of Achievement*, 143–4.
50  Ibid., 145.

51 Canada, Department of Trade and Commerce, 'Export Permit Application no. 167978,' Ottawa, 14 June 1949, LAC, RG 25, file 11044-AK-40, pt. 1, 1.

52 Canada, 'Washington D.C to External Affairs 2294 Priority Ref your Tel E1636 Oct 24 Arms and Munitions for Cuba,' telegram, Washington, D.C., 30 October 1957, LAC, RG 25, file 11044-AK-40, pt. 1, 2.

53 Jules Léger, 'Memorandum for the Minister: Proposed Export of Beaver Aircraft to Cuba,' 15 November 1957, LAC, RG 25, file 11044-AK-40, pt. 1, 2.

54 Léger, 'Memorandum for the Minister: Proposed Export of Beaver Aircraft to Cuba,' pt. 1, 1–3.

55 Sidney Smith, 'Memorandum for the Prime Minister: Proposed Export of Beaver Aircraft to Cuba,' 15 November 1957, LAC, RG 25, file 11044-AK-40, pt. 1, 1.

56 Canada, 'Washington D.C to External Affairs 2727 Priority Ref our Tel 2415 Nov 15 Sale of Aircraft to Cuba,' telegram, Washington, D.C., 27 December 1957, LAC, RG 25, file 11044-AK-40, pt. 1, 1.

57 Canada, Department of External Affairs, 'Ref: Your Telegram of 2727 Dec 27 Subject: Sale of Aircraft to Cuba,' telegram, Ottawa, 2 January 1958, LAC, RG 25, file 11044-AK-40, pt. 1, 1–2.

58 Jules Léger, 'Memorandum for the Minister: Export of Military Equipment to Cuba,' 14 May 1958, LAC, RG 25, file 11044-AK-40, pt. 1, 1.

59 Sidney Smith, 'Memorandum for the Prime Minister: Sale of Arms to Cuba,' 29 August 1958, LAC, RG 25, file 11044-AK-40, pt. 2, 3.

60 'Ottawa Sells 100 Fighters Not for Rebels,' Toronto Star, 4 September 1958, 99.

61 Canada, Department of External Affairs, 'URTEL1919 Aug20 Subject: Sale of Arms to Cuba,' telegram, 8 September 1958, LAC, RG 25, file 11044-AK-40, pt. 2, 1.

62 Jules Léger, 'Memorandum for the Minister, Subject: Sale of Arms to Cuba,' 1 October 1958, LAC, RG 25, file 11044-AK-40, pt. 2, 1–3.

63 M. Cadieux, 'Memorandum for the Under-Secretary – Export of Arms to Cuba Interim Report,' 5 November 1958, LAC, RG 25, file 11044-AK-40, pt. 2, 1.

64 Canada, Department of Trade and Commerce, 'Export Permit Application no. 453917,' 22 October 1959, LAC, RG 25, file 11044-AK-40, pt. 3.1, 1.

65 Canada, Department of External Affairs, 'Export of Military Equipment to the Caribbean Following for the Minister,' telegram, 11 November 1959, LAC, RG 25, file 11044-AK-40, pt. 3.1, 1–2.

66 Canada, Department of External Affairs, 'YourTEL155 of Nov.18 Subject: Export of Beaver to Cuba,' telegram, 2 December 1959, LAC, RG 25, file 11044-AK-40, pt. 3.1, 1.

67 Diefenbaker, *The Years of Achievement*, 142–3.
68 Sidney Smith, 'Prime Minister: Recognition of New Cuban Government,' memorandum, 8 January 1959, LAC, RG 25, file 10224-40, 1–2.
69 Canada, 'Numbered Dispatch D-131: Return of the Communist Party to Cuba,' telegram, Havana, 19 March 1959, LAC, RG 25, file 10224-40, 1–2.
70 Canada, 'Our Telegram 133 of January 22 and Earlier Correspondence, Subject: Situation in Cuba,' telegram, Washington, D.C., 27 January 1960, LAC, RG 25, file 10224–40, 1.
71 Wright, *Three Nights in Havana*, 64.
72 Diefenbaker, *The Years of Achievement*, 144–5.
73 Ibid., 127.
74 Canada, W.R. Martin, secretary, Privy Council Office, 'Meeting of Canadian Ministers and the United States Secretary of State in the Office of the Minister of Agriculture, Room 435, House of Commons, at 3:00 pm, Wednesday July 9, 1958,' LAC, RG 25, file 1415-E-40, pt. 1, 6.
75 Harold Greer, 'Alcan Admits U.S Factors Barred Big Sale to China: Firm Feared Effect on Better Customer,' *Globe and Mail*, 22 January 1959, 1.
76 Wright, *Three Nights in Havana*, 67.
77 Canada, 'Remarks by the Prime Minister,' pt. 1, 2.
78 Robert W. Reford, *Canada and Three Crises* (Lindsey: Canadian Institute of International Affairs, 1968), 162.
79 'Little Sign Cuban Cash-Trade Deals May Fizzle: Warning by PM,' *Globe and Mail*, 24 December 1960, 22.
80 Wright, *Three Nights in Havana*, 65.
81 Diefenbaker, *The Years of Achievement*, 142.
82 Ibid., 138.
83 Oakley Dalgleish, 'Equality Comes First,' *Globe and Mail*, 6 December 1960, 6.
84 Bruce Macdonald, 'Won't Sever Trade Ties Canada Says,' *Globe and Mail*, 30 January 1962, 1.
85 Ibid.
86 Diefenbaker, *The Tumultuous Years*, 72.
87 Peter Stursberg, *Diefenbaker: Leadership Gained 1956–62* (Toronto: University of Toronto Press, 1975), 162.
88 For a contemporary interpretation of Diefenbaker, see George Grant, *Lament for a Nation: The Defeat of Canadian Nationalism* [1965] (Ottawa: Carleton University Press, 1997), 41–52.
89 Wright, *Three Nights in Havana*, 81.
90 Diefenbaker, *The Years of Achievement*, 134–41.

# 4 Between Nation and Empire: The Fair Play for Cuba Committees and the Making of Canada-Cuba Solidarity in the Early 1960s

CYNTHIA WRIGHT

In December 1960 two Canadians[1] – Vernel Olson and Anne Olson – visited revolutionary Cuba as part of a 326-member delegation which had been organized by a U.S. group, the Fair Play for Cuba Committee (FPCC). Everybody was talking about Cuba, and the country was attracting what Lou Perez has called 'a new wave of foreign travelers, mostly the committed, some just curious, a few critical.'[2] As it turned out, the Fair Play for Cuba tour of Christmas 1960 would be the last chance for U.S. citizens to visit Cuba legally before the United States ended diplomatic relations and imposed a travel ban in January 1961.[3] Furious at the nationalization of U.S. businesses and property, the United States had already imposed an embargo in October 1960 and initiated covert action to destroy the regime. Indeed, rumours of an imminent U.S. invasion of Cuba formed the essential background to the Fair Play tour. As for Fair Play itself, which had been in existence for barely a year, it was ordered by the United States to register itself as a 'foreign agent'[4] – something the group refused to do. The December 1960 tour, composed chiefly of U.S. students, would mark 'the high point of Fair Play's brief existence.'[5] For their part, the Olsons, already committed revolutionary socialists long before this first trip to Cuba, would return to Toronto and form, in early February 1961, the first chapter of another network of Fair Play Committees – this time across Canada.

In his fascinating account, *Where the Boys Are: Cuba, Cold War America and the Making of a New Left*, U.S. historian Van Gosse analyses the startling appeal of Castro and early revolutionary Cuba to restless Cold War American (including many African American) intellectuals, bohemians, liberals, and leftists, many of whom would channel their support for the *Fidelistas* into the formation of US Fair Play for

Cuba committees. A blend of cultural studies and political history from below, Gosse's book addresses a set of omissions identified by Amy Kaplan in her *Cultures of United States Imperialism*: 'the absence of culture from the history of US imperialism, the absence of empire from the study of American culture; and the absence of the United States from the postcolonial study of imperialism.'[6] Gosse argues that many accounts of the U.S. New Left, including those produced from the left, have 'written out' the anti-imperialist strand of the movement's history, especially Cuba. For these writers, anti-imperialism appears as part of narratives of decline in which 'the move in the late 1960s towards confronting US imperialism in solidarity with the armed peasants of the Third World was a grievous and willful error and defines the closure or "death" of the New Left.'[7]

Consciously countering such narratives, Gosse excavates the remarkable early history of popular support for the Fidelistas which was fostered by Castro's tours of the northeastern United States in the years before the Revolution and just after 1959, as well as by journalist Herbert Matthews's early sympathetic accounts in the New York *Times*. Along the way, Gosse builds a gendered and raced account of how and why Fidel Castro came to appeal to so many 'young and restless' in the late 1950s and the early 1960s, as an unlikely coalition of liberals, beatniks such as Allen Ginsberg, and African Americans such as LeRoi Jones and James Baldwin came together around Cuba. Many of these same people involved with Cuba would also move into the New Left. As Gosse remarks of what he calls 'patriarchal imperialism': 'There was a problem with the all-encompassing narrative of the Free World and the American Century: it quickly became very boring.'[8] For young homosexual, African American, and/or beatnik men, Castro was far more interesting a masculine figure than Eisenhower.

The early U.S.-based Fair Play for Cuba Committees, as scholars have noted, were the first generation of a new political formation: conscious attempts to forge international links of support within the hemisphere and against U.S. policy.[9] But the U.S.-based FPCCs did not survive the witch-hunt that followed the accusation that Jack Kennedy's alleged killer, Lee Harvey Oswald, was a member of Fair Play. The organization – already adrift following a peak around the time of the Bay of Pigs, and under very heavy repression – was buried. As for organized Cuba-U.S. solidarity work, it would not be fully renewed until the celebrated Venceremos Brigades of the late 1960s.

The formation and trajectory of the Canadian Fair Play for Cuba

Committees would at first parallel, then very much depart from, that of their U.S. counterparts. Formed in early 1961 in the months before the U.S. FPCC went into decline, the Canadian FPCCs were much more long-lasting, surviving well into the late 1960s and beyond. Moreover, they were arguably far more influential than their U.S. counterparts in making space for debate about Cuba. For one thing, the Canadian FPCCs enjoyed the support of several members of the Co-operative Commonwealth Federation (CCF) and its successor organization, the New Democratic Party (NDP), some of whom were elected politicians, as well as liberals, revolutionary socialists, independent leftists, university professors, students, housewives, church people, writers, and others. Canadian supporters of Cuba, moreover, never faced the travel ban imposed on U.S. nationals, nor did Canada support the U.S. embargo, and this enabled visits to Cuba and active ties of solidarity that became very difficult in the U.S. case. Yet the story of the Canadian FPCCs is absent from accounts of the left in Canada, and has remained largely unknown. In part, this is because scholars have in many ways only begun to write serious histories of the post-war social movements in Canada, to consider how the Cold War shaped the New Left and the women's movement, and to produce more transnationally framed accounts. Cold War obliteration of particular histories and political subjects has also played a role, but so too has a persistent left nationalism which has often grounded a deeply limited understanding of left narratives and imaginaries in Canada.

Through an excavation of the forgotten story of the Fair Play for Cuba Committees in Canada, and especially the group's first two years, this chapter offers a very preliminary consideration of the impact of the Cuban Revolution on the development of left and solidarity politics in Canada, and on the making of what Gosse calls 'foreign policy from below.' In both the United States and Canada, the committees were part of the difficult process of opening up political dissent within the stifling context of McCarthyism and the Cold War consensus; they were also fundamentally linked to the early phase of the civil rights movement, Black Power, and the student movement.

## The Revolution Will Be Televised

When Vernel Olson and Anne Olson returned from Cuba and began organizing a Fair Play for Cuba Committee in Toronto in early 1961, the dominant ideological framing of the Cuban Revolution in the mainstream media was shifting dramatically. As in the United States, the role of positive media coverage of Castro in the period just before his seizure of power and after is central to understanding something of Fidel's early popularity. As Samuel Farber observes, 'contrary to the expectations of Gil Scott Heron, the revolution was televised, at least in the case of Cuba.'[10] Here Farber is echoing the work of Louis A. Perez, Jr, who has documented the high rates of TV ownership in Cuba even before the Revolution and the extent to which the revolutionary leadership would make use of the medium particularly after the seizure of power. But it is also true that in Canada and the United States, as well, television coverage was key to creating excitement about what the Cubans were doing and to sustaining the mystique of the Sierra Maestra. Right from the beginning, as many have observed, Castro was attuned to the need to cultivate the media so as to build support both within Cuba and, crucially, internationally.[11]

New York *Times* journalist Herbert Matthews's celebrated 1957 meeting with Castro in the Sierra Maestra caused a sensation at a time when many thought Fidel was dead. Not long after, U.S. journalist Robert Taber – who would go on to co-found the New York City Fair Play for Cuba Committee – produced the thirty-minute CBS documentary, *Rebels of the Sierra Maestra: The Story of Cuba's Jungle Fighters*.[12] Matthews's print journalism and Taber's documentary both circulated in Canada, but Canadian print and broadcast media were also very active on their own account for, as Gosse comments, 'there was a race on to find and "capture" Castro after Matthews' scoop.'[13] While Canadian diplomatic officials wildly miscalculated the popular support for Castro in Cuba,[14] Canadian media knew that they were on to a major – and popular – story. Indeed, as Robert Wright observes in his *Three Nights in Havana*, 'editorials and letters in the Canadian dailies throughout 1958 were overwhelmingly supportive of the guerillas.'[15]

Patrick Watson, a long-time journalist and former chair of the CBC, recalls sending a cameraman in 1958 to the Sierra Maestra. The resulting 'treasured footage,' Watson notes, was aired 'two days after Fidel Castro marched into Havana, along with a live feed from that city, and fresh footage.' Watson would himself go to Cuba a year later with the same cameraman. They spoke with Castro as well as numerous others to make the documentary *Castro's First Year of Power*.[16] Castro's brief April 1959 visit to Montreal, the only Canadian stop on a tour of the U.S. northeast, further built excitement about the Revolution. As Wright recounts, 'thousands … turned out in person to see him' while others listened as René Lévesque, then a Radio-Canada journalist, interviewed the Cuban leader.[17] Many working-class people in Canada in this era still did not own televisions and it was Cuban radio, rather than North American media, that formed their sense of the Revolution. Indeed, radio was central to the rebels' ability to build knowledge about, and support for, the Revolution in Cuba and abroad. After the formation of Fair Play in Canada, many people, including Howard Pawley, later the NDP premier of Manitoba, wrote to the Toronto office talking about how important Radio Havana was for them.[18]

While many journalists on both sides of the Canada-U.S. border initially sympathized with Castro's project, citing, for example, the corruption and violence of the Batista dictatorship, the love affair with Castro quickly began to fade in the months after the Revolution. Those U.S. journalists who remained critical of the new Cold War consensus on Cuba now lacked institutional spaces for their work; as Gosse notes, 'it is no accident that [the U.S.] Fair Play began as an alternative media outlet run by professional reporters.'[19] In the Canadian context, mainstream mass-circulation magazines such as *Maclean's* would also very soon close down the ideological space opened up by the Cuban Revolution's fundamental challenge to U.S. imperialism. This was evident to all by early 1961. Farley Mowat, for example, a key supporter of the Canadian Fair Play network who had planned to write on Cuba for *Maclean's*, complained to Vernel Olson that 'it was then decided that any report which I might make would be too much at variance with the accepted attitude toward Cuba of the US dominated press.'[20] In Canada, much of the shift in the press occurred in the context of the Canadian government's decision not to follow the United States in imposing an embargo against Cuba. Nor did Canada end diplomatic relations with Cuba, as had the United States in January 1961.

These diverging Canadian and U.S. positions on the embargo unleashed a firestorm. By early 1961, articles increasingly worried about 'anti-Americanism' among Canadians and 'anti-Canadianism' among Americans, the possibility of an open breach between Canada and the United States over Cuba, and the dangers of political identification between Cuba and Canada over the question of U.S. power. On the U.S. side, ideologues such as Arthur Schlesinger, Jr, railed against the failure to get behind Washington. A January 1961 *Maclean's* article, 'Why Castro's Cuba Is Wrong about Canada,' outlined what writer Ian Sclanders saw as Castro's misplaced faith in Canada and the dangers of assuming Canada would not ultimately back the United States. The argument is

articulated through a set of binaries which explicitly contrast the vola-
tility of Cuban people and Cuban food (*sic!*) with the peaceable and
orderly character of Canada. He quotes approvingly a Canadian living
in Havana who comments: "'Tossing a bomb … is the same to a Cuban as writing a letter to the editor is to a Canadian.'"[21] Of course, not
long after, the first bombs would explode in Quebec as a far-left radical nationalist movement appeared.[22] But the reference to a peaceable
Canada reveals how anxieties about 'foreign' policy are fundamentally
linked to anxieties about 'national' identity.

While Sclanders's article is full of absurdities, he was right about
one thing: there would be no official, serious break between the United
States and Canada over Cuba, including at the time of the Bay of Pigs,
even as demonstrations and public meetings erupted across the country and internationally. Indeed, while the diverging Canadian position
on Cuba infuriated many U.S. business interests, media, and citizens,
and led fringe anti-Castro groups to threaten Canadian interests, new
evidence suggests that, 'far from encouraging Canada to support the
embargo, the United States secretly urged Diefenbaker to maintain normal relations because it was thought that Canada would be well positioned to gather intelligence on the island.'[23] Also crucial was the fact
that the Cuban revolutionary government did not nationalize the Royal
Bank of Canada, which had very important interests in Cuba, and was
very gentle with the few Canadians who had private interests in the
island. Canadian business elites saw no particular call to get behind an
embargo of Cuba.

This, then, was the context in which the Olsons founded a Fair Play
for Cuba Committee in Canada. In the United States, Robert Taber's
January 1960 article in *The Nation*, 'Castro's Cuba,' was one of the key
catalysts in the formation of the U.S. Fair Play for Cuba Committee of
which Taber was a co-founder. A somewhat similar part was played
in Canada by an article written by the liberal historian Kenneth Mc-
Naught which appeared in the Canadian magazine *Saturday Night* in
January 1961, the same month the United States ended diplomatic relations with Cuba. McNaught's own intervention addressed the crisis in
Canada-U.S. relations over Cuba but was fundamentally aimed at re-
making the terms of a debate which, he argued, was split between those
who opposed 'betraying an American ally, and those that approved the
show of Canadian independence.'

McNaught reframed the question by situating Cuba within the context of the struggles of the Third World: 'Canada's policy toward the

Castro revolution will reveal not only the degree to which we are in-dependent in foreign affairs. It will confirm or modify the unflattering appraisal of "the West" at present held by a majority of the peoples of Afro-Asia and Latin America.'[24] McNaught's argument is anchored in a critique of U.S. actions on the first Cold War front, Asia, and he decries the long history of backing corrupt, violent, and undemocratic regimes in the name of anti-communism. The notion of 'fair play' deployed in McNaught's article accorded a genuine space for 'ex-colonial peoples' to 'feel their way toward independence and social justice'; it was, as Gosse notes in his own discussion of the concept, a somewhat archaic 'Anglo-American ideal' which allowed liberals to critique the long U.S. history of support for the deeply repressive Batista regime while also arguing that support for Cuba's independent development would keep it out of the communist orbit.[25]

As it turned out, McNaught's distrust of mainstream media sources on Cuba would provide an opening for linking his Canadian readers with Vernel and Anne Olson. McNaught noted that, ironically, U.S. sources on Cuba were more informative and more critical of the Cold War consensus: 'A Canadian seeking to understand the Cuban-American crisis will find his most complete sources of information (and criti-cism) in the reports carried by small-circulation American periodicals, or in several paperbacks published in the United States.'[26] His own ar-ticle opened with a paragraph-long citation from one of these influen-tial U.S. paperbacks, C. Wright Mills's 1960 best-seller, *Listen, Yankee: The Revolution in Cuba*. McNaught went on to add that, if a Canadian 'wishes to visit Cuba to see for himself he will find ready assistance from the American "Fair Play for Cuba Committee" – an organiza-tion supported by distinguished writers, artists, journalists, and other professional people.'[27] Interested Canadian readers who subsequently wrote to New York then had their addresses forwarded to Vernel Olson. Canadian media also picked up the story after press releases were sent out about the formation of Fair Play in Canada; this, too, helped build the group. Fair Play in Canada was launched.

### 'I Say You People Are Communists!': Building Fair Play for Cuba in Canada

In early 1961, as Fair Play was being formed, Vernel Olson approached a number of people to be sponsors of the group. He may have been following the lead of the New York FPCC, which had some thirty sponsors, some of whom were internationally known, including Simone de Beauvoir, Jean-Paul Sartre, C. Wright Mills, and James Baldwin. As Gosse notes, some eight of the thirty sponsors were African American, including Richard Gibson, a journalist who was to play a major leadership role in the New York chapter.[28] However, if the initial sponsors of the U.S. Fair Play were in many cases unaffiliated intellectuals and journalists increasingly critical of the ideological framework of the Cold War, the base of Fair Play in Canada was rather different. For one thing, the Canadian FPCC lacked a key element that made the New York FPCC important: significant membership by African Americans who also played a leadership role in the organization. There would be no Canadian equivalent of the celebrated Hotel Theresa moment in which Castro used a Harlem hotel as a base to connect with Third World, Latino, and African American supporters of Cuba, including Richard Gibson. The early sponsors of the Canadian FPCC were from the trade-union movement, the CCF, academia, the churches, and the senior professions such as medicine and law. Many had clear, and varying, ideological affiliations with the left, most notably Trotskyist currents, but Vernel also worked to make the group non-sectarian in orientation. He tried to reach unaffiliated writers and intellectuals, and figures such as Farley Mowat responded with enthusiasm. Other well-known Canadian writers such as Irving Layton were not so forthcoming. In the same month that Kennedy announced the Alliance for Progress and one month before the Bay of Pigs invasion, Layton wrote in a stinging letter to Vernel Olson: 'I am now satisfied that President Kennedy and his advisors are bent upon pursuing a genuine liberal policy with regard to backward and distressed countries, supporting genuine social and economic reforms there.'[29]

While the formation of Fair Play in Canada was clearly influenced by the U.S. example, the two national networks were distinct. In a 1961 letter to a supporter, Vernel noted: 'This question was thoroughly discussed at the time of the formation of the Committee and we chose to be completely independent. This decision was made despite a certain amount of pressure from New York.'[30] Some committee members, aware of real dangers of surveillance and harassment, feared the circulation of membership lists across the border. But Toronto Fair Play would go on to work relatively closely with the New York chapter of Fair Play during the latter's short life. It is likely that Vernel and Anne Olson met Richard Gibson of the New York FPCC for the first time in 1960 on the FPCC Christmas tour. There was a more or less constant circulation of literature, organizing ideas, and speakers between the two national contexts during the short period in which the two groups' existence overlapped. Supporters from Canada would also attend meetings and conventions of the FPCC in the United States. And, although Cuba solidarity was an international issue, as the global demonstrations against the Bay of Pigs invasion made clear, Fair Play in Canada seems to have had relatively little correspondence with solidarity groups besides those in the United States and in Cuba itself.[31]

Fair Play held its inaugural mass meeting in Toronto in February 1961 at the First Unitarian Church of which Vernel Olson was a member. Both Jean-Paul Sartre and C. Wright Mills, each with well-known books on Cuba, were originally sought as speakers, but unsuccessfully. In the end, Richard Gibson spoke, and the main attraction was a history professor from Michigan State, Samuel Shapiro. Shapiro had been in the Cuban countryside the previous summer and had subsequently published an article in the *New Republic*. According to a *Globe and Mail* report of the public meeting at First Unitarian, Shapiro argued, 'Within the next five years, we will see seven to 10 revolutions in Latin-America.' At one point during the question-and-answer period, a man in the audience 'screamed': 'I say you people are Communists.'[32] The meeting, which was attended by 300 people according to the *Globe* and 400 according to Vernel, passed a resolution recognizing 'the historical justification of the Cuban revolution and call[ing] upon the Canadian government to extend long term, low interest loans to Cuba for the purpose of greatly expanding Canada-Cuban trade.' Vernel Olson immediately embarked on an extensive speaking tour of western Canada, where he spoke to 400 people in Winnipeg, 175 in Regina, 125 in Edmonton, and 75 in Vancouver.[33]

Olson's speaking tour was significant for it led to the formation of Fair Play chapters in many of these centres. FPCC chapters appear to have been more or less self-organized and loosely coordinated with one another. It does not appear that the network of Canadian FPCCs ever met in convention, unlike its U.S. counterpart, although there was a fair amount of written correspondence between some of the Canadian committees and the Toronto office, and the FPCC bulletin updated chapters and general members alike. Sometimes members wrote to propose names of people who should be contacted because they were regarded as potential supporters of Fair Play; some of these same potential supporters were also recommended to the Cuban authorities in Canada as people who should be invited to visit Cuba. Hence it was that a Pierre

Trudeau of Westmount, Quebec, was suggested, as well as a handful of Queen's University professors, some of whom were described as very critical of the United States in their classrooms.[34] Gabriel Glazer, a lawyer active in Montreal Fair Play, wrote to suggest Dr Charles Moyo, 'one of a handful of black Nigerian physicians extant and outspokenly pro-Cuba.'[35] The reference here to newly independent Nigeria is a reminder of the crucial broader context of decolonization and of the formation of a Third World project with which Cuba was already deeply associated.

Indeed, these letters to the Toronto office of Fair Play are a fascinating indication of who supported Cuba, and why, in this early period of the group's existence. Interestingly, rarely did letter writers articulate political solidarity with Cuba through a Canadian nationalist position. One exception to this, a letter written by a woman in Owen Sound, Ontario, who described herself as 'a 35 yr. old housewife,' reads: 'With the amount of control the U.S. has over Canada's economy will Canada itself become the next Cuba? It is certain we intend to gain back this lost control eventually and intend doing so much sooner than the U.S.A. realizes.' A woman from Cranbrook, British Columbia, wrote one month after the Bay of Pigs invasion to say that 'we put a "Fair Play for Cuba" float in the local parade today.'[36] The occasion was Cranbrook's Victoria Day celebration, thereby making a rather startling juxtaposition of the Cuban Revolution with the British Empire but nonetheless offering a clear indication of popular support for Cuba in this period.

At least in the early years, FPCC chapters existed across the west and in Ontario and Quebec. Over time, the strongest chapters appeared to be in Toronto, Vancouver, and – to a far lesser degree – Montreal, although, as is often the case with political formations of this type, many of them faded in and out depending on the moment. Montreal had two committees, one anglophone and one francophone. Gabriel Glazer wrote Toronto in May 1961 to insist on the importance of Fair Play having a bilingual name, Amis du Peuple Cubain – FPCC, and indeed this bilingual name appears on Fair Play pamphlets and bulletins. In a subsequent letter, Glazer also noted that, while 'the French section is not as strong as the English speaking one, nevertheless, the majority of our members are French.'[37] Both Toronto and Vancouver would also develop student committees for Cuba based at the University of Toronto (under the name Student Committee on Cuban Affairs) and the University of British Columbia.[38]

A clear core constituency of Fair Play in Canada was the left wing of the CCF and people like Vernel Olson himself who were CCF supporters but whose own politics were closer to Trotskyist revolutionary socialism. (Vernel had more than once been rejected for CCF membership presumably because of his former adhesion to Trotskyist groups.) For him, the vast appeal of Cuba was related to the renewal of socialism and the fierce critique of Stalinism that was strongly nurtured within Trotskyist circles. As he wrote in the same month as the formation of Fair Play: 'Many others who have been disillusioned with socialism as a result of the degeneration of the Soviet Union can be brought back into activity when confronted by the Cuba Revolution which is led by a native leadership in the finest traditions of the socialist movements of the world.'[39]

In February 1961 Vernel wrote to William Irvine, a central figure on the left of the CCF, about the need to defend 'the Cuban people and their right to create a society in the image outlined in the Regina Manifesto.'[40] The comparison here between the Cuban revolutionary project and the CCF's 1933 anti-capitalist manifesto did elide some crucial differences between the Canadian and Cuban realities. At the same time, this was a period when the concept of state-led economic planning, albeit theorized and organized in a variety of different ways, was important across the 'three worlds.'[41] And clearly those on the left of the CCF did see some affinities between the Cuban project and their own political vision. Vernel Olson was writing to Irvine at a crucial time: leftists, trade unionists, and CCFers were debating the orientation of a new party formation, then called the New Party but later to be known as the New Democratic Party. Olson was signalling here his own commitment to a party that would clearly embody socialist aspirations and solidarity with Cuba. To that end, one of his earliest projects was the attempt to organize a delegation of New Party supporters to go to Cuba.

### Building Solidarity: Delegations and the Cold War Frontier

Vernel strongly believed that one of the best ways to build solidarity with the Cuban project was to provide people with the opportunity to see Cuba for themselves, and he worked tirelessly to organize group tours. Such delegations may seem commonplace today but they were profoundly important in this period for crossing 'the Cold War frontier'[42] and would subsequently play a significant role in creating a sense of an international left in the 1960s. Comparatively few Canadians, in contrast with U.S. nationals pre-1959, would have had direct experience of Cuba whether as permanent residents, tourists, or business investors. The Canadian tourist boom, which would begin in the 1970s, was still a long way off. Moreover, few Cubans lived in Canada; there were just 150 in 1961.[43] FPCC-organized tours offered, then, a unique opportunity to experience the Cuban revolutionary reality.

Olson was to encourage many such trips to Cuba, and an early priority was an FPCC tour for New Party sympathizers in 1961. The idea was to get them to Cuba for the 26 July celebrations – and just before the NDP convention of 31 July. Here he faced a major obstacle: what he saw as the complete incompetence of the Instituto Cubano de Amistad con los Pueblos (ICAP) in Havana, and this was to remain a theme in Vernel Olson's papers for years. Frustrated, he wrote Castro directly in early July 1961 to express his irritation.[44] However, it does not appear that the New Party tour ever took place.

As we have seen, the huge significance of Cuba for some Old Left Trotskyist sympathizers such as Vernel was that it represented a non-Stalinist revolutionary project. At the same time, the way in which Vernel organized tours provides a window into how he conceptualized the key political actors of the early 1960s, students and women among them. From the beginning, Fair Play in Toronto strongly encouraged student tours to Cuba, a fact that is important given that students would later contest the Vietnam War, the colonial oppression of indigenous people in Canada, and the profound Cold War disciplining of the university. A key point, too, is that student organizations in Havana had long played a central role in the revolutionary process, one that has often been obscured by the mythology surrounding the Sierra Maestra, and their activities well pre-date the student explosions of the 1960s in the global north.[45] The first FPCC-sponsored student tour to Cuba was in 1964 and was an intellectual boost for the important student committees for Cuba in centres such as Vancouver and Toronto. In 1965 Vernel was profoundly frustrated with the ICAP when a student tour was cancelled by it at the last minute, and the students were deeply disappointed.[46] Many students would eventually go, however, often on their own initiative, and give public talks and write literature about Cuba for Fair Play.

Another proposed visit, involving the Voice of Women for Peace (VOW) – a group founded in July 1960 and one of the midwives of second-wave feminism in Canada – and the Federation of Cuban Women (FMC) does not appear to have taken place, even though Anne Olson was a member of Voice of Women.[47] Women were few but very important in Fair Play; Anne Olson played an indispensable role in the

Toronto office and corresponded with other radical housewives from various classes, some of whom were enthusiastic readers of Betty Friedan's 1963 book, *The Feminine Mystique*. As Gosse has commented for the United States, and his argument is useful for Canada as well, peace groups from a variety of political orientations 'created the first public space within the United States for dissent within the orthodoxy of national security.'[48] Women's peace groups such as the VOW also had a much larger membership than the FPCC; the VOW, for example, had some 10,000 members in its first year.

Many in the peace movement strongly believed in organizing delegations of individuals to engage directly with the so-called 'enemy' and to try and solve global problems outside government frameworks; this approach also provided, crucially, an international framework for activists to network with each other. In the very early 1960s, for example, the VOW would sponsor a group of Soviet women to come to Canada to talk about peace, a major initiative in the context of the Cold War and 'patriarchal imperialism.' Voice of Women went on to emerge as an important actor in the early 1960s as debates erupted in Canada over the Cuban Missile Crisis, nuclear weapons, and the independence (or not) of Canadian foreign policy from the United States. Somewhat parallel developments occurred in the United States during the missile crisis, when, with Fair Play being increasingly in disarray and under heavy state surveillance, peace and progressive groups stepped into the breach.[49]

### A Fugitive and a Visit from the RCMP

Not unlike its counterpart in New York City, the Toronto Fair Play for Cuba Committee would have a deeply dramatic inaugural year full of internal and external crises. The most serious of the group's internal crises involved Kenneth McNaught and Leslie Dewart, both established university professors and important Fair Play supporters. Both resigned from Fair Play in late June 1961 and withdrew their sponsorship of the group. Vernel explained why in a long letter to Gabe Glazer which revealed the extent to which Fair Play, like its counterpart in the United States, was subject to surveillance and harassment: 'Their resignation followed an RCMP statement appearing in the Toronto papers which said that the mounties were "watching" the FPCC. They [McNaught and Dewart] called me into conference ten days ago and suggested that the Committee should write an anti-communist clause in its constitution and remove one person from the Toronto executive. They also suggested changing the name of the Committee because of the association with the American Committee which is under heavy attack from Eastland & Co.'[50] 'Eastland and Company' refers to the Internal Security Subcommittee chaired by Senator James Eastland, a southern Democrat. Along with the FBI, it was intent on destroying Fair Play in the United States. As Gosse comments of the Eastland hearings, 'among the organized liberals or the larger public, it was a clear stop-sign indicating an illicit taint.'[51]

For Vernel, however, calls for anti-communist language were all too reminiscent of the clauses adopted by many unions in the Cold War period and he refused to have anything do with them. He would be solidly backed up by the membership and other chapters of Fair Play. Montreal, for example, affirmed its support for Vernel. Making reference to the recent end of the repressive and anti-communist Duplessis regime, it noted, 'Quebecers only now breathing a little more easily. Bill of rights guarantees are meaningless unless they are used.'[52] While the organization was easily able to survive this crisis, it was to upset Vernel's health and disturb him for some time to come.

Not long after this episode, partly occasioned by RCMP surveillance, Fair Play would have another – much more serious – brush with the Mounties. In a September 1961 letter to a trusted comrade, Vernel wrote: 'We have been harassed at 21 Ellis gdns [Olson residence] for the past two weeks. We have had two visits from the RCMP and one from the Toronto homicide Squad …You will hear more about the case as time goes by.'[53] This, as it turned out, was a reference to what was easily the most dramatic incident that Fair Play in Toronto was involved with that year: assisting Robert F. Williams's safe passage to Cuba after he was framed for kidnapping a white couple in the United States.

Williams was a key African American supporter of Cuba (he had been at the meeting with Castro in the Hotel Theresa), a member of Fair Play in the United States, and a Unitarian. He had visited Cuba, where he was deeply impressed by revolutionary efforts to end segregation and racism, and, after being recruited by Robert Taber, he had spoken on a Fair Play platform in U.S. and Canadian cities. While often forgotten now, at the time Williams was an important bridge politically between the civil rights period and Black Power; his militant organizing in North Carolina was to influence figures such as Huey Newton of the Black Panthers. At one time the head of the most militant chapter of the National Association for the Advancement of Colored People

(NAACP) in the United States, Williams has recently been the subject of a documentary, *Negroes with Guns*, and studied by scholars interested in the formation of a U.S. Third World Left. He was the first of many African Americans to seek political refuge from U.S. racism in Cuba and to forge an identification between the Cuban Revolution and Black emancipation.[54]

When Williams's life was endangered in the United States, he and his wife, Mabel, turned to allies in Canada, hoping he could find refuge there from the FBI and the Klan. As Timothy Tyson observes in his biography of Williams, 'the Williams family's escape from Monroe [North Carolina] has been shrouded in mystery for decades. Some black residents still offer to show visitors where Fidel Castro's helicopters landed to spirit his friend away to Cuba.'[55] The truth is almost as sensational as the legend. In the United States and Canada, Mabel and Robert Williams were sheltered by a diverse network of people with connections to Fair Play and/or organized left-wing (often Trotskyist) politics. But Canada was no safe haven; as Williams told the story in his short 1962 memoir, also called *Negroes with Guns*: 'The Royal Canadian Mounted Police initiated a search that was just as vicious and carried out just as energetically as the FBI search. Since there were many Canadians who realized what the race situation was in the United States and who sympathized with me, the Royal Canadian Mounted Police started searching homes. They even searched a church in Toronto (and questioned the minister) where I had appeared while on a speaking tour the previous summer.'[56]

After spending six weeks in Toronto with Vernel and Anne Olson, and just narrowly escaping a raid, Robert and Mabel sought refuge separately; Robert headed for Nova Scotia, seen to be a safe place because of the size of the African Canadian population in the province. From Newfoundland, he escaped on a flight to Cuba, where he lived for many years before moving to China.[57] Mabel Williams, and the Williams's two children, would make their way to Cuba after Robert, through two different routes. Anne Olson would subsequently become the North American distributor for Williams's Black Liberation publication, *The Crusader*, a major undertaking given the journal's wide circulation. Anne and Vernel Olson would continue to correspond with Robert and Mabel Williams, and even send them the latest and best music to play on their Radio Havana program, *Radio Free Dixie*, which was broadcast to the United States and could be heard in some parts of Canada.

Indeed, one of the most interesting aspects of the Canadian FPCC's work was its relationship with American supporters of Cuba, whether they were living in the United States or in Cuba. The range of FPCC literature that can to this day be found in the archival and library collections of U.S. institutions or in the second-hand bookstores of border cities such as Seattle is testimony to this fact.

### Listen, Yankee: The Cuban Revolution in Circulation

In the first five years of the Castro regime, an extraordinary amount of literature was produced about the Cuban Revolution by non-Cuban observers. While much of the mainstream media debated whether Castro was communist, and whether he was intent on exporting the Cuban Revolution to all corners of the hemisphere, other writers were getting a hearing with a very different analysis.[58] The classic of this genre is the U.S. sociologist C. Wright Mills's *Listen, Yankee: The Revolution in Cuba*. Excerpted as the cover story in the December 1960 issue of *Harper's*, the book would go on to sell hundreds of thousands of copies in the United States and be translated into numerous languages, becoming, as Gosse notes, one of the first classics of the New Left.[59] In a 1961 letter to his parents, Mills wrote, 'I get from 7 to 10 letters a day from people all over the world thanking me for having written the book and many asking, "How can you help me to get to Cuba so I can help Fidel?"'[60] The book was also very popular in Canada, and was sold through Fair Play, as was Leo Huberman and Paul Sweezy's *Cuba: Anatomy of a Revolution*, described by Gosse as 'the first full examination of the revolution from a Marxist perspective, very widely read in 1960 and after.'[61]

In addition to sympathetic early accounts of the Cuban Revolution by radicals and Marxists, Fair Play circulated or produced materials in at least three additional categories: speeches by Fidel Castro and Ernesto 'Che' Guevara, always very popular; FPCC bulletins and pamphlets; and other sympathetic accounts of Cuba, most notably a pamphlet reprinted from a mainstream media source, *Jack Scott Takes a Second Look at Cuba*. Robert Wright has commented on Castro's 'resolve to speak English only when the political advantage of doing so was extraordinary' and argued that such a move has allowed mainstream North American English-language media to demonize Castro because anglophone publics lacked access to his speeches.[62] At the same time, many people on both sides of the Canada-U.S. border solved that problem by reading Castro's speeches themselves, and they obtained this literature through the Toronto office of the Canadian Fair Play for Cuba Committee. Indeed, Fair Play was constantly asking the Cubans for more literature so they could also meet U.S. demand, including demand for material in Spanish. For years, the Canadian FPCC acted as a key source for those resident in the United States who could not receive materials from Cuba or send any to the island.[63] The literature destined for Canada was in English mainly, since the country did not at that point have a sizeable Latin American population, although Mexican students, exiles from Franco's Spain, and a very small number of Cubans participated in Fair Play activities in Toronto. But Fair Play did ask the Cubans for Portuguese-language propaganda for Toronto's growing Portuguese community, whose labour as construction workers helped remake the city in the 1950s and 1960s.

The Canadian FPCC also produced an important body of literature of its own. FPCC pamphlets were often very detailed eyewitness accounts from people who had recently visited Cuba, and included titles such as the very popular *Four Canadians Who Saw Cuba* (1963), *The Real Cuba As Three Canadians Saw It* (1964), and *Canadian Students in Cuba* (1965), which came out of the 1964 student tour.[64] Another early pamphlet that enjoyed particular popularity was Leslie Dewart's *A Catholic Speaks on Cuba* (1961), based on a speech that Dewart had given at a May 1961 rally sponsored by Fair Play. One grateful reader wrote to Fair Play: 'Sorry I cannot at this time make a substantial donation. We have seven children. But you do have our prayers. We, too, are Catholics.'[65] Dewart, a philosophy professor at St Michael's, a Catholic college at the University of Toronto, was also Cuban, having come to Canada in his late teens in the early 1940s. His powerful affirmation of support for Cuba and Fair Play from a Catholic perspective, and from the standpoint of a Cuban who had experienced severe political violence, was very important politically at a period when much was being made of the repression of the Catholic Church in Cuba. Dewart's pamphlet likely stands as one of the very earliest Catholic faith-based sympathetic accounts of Cuba, and pre-dates statements on Cuba by leading radical U.S. Catholics such as Dorothy Day.[66] While Dewart, as we have seen, resigned from Fair Play, he would go on to write numerous works about the Cuban church.[67]

Perhaps the most popular document circulated by Fair Play was the twenty-eight-page pamphlet *Jack Scott Takes a Second Look at Cuba* (1963), introduced by NDP MP Bert Herridge. Jack Scott, who is not to be confused with the older west coast left-wing radical and trade un-

ionist of the same name, was a journalist with the Vancouver *Sun* who
was particularly popular with women readers. He visited Cuba twice
in the early 1960s, and his columns provide a sense of the possibilities of
political commentary on Cuba within the mainstream media during a
period in which there was less space for a pro-Cuba position than there
had been earlier. Eight of these columns from May and June 1963 were
collected to make *Jack Scott Takes a Second Look at Cuba*. Scott's pamphlet
was among the few circulated by FPCC to address, in however limited
a way, the situation of Cuban women in the context of the Revolution.

Scott describes his political outlook by comparing himself to another
correspondent in Cuba: 'Like me, he's a pale, non-toxic socialist of the
British Labor Party-type with certain natural reservations about this
affair. His fascination, like mine, is a simple matter of ceaseless admiration and gratitude for a society that, alone in the Caribbean or in Central America, respects the human race.'[68] Scott linked Cuba, as did C.
Wright Mills, to the broader story of 'the hungry nations' of the global
south. But Scott was no C. Wright Mills; his work has none of the sheer
power of *Listen, Yankee* and at times he strikes the reader as somewhat
of a total 'gringo.' For one thing, he spends a ridiculous amount of time
commenting on the rear ends of Cuban women. (Most of these rear
ends, according to Scott, were no longer encased in girdles because of
the difficulty of accessing, post-embargo, the elastic which went into
undergarments.) If anything, Scott found Cuban revolutionary society
rather too tame: 'It often seems that they've declared a moratorium
here on sex and the nicer sins, generally, since the prevailing atmosphere is very similar to what might be found at a well-run young people's summer Bible school.'[69] Scott's description, arguably, is haunted
by pre-revolutionary representations of the island 'as the Mafia's Caribbean sewer.'[70] Yet his discussion of Cuban women has curious echoes of
Betty Friedan's diagnosis of North American women's discontent, *The
Feminine Mystique*, also published in 1963.[71] Observing a group of Afro-
Cuban women, Scott observes, 'These four particular young women
certainly have none of the problems of boredom or restricted interests
that afflict so many North American women ... All four of these women
wholeheartedly support the revolution, two of them being downright
fierce about it, since Fidel Castro has given them what money couldn't
buy in earlier days, the full dignity of equality now accorded the
Negro.'[72]

As Daniel Horowitz's extraordinary biography has made clear, Betty
Friedan was a consummate negotiator of the political shifts occasioned

by the Cold War disciplining of the left and the labour movement; her mainstreaming of feminism would have profound influence.[73] But, precisely because *The Feminine Mystique* was a Cold War product, it could have nothing to say about Cuban women or revolutionary challenges to racism. Those radical housewives in Canada who read her, including FPCC supporters, would have to turn elsewhere for accounts of Cuban women's lives. It does not appear that the FPCC ever produced a pamphlet on Cuban women, although plans for one were discussed in the FPCC bulletin in 1966. It would be almost a decade before the resurgence of the women's movement provided a context for the 1974 publication by Toronto's socialist-feminist Women's Press of Margaret Randall's path-breaking book of interviews with Cuban women.[74] By then, however, the FPCC was dissolved and Cuban solidarity work was on an altogether new terrain.

## Conclusions and Trajectories

The 1963 assassination of President John F. Kennedy was to have a profound effect on the U.S. Fair Play for Cuba Committees. The subsequent heavy surveillance vastly contributed to the destruction of the group and to the fostering of internal divisions within Fair Play. Meanwhile, in Canada, one leading member of Fair Play in Vancouver, as he watched news unfolding of Kennedy's assassination on television, feared the imminent arrival of the RCMP at his door. He gathered up three cardboard boxes of Fair Play files he had at home and asked an unsuspecting neighbour to look after them for a week.[75] A panicked supporter of Fair Play tore up his membership card in front of witnesses and wrote to the Toronto office suggesting that the group disband itself.

But, in the end, a central difference between the Fair Play for Cuba Committees on both sides of the border was their experience of state repression. The Canadian network survived; the U.S. one did not. The Canadian FPCCs knew that they were under surveillance, but they continued even after Vietnam became the urgent priority of anti-imperialist and anti-war work. It is striking that, as the U.S. Fair Play was being destroyed, Canadian Fair Play members and supporters were continuing to visit Cuba and to produce detailed pamphlets on Cuban conditions. Jack Scott's popular pamphlet circulated in the same year as Kennedy's assassination. But there was more political space in Canada generally; the existence of the CCF, and later the NDP, was critical since CCF/NDP activists were often supportive, openly or quietly, of Cuban solidarity work. A Trotskyist group, League for Socialist Action (LSA), also founded in 1961, was very important too since many of its members and sympathizers were in the leadership of Cuban solidarity efforts. Indeed, left-wing CCF/NDP and LSA members were the backbone of Fair Play in Canada. No doubt, the fact that Fair Play in Canada was led by politically experienced leftists who already knew how to deal with repression helped them to survive surveillance and harassment.

This relatively longer history meant that interest in, and engagement with, Cuba was carried on in different ways throughout the 1960s and beyond by the NDP, left-wing English and French Canadian nationalists, and the peace and feminist movements. George Grant's *Lament for a Nation*, arguably the founding text of English Canadian nationalism and produced in the wake of the Cuban Missile Crisis, sustained a hostility to U.S. hegemony, at least to its manifestation in Canada. The influence of Cuba and Che Guevara on the left wing of the Quebec sovereignty movement and nationalist politics generally, not just the Front de Libération du Québec (FLQ), deserves further research. It suggests a relationship with its own dynamics of identification, and one that in certain ways parallels that between African Americans and Cubans.

Student interest in Cuba on more than one Canadian campus suggests another important avenue for further research into the political trajectory of those who politicized around Cuba and/or who participated in the 1964 FPCC student tour of Cuba. It also suggests the need to attend more closely to the question of the relationship between Old and New Lefts in Canada, and to examine the ways in which younger radicals were often schooled by those with Old Left histories. The role of the Canadian FPCCs in fostering student trips to Cuba is an important example. As Andrew Hunt has argued for the United States, 'the so-called "Old Left" played a more vital role in the movement than scholars have supposed, and its impact on young radicals was constantly in evidence.'[76]

The North American influence of socialist-feminist Margaret Randall, who exited the Cold War United States first via bohemianism and later through Mexico, Cuba, and Nicaragua, was very important for many women in the 1970s and after. She published widely in Canadian feminist and left printing houses, carrying on a tradition in which U.S. supporters of Cuba circulated their work through Canadian organizations. The leadership within activist communities in Canada of immigrants and political exiles from Latin America and the Caribbean also sustained attention to an anti-imperialist politics. The relative liberalization of historically racist immigration laws in the later 1960s and afterwards meant that Third World immigrants and refugees would begin to realign profoundly the boundaries of left-wing, solidarity, and feminist politics in Canada.

But, by the early 1960s, the Communist Party would challenge Fair Play by forming its own Cuba solidarity group, and the later influence of Maoism meant that cities such as Vancouver would end up with three Cuba solidarity groups, each attracting hundreds to 26 July banquets. By the mid-1960s, Vietnam overshadowed Cuba as the main priority of anti-imperialist work. Today, Cuba is no longer – for a variety of reasons – at the centre of solidarity projects within the broad spectrum of the left in Canada and has not been for many years even as active solidarity committees exist all across the country. At the same time, however, the recent resurgence of left projects within Latin America makes critical reflection on the revolutionary past, including Cuba's, more important than ever.

## NOTES

1  I have not yet been able to determine if other Canadians went on this tour. James Endicott, for example, a key founder of the Canadian Peace Congress, was in Havana in December 1960, but it is unclear whether he was there as part of the FPCC tour. It seems very likely that he would have encountered tour members while in Cuba. See also James G. Endicott, *Rebel out of China* (Toronto: University of Toronto Press, 1980), 338, 339.

2  Louis A. Perez, Jr, *Cuba: Between Reform and Revolution*, 3rd ed. (Oxford: Oxford University Press, 2006), 352.

3  Indeed, the FPCC tour was still in Cuba when news came of the ending of diplomatic relations and the imposition of a travel ban.

4  Van Gosse, *Where the Boys Are: Cuba, Cold War America and the Making of a New Left* (London: Verso, 1993), 263.

5  Van Gosse, *Rethinking the New Left: An Interpretive History* (New York: Palgrave Macmillan, 2005), 61. For more on the tour, see Gosse, *Where the Boys Are*; Mark Schleifer, 'Cuba Notebook,' *Monthly Review* (July/August 1961): 72–83.

6  Amy Kaplan. 'Left Alone with America: The Absence of Empire in the Study of American Culture,' in Amy Kaplan and Donald Pease, eds., *Cultures of United States Imperialism* (Durham, N.C.: Duke University Press, 1991), 11.

7  Gosse, *Where the Boys Are*, 8.
8  Ibid., 52.
9  Roger Burbach and Orlando Nunez, *Fire in the Americas: Forging a Revolutionary Agenda* (London: Verso, 1987), 81; Van Gosse, 'Active Engagement: The Legacy of Central American Solidarity,' *NACLA Report on the Americas*, 27, no. 5 (1995): 24.
10  Samuel Farber, *The Origins of the Cuban Revolution Reconsidered* (Chapel Hill: University of North Carolina Press, 2006), 130.
11  Robert Wright, *Three Nights in Havana: Pierre Trudeau, Fidel Castro and the Cold War World* (Toronto: HarperCollins, 2007), 41. See also Gosse, *Where the Boys Are*.
12  For discussion of this documentary, see Gosse, *Where the Boys Are*, 82–6.
13  Ibid., 82.
14  Wright, *Three Nights in Havana*, 39–41. See also John M. Kirk and Peter McKenna, *Canada-Cuba Relations: The Other Good Neighbor Policy* (Miami: University Press of Florida, 1997).
15  Wright, *Three Nights in Havana*, 45.
16  Patrick Watson, 'Remember How Fidel Castro Started,' *Globe and Mail*, 14 May 1998, A21. See also Watson's memoir, *This Hour Has Seven Decades* (Toronto: McArthur, 2004).
17  Wright, *Three Nights in Havana*, 23, 24. For an account of Castro's U.S. tours, see Gosse, *Where the Boys Are*. Fidel's celebrated tours of the U.S. northeast before and just after the Revolution enabled him to raise money and connect with political supporters. It does not appear that any organized Cuban solidarity constituency developed in this period in Canada, with the important exception of Andy McNaughton, who ran guns to the revolutionaries and became an honorary Cuban citizen. For more on McNaughton, see Wright, *Three Nights in Havana*, 31. On running guns and the Revolution, see Julia E. Sweig, *Inside the Cuban Revolution: Fidel Castro and the Urban Underground* (Cambridge, Mass.: Harvard University Press, 2002).
18  Library and Archives Canada (LAC), Ross Dowson Papers, Series 26, Howard Pawley to Vernel Olson, 10 October 1961. All subsequent archival references are to this collection; 'VO' refers to Vernel Olson.
19  Gosse, *Where the Boys Are*, 109–110.
20  Farley Mowat to VO, 13 February 1961.
21  Ian Sclanders, 'Why Castro's Cuba Is Wrong about Canada,' *Maclean's*, 28 January 1961, 44.
22  On Cuba and the FLQ, see Wright, *Three Nights in Havana*, 105–10.
23  Ibid., 65, 70. See also Don Munton and David Vogt's contribution to this volume.

24  Robert Taber, 'Castro's Cuba,' *The Nation*, 23 January 1960; Kenneth McNaught, 'Canada, Cuba, and the US,' *Saturday Night*, January 1961. McNaught's article was subsequently reprinted in the U.S.-based independent socialist magazine, *Monthly Review*, 12, no. 12 (1961): 616–23. References here to McNaught are from the *Monthly Review* reprint, 617.

25  Gosse, *Where the Boys Are*, 157.

26  McNaught, 'Canada, Cuba, and the US,' 620.

27  Ibid.

28  Gosse, *Where the Boys Are*, 141.

29  Irving Layton to VO, 9 March 1961.

30  VO to Anthony Mardiros, 12 July 1961.

31  Exceptions include scattered correspondence with a Tel Aviv-based Israel-Cuba solidarity group and a British-Cuban one.

32  'Professor Urges Neutral Canada as Aid to Cuba,' *Globe and Mail*, 20 February 1961.

33  The first Fair Play bulletin, published early in 1961, contained news of the speaking tour; for the resolution, VO to Robert Horn, 1 March 1961.

34  Pierre Trudeau visited Cuba in 1964; however, available evidence suggests that he did so on his own initiative, as he had in 1949. See Wright, *Three Nights in Havana*.

35  Gabriel Glazer to VO, 8 June 1961.

36  Madge Silcock to VO, 26 April 1961; Mrs M. Anderson to VO, 22 May 1961. Silcock would go on to keep up a correspondence on socialist issues with the Olsons.

37  Gabriel Glazer to VO, 7 May and 8 June 1961.

38  See below for more on students and Cuba.

39  VO, 28 February 1961. The story of the Canadian FPCC is closely linked both to the tangled history of Trotskyism and to early debates within Trotskyist circles about the nature of the Cuban Revolution, a very important subject that I do not have the space to detail here.

40  VO to William Irvine, 8 February 1961.

41  Michael Denning, *Culture in the Age of Three Worlds* (London: Verso, 2004), 27.

42  Carole Fink, Phillipp Gassert, and Detlef Junker, 'Introduction,' in Fink et al., *1968: The World Transformed* (Washington, D.C.: German Historical Institute, and Cambridge: Cambridge University Press, 1998), 19.

43  Wright, *Three Nights in Havana*, 37–9; on Cubans in Canada, see ibid., 96. While the Cuban community in Canada was small, Canada nonetheless was often used by right-wing Cuban exiles as a staging ground for organizing and for violence especially during the 1970s, as Wright makes clear (112–15).

44  VO to Fidel Castro [in Spanish], 6 July 1961.
45  Jaime Suchlicki, *University Students and Revolution in Cuba, 1920–1968* (Coral Gables, Fla.: University of Miami Press, 1969).
46  The summer-fall 1965 FPCC bulletin airs these grievances in detail, including from the Cuban side (21–8). Indeed, the student tour was linked to the complex story of how the FPCC tried to gain the trust of Cuban authorities and also manage the political tensions involved in the relationship, a crucial theme on which I cannot elaborate here for reasons of space.
47  Barbara Roberts, 'Women's Peace Activism in Canada,' in Linda Kealey and Joan Sangster, eds., *Beyond the Vote: Canadian Women and Politics* (Toronto: University of Toronto Press, 1989).
48  Gosse, *Rethinking the New Left*, 55.
49  For a brief discussion of the Cuban Missile Crisis and the Canadian peace movement, see Endicott, *Rebel out of China*; on the United States, see Gosse, *Where the Boys Are*, 235–40.
50  VO to Gabriel Glazer, 5 July 1961.
51  Gosse, *Where the Boys Are*, 243.
52  Excerpt from a one-page, undated report prepared by VO, which cites the Montreal statement.
53  VO letter, 19 September 1961.
54  For some of the literature on Williams, see Ruth Reitan, *The Rise and Decline of an Alliance: Cuba and African-American Leaders in the 1960s* (East Lansing: Michigan State University Press, 1999); Cynthia A. Young, *Soul Power: Culture, Radicalism, and the Making of a U.S. Third World Left* (Durham, N.C.: Duke University Press, 2007); Timothy B. Tyson, *Radio Free Dixie: Robert F. Williams and the Roots of Black Power* (Chapel Hill: University of North Carolina Press, 1999).
55  Tyson, *Radio Free Dixie*, 282.
56  Robert F. Williams, *Negroes with Guns* (Detroit: Wayne State University Press, 1998 [1962]), 63–4.
57  The most reliable published account of Williams's escape is likely that found in Tyson, *Radio Free Dixie*, 282–5. However, Tyson is under the impression that Nova Scotia is in 'French Canada' [!].
58  For one example, see William Eccles, 'Cuba's Program to Export Revolution,' *Maclean's*, 75, no. 5 (1962): 21–3, 44–6.
59  Gosse, *Where the Boys Are*, 176.
60  C. Wright Mills, *Listen, Yankee: The Revolution in Cuba* (New York: Ballantine Books, 1960); Kathryn Mills with Pamela Mills, eds., *C. Wright Mills: Letters and Autobiographical Writings* (Berkeley: University of California Press, 2000), 326.
61  Gosse, *Where the Boys Are*, 159.

62  Wright, *Three Nights in Havana*, 29–30.
63  There is an important parallel here with the *Canadian Far Eastern Newsletter*; the small group of individuals behind that publication worked very hard to build readerships 'in the United States where publications coming directly from the People's Republic were illegal and banned from the mails.' Endicott, *Rebel out of China*, 344.
64  The first two of these pamphlets are online at www.socialisthistory.ca. I intend to prepare a full inventory of FPCC pamphlets and bulletins in the course of my research.
65  George Vaughan to FPCC, 5 November 1961.
66  For more on Dorothy Day and U.S. Catholic positions on Cuba, see Gosse, *Where the Boys Are*, 237–8.
67  One of these, *Christianity and Revolution: The Lesson of Cuba* (New York: Herder and Herder, 1963), was sold through the FPCC.
68  Jack Scott, *Jack Scott Takes a Second Look at Cuba* (Toronto: Fair Play for Cuba Committee, 1963), 7 [in author's possession].
69  Ibid., 15.
70  Gosse, *Where the Boys Are*, 83.
71  Betty Friedan, *The Feminine Mystique* (New York: Dell Publishing, 1963).
72  Scott, *Jack Scott*, 19.
73  Daniel Horowitz, *Betty Friedan and the Making of the Feminine Mystique: The American Left, the Cold War and Modern Feminism* (Amherst: University of Massachusetts Press, 1998).
74  Margaret Randall, *Cuban Women Now* (Toronto: Women's Press, 1974). On Randall's importance, see Timothy Brennan, *At Home in the World: Cosmopolitanism Now* (Cambridge, Mass.: Harvard University Press), 303.
75  Personal communication to author, September 2001.
76  Andrew Hunt, 'How New Was the New Left?' in John McMillian and Paul Buhle, eds., *The New Left Revisited* (Philadelphia: Temple University Press, 2003), 144.

# 5 Cuba's Long Shadow: The Progressive Church Movement and Canadian-Latin American Relations, 1970–87

DAVID SHEININ

After 1970, the progressive church movement in Canada (PCM) exploded into local and national politics both in the intensity and in the breadth of its members' actions. On indigenous poverty, refugee law, and the problem of human rights, among a range of critical issues, the PCM saw its role as leading Canada towards a more humane and more generous foreign and domestic policy. Through church organizations, in alliance with non-religious political and community groups in Canada and Latin America, and following quickly on the emergence of an equivalent movement in the United States, church leaders spearheaded a Canadian 'discovery' of dictatorship and U.S.-influenced violence in the Americas. This chapter examines how the Cuban Revolution helped shape the PCM while conditioning how PCM members understood human rights and dictatorship and worked to change Canadian-Latin American relations.[1]

How PCM members approached the Cuban Revolution determined the evolution of church politics in Canada on Latin America in three ways. First and most important, PCM analysis of authoritarian ills in the Americas almost always excluded Cuba so as to make it irrelevant as a target for change in most discussions of human rights, dictatorship, and Canadian foreign policy. At the same time, a Cuban shadow loomed large over the PCM, identifying the movement with anti-imperialism and positioning it in often sharp opposition to what its leaders felt to be a disgracefully pro-business Canadian foreign policy, insufficiently distant from that of the United States.[2]

Secondly, the Cuban Revolution became a reference point for many on the left and centre-left throughout the Americas as they developed an increasingly radicalized national and international politics. In the

United States and Canada, the Cuba reference point was especially poignant since it was juxtaposed against often dominant Cold War cultures that excoriated a supposedly Soviet-inspired Cuban menace. In the PCM, the Cuban example did not prompt blind adherence to the Revolution. But, as in other left and centre-left circles in Canada and the United States, it served as a starting point for the shaping of domestic and foreign policy analysis in a way that, if not explicitly Marxist in synthesis, modelling, and conception, invoked Marxist analysis on praxis, imperialism, and the role of corporations in capitalist society.[3]

A third, less significant Cuba connection for the PCM was related to the first two. In the early 1980s, and in the aftermath of the overthrow of the Nicaraguan dictator Anastasio Somoza by Sandinista rebels, progressive groups in North America and Europe following human rights violations and dictatorship in Latin America shifted their attention from state terror in Chile and Argentina to intensifying repression and violence in Central America. As in the United States, and primed in part by the international outcry over of the assassination of Salvadoran Archbishop Oscar Romero by a right-wing death squad, the PCM spearheaded a vociferous denunciation of right-wing terror in the region in a manner that – as had Romero – linked human rights activism, left politics, opposition to U.S. foreign policy, and liberation theology. Likely taking a cue from the growing linkages between church progressives like the Maryknolls in the United States and the surge in North American protest over U.S. interventionism, Fidel Castro and other Cuban authorities began to relax state restrictions on religious organizations. The PCM took advantage of the change to re-establish old ties and foster new ones with church groups in Cuba, and to reinforce the argument that left-wing activism was not anathema to spirituality.[4]

### In the Beginning: The Inter-Church Committee on Human Rights in Latin America

The PCM was neither amorphous nor restricted to a particular religion or denomination.[5] By the mid-1970s, it comprised a range of groups and individuals – secular and religious – from most regions of the country. But after 1970, one group emerged as the strongest and most influential voice of the PCM on Latin America. The Inter-Church Committee on Human Rights in Latin America (ICCHRLA) began operations in January 1977 after the dissolution of its predecessor, the Inter-Church Committee on Chile (ICCC). Members of the group included the Anglican Church of Canada, the Canadian Conference of Catholic Bishops (English and French), the United Church of Canada (UCC), the Lutheran Church in America (Canada Section), the Presbyterian Church in Canada, the Religious Society of Friends, the Canadian Council of Churches, the Scarborough Foreign Mission Society, and the Latin American Working Group (LAWG). Based in Toronto, ICCHRLA maintained strong ties with the Comité Chrétien (Christian Committee on Human Rights in Latin America) in Montreal and with a number of Latin American immigrant and exile organizations in Canada. The first executive secretary of ICCHRLA was Frances Arbour, and representing the UCC – the most progressive of the churches represented on the committee – were Garth Legge (United Church Division of World Outreach) and John Foster (United Church Division of Mission in Canada).[6]

Inspired in large measure by the Vicario de la Solidaridad (Santiago, Chile) and other Latin American church bodies that tied faith to political action, ICCHRLA explained its founding as a prophetic response to human rights abuses in the Americas. Beginning in the 1950s, after the U.S.-backed toppling of the democratically elected government of Guatemala in 1954, most Latin American nations went through periods of ferocious dictatorial rule and violent, state-sponsored internal wars. Canadian church groups were slow to react. But, with the U.S. Central Intelligence Agency (CIA)-supported coup d'état against the government of Salvador Allende in Chile, Canadian church leaders sat up and took notice. They began to work together as a movement with two central objectives – the motivation of Canadians to view suffering in the Americas as their problem, and an attendant shift in Canadian foreign policy to place pressure on military governments to end human rights abuses. ICCHRLA understood the identity of its backers in Canada as Christian constituencies, and it came quickly to depend on a network of progressive Christian volunteers. At the same time, the PCM faced an ongoing budget crisis that seemed to church leaders to place their work in perpetual jeopardy.[7]

In formal correspondence, public documents, and sponsored publications, the PCM stressed the ties between its Latin America politics and spiritual interpretations of Christ's mission on earth. Privately, however, leaders of the movement showed that they were influenced less by new currents in theology since 1960 than by political change in the hemisphere dominated by U.S.-Cuban conflict. In May 1972, just over a year before the military coup d'état in Chile that brought General Augusto Pinochet to power, John Foster wrote of his experiences on a recent stay in Chile. Here, as elsewhere in the private correspondence of PCM leaders, Foster's language is more radically political than his public statements and thus reveals more of the Cuba connection to PCM politics and action than many public documents. First, his private analysis of Canadian government policy in Latin America was systemic and shaped by predominant socialist intellectual currents deriving from the Cuban Revolution and dependency theorists.[8] Foster's assessment saw little prospect of a Canadian foreign policy more 'liberal' than what he viewed as the country's retrograde domestic policies. How, he asked, could the Canadian government be expected to take a progressive approach to poverty in Latin America, with responsibility for the actions of corporate Canada abroad and the 'international division of labour,' when domestic policy on related issues was 'lousy'?[9]

ICCHRLA and the PCM more generally took theological inspiration from key liberation theologians[10] in crafting an understanding of human rights, freedom, and other problems that integrated philosophical, spiritual, and political components. That interest in liberation theology and its shaping of popular notions of the linkages between spirituality, political action, and human rights was fostered, in turn, at a grass-roots level in Canada.[11] But, in addition, PCM leaders made reference to the work of Latin American spiritual leaders who went much further in their condemnation of repression, dictatorship, and U.S. imperialism. Canadian church leaders drew directly on Pope Pius XI's *Quadragésimo anno* in condemning the 'international imperialism of money.' They cited explicitly a statement by the Conference of Latin American Bishops, meeting in Puebla, Mexico, in 1968, that rejected the United States National Security Doctrine (NSD), a Cold War era set of policies that drew on the violent French response to 1950s independence movements in Algeria. The NSD posited a new form of warfare in the Americas. There would no longer be traditional troop movements on battlefields. Conflict would be urban- and jungle-based. The 'enemy' might as easily be a child as a uniformed soldier. The PCM correctly identified NSD as a terrifying ideological basis for the dictatorial denial of human rights in Latin America and bloody United States interventions.[12]

## Cuba as Stealth Model

In emphasizing theological and political ties, for fear of alienating Canadians who might balk at what smacked of a pro-Cuba leaning, PCM leaders were circumspect about identifying their ideological and political ties to the Cuban Revolution. Frequently accused of 'Marxism,'[13] they rarely made it known publicly that their political influences were, in fact, Marxist- and Cuban Revolution-inspired. John Foster wrote privately in 1979 that his understanding of political and economic matters was shaped by *The Nation*, the *Monthly Review*, and the *New Left Review*, among other left-wing journals. Like Foster and other PCM leaders, these prominent publications on the left did not count themselves as backers of Cuban communism. But each excoriated U.S. aggression towards Cuba. Foster also cited Marxist theorists Antonio Gramsci, Louis Althusser, and Noam Chomsky as important influences on his current thinking.[14] While the views of each of these thinkers might be viewed as antithetical to the authoritarian turn of the Cuban Revolution after 1962, their popularization in North American intellectual circles in the 1960s was tied closely to pro-Cuba sensibilities in the Canadian and American lefts.

Foster's understanding of UCC efforts in the 1970s to expand its base politically beyond the church itself was pitched to the public as left-liberalism – a liberation theology-inspired move to integrate the spiritual and political realms. In church-sponsored events, in dozens of pamphlets, newsletters, and other publications, and in other ways, church progressives made no reference to Cuba when pressing Canadians to define human rights through abuses in Latin America.[15] Only rarely – as in the case of a 1986 ICCHRLA letter of concern to Nicaraguan president Daniel Ortega over the expulsion of Bishop Pablo Antonio Vega Mantilla from Nicaragua – did the church community waver in its often unstated sympathy for socialist revolutionary movements and its condemnation of right-wing terror.[16]

Privately, Foster and other PCM leaders expressed strong sympathy for the Cuban revolutionary model. Foster recognized that his public positions were further to the right than his actual beliefs. 'My life,' he wrote, 'has taken a turn for the public, active and to some extent "middle of the road."' Moreover, Foster's confidential criticisms of what he regarded as PCM political weakness invoked Marxist terminology and analysis that he would not have used in public; the PCM lacked a 'dialectic tension with an "outside-church" "outside the faith" reality.'[17] The public-private dichotomy reflected the difficulties church activists faced in appealing to a religious constituency potentially hostile to the Cuban Revolution. Citing Che Guevarra privately in a manner that would have been impossible in a public forum, Foster backed Latin American governments that favoured the nationalization of industry,

wide-ranging land-reform policies, and a state monopoly on trade. He
was impatient with the ambiguities of 'the general charitable questions
about international good will.'[18] He told Garth Legge what church
leaders would not have recognized publicly – that Canadian roles in
supporting Latin Americans would have to stress 'the hard class, ethi-
cal, strategic, material questions about the sort of society one wants to
build.'[19] With reference to socialism in Chile, Foster emphasized the
need to spread the idea that Christianity, socialism, and guerrillas were
not mutually exclusive. In UCC publications, progressive politics were
tied loosely to spiritual references and to ending poverty; Foster la-
mented the passing of a more aggressive church politics in Canada with
explicit Marxist objectives. 'It is the acceptance of a class perspective,'
he wrote, 'and a dedication to the working man, which has not been
talked of too much in the Canadian tradition since the halcyon days of
J.S. Woodsworth in Winnipeg.'[20]

Two years later, in 1974, the public-private dichotomy remained
sharp. The language of public documents was moderate, concealing
the political fervour and structural analysis that tied the PCM intel-
lectually to the Cuban Revolution. Writing now as a member of the
UCC's Department of Church in Society, John Foster, in an open letter
to supporters, explained the church's work with immigrant women in
Toronto. His tone and language were left-liberal, the very thing he had
excoriated elsewhere as too moderate. He noted the work of the PCM
in assisting Latin American immigrant women with childcare, medical services, and legal support. In a 15 November 1974 fund-raising
letter for the Latin American Working Group, he made no mention of
capitalism or the class perspective. Instead he wrote of LAWG's work
providing information to Canadians and its support for the 'struggle
for justice in Latin America.'[21] But, by contrast, a 1974 LAWG internal document reprised the more radical socialist politics that Foster
had raised earlier. Here LAWG's objectives were cast by its leaders in
starker political terms, beginning with the need for 'an insertion of an
international perspective, specifically on L.A. [Latin America], of imperialism and the inter-connectedness of the present capitalist system glo-
bally for the Canadian struggle.' The LAWG internal manifesto called
on Canadians to 'aid in the LA struggle by screwing up the works of the
Canadian front of mechanisms of exploitation (aid, trade, investment,
MNCs [multinational corporations], etc).'[22]

The progressive *United Church Observer* expressed the moderate public face of the PCM stand on why 'Christians support Marxist Chile.'

In reference to the democratic-socialist government of Chilean president Salvador Allende, here as elsewhere in public fora, the United Church backed leftist politics but downplayed precisely the systemic arguments set out in internal communications. Reasons for support of 'Marxist Chile' in the aftermath of the brutal coup d'état of General Pinochet in September 1973 included the legal election of assassinated president Salvador Allende, the latter's 'distinguished and humanitarian' qualities, and the social-justice objectives of the deposed government. The periodical also cited the cooperative relationship Allende had cultivated with the Catholic and Methodist churches in Chile. It reprinted Chilean Cardinal Raúl Henriquez's enjoinder that 'there are more Christian values in socialism than in capitalism.'[23]

If Cuba represented an ambiguous model for PCM leaders – inspirational, anti-imperial, but at the same time problematic for its authoritarian and anti-religious components – Salvador Allende's Chile was something else again. It was the 1973 coup d'état in Chile that focused PCM attention on Latin America and turned Allende's Chile into a model in retrospect for democratic, egalitarian government. Reports of the ferocity of the coup d'état, emerging evidence of CIA involvement in the military takeover, and information on massive human rights violations in Chile all shaped PCM approaches to Latin America. The ties between Canadian businesses (including Noranda, Falconbridge, and the Royal Bank of Canada) and the Chilean *golpistas* – authors of the coup d'état, or *golpe* – alarmed PCM members and underlined the tight relationship between the Canadian government and Canadian and American corporate structures in an ugly imperial project. While Chile was the country under attack, the Cuban model became still more poignant in this context as a foil to Canadian-American corporate might.

In the 1970s the PCM increasingly addressed the question of human rights and dictatorship in Latin America through the prism of corporate responsibility and the question of morality in Canadian foreign policy and business practices. In an ongoing representation of the strength of Marxist models within the movement, the PCM understood the problem of corporate responsibility as one inherent to international capitalism and framed the problem as such in its planning – though, again, not in its presentation of related issues to potential supporters in Canada. 'We live close to the heart of the capitalist system,' John Foster wrote. 'If they twitch on Wall St. and shiver on Bay St., or down the street in Calgary, they literally shake in Lima or Kinshasa.' The PCM understood Canadian-based and American-based corporate giants as the 'econom-

ic arm' of U.S. policy in Latin America, on their own and 'in bodies like
David Rockefeller's [!] Trilateral Commission.' After the Chilean coup,
Foster and others in the movement were hard-pressed to see the difference between Canada and the United States when considering the
violence of international capitalism.[24]

Not surprisingly, the PCM condemned and worked to counter Canadians who joined the Cold War chorus against Cuba, activity that
frequently melded into a criticism of Canadian policy on a range of
issues with nothing at all to with the Cuban Revolution. Progressive
Conservative Party MP Otto Jelinek was among a number of prominent Canadians who opposed changes to Canadian refugee laws in the
1970s that would have expanded opportunity to those fleeing dictatorship. In 1975 Jelinek accused an unnamed Cuban diplomat in Ottawa of
backing 'revolutionary' Chilean refugees in Toronto who were working
to topple the dictatorship in Chile.[25] The accusation underlined that
Cuba had become a political touchstone (in this case, a lightning rod)
for conservatives as well progressives. Jelinek's accusation typified the
opposition that the PCM felt it had to overcome in pressing for a new
Canadian foreign policy in the Americas more sympathetic to human
rights and more antithetical to dictatorial violence. Many Canadian
conservatives were quick to invoke Cuba to demonize a broad range
of progressive causes. Their ideological positions on Cuba often dove-
tailed with those of American conservatives. In this case, Jelinek's stand
was not only without merit, but it also skilfully and insidiously labelled
the Chilean refugee community subversive – precisely the chilling designation that, in the context of post-Allende state terror in Chile, had
prompted their escape to Canada.

Where progressive church groups worked with refugee organizations and other secular bodies, which they did with increasing frequency after 1970, those contacts underscored what church leaders already
believed – that the human rights crisis in Latin American was confined
to countries under right-wing dictatorships. Chilean, Argentine, and
other refugees from Latin America had generally not thought much
about Cuba before their arrival in Canada. But their politicization in
Canada – around issues that went far beyond the national or regional
struggles that had formed them before their exile – engendered a sympathy for the Cuban Revolution that, in turn, reinforced PCM understandings of Cuba, animosities towards right-wing dictatorships, and
determination to end Canadian economic and diplomatic ties with the
extreme right in Latin America. In 1979 the UCC Division of Mission

backed New Brunswick workers who refused to load heavy water for shipment to Argentina to service a Canadian-built CANDU nuclear reactor.[26] In 1983 the Catholic Women's League (CWL) worked with the Group for the Defence of Civil Rights in Argentina, the Emergency Committee for Argentine Political Prisoners, and the No Candu for Argentina Committee – Canadian grass-roots organizations focused on human rights abuses in Argentina – in bringing a representative of an Argentine human rights group, the Grandmothers of the Plaza de Mayo, to the annual CWL convention.[27]

## Confronting the Canadian Government and Reworking Foreign Policy

Beyond protesting the refusal of the Canadian government to acknowledge its complicity in the success of right-wing terror in the Americas, the PCM adopted a strategy for change that emphasized the need for new Canadian policies on refugee admission and corporate responsibility. In each case, the PCM made its appeal to the public and to government leaders by highlighting human rights violations. And in each case, Cuba was almost always absent from the public discourse. It simply did not exist in the Latin America or Caribbean that the PCM brought to light in Canada as violent and repressive. ICCHRLA's mandate excluded Cuba when making reference to Latin America as an arena of contention pitting 'disadvantaged masses' against local elites supported by powerful, international interests. It identified repression through reports from Christians in Argentina, Uruguay, Paraguay, and Chile – all countries with ferocious right-wing dictatorships, supported militarily and economically by the United States in a war of terror against their own civilian populations.

Through the 1970s, ICCHRLA and the PCM more generally worked for three key objectives. First, they sought to influence Canadian government policy on human rights and dictatorship with special reference to Chile, Argentina, and other nations under right-wing dictatorial rule. They lobbied for amendments to Bill C-24 on immigration to expand the definition of refugees and facilitate their arrival in Canada. They also worked in support of Bill C-404, sponsored by MP David McDonald, on human rights and foreign aid. McDonald's bill sought to end Canadian foreign aid to any country identified by the government as a human rights violator. Secondly, ICCHRLA's educational mandate committed it to disseminating information on human rights abuses and dictatorship in Latin America. Thirdly, the committee worked with refugees from right-wing dictatorships to help smooth their arrival in Canada.[28] Cuba simply never registered as a problem for members of the PCM in any of these contexts. In October 1976 a group of scholars and church leaders from Canada and Latin America came together in Toronto to analyse tripartite Canadian-U.S.-Latin American relations and to consider 'political alternatives and strategies seen as possible for the coming years.' Reflecting what PCM leaders viewed as crisis spots in the Americas, the focus was on five nations, Argentina, Chile, Brazil, Panama, and Peru.[29]

Because of the Cuban Revolution's hostility to organized religion, the church movement remained cautious in invoking the Cuban example or even citing relations with Cuban institutions. Moreover, references to Cuban church activity tended always to be positive and encouraging. In May 1986 Jane Maxwell reported to ICCHRLA on a trip that she and Anglican Archbishop Ted Scott had recently made to Cuba, and more specifically to representatives of the Episcopal Church of Cuba. To be sure, while progressive church members in Canada like Scott and Maxwell were sharp in their criticisms of U.S. and Canadian imperialism in Latin America, that criticism never extended past the links between business and politics to include church activity. Maxwell noted that the Cuban Episcopal Church had lost three-quarters of its adherents since 1959, but she nonetheless talked optimistically of the church's revival there, citing two key factors as evidence: the impact of government-church cooperation in revolutionary Nicaragua as a possible example for Cuba, and the commitment of Cuban churches to work in the context of revolutionary change. The influence of the PCM in Latin America is reflected in the access Maxwell and Scott had to high-ranking Cuban officials. In addition to several discussions with the director of religious affairs, the two had a forty-five-minute meeting with Fidel Castro, who, besides asking 'very many questions about the Anglican Church,' 'demonstrated his great intellectual capacity and an impressive knowledge of and interest in religious affairs.'[30]

In 1975 United Church minister A.C. Forrest interviewed the secretary of state for external affairs, Allan J. MacEachen, for the *United Church Observer*. In the interview, MacEachen tried to thread the needle on what he described on the one hand as a 'new left-wing policy' in External Affairs and, on the other, the constraints on policy imposed by economic uncertainties in Canada. Forrest would have none of it, pressing him on Cuba with regard to what he and other PCM members viewed with suspicion as 'the so-called new left-wing policy.' Had it changed Canadian relations with Cuba? In what practical way was the government trying to improve relations with Cuba? 'If I remember correctly,' Forrest noted wryly, 'we're buying an awful lot of sugar from South Africa and very little from Cuba.'[31] MacEachen reacted defensively to Forrest's questioning, insisting that Canada-Cuba relations were improving steadily in trade, diplomacy, and other areas.

In 1987 the UCC organ *The Refugee as Neighbour* presented an introduction to the reforms needed in Canadian refugee law. Its discussion included definitions of asylum and resettlement under international law, Old and New Testament bases for the granting of asylum, and an explanation of what the UCC considered the root causes of the international crisis now producing thousands of refugees annually. The publication was at pains to point out that there were refugees with legitimate asylum claims from both Eastern European communist nations and right-wing dictatorships in Latin America, Africa, and Asia. Citing Noam Chomsky, and without reference to Cuba, it blamed some analysts for falsely identifying popular reform and revolutionary movements in Latin American with Soviet communism. Cuba was identified only peripherally as the source of a modest 2,000 refugees in 1987.[32]

PCM opposition to U.S. foreign policy in the hemisphere drew explicitly from the Cuban example and the dangers that the Cuba-U.S. relationship highlighted for other nations in the region. As early as August 1966, UCC and Anglican youth met at Lac Joseph, Quebec, to hear reports from some of their number returning from Puerto Rico, the first trip sponsored and organized by the churches with the goal of exposing some of their young members to conditions in Latin America. At Lac Joseph, they discussed the necessary political and spiritual responses to recent developments in the Americas, including the U.S. invasion of the Dominican Republic in 1965, the coup d'état in Brazil a year before, and the Cuban Revolution and U.S.-inspired attempts at counter-revolution. 'Latin Americans,' one attendee wrote, 'found the imperial fist planted firmly in their stomach. Canadians with friends in Latin America were hardly immune to the implications.'[33] The key outcome of the Lac Joseph meeting was the formation of the Toronto-based Latin American Working Group, which dedicated itself to disseminating information in Canada about U.S. imperialism in Latin America and to undertaking projects supportive of Latin American peoples.

PCM work on refugee law came as a result of the brutality of the Chilean dictatorship that seized power in 1973.[34] The movement took its inspiration from events in Chile and Argentina in the 1970s and developed a program for refugee reform based on the nature of state oppression in those countries and, later, Central American nations. A 1980 Canadian Council of Churches 'Refugee Concerns Project' made reference to Cuban asylum seekers among a list of priorities that included Chilean and Salvadoran state-terror victims and family reunification. But Cuba was marginal to the church effort on refugees and associated criticisms of Canadian policy in Latin America.[35]

In a 1980 letter to Employment and Immigration Minister Lloyd Axworthy, Canadian Council of Churches General Secretary Donald Anderson illustrated another PCM tactic, adapting political action to immediate crises. Anderson urged that Canada admit 3,000 refugees in 1980, making reference to Haiti, Chile, Bolivia, Argentina, and El Salvador, all nations under violent right-wing repression, but not to Cuba, where there was no crisis by the terms of PCM analysis.[36] The absence of Cuba in PCM thinking on refugees from Latin America and the larger problem of Canadian refugee policy underlined the impact that the movement had had on Canadian foreign policy, where, on the question of human rights and dictatorship, Canadian policy had begun to move further from the U.S. government line on Cuba and the Cold War and closer to an association of dictatorship, military government, human rights violations, and U.S. policy in the region.[37]

During the 1970s, in the latter stages of the violent Somoza dictatorship in Nicaragua, the PCM supported the overthrow of that regime in favour of the Sandinista revolutionaries. In September 1978 a coalition of church leaders that included Michael Czerny (Jesuits), Thomas M. Anthony (director, National and World Program, Anglican Church of Canada), Dennis Murphy (Canadian Catholic Conference of Bishops), and Donald Day (general secretary, UCC) wrote to Prime Minister Pierre Trudeau calling on him to break diplomatic ties with the Somoza government as a human rights abuser, to end bilateral trade with and aid to the country, to urge the Carter administration to halt U.S. economic and military support for Somoza, and to indicate a willingness to support a provisional democratic government that would include the Sandinistas.[38]

PCM contacts in Latin America were among the most radical of church and other organizers, some of whom clearly identified themselves as Cold War enemies of the United States. In September 1978, responding to an urgent appeal from the Sandinista leader, Catholic priest, liberation-theology exponent, and future Nicaraguan foreign minister Ernesto Cardenal, Garth Legge arranged for the immediate transmission of $12,000 in support of Nicaraguan refugees in Costa Rica. More important, Legge sounded the alarm on new revelations of Somoza's state-sponsored terror in Nicaragua to the World Council of Churches in Geneva.[39] A month later, ICCHRLA sponsored a visit of Ernesto Cardenal to Canada to raise support for the Nicaraguan Revolution. In an invitation to Donald Ray, secretary of the General Council of the United Church of Canada, to a reception for Cardenal at Friends House (Canadian Friends Service Committee) in Toronto, ICCHRLA executive secretary Frances Arbour openly supported the Sandinistas' cause. Cardenal, she wrote, was in Canada to promote the hopes of the Nicaraguan people 'for overcoming the Somoza regime.'[40] One month later, drawing on positions expressed by Cardenal during his November visit, the PCM reiterated its strong commitment to the Nicaraguan Revolution and forcefully called on Canadians to support the Sandinistas and oppose the growing threat of U.S. military intervention.[41]

Progressive church politics in Latin America frequently intersected with secular projects. In early 1981, for example, church activists took part in a delegation of Canadian progressives who travelled to Nicaragua for three weeks to find ways to cooperate with the new revolutionary government.[42] Once it became clear that the U.S. government planned to destabilize Nicaragua through military and other forms of intervention, church progressives established broad-based coalitions in the progressive community to press the Canadian government to take action in support of the Sandinistas. While progressive Canadians had not expressed similar alarm over the risk to the nascent Cuban Revolution twenty years earlier, the Cuban case clearly influenced an emerging sense of crisis and urgency that progressives now applied to Nicaragua.

The newly formed group 'Non-Intervention in Nicaragua, Canadians for Self-Determination' included Meyer Brownstone (Oxfam-Canada), George Cram (Anglican Church of Canada), Michael Czerny (Jesuit Centre for Social Faith and Justice), John Foster (United Church of Canada), Murray Thomson (Project Ploughshares), Eugene Forsey, Dan Heap, and George Ignatieff. The group drew directly on a Washington *Post* report from 14 February 1982 that posited a crisis reminiscent of the origins of the Bay of Pigs invasion; now President Ronald Reagan had approved a plan that included an 'advising and supporting force made up largely of anti-Sandinista exiles in Honduras in a position to harass the Nicaraguan regime.' Indicators of U.S. aggression, according to the group, included the CIA's sending of millions of dollars into the region to train opponents of the Revolution as well as many *Somocista* exile attacks on targets in Nicaragua, leading to 'dozens of deaths.'[43]

The Cuban example helped raise the spectre of a Nicaraguan crisis triggered by U.S. terror. In 1984 the New Democratic Party executive in the riding of Spadina (Toronto) sent federal MP Dan Heap and Rob Adamson to Central America to try to foster stronger ties between Nicaragua and Canada. The pair was guided in their assessment of the Nicaraguan Revolution and the potential for improved bilateral ties by their contacts with progressive church members in Canada and in Nicaragua and by progressive church attitudes towards the conservative Catholic Church in Nicaragua. Meeting with the Canadians, Monsignor Bosco Vivas, auxiliary to the Catholic archbishop of Managua, accused the revolutionary government of repression in a manner reminiscent of earlier church attacks on the Cuban revolutionary leadership. Heap and Adamson characterized Vivas's remarks as 'half-truths, in light of conversations with other clergy and lay people and documents given to us by church based institutions ... When we asked whether the church had spoken against the killings and sabotage by the contras as it has against the conscription law and other actions of the government, he hedged.'[44] By contrast, the Canadians found that several progressive clergy and lay people they spoke with (including the U.S. bishop at the head of the Protestant Episcopal Church) more optimistic and more credible on the subject of church-government ties. Heap and Adamson called for a multifaceted Canadian response to the Nicaraguan Revolution that would include the activity of progressive church organizations.[45]

Cuba formed the backdrop to the PCM's identification of U.S. Cold War imperialism as the culprit in much of what its members wanted changed. This was particularly clear on occasions in which Canadians cooperated with their American counterparts on pro-human rights and anti-dictatorship projects in Latin America. In 1975, for example, a human rights ad hoc committee from the United States and Canada chose the Dominican Republic for a site visit in a manner explicitly designed to counter U.S. government targeting of Cuba as the hemisphere's principal rights violator. The committee consisted of public figures from both countries who had identified themselves as opponents of U.S. policy in Cuba. They included Philip Wheaton, adviser to the Latin American Working Group of the United States National Council of Churches, Edouard Morin, as representative of the Canadian Anglican, Catholic, and United churches, and Leonard Woodcock of the United Auto Workers, among others.[46]

The choice of the Dominican Republic for a site visit came ostensibly at the request of unnamed Dominican organizations. But the political significance of calling the Dominican government on the carpet for human rights abuses was clear. This was a government that had come into power as a Cold War test case, in the aftermath of the U.S. invasion of the Dominican Republic a decade earlier to prevent the purported rise of a 'Cuban style' communist regime in another Caribbean island nation. The group meant to expose U.S. policy in Latin America in support of so-called democratic, anti-communist governments for what it was – the backing of atrocious human rights violators. A visit to the U.S. embassy in Santo Domingo underscored what the group found disingenuous about U.S. policy. The embassy political officer, Leonardo Neher, insisted that charges against the Dominican government had to be understood in a 'historical context' where, by comparison to some other nations, the human rights abuses in the Dominican Republic were modest. The Canadian and American visitors rejected Neher's assertion, arguing that the relevant historical context was one defined by U.S. military invention in 1965 and 'within the economic context of the massive penetration of the Dominican economy by trans-national corporations based in the United States and Canada, particularly Gulf and Western, Falconbridge, and Rosario Mining.'[47]

PCM leadership understood the 1970s crises in the Dominican Republic, Chile, Argentina, and other Latin American countries through a Cuban lens. In 1975 LAWG described the 1965 U.S. invasion of the Dominican Republic as an attempt to prevent 'another Cuba.' The result was a nightmare for working Dominicans that cast the Cuban Revolution as a successful alternative to U.S. militarism and state terror, and the repressive, U.S.-backed government of Joaquin Balaguer as a pathetic and repressive extension of the brutal Rafael Trujillo dictatorship, with a grotesque Canadian economic presence. The PCM excoriated the government of Lester B. Pearson for having supported the U.S. invasion of the Dominican Republic ostensibly on behalf of the Dominican people. As far as PCM leaders were concerned, Canadian policy towards Latin America had been formed by that subservience to U.S. aggression in the region. The PCM also opposed Canadian corporate links to the Dominican Republic, particularly citing Falconbridge, which had taken advantage of the U.S.-imposed post-1965 political repression to establish a permanent Dominican plant in 1968. The refinery began operations in 1972, establishing Falconbridge as the largest foreign private investor in the country, second in importance to Gulf and Western in the Dominican economy. Moreover, not only had Falconbridge come under the majority ownership of Texas millionaire Howard B. Keck (giving an even murkier, U.S.-influenced multinational character to corporate Canada), but the PCM accused the company of exploiting the Dominican people.[48] A final key player in Canadian complicity in the promotion of right-wing repression was the Royal Bank of Canada and other financial institutions that underwrote oppression. At the time of the Dominican invasion, Canadian banks held almost 70 per cent of the assets of all foreign banks in the island nation.[49]

The PCM's concept of exploitation in the case of the international sugar trade both excluded and included the Cuban case. On the one hand, Cuba was a major sugar supplier to Canada – fourth after Australia, Mauritius, and South Africa in 1974. Its 98,145 tons of sugar represented more than all of the sugar imported from the remaining five major foreign suppliers. Most of the Cuban sugar consignment went to the Atlantic refinery owned by Jannock, a Toronto holding company, in Saint John. Nevertheless, because so much of Cuban sugar went to the Soviet Union and its allies, and because Cuba fell outside the norm in international marketing, purchasing, and pricing arrangements, the PCM, as in other cases, simply discounted Cuba as relevant to the problem of Canadian foreign policy, sugar consumption, and exploitation of poor foreign workers. Commodity and futures markets, the dominance by and monopolization of national and regional markets in Canada by the six refining companies, the international control of sugar prices by governments and refiners in wealthy nations, and the low price paid by Canadians for sugar all contributed to Canadian exploitation of foreign sugar workers. But, while the PCM movement specifically identified workers in South Africa and the Philippines as victims of Canadian imperialism, Cuban workers remained outside the orbit of that exploitation and a model for worker dignity in the sugar sector.[50] Indeed, the PCM celebrated the manner in which Cuba shared $2 billion in annual sugar profits among all citizens. Before the Cuban Revolution, 'the industry was so completely controlled by American interests that virtually no profit accrued to the Cubans themselves.' Castro's nationalization of the sugar industry without compensation to the American firms expropriated was deemed to be a triumph for sugar workers and the management of sugar production.

The PCM succeeded in pushing the Liberal Party, and even more so the Progressive Conservative Party, to the left on three specific foreign policy issues that church leaders had emphasized after 1970 – human rights protections, opposition to dictatorship and state terror, and refugee policy. But the caution PCM leaders showed towards the Cuban model and the public face of their movement underscored the position of the church leadership as a fulcrum between the Liberal and Conservative governments that it pushed to the left on refugee and human rights policy (though not far enough left, as far as John Foster, Frances Arbour, and other PCM leaders were concerned) and a Canadian public that sometimes frustrated church leaders for its conservatism on Cuba, refugees, and issues of development and poverty.

**Conclusion: The Gramscian Vision**

Ironically, even though PCM leaders looked to a Cuban model for social change and a reversal of capitalist ills, theirs was a Gramscian vision of their own role in promoting social and political change in Canada. As early as the late 1960s, PCM leaders believed that government policy reform would not only not be primed by a progressive Canadian public, but that Canadians would have to be pushed (perhaps even dragged) towards progressive reform by an intellectual and political vanguard – the PCM leadership itself. During the 1970s and 1980s, the PCM leadership was more progressive than congregants, whom church leaders frequently regarded as a difficulty, if not an obstacle to change. While church leaders were critical of what they regarded as Canadian apathy on human rights, dictatorship, and international corporate responsibility, they were also profoundly aware of public opinion and believed that, to shape it, they had to win hearts and minds.

The UCC Division of Mission thought it important, for example, to challenge the 'public utterances by some persons' that the churches had done nothing in support of the Vietnamese 'boat people' refugees. Not only did the church believe it important to counter a public perception of a 'don't care' attitude on the part of the religious community, but it blamed congregant ignorance and apathy for the conundrum. The UCC's answer to its public-relations dilemma was to educate its constituency. Among other actions, it circulated a letter from a community group in Windsor, Ontario, showing how individuals and groups might undertake refugee sponsorship. If congregants were apathetic and giving the churches a black eye for their alleged disinterest in refugee sponsorship, PCM leaders would change their attitudes.[51]

In 1975 United Church minister (and future church moderator) Lois Wilson – a pastor at the time in Hamilton, Ontario – broached with her congregation the idea of the local church sponsoring a block of subsidized apartments for refugees from Latin America and elsewhere. On pitching the idea, she recalls, she was met with the blank stares of a community of good people who simply could not grasp the notion of non-profit apartments for refugees to Canada. She also remembers a second incident when, as church moderator in 1980, she made a visit to a United Church mission in India. To her dismay, she found that church members there were trying to 'convert' Indians to Protestant Christianity.[52] Here and on dozens of other occasions, the PCM felt it had to educate Canadians. 'Public attitudes, our attitude, help create an atmosphere for or against human rights. Our attitudes create laws, through our votes, and laws safeguard justice (or suppress it).'[53] And, in the end, the Gramscian model produced significant and rapid change that included new, more generous refugee laws after 1977, the 1980s disappearance of the Cuban lightning rod for conservative cold warriors in Canada, a foreign policy generally sympathetic to the Nicaraguan Revolution, and a dramatic realignment of Progressive Conservative Party policy on human rights, most evident in the leadership of Prime Minister Brian Mulroney's government within the Commonwealth in isolating South Africa during the 1980s.

NOTES

1  'Remi De Roo Prepares to Retire with Bright Hope for the Continuing Legacy of Vatican II,' *Catholic New Times*, 14 February 1999, 3; Murray Polner, *Disarmed and Dangerous: The Radical Lives of Daniel and Philip Berrigan* (Boulder, Colo.: Westview Press, 1998); Brian J.R. Stevenson, *Canada, Latin America, and the New Internationalism: A Foreign Policy Analysis, 1968–1990* (Montreal and Kingston: McGill-Queen's University Press, 2000).
2  Morris H. Morley, *Imperial State and Revolution: The United States and Cuba, 1952–1986* (Cambridge: Cambridge University Press, 1987); Robert W. Wright, *Three Nights in Havana: Pierre Trudeau, Fidel Castro and the Cold War World* (Toronto: HarperCollins, 2007).
3  Jonah Raskin, *For the Hell of It: The Life and Times of Abbie Hoffman* (Berkeley: University of California Press, 1996), 21, 88; Van Gosse, *Where the Boys Are: Cuba, Cold War America and the Making of a New Left* (New York: Verso, 1993).
4  Timothy Shortell, 'Radicalization of Religious Discourse in El Salvador: The Case of Oscar A. Romero,' *Sociology of Religion*, 62, no. 1 (2001): 87–103;

Maryknoll Missioners' Conference, *The Modern Mission* Apostolate (Maryknoll, N.Y.: Maryknoll Publications, 1965); James Hodge, *Disturbing the Peace: The Story of Father Roy Bourgeois and the Movement to Close the School of the Americas* (New York: Orbis, 2004); Fidel Castro, *Fidel y la religion: conversaciones con Frei Betto* (Havana: Oficina de Publicaciones del Consejo de Estado, 1985).

5 In fact, the movement included a number of outspoken rabbis and synagogue congregations, including, most prominently, Gunther Plaut and Toronto's Holy Blossom Temple.

6 Christopher Lind and Joseph Mihevc, *Coalitions for Justice: The Story of Canada's Interchurch Coalitions* (Ottawa: Novalis, 1994).

7 Frances Arbour, Bill Fairbairn, Gloria Shepherd, Gabrielle Iribarne, and Ana Ortega to ICCHRLA, 3 May 1985, 91.169C, United Church of Canada Archives (UCCA), Toronto; Frances Arbour, 'Canada: The Inter-Church Committee on Human Rights in Latin America,' in Virginia Fabella and Sergio Torres, eds., *Doing Theology in a Changing World* (Maryknoll: Orbis Books, 1984), 45–50.

8 Magnus Blomstrom and Bjorn Hettne, *Development Theory in Transition: The Dependency Debate and Beyond* (London: Zed Books, 1984).

9 Foster to Graham Legge, 7 May 1972, 83.054C, UCCA.

10 See, for example, Gustavo Gutiérrez, *Gustavo Gutiérrez: textos esenciales, acordarse de los pobres* (Lima: Fondo Editorial del Congreso del Perú, 2004); Leonardo Boff, *Qué es hacer teología desde América Latina* (Lima: MIEC-JECI, Secretariado Latinoamericano, 1977).

11 Betty Marlin, Alberta Conference, UCC, to Louise Rebonczy, senior programme officer, Human Resources Programme, International Development Research Centre, 31 January 1979; Clinton Mooney, Coldstream Pastoral Charge, UCC, Truro, N.S., to Clarke MacDonald, deputy secretary, Division of Mission, UCC, 23 March 1979, 83.055c, UCCA.

12 Joseph Comblin, *A idelogia a Seguranca Nacional*, 3rd ed.(Sao Paulo: Civilizacao Brasileira, 1980); Salvador María Lozada, *Las fuerzas armadas en la política hispanoamericana* (Buenos Aires: Columbia, 1967); Salvador María Lozada, *La ideología de la Seguridad Nacional: el aporte del Padre Joseph Comblin* (Buenos Aires: Editorial Derechos Humanos, 1982), 3–13; Jorge Novak, *Esa difícil página del evangelio* (Quilmes: Comisión diocesana, 1983).

13 Legge to Brenda Moyes, 2 April 1980, 82.002c, UCCA.

14 Foster to Mooney, 28 February 1979; Foster, 'New Dimensions in Corporate Responsibility,' 19 July 1978, 83.055c, UCCA.

15 'Ottawa Is Urged to Push for Central American Peace,' Toronto *Star*, 12 April 1986; Joe Clark, secretary of state for external affairs, to Bishop Adol-

phe Proulx, chair, ICCHRLA, 30 April 1986; Taskforce on the Churches and
Corporate Responsibility, 'Canadian Economic Relations with Countries
That Violate Human Rights,' A Brief to the Sub-Committee on Latin
America and the Caribbean of the Standing Committee on External Affairs
and National Defence, June 1982, 91.162c, UCCA.
16  ICCHRLA to Ortega, 9 July 1986, 91.169c, UCCA.
17  Foster to Greg Chisolm, 1979; Bob Lindsey to members of the Working
Unit on Social Issues and Justice, Division of Mission, UCC, 6 July 1979,
83.055c, UCCA.
18  Ibid.
19  Ibid.
20  Foster to Legge, 7 May 1972, 83.054C, UCCA.
21  Foster to 'whom it may concern,' 11 October 1974; Foster to David Heath,
15 November 1974, 83.054c, UCCA.
22  'A LAWG, LAWG Way to Go: Programming for Sept./74 to June/75,' 1974,
83.054c, UCCA.
23  'Why Christians Support Marxist Chile,' *United Church Observer*, November 1973, 35.
24  Foster, 'New Dimensions in Corporate Responsibility,' 18 July 1978; Bob
Carty, 'Corporate Investments and Political Economy,' February 1979;
Tony Clarke, Peter Hasel, and Paul Hansen, 'Taskforce on the Church and
Corporate Responsibility: A Working Paper,' May 1979, 83.055c, UCCA.
25  'Cuba Aids Chilean Subversives,' Toronto *Star*, 13 November 1975.
26  Foster to MacDonald, 1 June 1979, 83.055c, UCCA.
27  'Argentina Entering a New Phase,' *Canada/Argentina Bulletin*, December-
January 1983, 2; 'Welcome,' C.W.L. National Convention (1983); 'Why 1%,'
Catholic Women's League of Canada; 'Argentine Women Mount a Search
for Grandchildren,' *Globe and Mail*, 14 August 1983; 'To Let the Oppressed
Go Free,' Canadian Catholic Organization for Development and Peace
(1983); 'Letter to Canadian Catholics Calls for Action,' *Global Village Voice*
(Toronto: Canadian Catholic Organization for Peace and Development
(January-March 1980): 4; Emergency Committee for Argentine Political
Prisoners and Refugees, *Sponsorship of Argentine Political Prisoners: Why and
How*, n.d.
28  ICCHRLA, 'Newsletter,' May 1977; George Cram, chair, ICCHRLA, to
Donald Ray, secretary of the General Council of the United Church of
Canada, 8 September 1977, 85.035c, UCCA.
29  Herbert Souza, Bob Carty, John Foster, and Ray O'Toole to 'Perspectives
for Development – Latin America/Canada' participants, 9 December 1976,
85.035c, UCCA.

30  Minutes, ICCHRLA meeting, 21 May 1986, 91.169c, UCCA.
31  'Interview of the Secretary of State for External Affairs, the Honourable Allan J. MacEachen, with Rev. A.C. Forrest of the *United Church Observer*, November 18, 1975,' 85.035C, UCCA.
32  Editorial, *The Refugee as Neighbour* (April 1987): 1; 'Reflections upon Root Causes,' *The Refugee as Neighbour* (April 1987): 3.
33  'Snapshots: LAWG's First Decade,' *Quarterly Report, Latin American Working Group* (summer 1986): 1.
34  Tim Ryan, 'In Search of Accountability in Canada's Human Rights Policy: An NGO Perspective,' in Irving Brecher, ed., *Human Rights Development and Foreign Policy* (Halifax: Institute for Research on Public Policy, 1989), 422–4; Ninette Kelly and Michael Trebilcock, *The Making of a Mosaic: A History of Canadian Immigration Policy* (Toronto: University of Toronto Press, 1998), 365–9.
35  Canadian Council of Churches, 'Refugee Concerns Project,' 1980, 91.110C, UCCA.
36  Anderson to Axworthy, 24 September 1980; Brief Follow-up Working Group to Refugee Concerns Project Committee, Canadian Council of Churches, 25 June 1980; Minutes of Meeting, Canadian Council of Churches and Lloyd Axworthy, 9 May 1980; Cranford Pratt, 'A Report on the Annual Conference on Canadian Foreign Policy and Human Rights Organized by the Canadian Human Rights Foundation,' 1985, 91.110c, UCCA; *The Displaced of El Salvador: Six Years of War* (Toronto: Canadian Jesuit Refugee Program, 1986).
37  Andrew Brewin, Louis Duclos, and David MacDonald, 'One Gigantic Prison: Report of the Fact-Finding Mission to Chile, Argentina, and Uruguay,' November 1976, ICCHRLA; Betsy Anderson, 'Canada Joins the Big Leagues in Bankrolling Chile's Junta,' *Last Post* (Toronto: Canadian Council of Churches), November 1978.
38  Czerny, Anthony, Ray, and Murphy, 'Message to Prime Minister Trudeau,' 19 September 1978, 85.035c, UCCA.
39  Legge to World Council of Churches, 21 September 1978; Legge to Cardenal, 21 September 1978; Legge, 'Background Information on Nicaragua,' 12 September 1978, 85.035c, UCCA.
40  Arbour to Ray, 31 October 1978, 85.035c, UCCA; ICCHRLA, 'Newsletter,' November 1978.
41  ICCHRLA, 'Nicaragua Conflict Escalates: Churches Call for Action' (press release), 24 November 1978; John Foster, director, ICCHRLA, to Donald Jamieson, secretary of state for external affairs, 22 November 1978; 'Report and Recommendations of an Ecumenical Delegation to Nicaragua' (Wal-

lace Collett, chair, Board of the American Friends Service Committee; Alan McCoy, president of the Conference of Major Superiors of Man in the U.S.A. [Roman Catholic Church]; Dwain C. Epps, National Council of Churches of Christ in the U.S.A.; Michael Czerny, ICCHRLA), 8 November 1978, 85.035c, UCCA.

42  'The Women of Nicaragua,' *Leftwords*, 3, no. 2 (1981): 8–9.

43  Non-Intervention in Nicaragua, Canadians for Self-Determination, 'Urgent Public Appeal,' n.d.; Brownstone to 'Friends,' 6 January 1982; Brownstone to Allan J. MacEachen, 17 December 1982; 'Nicaragua: An Inside Look,' Windsor *Star*, 21 April 1983; 'The Cross and the Collective,' *Globe and Mail*, 3 June 1980; 'The Contra Obsession,' *Globe and Mail*, 5 November 1986.

44  Dan Heap and Rob Adamson, 'Report on Visit to Nicaragua and Costa Rica,' 1984; 'Nicaragua's Two Catholic Churches Tearing Nation Apart,' *Globe and Mail*, 14 February 1987; Foster to Executive Staff Committee, 18 January 1979, 83.055c, UCCA.

45  'Spadina NDP Proposal,' January 1984; Peter Downs, 'Religious Dilemma in Nicaragua,' *Humanist in Canada* (summer 1984): 11–12.

46  'Human Rights Ad-Hoc Committee from the United States and Canada,' 1975, 85.035c, UCCA.

47  'Un comité de organizaciones de Estados Unidos y Canadá dice RD prevalence repression,' *Ultima Hora* (Santo Domingo), 11 September 1975; 'Organismos EU dicen hay repression en RD,' *El Nacional de Ahora* (Santo Domingo), 11 September 1975; 'Dirigentes EUA piden respeto libertades RD,' *La Noticia* (Santo Domingo), 11 September 1975; 'Exposición presentada por el sindicato de trabajadores Falconbridge Dominicana, CXA, a la conmisión ad hoc de los Estados Unidos y Canadá por los derechos humanos,' 11 September 1975, 85.035c, UCCA.

48  'The Canadian Connection,' *LAWG Newsletter*, April-May 1975, 4–7; John Deverell and the Latin American Working Group, *Falconbridge: Portrait of a Canadian Mining Multinational* (Toronto: James Lorimer, 1975).

49  'The D.R. – Another Cuba?' *LAWG Newsletter*, April-May 1975, 20–1.

50  ICCHRLA, 'Sugar – Who Pays the Price?' 1975, UCCA.

51  Clarke MacDonald, deputy secretary, Office of Church in Society, UCC Division of Mission, to 'Friends,' 31 January 1979; UCC Division of Mission, 'Refugees – Boat People,' January 1979, 83.055c, UCCA.

52  Interview with Lois Wilson, 20 October 2002.

53  Clarke MacDonald, deputy secretary, Office of Church in Society, UCC Division of Mission, to 'Friends,' 31 January 1979; UCC Division of Mission, 'Refugees – Boat People,' January 1979, 83.055c, UCCA.

# 6 *Viva el pueblo cubano*: Pierre Trudeau's Distant Cuba, 1968–78

GREG DONAGHY AND MARY HALLORAN

Following his election as prime minister in the spring of 1968, Pierre Trudeau set out to challenge the narrow orientation of Canada's foreign policy, which had traditionally emphasized close relations with Western Europe and the United States. Within a few short years, his government had recognized Communist China and sought novel economic links with the European Community and Japan. Latin America, too, was a Trudeau priority, and in January 1976 he became the first prime minister in fifteen years to visit the region, capping his tour with a high-profile meeting with Cuban dictator Fidel Castro. The dramatic encounter between these two charismatic men captured world attention and immediately became a defining moment in Trudeau's career. On his death, some twenty-four years later, admirers and critics alike continued to cite the visit as one of the main highlights of the Canadian's premiership.[1]

Trudeau's Havana sojourn has exerted a similar fascination on scholarly treatments of Canada-Cuba relations in the 1970s. In their influential monograph, *Pirouette: Pierre Trudeau and Canadian Foreign Policy*, Jack Granatstein and Robert Bothwell, for instance, focus on the visit, dismissing it and Canadian policy in Cuba as an ill-considered 'misadventure.'[2] Others are more sympathetic, though they, too, assign more weight to the visit than it merits. Political scientists John Kirk and Peter McKenna depict the voyage as the triumphant apex in a lengthy policy struggle between an engaged, liberating prime minister and his 'conservative' advisers, whose policies were marked by 'consistent deference to Washington.'[3] Author Robert Wright's recent study, *Three Nights in Havana*, echoes this view, using the trip as a prism through which to explore Canada's Cold War role, the development of Canada-Cuba relations, and the intense personal relationship uniting Castro and Trudeau.[4]

The perspective here is different. Cuba was rarely a top-of-mind issue for Canada's fifteenth prime minister, or even one in which he showed much sustained interest. Indeed, despite his admiration for Castro, which surged after his visit to the small Caribbean island, Trudeau tended to follow the advice of his diplomatic advisers on matters related to Cuba. While welcoming the prime minister's desire to develop more active relations with Latin America, these advisers carefully located their Cuban policy within a broad multilateral framework where Latin American, not American, considerations dominated. Against a backdrop of a looming Cuban-American rapprochement and the quickening pace of Canada-Cuba relations, Trudeau's visit was a calculated effort to maintain this balanced approach, an effort that became increasingly unmanageable following Cuba's intervention in Africa in 1975.

Trudeau gave early notice of his intentions with regard to Latin America. 'Canada and the World,' his principal foreign policy statement of the general election campaign of 1968, announced his government's plan to send a special ministerial mission to Latin America before the end of that year 'to demonstrate the importance the Government attaches to strengthening our bilateral relations with leading Latin American countries.'[5] Following the Liberals' overwhelming victory at the polls, the month-long mission set out as planned in late October, under the leadership of Mitchell Sharp and Jean-Luc Pepin, ministers respectively of external affairs and trade and commerce. With an entourage that included officials from ten government agencies as well as journalists and an itinerary of nine countries, it was the largest mission that Canada had yet sent abroad. Though the tour could claim few concrete accomplishments, it produced a surge of goodwill between Canada and the host countries, and signalled the government's determination to follow through on its declared interest in the region.[6]

A preliminary report on the ministerial mission served as the starting point for the government's subsequent review of Latin American policy. Soon after the report was tabled in the House of Commons on 24 January 1969, an interdepartmental task force was convened, chaired by James Langley, the assistant under-secretary for western hemisphere affairs, and coordinated by Paul Bridle, head of the Latin American Division in the Department of External Affairs. Its deliberations continued for much of the year. By the time their work was almost complete, task force members were able to draw on the experience of their colleagues who had developed the government's policies on Western Europe and NATO, and had learned the hard way the importance of couching their recommendations in terms pleasing to the prime minister. This the authors of the Latin American paper did, carefully incorporating in their report the cabinet's new foreign policy priorities.[7]

The Latin American policy review was one of the six component parts of *Foreign Policy for Canadians*, the Trudeau government's much anticipated policy statement tabled in the House of Commons in June 1970 and distributed widely in the form of glossy, pocket-sized booklets. It stressed the ways in which expanding ties with Latin America could advance the foreign policy objectives of the government, including the enhancement of quality of life in both Canada and Latin America and the promotion of social justice and economic growth. The most important question it addressed was possible membership in the Organization of American States (OAS), an option it weighed but rejected for the immediate future. Instead, the authors proposed that Canada 'should draw closer to individual Latin American countries and to selected inter-American institutions' through a 'systematic strengthening of links' in the realm of trade, culture, science, and development assistance.[8]

The quest for stronger Latin American ties was given further impetus by the 'Third Option,' the name given to the strategy adopted in the wake of the Nixon administration's sudden imposition of a 10 per cent surcharge on imports in August 1971. In addition to dealing with the immediate impact of the crisis, Trudeau set in train a reassessment of Canada's relations with the United States, the one major lacuna in *Foreign Policy for Canadians*. The result was the proposal put forth by the Department of External Affairs, and accepted by the cabinet in November 1971, 'to pursue a comprehensive, long-term strategy to develop and strengthen the Canadian economy ... and in the process to reduce the present Canadian vulnerability.' It invoked the notion, by no means original, that 'Canada's interests are best served by policies that seek to diversify those interests on a global basis as a means of avoiding excessive reliance on the United States.'[9] In practical terms, this meant forging new and stronger ties with trading partners beyond North America. The markets of Western Europe and Japan beckoned, but so too did those of Latin America. In all this, there was no specific mention of Cuba, except for a solitary note in *Foreign Policy for Canadians* indicating that it was indeed one of the three Caribbean countries, along with the Dominican Republic and Haiti, which was included within the definition of 'Latin America.'[10]

Nevertheless, even as policy makers worked to articulate this broad new framework for Canada's foreign policy, it was clear that relations with Cuba were going to intensify under Trudeau. Calling on the prime minister in December 1968, the new Cuban ambassador, Jose Fernandez de Cossio, picked up on Trudeau's interest in Latin America and urged him to extend trade credits to the Caribbean island. Regarded in the Department of External Affairs as 'the most astute and hardest working head of post in Ottawa,' de Cossio made it clear to Trudeau and Sharp that providing credits, as Western Europe already did, would result in increased exports of Canadian fertilizer, agricultural goods, and steel.[11] Trudeau was intrigued, and asked both Sharp and Pepin for their views. Meanwhile, he heeded the advice offered by his foreign service advisers and refrained from mentioning trade credits during his March 1969 visit with U.S. President Richard Nixon.[12]

Trudeau's interest in trade with Cuba was welcomed in the departments of external affairs and industry, trade and commerce, where senior officials were already aware of the prime minister's views on expanded ties with Latin America. Like the prime minister, they, too, recognized that there was 'considerable scope for [the] expansion of trade with Cuba if we are prepared to cooperate with regard to export credit.'[13] Indeed, there were already prospects for a $10-million sale of Holstein cattle, provided credits were forthcoming. The small size of this sale and the obvious need to match the terms of Canada's more aggressive European competitors convinced officials in May 1969 that now was an opportune moment to adjust Canadian policy and offer Havana some form of credit for the first time since the Revolution.

Officials cautioned that there were grounds for moving carefully. The United States and its OAS allies had repeatedly opposed steps reducing the effectiveness of the economic embargo against Cuba and were expected to view Ottawa's new policy as an unfortunate precedent. To forestall criticism, Sharp recommended that the government offer Havana only export-credit insurance rather than more generous government-to-government credits. More important, the provision of credit insurance was to be linked explicitly with progress towards settling Cuba's outstanding commercial debts, especially the $1.3 million owed to the Canadian International Paper Company.[14] This restrained and self-interested program for improved bilateral trade was approved by Trudeau in the spring of 1969.[15]

The American reaction to the tentative Canadian initiative was reassuring. State Department officials noted it 'with interest' and did not

Prime Minister W.L. Mackenzie King (third from left) at Havana Pier in 1938. Canada's longest-serving prime minister, King arrived in Havana on the steamship *Rotterdam* and stayed for three days. He was accompanied by the founder of Canada's foreign service, Dr O.D. Skelton (left), and greeted by the most prominent Canadian in the city, J.K. Stewart, supervisor of the Royal Bank of Canada. (Library and Archives Canada/C-71085)

First Canadian embassy in Havana, 17 Avenida de las Misiones (top two floors), Old Havana, 1951. (Courtesy of Kenneth and Ruth Brown)

Journalist René Lévesque interviewing Fidel Castro in Montreal. Lévesque, the famous Quebec radio and television journalist, interviewed Castro on his first visit to Canada in 1959. Lévesque went on to found the Parti Québécois and was premier of Quebec from 1976 to 1983. (Paul-Henri Talbot/*La Presse*)

Fidel Castro at a meeting of the United Nations General Assembly, 22 September 1960. (Warren K. Leffler/Library of Congress; Courtesy of Canadian Press)

Thousands of Cuban people along the streets in Havana greet Prime Minister Pierre Elliott Trudeau as he drives through the city on 26 January 1976. Along with him in an open car are *Comandante* Fidel Castro and the president of Cuba, Osvaldo Dorticós Torrado. (CP PHOTO/Fred Chartrand)

Fidel Castro with Foreign Minister Lloyd Axworthy, in the Canadian Official
Residence. As part of the Canadian government's engagement policy with
Cuba in the 1990s, Axworthy visited Cuba in January 1997. (Estudios Revolu-
ción, Consejo de Estado de la República de Cuba)

Justin, Margaret, and Alexandre (Sacha) Trudeau, Deborah Coyne, Romeo Leblanc, and Cuban president Fidel Castro (clockwise from left) watch as Cardinal Jean-Claude Turcotte blesses the casket during the state funeral for former prime minister Pierre Trudeau, Tuesday, 3 October 2000, in Montreal. (CP PHOTO/Paul Chiasson)

A woman walks past graffiti depicting revolutionary hero Ernesto 'Che' Guevara in Havana, Wednesday, 8 October 2008. (AP Photo/Javier Galeano)

voice 'any regret at this new development.'[16] Havana's response was also encouraging. Canada's commercial debts were soon settled and plans made to address the remaining claims of Canadians for compensation for property nationalized during the early 1960s.[17] Building on these developments, Industry, Trade and Commerce appointed a trade-promotion officer to Havana in July 1970, carefully hiding his economic function by designating him a second secretary.[18] Stimulated by the increasingly normal character of the economic relationship, bilateral trade flourished. Canadian exports grew from $40.74 million in 1968 to $56.07 million in 1971 and $145 million in 1974. Exports from Cuba grew steadily as well, from $5.11 million in 1968 to $10.36 million in 1971 and $76.76 million in 1974, leaving Canada with a comfortable and persistent trade surplus. Significantly, while these figures underlined the growth in bilateral trade and Canada's emergence as Cuba's second most important non-communist trading partner, they were not out of line with the growing pace of Canadian trade elsewhere in Latin America. Combined exports to Canada's three largest Latin American partners – Brazil, Argentina, and Venezuela – similarly grew from $198.87 million in 1968 to $261.36 million in 1971 and $667.25 million in 1974. Maintaining this kind of appropriate balance in relations with Cuba was the central characteristic of the Trudeau government's approach to Havana.[19]

The trade relationship was given a vital political dimension in the fall of 1970, when Havana agreed to provide a safe haven for Front de Libération du Québec (FLQ) terrorists involved in the kidnapping of British Trade Commissioner James Cross. Canadian policy makers, including the prime minister, were grateful for Castro's help, especially his undertaking not to allow his new guests to use Cuba as a platform for anti-Canadian activities, a promise scrupulously observed.[20] Encouraged by the quickening pace of bilateral ties, Canada's new ambassador to Cuba, Ken Brown, urged Ottawa, which was shaping its first aid program for Latin America, to include Cuba as an eligible country. In Brown's view, Canadian aid would serve three key foreign policy objectives. It would reinforce a political relationship that had already proved its worth in dealing with the FLQ. Aid would also be helpful in encouraging Cuba to refrain from exporting its revolutionary ideology, representing a small step towards the 'normalization of relations in the hemisphere.'[21] Finally, aid would help encourage exports, the principal reason why France, Israel, and Sweden were all involved in aid projects in Cuba.

Brown dismissed fears of U.S. opposition, citing Washington's attitude towards the provision of credit and the recent 'low-key American approach to Cuba.' Marcel Cadieux, now ambassador in Washington, was not so cavalier. A tough-minded and fervent anti-communist, he thought there was a profound difference between aid, where most of the benefits went to Cuba, and credit, where the benefits flowed both ways. An initiative that made Canada the first Western country to offer Cuba regular aid and possibly the largest donor after the Soviet Union would be 'particularly ill-received' in Washington and elsewhere in Latin America.[22]

Cadieux's analysis was greeted sceptically in the Department of External Affairs. Ed Ritchie, the under-secretary, had served as ambassador in Washington from 1966 to 1970 and doubted that the United States would object to small amounts of aid.[23] This view was largely shared by the director general responsible for policy in the western hemisphere. But, while Klaus Goldschlag, whom diplomat and diarist Allan Gotlieb later characterized as 'the best foreign policy mind in the department,'[24] readily acknowledged the strong arguments in favour of Canadian aid, he found no compelling reason why Cuba should be among the first group of Latin American countries to receive official Canadian aid on a government-to-government basis. Instead, Goldschlag proposed to defer the aid decision, while Canada further developed its broader links with Latin America and defined its relationship with both the OAS and the Inter-American Development Bank (IADB).[25] Canadian aid to Cuba, like Canada's trade relations, would be firmly rooted in a balanced, hemispheric policy, an approach cabinet approved in July 1971.[26]

Growing trade and the prospect of aid generated pressure for faster progress. Brown complained loudly about the slow pace of developments, fretting that relations with Cuba were 'bogged down' and 'had not improved in the past year because of a lack of initiative, caused by a "Washington Syndrome."'[27] Goldschlag dismissed such complaints. He insisted that Cuban policy had to be considered in the context of Canada's increasing engagement in Latin America rather than as a function of Canada-U.S. relations. 'In that perspective,' he concluded, 'there was no reason to think that Canadian-Cuban relations were seriously out of focus.'[28]

Maintaining that balanced focus soon grew more difficult. Following the appointment of a permanent observer to the OAS and agreement to join the IADB, cabinet agreed in May 1972 to send aid to Cuba on project-by-project basis. The decision was greeted with particular warmth in the Canadian International Development Agency (CIDA).

Flush with cash, the agency and its young, idealistic staff, who tended to regard Castro's improvements in health and education as a model for the developing world, were anxious to help. By mid-summer, CIDA had all but abandoned the restrained ad hoc approach outlined in the May memorandum to cabinet, assuring Cuban officials that it had set aside $1 million per year for the next three years for their projects.[29] Officials in External Affairs tried to rein in their colleagues across the Ottawa River, time and again emphasizing 'the need for caution in developing our aid to Cuba to ensure that it remained in balance with that of other Latin American and Caribbean countries and with the development of our relations with Cuba generally.'[30]

CIDA and its imperious president, Paul Gérin-Lajoie, were unpersuaded. Indeed, by August 1973, Gérin-Lajoie was speculating about an annual allocation of $2–3 million and a program rivalling Canadian efforts in Columbia, Brazil, and Peru.[31] External Affairs was aghast. Pierre Charpentier, the new head of the Latin American Division, worried that CIDA's ambitious plans would irritate the United States, upset the balance of Official Development Assistance (ODA) expenditures in Latin America, and alarm a large segment of the Canadian public. 'Total aid,' the under-secretary reminded Gérin-Lajoie that fall, 'should not be out of proportion to our interest in Cuba or Latin America.'[32] To forestall CIDA's campaign for more aid for Cuba, Ritchie suggested that any new ODA take the form of low-interest loans. Gérin-Lajoie, slated to visit Havana early in 1974, was non-committal, prompting another reminder from the under-secretary. Repeating a well-worn refrain, Ritchie insisted that 'we should not ... encourage the Cubans to believe that we are willing to proceed with aid projects more rapidly than is in fact the case' and should 'do nothing to encourage Cuban expectations until the current review of Canada's aid programme is concluded and we can see clearly where we are headed in the region as a whole.'[33]

As CIDA and External Affairs sparred over the appropriate shape of Canada's aid program, Havana erupted in a flurry of activity, signalling its interest in still closer relations. In early January 1974, Castro himself freed Ronald Lippert, a Canadian serving a thirty-year sentence for smuggling munitions into Cuba for the Central Intelligence Agency, resolving a consular case that had become a persistent bilateral sore. The Cuban leader also accorded the new Canadian ambassador, Malcolm ('Mac') Bow, a rare interview when he presented his credentials and later dropped into a reception for a visiting delegation of Canadian Members of Parliament. Nervous External Affairs officials warned their minister that relations 'seem to be entering a new and accelerated phase.'[34]

Indeed. Gérin-Lajoie's visit to Cuba in February 1974 blew Cuban expectations sky high. Not only did he deliver an annual aid program of $3–4 million in grants and $6–7 million in soft loans over three years, he invited the Cubans to ask for more. And they did. By July 1974, CIDA was pushing for an aid package totalling $23.5 million over the next four years. Gérin-Lajoie's mission, the escalating aid allocations, and the prospect of a return ministerial visit worried Ritchie, who tartly observed that this was 'surely rushing things.'[35] An invitation for Trudeau to visit Castro soon followed, providing the under-secretary with a welcome opportunity to strike an interdepartmental task force to get a handle on relations with Cuba.[36]

Guided by D'Iberville Fortier, the acting assistant deputy minister for Latin America, the ad hoc interdepartmental committee on Cuba reported to cabinet in the fall of 1974. It re-emphasized the importance of placing Canada-Cuba relations firmly in a balanced hemispheric context and reminded ministers (and CIDA) that relations with the United States, Mexico, Brazil, and Venezuela were all 'more important than those with Cuba.' Consequently, initiatives towards Cuba must be 'continually measured' against those directed at these other countries and care taken not to disturb relations with them.

However, as the memorandum pointed out, these countries were all moving towards improved relations with Cuba, and possibly none more quickly than the United States. Rumours that U.S. Secretary of State Henry Kissinger had a secret task force at work on Cuba, combined with Kissinger's successful pursuit of detente with the USSR and China, generated fears in Ottawa that a U.S-Cuba rapprochement might quickly follow congressional elections in November 1974. A series of recent high-profile visits by U.S. senators to Havana and the conclusion in February 1973 of a U.S.-Cuba agreement on hijacking reinforced these fears. Indeed, the implications for Canada of a renewed U.S.-Cuba relationship had been made very clear a year earlier, when Havana abruptly suspended its two-year-old talks with Ottawa on a hijacking agreement in order to pursue its negotiations with Washington. Only an appeal by Sharp to the Cuban foreign minister avoided the embarrassment of seeing Washington sign its agreement with Castro before Canada. Anxious to reinforce Canada's standing in Havana before a possible U.S.-Cuba rapprochement, the committee urged ministers to intensify the government's efforts to strengthen relations with Havana and recommended a program of visits for 1975 by senior ministers, possibly including one by the prime minister.[37]

The Department of External Affairs received its first indication that the prime minister was interested in travelling to Latin America in March 1975 when the Venezuelan ambassador, during an introductory meeting, invited Trudeau to visit. Intrigued by the possibility of a visit to both Venezuela and Mexico, which had invited him earlier in 1974, Trudeau asked the department for recommendations.[38] In the department's view, the quickening pace of relations between Canada and Venezuela clearly made a trip there worthwhile. A southern visit in early 1976 would also make it possible for the prime minister to go to Mexico, whose earlier invitation and older ties with Canada made it a priority. The department suggested that it might be appropriate to round out the trip with a voyage to Cuba. A visit by Trudeau would be an appropriate sequel to the Cuban mission scheduled in March 1975 by two senior ministers, Marc Lalonde and Alistair Gillespie. Despite hesitations from the domestic side of the Prime Minister's Office, which thought the prime minister had been travelling too much, Trudeau agreed in mid-June to visit Mexico, Cuba, and Venezuela in January 1976.[39]

Preparations for the visit proceeded quickly and smoothly. Only the Cuban leg of the trip provoked any real concern. Initially, Canadian officials worried mainly about the visit's potential to embarrass the government and warned the RCMP Security Service to be ready to respond if Cuban intelligence operations in Montreal became public or a prominent Cuban tried to defect.[40] As the date for the visit approached, however, the Department of External Affairs grew increasingly preoccupied with the problems generated by Castro's decision in November 1975 to send Cuban troops to Angola in support of left-wing elements in the widening war for control of the newly independent state. Allan MacEachen, Sharp's successor as secretary of state for external affairs, handled the file gingerly and avoided staking out a Canadian position until he had heard from his NATO allies. Although Kissinger tried to cast the Angolan civil war as part of the East-West conflict at NATO's December ministerial meeting, MacEachen eventually sided with the British foreign secretary, who insisted that this was a problem for Africans to resolve. Echoing his British colleague, MacEachen agreed that all foreign forces should be withdrawn and a government of national unity encouraged.[41]

Too committed to the prime minister's Cuban visit to cancel it without gravely offending Havana, but clearly worried that Castro's African adventure might cast a pall over the trip, the government searched over the holidays for an initiative which might encourage an end to foreign intervention. Meanwhile, it was guarded in its public statements on the situation. By early January, however, the minister was faced with growing pressures to adopt a more explicit stand. American officials, who had welcomed Trudeau's visit to Cuba when briefed about it in July, warned that Angola had altered the equation and that Washington would follow the visit closely.[42] Jim Hyndman, who succeeded Bow as Canada's ambassador to Cuba, was also growing concerned and pressed for clear statement of policy that might take some of the sting out of the issue before Trudeau encountered Castro.[43] As a result, the department urged MacEachen to issue a 'strong statement' that called for a cease-fire, condemned foreign intervention, and encouraged the parties to the civil war to seek a negotiated settlement.[44] MacEachen issued the statement on 20 January 1976.

The minister's belated statement failed to deter opposition critics from attacking the prime minister's decision to continue with the visit to Cuba for the support it seemed to lend Castro's regime as it intervened in Africa. As a result, the visit to Cuba overshadowed the two other destinations and reduced them to bookends for the expedition to Havana. That was perhaps not entirely surprising given the trip's failure to generate much in the way of concrete achievements. Efforts to negotiate a new Canada-Mexico air agreement had bogged down in the fall of 1975 and left only a cultural agreement with Mexico (as well as a minor sports agreement with Cuba and Mexico) for Trudeau to sign during his travels.

In Mexico, which set the pattern and tone for the entire trip, the prime minister was greeted warmly at the airport as a head of state by President Luís Echeverría and enjoyed almost five hours of talks with the Mexican leader and his cabinet. The Mexicans made appreciative noises about Canadian transportation and nuclear technologies, though the prime minister's sales pitch was ultimately in vain. If Trudeau was a little annoyed by the anti-Americanism he encountered in Mexico City and the lack of time available for him to make his points, External Affairs was well satisfied with the visit, which it judged a 'significant success in focussing attention of the Mexican government and public on Canada.'[45]

The results of the visit to Venezuela, with whose foreign minister MacEachen was co-chairing an international conference on North-South cooperation, were more promising. Trudeau and Venezuelan President

Carlos Andrés Pérez got on well and agreed to consult informally on 'matters of mutual concern.' Pushed by Pérez, who was anxious to off-set American influence in Latin America with a stronger Canada presence, Trudeau agreed to re-examine the institutional basis of Canada's relations with Latin America, especially the Sistema Económico Latinoamericano y del Caribe (SELA). In return, the Venezuelans proved surprisingly willing to help address Canada's billion-dollar bilateral trade deficit and promised to begin early negotiations on an 'umbrella agreement on economic cooperation.'[46]

There were fewer economic gains in the visit to Cuba, although D'Iberville Fortier later thought that it reinforced Canada's standing as Cuba's third most important supplier, after the USSR and Japan. The political dividends were more significant. On his arrival on 26 January, Trudeau and his delegation were greeted at the airport by Castro and his senior ministers, and saluted by large crowds of 'carefully stage-managed' Cubans during the cavalcade to Havana. After a round of fruitless trade talks the next morning and a series of visits to local development projects, Castro, Trudeau, and a reduced entourage then boarded a helicopter for a day's diving and fishing on the small island of Cayo Largo.[47]

In this beautiful but spartan setting – dinner was served on a 'long trestle table with benches' – the two leaders enjoyed several hours of uninterrupted conversation. The presence of the prime minister's wife, Margaret, and their infant son, Michel, who joined the fishing expedition over the furious protests of the prime minister's foreign policy adviser, Ivan Head, reinforced the informality of the gathering, where the two men quickly developed a close, personal rapport.[48] In private, Trudeau found the Cuban dictator to be 'quiet-spoken' and 'very thoughtful.'[49] For his part, Castro was drawn by the Canadian's 'personality and intellect, by his philosophical bent ... and by his curiosity and interest in Cuban realities and problems.'[50] This did not, however, produce a meeting of minds, and the two leaders spent much of their time together debating Cuba's Angolan intervention in talks that Trudeau later described as 'brutal and frank.'[51]

The visit ended the following day with a 'mass rally' in Cienfuegos. Clearly moved by his encounter with Castro, Trudeau warmed to the crowd of 25,000, concluding his speech with an enthusiastic chorus of *vivas*: *Viva Cuba y el pueblo cubano! Viva el Primer Ministro Fidel Castro! Viva la amistad cubano-canadiense!* While the phrases were reportedly the work of a dutiful foreign service officer, the warmth of the cheer added to the controversy in Canada.[52] Nonetheless, Trudeau returned home genuinely pleased with the trip, which he thought broke new ground in developing closer relations with all three countries.[53] In view of the differences between Ottawa and Havana over Cuba's role in Angola, however, the personal triumph that the visit represented for Trudeau complicated matters for Canadian policy makers. Unhappy about the prospect of Canadian aid being funnelled through Havana to anti-Western forces in Angola, MacEachen wondered soon after the visit about suspending aid to Cuba. His senior advisers were not encouraging. Having acknowledged the importance of the aid program in a routine Castro-Trudeau press communiqué, they warned in February 1976 that it would be 'very difficult' and 'impolitic' to bring the program 'to an abrupt halt in the months to come.'[54] Even so, it was clear by the early spring that the tensions created by Castro's intervention in Angola, soon to be compounded by new revelations about Cuban espionage activities in Montreal, had begun to eat away at bilateral relations.

This might even have seemed obvious to Castro, who paid an extraordinary visit to Ambassador Hyndman's residence in May to deliver a stuffed fish for Trudeau, cigars for Margaret, and a stout defence of his African policies.[55] Trudeau was unimpressed. His reply congratulated the Cuban leader on some recent troop withdrawals from Angola but insisted that 'the resolution of the basic political problems of that country, and the achievement of permanent stability, will be hastened by the removal of all elements of foreign involvement.'[56] However unhelpful, at least this was dialogue, a point Hyndman often underlined, urging Ottawa to exploit the rapport between the two leaders and Canada's status as the only Western country (other than neutral Sweden) sending economic aid to Cuba. Increased contacts, more high-level visits, and continued aid would consolidate Canada's position, serving 'not only our direct commercial and political interests, but also our wider interest in moderating Soviet influence in Cuba' and encouraging Cuba's 'reintegration within the Latin American community and normalisation with the USA.'[57]

Hyndman's pious hopes were not warmly received in Ottawa, where 'incontrovertible evidence' of a Cuban spy ring was discovered in early January 1977. The Cuban group included the consul general and vice-consul in Montreal, the third secretary at the embassy in Ottawa, a postgraduate student in Montreal, and a representative of a Cuban firm. They had engaged an American to supply information about the National Front for the Liberation of Angola and the National Union for the Total Independence of Angola and had trained him in intelligence and counter-surveillance techniques. Two of the diplomats were to leave the country as soon as possible, while the third, who was out of the country, would not be allowed to return. The non-diplomats were deported. The government made public the facts of the case on 10 January, once it was clear that the story was about to break in the media.[58]

Meanwhile, behind the scenes, the Department of External Affairs vented its displeasure in a series of testy exchanges with officials in Havana and with the Cuban ambassador in Ottawa. Although Ottawa hoped to minimize the incident's impact on bilateral relations, both Foreign Minister Isidoro Malmierca and Vice-Foreign Minister Pelegrin Torras were surprised by Canada's tough line. After all, they argued, Canada was not the target.[59] Ottawa showed little sympathy for such complaints, since 'it was the Cuban hand which was in the cookie jar.'[60] A few weeks later, Cuba replied with a sharply worded protest of its own. It charged Ottawa with mishandling the matter and claimed that the RCMP had tried to recruit a Cuban involved in the Montreal incident. Moreover, Havana accused Canadian citizens in Cuba of spying and threatened their arrest if the Montreal case was not settled satisfactorily.

While Hyndman convinced Deputy Prime Minister Carlos Rafael Rodríguez to withdraw the offensive Cuban note and the threat to Canadians in Cuba, the affair reminded the government that its policies towards that country left it open to criticism. Indeed, soon after the story broke, the Conservative opposition seized on the incident and called for an immediate end of aid for Cuba. 'Whatever good CIDA's agricultural projects are doing in Cuba,' declared their critic, Douglas Roche, 'it is not possible to support them when Cuba finds the resources to send troops to Angola and also to train guerrillas for war against Rhodesia's white minority.' Furthermore, Cuban activity on Canadian soil 'raises further questions about CIDA being duped.'[61]

Increasingly embarrassed by its Cuban connection, Trudeau's government slowly retreated. In December 1977 the new secretary of state for external affairs, Don Jamieson, tactfully dodged an invitation to visit Havana, fearful of the domestic fallout.[62] Ottawa tightened visa procedures too, overriding objections from External Affairs, which hoped to save the goodwill it believed necessary 'if we are to preserve an important share of the Cuban market.'[63] Worse was to come. In early 1978 Cuban intelligence tried to recruit a Canadian tour guide and then jailed a Canadian engineer for sabotage. There was now no chance that Jamieson would visit Cuba.[64]

It was in light of these problems and of continuing media interest in Canada-Cuba relations that the Latin American Division, in March 1978, prepared a discussion paper on the subject. Although the state of the Cuban economy meant that there was little scope for growth in trade between the two countries, the paper noted that Cuba remained an important market, and one worth protecting against the competition that would ensue should U.S.-Cuba relations improve. Politically, maintaining the link with Cuba was seen as helping to lessen its dependence on the Soviet bloc, while Cuba's leadership role in the Third World served Canada's interests in the North-South dialogue. Moreover, strong relations with Cuba helped differentiate Canadian policy from that of the United States. But there were costs. The conviction by Cuban courts of a Canadian citizen on flimsy charges and Cuban intelligence activities on Canadian soil had gone forward despite the good relations boasted of by both countries, while Cuba's role in Africa continued to attract public criticism. Because relations with Cuba 'run the risk of being construed both domestically and internationally as implying tacit acceptance of Cuban initiatives abroad,' the paper argued for a more cautious approach to the relationship.[65]

As the Department of External Affairs continued to review policy towards Cuba, it sought opinions from the British Foreign Office and the U.S. State Department 'on the value of the present Canadian relationship with Cuba for the Western community as a whole.' The British were supportive, drawing parallels with their own policy towards Cuba and stressing the value of showing Cuba 'that the West was not a monolithic whole' and that 'some doors remained open.'[66] The Americans, who opened a quasi-diplomatic U.S. Interests Section in Havana in 1977, were less encouraging. Admittedly, Canada produced some useful intelligence on trade, aid, and human rights, and was a trusted spokesman for the Western point of view. Overall, however, the Washington embassy concluded, 'Canada's links with Cuba are perceived by the USA to be of limited and perhaps diminishing value to the Western allies.'[67]

As the department continued to re-evaluate its policy towards Cuba, Havana made a surprising gesture: most of the Cuban nationals on Canada's list for family reunification were to be allowed to leave. But this signal of Cuba's continuing desire for strong political and economic ties with Canada was too little, too late.[68] In External Affairs, a consensus was emerging that Cuba's military involvement in Africa was making the future of Canadian aid to that country untenable. As Allan Gotlieb, the under-secretary, put it to the minister, Cuba's Angolan adventures had 'placed political constraints on our aid relationship. [The Cuban government] should therefore understand why there can be no early implementation of the future aid projects to which they attach importance.'[69] Gotlieb recommended that Canada's relations with Cuba 'should be readjusted to correspond more to the sort of ties that Canada would be expected to have with a country of such different interests and policies.' In addition to the suspension of aid, the department recommended that no new lines of credit should be granted, though individual credits should be available on a case-by-case basis.[70]

Jamieson made the case for the termination of CIDA programs in Cuba at cabinet meetings in June and July. Most of his colleagues needed no convincing, but the prime minister opposed the suggestion that the decision be linked to Cuba's continuing intervention in Angola. After all, Trudeau pointed out, he had received only twenty letters on the subject in the recent past, indicating that it was becoming an old subject. Jamieson countered that the prime minister's mail was not a true measure of popular opinion, which had come to view Cuba as an impediment to peace in Africa and Canada as soft on Cuba. His colleagues agreed, forcing Trudeau to give way. Cabinet endorsed a handful of other measures recommended by the department, including the cancellation of a proposed baseball game between the Montreal Expos and a team from Cuba, and a moratorium on ministerial visits. Visitors from Cuba in future were to require visas, but, at the prime minister's instruction, Jamieson and his counterpart at Employment and Immigration, Bud Cullen, drew up a list of other countries to which that regulation would apply so as not to single out Cuba. Significantly, there was general agreement that there should be no disruption in trade with Cuba, and to that end the Export Development Corporation should continue to extend to it lines of credit.[71]

The Cuban response to the Canadian measures was muted. When Hyndman's successor, Gary Harmon, announced the end of Canadian aid, it clearly came as no surprise to the Cuban vice-prime minister. Though the Cubans were quietly 'puzzled even troubled' by the state of their relations with Canada, there was no interest in Ottawa in patching things up. Gotlieb suggested that minor working-level visits might be considered as a means of reassuring Havana. But there was no doubt that the government's decision in the summer of 1978 brought to a close a chapter in the Trudeau government's relations with the Castro regime. From that point on, its dealing with Cuba would be 'more in line with relations with other communist countries.'[72]

In summary, despite the unique personal bond that joined Castro and Trudeau, Canada's relations with Cuba were never very special. Initially inspired by Trudeau's desire to expand Canada's links beyond the familiar North Atlantic to embrace Latin America, Canada's rapprochement with Cuba was carefully managed from the start by the prime minister's diplomatic advisers in the Department of External Affairs. Rather than hindering his initiative, they welcomed it, rooting the policy in a broad hemispheric approach that reflected a judicious grasp of Canada's interests elsewhere in Latin America. This balanced and moderate approach was simultaneously restrained and inspired by U.S. preoccupations in the Caribbean, but never determined by them. It was also typical of Canada's historical role in the region. Indeed, this chapter reinforces the broader view in the literature that, since 1945, Canada's interest in Latin America and the Caribbean, and in particular Cuba, has been episodic and transitory. As a former deputy undersecretary, Klaus Goldschlag, once quipped, 'in the Caribbean, we have interests but no foreign policy. In Africa, we have a foreign policy, but no interests.'[73]

## NOTES

1  See, for example, 'Castro Arrives to Offer His Respects,' Toronto *Star*, 3 October 2000, A1, and John Harbron, 'The Cuban Connection,' *Globe and Mail*, 4 October 2000, A21. For a more critical perspective, see Jamie Glaznov, 'Trudeau and his Communist Friends,' 16 October 2000, http://www.enterstageright.com/archive/articles/1000trudeau.htm. Of course, the Cuban trip echoed in the popular memory long before Trudeau's death. See Peter Desbarats, 'Trudeau's Visit to Cuba Was So Memorable,' Ottawa *Citizen*, 23 April 1998, A7. Two years later, an Angus Reid poll ranking Trudeau as the most important prime minister of the twentieth century cited the visit as one of his major successes. See Anne McIlroy, 'Canada United in Voting Trudeau "PM of Century,"' *Globe and Mail*, 3 January 2000, A4.
2  Robert Bothwell and J.L. Granatstein, *Pirouette: Pierre Trudeau and Canadian Foreign Policy* (Toronto: University of Toronto Press, 1990), 273–5.
3  John M. Kirkand and Peter McKenna, *Canada-Cuba Relations: The Other Good Neighbor Policy* (Gainesville: University Press of Florida, 1997), 88, 96–7.

4  Robert Wright, *Three Nights in Havana: Pierre Trudeau, Fidel Castro and the Cold War World* (Toronto: HarperCollins, 2007).

5  Department of External Affairs (DEA), *Statements and Speeches*, 68/17, 'Canada and the World,' 29 May 1968.

6  DEA, Annual Report 1968. The visit to Mexico led to the establishment of a joint Mexico-Canada committee for bilateral consultation on political, economic, and commercial questions, the first such tie Canada forged with a Latin American country.

7  'Meeting of the Latin American Task Force,' 18 February 1968, RG 25, vol. 8813, file 20-1-2-LATAM-1, Library and Archives Canada (LAC); Geoffrey Murray, 'The Foreign Policy Review Process, 1967–1972,' Department of Foreign Affairs and International Trade, Historical Section, chapter 4, 29–32.

8  Secretary of State for External Affairs, *Foreign Policy for Canadians: Latin America* (Ottawa: Information Canada, 1970), 8–18, 20–4.

9  Mitchell Sharp, 'Canada-US Relations: Options for the Future,' *International Perspectives* (autumn 1972): 13, 17, 22.

10  *Foreign Policy for Canadians: Latin America*, 4.

11  Paul Bridle, head, Latin American Division, to file, 31 December 1968; J.C. Langley, Memorandum for Bridle, 30 January 1969; Bridle to Langely, 12 February 1969, RG 25, vol. 8636, file 20-1-2-Cuba, LAC.

12  Bridle, Briefing Note for the Prime Minister, 14 March 1969, RG 25, vol. 8636, file 20-1-2-2-Cuba, LAC. Kirk and McKenna cite Trudeau's remarks during his Washington visit about Canada's willingness to trade with Cuba to hint at a difference between Trudeau and the Department of External Affairs over Cuba and his willingness to press it for a more forward-looking Cuban policy. See *Canada-Cuba Relations*, 96–8. Trudeau, however, went no further than to reflect established Canadian policy, equating trade with Cuba and trade with Communist China. See Pierre Trudeau, Transcript of Press Conference, National Press Club, 25 March 1968.

13  Mitchell Sharp, Memorandum for the Prime Minister, 16 April 1969, RG 25, vol. 8636, file 20-1-2-Cuba, LAC.

14  William Brett to T.M. Burns, assistant deputy minister of industry, trade and commerce (IT&C), 24 April 1969, and Marcel Cadieux to Jake Warren, deputy minister, IT&C, 24 April 1969, RG 25, vol. 8636, file 20-1-2-Cuba, LAC.

15  Ottawa to Havana, tel XL-341, 29 May 1969, RG 25, vol. 8636, file 20-1-2-Cuba, LAC.

16  Cadieux to Warren, 30 May 1969, RG 25, vol. 8636, file 20-1-2-Cuba, LAC.

17  A.E. Ritchie, Draft Memorandum for the Minister [20 February 1970], RG 25, vol. 8636, file 20-1-2-Cuba, LAC.

18  On this subterfuge, see Ottawa to Havana, tel APO-979, 14 March 1972, RG 25, vol. 8637, file 20-1-2-Cuba, LAC.

19  Figures drawn from Statistics Canada, *Canada Year Book 1973* (Ottawa: Information Canada, 1973), 761, and Statistics Canada, *Canada Year Book 1975* (Ottawa: Statistics Canada, 1975), 731–2.

20  Trudeau to Castro, 14 December 1970, RG 25, vol. 8636, file 20-1-2-Cuba, LAC; see also Kirk and McKenna, *Canada-Cuba Relations*, 102–5.

21  Havana to Ottawa, tel 375, 11 March 1974, RG 25, vol. 8638, file 20-1-2-Cuba, LAC.

22  Washington to Ottawa, tel 30, 5 January 1971, RG 25, vol. 8636, file 20-1-2-Cuba, LAC.

23  Ritchie's marginalia on ibid.

24  Alan Gotlieb, *The Washington Diaries* (Toronto: McClelland and Stewart, 2006), 6.

25  Goldschlag to Ritchie, 4 March 1971, RG 25, vol. 8636, file 20-1-2-Cuba, LAC.

26  Cabinet Conclusions, 13 July 1971. Goldschlag's recommendation, which cabinet also approved, included the suggestion that government funds might be directed to third parties – like the Canadian University Services Overseas (CUSO) – already working on Cuban development projects.

27  Memorandum for File, Ref. 22/600-CUB, 15 November 1971, RG 25, vol. 8636, file 20-1-2-Cuba, LAC.

28  Dilys Buckley-Jones to file, 15 November 1971, RG 25, vol. 8636, file 20-1-2-Cuba, LAC. Kirk and McKenna use a different and less reliable account of this meeting to reach the opposite conclusion – that Canada policy was subject to the 'Washington Syndrome.' See *Canada-Cuba Relations*, 98. Their source is Memorandum for File, Ref. 22/600-CUB, 15 November 1971, RG 25, vol. 8636, file 20-1-2-Cuba, LAC.

29  J.F. Godsell to Paul Gérin-Lajoie, 2 August 1972, and Goldschlag to L.A.H. Smith, director, Aid and Development Division, Export Development Corporation (EDC), 19 October 1972, RG 25, vol. 11922, file 38-1-7-Cuba, LAC.

30  D.R. Hill to Goldschlag, 16 February 1973, RG 25, vol. 11922, file 38-1-7-Cuba, LAC.

31  Pierre Charpentier, head, Latin American Division, to Ritchie, 15 August 1973, RG 25, vol. 11922, file 38-1-7-Cuba, LAC.

32  Ritchie to Gérin-Lajoie, 19 September 1973, RG 25, vol. 11922, file 38-1-7-Cuba, LAC.

33  Ritchie to Gérin-Lajoie, 28 November 1973, cited in EDC to Ritchie, 4 March 1974, RG 25, vol. 11922, file 38-1-7-Cuba, LAC.

34  Havana to Ottawa, tel 26, 9 January 1974, and Charpentier to Press Office

and attached Notes for the Minister, 25 January 1974, RG 25, vol. 8638, file 20-1-2-Cuba, LAC.

35 Ritchie's marginalia on Havana to Ottawa, tel 215, 12 February 1974, RG 25, vol. 8638, file 20-1-2-Cuba, LAC.

36 Charpentier's marginal notes on ibid. and Fortier to Latin American Division, RG 25, vol. 8638, file 20-1-2-Cuba, LAC.

37 Michael Dupuy, Memorandum for the Secretary of State for External Affairs (and the ministers of IT&C, Finance, Agriculture, and Transport), 1 October 1974, RG 25, vol. 8638, file 20-1-2-Cuba, LAC.

38 Charpentier to J.-P. Carrier, 23 January 1975, RG 25, vol. 8801, file 20-1-2-Venz, LAC.

39 Fortier for H.B. Robinson, under-secretary of state for external affairs, 21 May 1975, and Ivan Head to MacEachen, 11 June 1975, RG 25, vol. 9293, file 20-Cda-9-Trudeau, LAC.

40 Confidential Source. See also PSP [Malcolm Bow] to Charpentier, 12 January 1976, RG 25, vol. 9243, file 20-Cda-9-Trudeau-Latam, LAC.

41 Robinson, Memorandum for the Minister, 19 December 1975, RG 25, vol. 8613, file 20-1-2-Angola, LAC.

42 Glen Shortliffe, head, USA division, to Charpentier, 8 January 1976, RG 25, vol. 9243, file 20-Cda-9-Trudeau-Latam, LAC.

43 Havana to Ottawa, tel 34, 8 January 1976, RG 25, vol. 9243, file 20-Cda-9-Trudeau-Latam, LAC.

44 Robinson, Memorandum for the Minister, 8 January 1976, RG 25, vol. 11089, file 21-3-Angola, LAC.

45 Ibid.

46 Ibid.

47 Havana to Ottawa, tel 280, 4 February 1976, vol. 9243, file 20-Cda-9-Trudeau-Latam, LAC. For an excellent and detailed account of the visit, see Wright, *Three Nights in Havana*, 161–213.

48 Margaret Trudeau, *Beyond Reason* (New York: Paddington Press, 1979), 201.

49 Pierre Trudeau, *Memoirs* (Toronto: McClelland and Stewart, 1993), 212.

50 Havana to Ottawa, tel 331, 11 February 1976, vol. 9243, file 20-Cda-9-Trudeau-Latam, LAC.

51 Canada, House of Commons, *Debates*, 3 February 1976, 10571.

52 Richard Gwyn, *Northern Magus: Pierre Trudeau and Canadians* (Toronto: McClelland and Stewart, 1980), 303.

53 Latin American Division, 'Report on the Prime Minister's Visit to Mexico, Cuba and Venezuela,' March 1976, RG 25, vol. 9243, file 20-Cda-9-Trudeau-Latam, LAC.

54  Fortier to Robinson, 5 February 1976, RG 25, vol. 11922, file 38-1-7-Cuba, LAC.
55  Confidential Source.
56  Head to Robinson, 15 September 1976, and enclosure, Trudeau to Castro, 10 August 1976, RG 25, vol. 11431, file 20-CUBA-1-3.
57  Havana to Ottawa, tel 2807, 6 December 1976, Havana to Ottawa, tel 0002, 4 January 1977, RG 25, vol. 11431, file 20-Cuba-1-3.
58  Ottawa to Havana, tel GWP-2, 9 January 1977, RG 25, vol. 11127, file 20-22-3-CUBA; *Canadian Annual Review of Politics and Public Affairs*, John Saywell, ed. (Toronto: University of Toronto Press) (hereafter *CAR*), 1977, 267.
59  Havana to Ottawa, tel 0057, 10 January; tel 0085, 12 January; and tel 0088, 12 January 1977; Ottawa to Havana, tel GWP-05, 11 January 1977, RG 25, vol. 11127, file 20-22-3-CUBA.
60  Ottawa to Havana, tel GWP-05, 11 January 1977, RG 25, vol. 11127, file 20-22-3-Cuba.
61  Quoted in *CAR*, 1977, 267.
62  T.A. Williams, director, Latin American Division, to Gary Harmon, ambassador in Havana, 28 December 1977, RG 25, vol. 8638, file 20-1-2-CUBA.
63  Williams to Goldschlag, deputy, USSEA (under-secretary of state for external affairs), 9 January 1978, RG 25, vol. 8638, file 20-1-2-CUBA.
64  Jamieson to Malmierca, 20 January 1978; Malmierca to Jamieson, 8 February 1978; and Goldschlag to Michael Pitfield, clerk of the Privy Council, 23 January; Gotlieb, Memorandum for the Minister, 21 March; Ottawa to Havana, tel GSL-292, 6 April 1978, RG 25, vol. 8638, file 20-1-2-CUBA.
65  Latin American Division, 'Discussion Paper – Canada-Cuba Relations,' 9 March 1978, RG 25, vol. 8638, file 20-1-2-CUBA.
66  London to Ottawa, tel 0681, 20 April 1978, RG 25, vol. 8638, file 20-1-2-CUBA.
67  Washington to Ottawa, tel 1888, 18 May 1978, RG 25, vol. 8638, file 20-1-2-CUBA.
68  Havana to Ottawa, tel 1133, 12 May 1978, RG 25, vol. 8638, file 20-1-2-CUBA.
69  Gotlieb, Memorandum for the Minister, 17 May 1978, RG 25, vol. 8638, file 20-1-2-CUBA.
70  Gotlieb, Memorandum for the Minister, 28 June 1978, RG 25, vol. 8638, file 20-1-2-CUBA.
71  Confidential sources.
72  Gotlieb, Memoranda for the Minister, 6 November and 29 November 1978, RG 25, vol. 8638, file 20-1-2-CUBA.
73  Cited in Allan Gotlieb, *The Washington Diaries, 1981–1989* (Toronto: McClelland and Stewart, 2006), 179.

# 7 Canadian-Cuban Relations: Muddling through the 'Special Period'

PETER McKENNA AND JOHN M. KIRK

Relations between Canada and revolutionary Cuba have been intriguing, complicated, and, at times, unusually fluid. Successive governments in Ottawa have varied in their approaches to the island state, with some choosing a more engaged approach and others a considerably more restrained policy stance. Relations arguably peaked under the worldly and watchful eye of former prime minister Pierre Trudeau, and reached a low point during Brian Mulroney's tenure from 1984 to 1993.[1] The more recent Liberal majorities led by Jean Chrétien saw relations between the two countries fluctuate between the highs of important political visits (by the prime minister himself, then Foreign Affairs Minister Lloyd Axworthy, and when Fidel Castro attended Trudeau's funeral in the fall of 2000) to the lows in later years of shrill remarks by both sides about 'enemy territory' and 'northern ice.'[2] With the passing of the Chrétien torch in late 2003 to long-time Liberal Party rival Paul Martin, the Canadian-Cuban dynamic effectively returned to the autopilot-like days, at least from a policy-making standpoint, of Prime Minister Lester Pearson.[3]

As the succession process in post-Castro Cuba continues to unfold, and arguably firms up around the leadership of Raúl Castro, Canada's response to date can best be characterized as a 'wait-and-see' posture. This spectator-like approach to revolutionary Cuba is perfectly consistent with official Ottawa's natural predilection for muddling through when it comes to Canadian-Cuban relations. Particularly since the beginning of Cuba's 'Special Period in Peacetime' in the early 1990s, Canada's relationship with Cuba has been marked by irregular periods of moving forwards and backwards, in fits and starts, and turning at times hot and cold. And from the late 1990s onward, and right up to the present-day minority Conservative government of Stephen Harper, the bilateral tango between Canada and Cuba has been placed in a semi-permanent deep freeze – or worse, suspended political animation.

Little is likely to change in Cuba for the foreseeable future, where stability and normality are the common denominator during the interim leadership of Raúl Castro. (However, with the Obama administration expressing an interest in reaching out to Cuba and moving to close down the Guantánamo detention centre, changes in U.S.-Cuba relations may well be in the air.) Still, as Cuba's Special Period continues (even as Cuba's economy shows signs of significant positive growth, posting the best GDP growth for all of Latin America and the Caribbean in 2006), the Canada-Cuba relationship is unlikely to change in any fundamental way in the short term.[4] While Stephen Harper obviously brings a different set of values and a distinctly conservative ideological prism to Ottawa, it has only periodically filtered into Canada's relations with Havana. Rather, the continuation of a 'stay-the-course' Cuba policy – with some minor wrinkles here and there – appears to be the order of the day. Of course, this apparent pause or drift in the Canada-Cuba diplomatic policy game should not be misconstrued as any significant rupture or downturn in official relations. But this bilateral paralysis, if you will, even in the post-Fidel Castro period, could change if Prime Minister Harper is re-elected with a majority-government mandate.

In an interesting sort of way, the two countries actually need each other – though for obviously different reasons. From the beginning of the Special Period, Canada has used its burgeoning relationship with Cuba to differentiate itself from its superpower neighbour, as well as to seek out hemispheric 'counterweights' to the United States and to reaffirm a 'Made in Canada' foreign policy posture. Pointing to continued relations with Cuba, and thus effectively poking the U.S. hyperpower in the eye, has also been smart electoral politics in Canada. The Cubans, on the other hand, have traditionally sought to secure increased economic/developmental assistance from Ottawa, growth in Canadian foreign investment, and a patina of international credibility and legitimacy from interacting diplomatically with Canada. Havana also recognizes that showcasing cordial relations with Ottawa highlights the extent to which Washington is out of step with one of its close continental allies. So no matter how wonderful, or even how poor, relations between the two countries can get, they both realize that it would be counter-productive to sever what has always been a beneficial relationship for both partners.

The first aim of this chapter is to identify how this apparent symbiosis has manifested itself in the general conduct of bilateral relations since the Special Period of the early 1990s. Secondly, it strives to reveal what the driving forces or explanatory determinants of the overall bilateral relationship have been (and continue to be). Thirdly, it addresses briefly the state of Canadian-Cuban relations under the conservative and right-leaning government of Stephen Harper. Finally, the chapter concludes with some basic observations about the nature and extent of Canadian-Cuban relations during the Special Period – and what policy lessons, for future Canadian (and perhaps even foreign) governments, can be drawn from this bilateral engagement and dialogue.

### Chrétien 'Constructively Engages' Cuba

It was abundantly clear from the very beginning of 1994 that the Liberal government of Jean Chrétien would base its Cuba policy on what became known in political and bureaucratic circles as 'constructive engagement' or 'principled pragmatism.'[5] While this approach (which was heavily influenced by the thinking of Lloyd Axworthy) differed starkly from that of Washington officialdom, there was considerable debate within the Liberal Party and the foreign policy establishment over its efficacy and its ability to secure meaningful change in revolutionary Cuba. Simply put, it hinged on whether dialogue and interaction should trump vitriolic diatribes and isolation – as had been Washington's modus operandi since 1961, when the United States broke off diplomatic relations with Cuba.[6] At the centre of this whole debate was always the key question: What precisely is the most optimal way of facilitating positive and substantial political and economic reforms in Cuba? During the Chrétien period (at least during the first half of his mandate), the answer appeared to be clear and consistently articulated – specifically, it made eminently more sense to engage Cuba across a wide variety of policy and issue areas as a means of promoting positive change than it did to ostracize it as an international pariah state and close the door to a bilateral conversation.

At the June 1994 annual General Assembly of the Organization of American States (OAS), the secretary of state for Latin America and Africa, Christine Stewart, indicated strongly that it would be more beneficial for everyone if Cuba were fully integrated into the inter-American fold. In her subsequent address to the plenary session, Stewart deftly pointed out that Cuba's continued 'exclusion' from the OAS – which had been largely orchestrated by the United States in the early 1960s –

was decidedly unhealthy for both Cuba and all of the other countries of the Americas.[7] And, with an unmistakable eye towards Washington's confrontational Cuba policy, Stewart went on to explain: 'It is in all our interests, individually and as an organization, as well as in the interests of the people of Cuba, that we support a process of change in Cuba that is positive and orderly.'[8] The Chrétien government's policy preference for carrots over sticks, then, was sent out to a host of audiences: in Canada, Cuba, and the United States and within Canada's own foreign policy bureaucracy.

A few weeks later, Stewart announced with some fanfare that Cuba would once again be eligible for Canadian Official Development Assistance (ODA) – which had been suspended in 1978 by the government of Pierre Trudeau over the question of Cuban involvement in the Angolan war. After a rather desultory series of negotiations, both governments finally agreed in March 1996 to set up a formal government-to-government bilateral-aid program, with the Canadian International Development Agency (CIDA) front and centre, beginning with the modest sum of $30 million over five years. Consequently, Canada quickly became one of the largest donor countries in Cuba and thus placed itself in a better position to influence Cuba's decision-making process, if only marginally.[9] A sizeable portion of the funding was actually earmarked for 'good governance' and strengthening 'civil society' in Cuba, including financial support for Cuban non-governmental organizations (NGOs), human rights institutions, and various ministries within the Cuban government apparatus. Most important, especially from the Cuban standpoint, was the fact that the foreign-aid program was not conspicuously linked to any measurable progress in human rights protections, increased democratization, or economic liberalization in Cuba.

This positive approach of engaging the Cubans – as witnessed by Canada's modest aid program and ministerial exchanges – manifested itself again at the inaugural Summit of the Americas in late 1994. With the notable exception of Cuban President Fidel Castro, the Miami gathering brought together all the political leaders of the Americas. In response to U.S. President Bill Clinton's disparaging remarks about Cuba's lack of representative democracy, Prime Minister Chrétien challenged the prevailing view from Washington that isolating and ostracizing Cuba was beneficial for hemispheric affairs. As he declared pointedly: 'We have a right to disagree with that position. For us, it is the normalisation [of relations] that will lead to more democracy.'[10]

Highlighting once again Canada's Cuba policy of principled pragmatism, Secretary of State Christine Stewart indicated in Miami that Canada 'would hope that when other summits are held in the hemisphere that Cuba be present at the table. We as a nation will work to see that happens, and we will work with others in the hemisphere to see that happens.'[11]

On the official ministerial front, dialogue continued with the marking of the fiftieth anniversary of the formal establishment of Canadian-Cuban diplomatic ties in March 1995. On a high-profile visit to Ottawa, Cuban Foreign Minister Roberto Robaina met with a group of senior Canadian officials, including the foreign affairs minister, the secretary of state for Latin America, and the minister for international trade.[12] The discussions focused on trade and commercial issues, wider international political developments, and specific questions about fisheries cooperation and economic development in Cuba; unsurprisingly, the working visit drew pointed criticism from Capitol Hill, as some members of the U.S. Congress accused Canada of coddling a dictatorial government with a questionable human rights record. True to form, Canadian officials once again raised the thorny issue of human rights with their Cuban counterparts, outlining concerns about the lack of democratic pluralism, fundamental freedoms, and respect for basic political and civil rights.

In the wake of the unfortunate 24 February 1996 downing of two civilian Cessna aircraft by Cuban MiG fighter jets (precipitated by the provocative actions of the Miami-based Brothers to the Rescue anti-Castro group), which Canada and other countries understandably condemned, Ottawa still held firmly to its engagement approach. In fact, at the OAS General Assembly in June of that year, the Canadian delegation restated its opposition to the U.S. policy of treating Cuba as a pariah state in the hemisphere – even linking it expressly to the horrific shooting down of the two Cessna planes. According to Stewart, 'policies of isolation do not prevent such tragedies; indeed, they only give rise to the hardening of militant policies and reinforce the wrong kind of nationalism and political rigidity.'[13] Once again, Ottawa was underlining the costs of isolation and, by implication, emphasizing the potential benefits of engaging the Cubans.

In the initial phase of the Chrétien years, Foreign Affairs Minister André Ouellet captured the essence of Canada's Cuba policy when he said: 'It is time to turn the page on Cuba. The Cold War is over.'[14] It is worth noting, though, that the profile of Canada-Cuba relations was enhanced considerably with the early 1996 appointment of Lloyd Axworthy as Canada's new minister of foreign affairs. Not only did he exhibit a personal interest in the Cuban file, but, as a strong advocate of engaging the Cubans constructively and comprehensively, he was anxious to hold serious government-to-government discussions with Havana. And, because Canada was in the forefront of opposing the anti-Cuba Helms-Burton law (which was quickly signed into law by President Bill Clinton after the two Cessnas were shot down), the Cubans carefully put out the diplomatic feelers to see whether the Canadians would like to sit down with them. Not long after assuming his new portfolio, Axworthy met informally with Cuban Vice-President (responsible for economic development) Carlos Lage in an airport dining room just outside Heathrow airport. While the Cubans were clearly interested in obtaining increased economic and commercial assistance from Canada, the Canadians were looking to bolster any economic package with some language on human rights (especially in terms of political rights and freedoms); as Axworthy himself explained: 'Lage defended his government's use of police power as protection against American efforts to dislodge the regime, while I argued that joining international covenants on human rights and opening up political space for Cuban society was a better way to preserve their position.'[15] Discussion around this issue – off and on and with various degrees of intensity – would continue throughout Axworthy's tenure, and with arguably mixed results and no major breakthroughs.[16]

Still, and in conjunction with these exploratory talks, Axworthy undertook a two-day visit in late January 1997 to Havana, where he proudly brandished a fourteen-point Canada-Cuba Joint Declaration for bilateral cooperation in a variety of areas (including the sensitive topic of human rights) as a result of his efforts. This rather extraordinary trip, which was vigorously opposed by the Clinton White House, actually marked the first time in almost forty years that a foreign minister from Canada had set foot on Cuban soil in an official capacity. Harkening back to former prime minister Pierre Trudeau's high-profile state visit to Cuba in 1976, Axworthy's cordial meetings with President Castro (often stretching late into the evening and early morning) and senior Cuban officials generated a fair amount of media interest in both Cuba (where it was front-page news) and Canada (where the tone of the coverage proved to be overwhelmingly negative). In one representative (and rhetorically overheated) editorial, the *Globe and Mail* stated:

'The Axworthy visit is the best gift Mr. Castro has received since his beard was black.'[17]

The visit by Axworthy also engendered a flicker of press and political attention in media-saturated Washington, which normally reserved stories about things Canadian to the back pages.[18] In uncharacteristically blunt diplomatic parlance, U.S. State Department spokesperson Nicholas Burns harshly attacked Canada for allowing the visit to Cuba to happen in the first place. As he went on to lecture Ottawa: 'It doesn't make sense to reward a dictator in our own hemisphere who's completely behind the times. You reward him by sending your foreign minister down to visit, by having visits as usual, by trading. And we think that's wrong.'[19] Not to be outdone, virulent anti-Castro campaigner Senator Jesse Helms was typically livid about the Axworthy visit, and did little to disguise his displeasure with the Chrétien government. Indeed, he breathlessly invoked the bizarre analogy that Canada's dealings with Cuba in the 1990s were tantamount to former British prime minister Chamberlain's appeasement of Germany's Adolf Hitler in 1938: 'You had someone named Neville Chamberlain, he went over and sat down with Hitler and came back and said, "We can do business with this guy," and you saw what happened. Now if we're going to forget all principle and let Fidel Castro get by with all of his atrocities, then we [had] better look at the status of our principles and Canada certainly should look at hers,' he said defiantly.[20] Not surprisingly, official Ottawa was not impressed with the harsh language emanating from south of the border.

In fact, Nicholas Burns's critical remarks and Senator Helms's hyperbole did little to dissuade the Canadian government from continuing to engage the Cubans constructively and professionally. What these discordant voices seemed to highlight more than anything else were the fundamental differences in philosophical approaches towards Cuba – which was also evident when Prime Minister Chrétien visited Washington in early April 1997. Both Chrétien and President Clinton, though quickly building a strong personal bond, simply agreed to disagree politely on the question of Cuba and the Helms-Burton law. Clinton's view had not changed appreciably from the position that he had enunciated on the occasion of Axworthy's trip in January, when he stated confidently: 'I'm skeptical, frankly, that ... the recent discussions between the Canadians and the Cubans will lead to advances. I believe that our policy is the proper one.'[21] In his talks with congressional party leadership on the Hill, Chrétien was equally convinced that Canada's practical approach would, over time, bear the most fruit. He even bluntly told Senate majority leader Trent Lott: 'If you want to have an isolationist policy, that's your business. But don't tell us what to do. That's our business.'[22]

Arguably the most significant component of Canada's charting its own policy course and constructively engaging the Cubans material-ized in the first part of 1998. To the surprise of many, it was announced at the mid-April Santiago Summit of the Americas that Prime Minister Chrétien would be making a state visit to Cuba towards the end of that same month. Deliberately leaked by the U.S. delegation to the summit, and sharply criticized by President Clinton's national security adviser Sandy Berger, the announcement forced a noticeably angry Chrétien to disclose details of the surprise visit to a clutch of news-hungry Ca-nadian reporters.[23] As the prime minister explained things, President Clinton had been notified in general about the impending trip some ten days prior to the summit meeting in Chile. But at no time did he indi-cate his displeasure with Chrétien or his government for undertaking such a high-profile visit. In his closing comments at the final press con-ference, Chrétien added that most of the other leaders at the gathering 'talked to me very positively about this decision' and that, 'in consulta-tion with the Vatican' [since the pope had visited Cuba in January], the government thought 'it was good to go at this time.'[24]

While the Chrétien-Castro meeting did not produce any major po-litical or economic breakthroughs, the symbolic importance of the visit was unmistakable. And both governments could come away with their own small victories; Canada could fortify its independence from U.S. policy on Cuba and Havana could point to the diplomatic recognition of a leading G-7 country. Still, relations between the two countries start-ed to deteriorate, admittedly over a long period of time, once Chrétien's Airbus aircraft departed from José Martí international airport. It was evident that the Cubans did not appreciate the heavy-handed approach of the Canadians, especially the rather gruff demands for the immedi-ate release of a handful of notable political dissidents. Bilateral rela-tions were further strained by the March 1999 decision of the Cuban government to sentence the so-called Group of Four political dissidents to various prison terms – without giving much thought to Chrétien's earlier pleas.

Consequently, Ottawa wasted little time in expressing its deep dis-satisfaction with the actions of the Castro government; as the former prime minister indicated at the time: 'Cuba sends an unfortunate signal to her friends in the international community when people are jailed for peaceful protest.'[25] Not long afterward, Chrétien ordered a full review of official bilateral relations, including the re-evaluation of Canada's efforts to reintegrate Cuba into the inter-American fold, the freezing of a joint Canada-Cuba development-assistance project in Haiti, and the suspension of high-level ministerial exchanges. While it was clear that Ottawa would not completely sever diplomatic relations with Cuba or impose punishing economic sanctions, the government's actions did signal a noticeable shift in Canada's long-standing policy of constructive engagement with Cuba.[26] No one could mistake the fact that the Canada-Cuba diplomatic winds were beginning to turn from warm and tropical to something akin to brisk and cold.

After several months of reviewing Canada's Cuba policy, Prime Minister Chrétien awkwardly stated that Ottawa was going to put 'some northern ice' into Canadian-Cuban relations for now. Word also went out that Cuba should not expect an invitation to be forthcoming any time soon for the April 2001 Summit of the Americas in Quebec City; as one Canadian official working on the review quipped: 'We now have a Cuba policy of continued engagement, curtailed activity.[27] The relationship hit another snag in late July when President Castro derided the 1999 Pan American Games, which were being staged in Winnipeg, for their 'tricks' and 'filth' and, most objectionably, for taking place on 'enemy territory.'[28] These comments were largely in response to insufficient protection for the Cuban athletes, who were being provoked by Miami-based exiles. It also did not help that the right-wing local paper, the *Sun*, held a competition inviting readers to guess the number of Cuban defectors – and with a week's vacation in Varadero as the major prize. Needless to say, 1999–2000 marked a low point in bilateral relations – from which they have never fully recovered, despite the solid efforts in recent years of Canadian Ambassador Alexandra Bugailiskis and her Cuban counterpart, Ernesto Sentí.

To be sure, bilateral relations seemed to lurch from bad to worse when a strange diplomatic brouhaha erupted in March 2000. What was supposed to be a political favour to the Cuban government – namely, the issuing of a forty-eight-hour transit visa for a Cuban diplomat expelled from Washington, José Imperatori, to expedite his swift return to Cuba – turned into a minor embarrassment for both Canadian and Cuban authorities; in a rather bizarre twist of fate, Imperatori simply refused to leave the safe confines of the Cuban embassy in Ottawa, even after his temporary visa had expired. After a series of high-level discussions, a clearly annoyed Lloyd Axworthy managed to secure a promise from Havana that Imperatori would end his self-imposed hunger strike and immediately make his way safely back to Cuba via Montreal.[29] But the incident left Canadian officials slightly annoyed about being caught in the middle of the seemingly never-ending U.S.-Cuba propaganda war (and being needlessly exploited as a platform for the Cubans), with many wondering out loud about what exactly the Cuban authorities' intentions were – other than to make life a little more difficult for official Washington.[30]

For the next several months, a drifting Canada-Cuba relationship muddled through with what would become a familiar pattern of mostly low-level official exchanges. Then, shortly after the funeral for former prime minister Pierre Trudeau in Montreal, where President Fidel Castro served as one of the honorary pallbearers (together with former U.S. President Jimmy Carter), both Chrétien and Castro met informally for about thirty minutes. While there were no efforts to initiate any melting of the bilateral ice, both leaders reportedly had a friendly exchange of personal anecdotes about Trudeau. It was clear, though, that both sides saw this meeting as purely a courtesy call, and not one intended to repair the strained Canada-Cuba relationship.

More ominously, Prime Minister Chrétien, after the November 2000 federal election, appointed the conservative-minded John Manley as Canada's new foreign affairs minister. Initially, Manley said precious little about Canadian-Cuban relations as he digested the copious files of the department and immersed himself in the finer points of international diplomacy. However, during the course of his appearance before the House of Commons Foreign Affairs and International Trade Committee, his aversion to revolutionary Cuba became slightly more detectable. When asked by one committee member whether Cuba would be invited to the April 2001 Summit of the Americas in Quebec City, his terse reply spoke volumes about his own personal view. In a rather nonchalant and abrupt manner, he stated the following: 'Not at the present time. There hasn't been any demonstration of an acceptance of democratic standards [there].'[31] And, as far as he was concerned, 'Canada agrees that Cuba is not ready to participate in the summit because it lacks commitment to democratic principles.'[32] Excluding Cuba from the summit process clearly marked a change from the Liberal government's previous position of calling for Cuba to take its rightful seat at the conference tables in both Miami and Santiago. In addition,

Manley's coolness towards Havana did not augur well for any future thaw in diplomatic relations.

Significantly, just days before the summit's opening ceremonies, Manley reiterated his own view that Cuba's absence from the hemispheric gathering was no one else's fault but that of the Cubans themselves. For him, it was not a question of Cuba being consciously and deliberately snubbed or excluded from the official proceedings, but rather an issue of Cuba's inability to endorse the summit's various declarations on safeguarding representative democracy in the Americas. In a newspaper interview, he sought to clarify his position on Cuba even further by noting: 'I think the Prime Minister expressed the view, I guess probably after Santiago, that it would be desirable if Cuba was there ... but we haven't seen progress in Cuba. We have seen continuing failure to respect human rights, freedom of expression [and] democratic norms and so it is not surprising there should be no particular movement to include Cuba in this process.'[33] Manley's comments were clearly more critical than anything that his predecessor, Lloyd Axworthy, had ever uttered on the subject of Canada's position towards revolutionary Cuba. It was painfully obvious to the Cubans that the Canada-Cuba relationship had now entered a new, and seemingly less auspicious, bilateral phase.

After roughly twenty months of bilateral relations holding steady in a veritable political deep freeze, some signs of an early thaw eventually began to appear. In November 2002 the Chrétien government dispatched a junior cabinet minister to visit Cuba to take stock of the overall bilateral relationship. This minister was Denis Paradis – the secretary of state for Latin America and Africa – and he was charged with leading a trade mission (along with a handful of parliamentarians and representatives from some seventy Canadian businesses) to participate in the 20th Havana International Trade Fair. This mission was also informed by the concerns of Canadian exporters, who were worried about U.S. competitors moving into a trade market that they had traditionally dominated. While visiting the country, Paradis met with senior Cuban officials, inaugurated a cultural exhibit commemorating the life of Pierre Trudeau, and spoke with interested students at the University of Havana.[34]

However, just as signs of improvement were looming on the horizon, bilateral relations suffered another blow only five months later – this time, ostensibly as a result of the controversial actions of the Cuban government. The highly publicized 2003 March-April crackdown on some seventy-five Cuban dissidents was clearly a major setback for the Canadian-Cuban relationship. Ottawa was quick to respond, with Foreign Affairs Minister Bill Graham protesting against the arrests, the subsequent trial process, and the harsh prison sentences – ranging from six to twenty-eight years – and arguing that none of this could be justified on national security grounds.[35] Cuba's ambassador to Canada was also hastily called in to the Department of Foreign Affairs and International Trade and told bluntly that Ottawa was 'deeply' disturbed by these unacceptable actions.[36] Additionally, a protest letter was handed to the Cuban emissary to present to Cuba's foreign minister, Felipe Pérez Roque. Two weeks later, Canada supported an OAS resolution condemning human rights abuses in Cuba and calling on Havana 'to immediately free all unjustly arrested Cubans.'[37] And at the annual OAS General Assembly, held in Santiago, Chile, in June 2003, Graham let it be known that Canada would support an OAS-backed resolution on imposing 'non-economic' measures against Cuba – such as halting all high-level ministerial meetings with Cuban officials.

It was clear, if it had not been realized by both countries already, that relations had hit another rough patch of ice in the bilateral road. While Prime Minister Chrétien had initiated a revitalization of bilateral relations with Cuba – based largely on the organizing principle of constructive engagement – he left office at the end of 2003 with both countries barely speaking to one another. In short, the muddling-through approach that had characterized much of Canada-Cuba relations throughout much of the 1980s and early 1990s had once again reared its ugly head in the early years of the twenty-first century. Granted, interaction and dialogue between the two countries would continue, but it would take place without any clearly defined policy goals, in a directionless and bureaucratic vacuum, and with little top-level political commitment or interest by both sides.

Indeed, after Paul Martin was sworn in as Canada's twenty-first prime minister in mid-December 2003, followed by his narrow election victory in late June 2004, very little changed in terms of Canada-Cuba relations. A noticeable chill continued to characterize the overall relationship, and no significant ministerial exchanges between the two countries took place.[38] Martin's few public remarks on the matter, most notably at the special Summit of the Americas in January 2004 in Monterrey, Mexico, shed very little light on what shape a Martin policy towards Cuba would take.[39] During his concluding press conference at the summit, Martin was asked whether he would use the good offices of Canada to encourage positive reform in Cuba. He responded rather vaguely by noting: 'We have in the past used or sought to basically deal with our relationship with Cuba in a way that provides greater benefit obviously for Cuba but also for all of the surrounding states.'[40] Until his defeat in the federal election of January 2006, Martin's approach to Cuba was essentially to do and say as little as possible – perhaps demonstrating his unwillingness to ruffle needlessly some feathers in Washington.[41] This point is particularly important, given the extremely poor relations between President George W. Bush and former prime minister Chrétien, and the consequent determination of Paul Martin to repair those strained bilateral ties.

To understand Martin's inaction on the Cuba file, one has to factor into all of this the issue of atonement for Canada's decision to refrain from participating militarily in the 2003 U.S.-sponsored war in Iraq. There is no question that Ottawa's decision not to dispatch troops to participate in the U.S.-led coalition triggered a deterioration in Canada-U.S. relations; as the U.S. ambassador to Canada, Paul Cellucci, said at that time: 'There is no security threat to Canada that the United States would not be ready, willing and able to help with. There would be no debate ... And that is why so many in the United States are so disappointed and upset that Canada is not fully supporting us now.'[42] As for Canada-Cuba relations, the Martin government's strategy was straightforward: it took a 'don't ask, won't tell' position on Cuba in hopes of regaining some of the diplomatic capital and good graces that Canada had lost over the Iraq war decision.[43] For Martin, the less one heard about revolutionary Cuba, the better it was for his government and, more important, for his attempt to refurbish Canada-U.S. relations.

One could make the same argument for the minority Conservative government of Stephen Harper, which took office in January 2006 and was re-elected in October 2008. The Harper government has displayed not only its affection for much warmer relations with Washington but also a cautiously right-leaning policy agenda. Overall, there has been much chatter by the punditry about the lack of direction in the conduct of Canada's foreign policy – with a great deal of finger-pointing at both the prime minister and his former foreign affairs minister, Peter MacKay.[44] If anything, the guiding principle for Canada's engagement in international affairs under a Harper government appears to be centred around a decidedly 'Anglosphere' underpinning and focus. As *Globe and Mail* columnist John Ibbitson explained: 'Rather than cleaving to the multilateral consensus (read the United Nations), the Harper government has chosen to stick close to Canada's traditional allies, with the United States at the centre, Great Britain and Australia not far removed, and continental Europe a distant object.'[45]

Many observers both inside and outside Canada are probably still wondering what shape a Harper foreign policy will eventually take. Of course, no one is sure exactly what his overarching priorities will be – other than a laser-like focus on repairing the troubled Canada-U.S. relationship (and perhaps picking a needless fight with the Chinese). On the face of things, his foreign policy has reflected a significantly more pro-Washington bent than previous Liberal administrations – as indicated by his robust support for the Afghanistan war and the so-called war on terror and his tough talk on North Korea and Iran. His staking out of a more pro-Israeli position in the Middle East (calling Israel's attacks on Lebanon in the summer of 2006 'measured') – and freezing of diplomatic contacts with Hamas – mark a sharp departure from Canada's nuanced and neutral Middle East policy.

Curiously, the one area where Harper and his Conservative government have said very little publicly is the issue of Cuba and particularly the succession process that ultimately led to Raúl Castro's assumption of the presidency in February 2008.[46] This seems odd since, from 2006 on, media reports of Castro's 'grave illness' and doubts about his return to good health reverberated around the world. It is almost as if Canada's Cuba policy is effectively locked on autopilot – or simply continuing on with Canada's predilection for muddling through.

One news report in December 2006 did quote a senior U.S. State Department official as saying: 'I do believe that this government (in Canada) really is committed to promoting a democratic future for Cuba, and Canadians have been able to maintain relationships both with the regime and with members of Cuban society and Cuban dissidents, and that's no small feat. Only a few countries have been able to do that.'[47] And in January 2007 another U.S. official approached Ottawa about accepting about forty-five Cubans then warehoused in the Migrant Operations Centre at the naval base in Guantánamo Bay. As Ellen Sauerbery stated: 'We talked to Canada at many opportunities in the past and urged them to see what can be done in terms of making an exception ... Some of these people have been at the migrant centre for as long as two years. And they're very frustrated they are not being resettled.'[48] So far, there has been no response from official Ottawa on this request.

By mid-February 2007, Canada's ambassador to the United States, Michael Wilson, was also speaking openly about using Canada's cordial relations with Cuba as a 'bridge' between Havana and Washington in a post-Fidel Cuba. 'We have a dialogue, and that is different from the United States because they have nothing like this type of dialogue ... Because of that dialogue, we have an understanding of how Cuba thinks. We also have an understanding of how Washington thinks. Cuba sees us as a North American country with which they can have some sort of dialogue. We can build a greater understanding between the two countries.'[49] In December 2006, Raúl Castro acknowledged that he was open to normalizing relations with the United States as long as no pre-conditions were attached to any bilateral talks – a position he has repeated twice since then. Sadly, Washington has rebuffed this offer in no uncertain terms, indicating a clear lack of interest in any such initiative. One key question in this potential development remains, however: Would Canada's offer, especially coming from the Harper Conservatives, be viewed by the Cubans as a welcome intervention, or as merely a stalking horse for Washington?

Significantly, there is a real concern among some sectors that the historically cordial Canadian-Cuban relations could be supplanted by an overriding plan to improve relations between Canada and the United States (and possibly to mimic U.S. policy towards Cuba). This could occur if an election were to be called and a Harper majority government elected. In this context, there is some speculation that the prime minister might take a tougher line towards Havana. It is conceivable (but unlikely), for example, that a Harper government might also wish to revisit Canada's long-standing opposition to the U.S. economic embargo, which Ottawa has consistently voted against when it has come before the United Nations every fall. One might also expect more critical comments by Harper himself about the Cuban government and its record on human rights and democratic development (not unlike the case of China). In December 2006 Jason Kenney, just prior to being appointed the new secretary of state for multiculturalism and Canadian identity, said that issues about the rule of law, democratic freedoms, and human rights 'are relevant to the foreign affairs policy in general, and not just to China.'[50] In addition, an already conservative-minded and largely critical foreign policy establishment in Ottawa might be turned loose to express its displeasure with Havana and Raúl Castro in unusually tough diplomatic language. These are all possible developments should a Harper government form a majority government, which admittedly looks less likely today.

We did get a glimpse of Harper's approach to Cuba during his July

2007 visit to Latin America and the Caribbean – with his conspicuous omission of a stopover in Cuba. Prior to leaving on his Latin American trip, he did say in a media interview that he was prepared to accept the right of Cuba to determine its own internal political and economic system. But, when he was asked about revolutionary Cuba during a press briefing in Barbados, he responded curtly by mentioning the incompatibility of the Cuban system with Canada's and went on to express concerns about aspects of governance and human rights in Cuba. While in Barbados, Harper also outlined some fundamental differences between Canadian and Cuban objectives, emphasizing the values that his government would be advancing throughout the region: 'to promote basic democratic values, to strengthen economic linkages, and to meet new security challenges.'[51] As an indication perhaps of the Canada-Cuba relationship during the Harper period, the Cuban ambassador to Canada sent the prime minister a box of Cohiba Habanos cigars without first realizing that Harper's asthma would prevent him from smoking them.[52]

On 21 May 2008 the Canadian government issued a declaration encouraging the Cuban people to continue their struggle towards democracy.[53] Significantly, 20 May is a date celebrated in Miami but not in Havana. Also noteworthy is the fact that no other Canadian government had ever marked this anniversary (the withdrawal of U.S. troops in 1902 from Cuba after a three-year military occupation) since 1959, knowing that it would be offensive to the revolutionary government. In terms of political symbolism, the Harper government was thus supporting a Bush initiative – a failed one too, since the communiqués issued both in Washington and in Ottawa were released one day late!

The irony of this potential hardening of the diplomatic arteries is, of course, that it would occur precisely at a time when there is significant pressure in the United States to overturn a clearly failed policy of nearly five decades in duration and to seek a normalization of relations with Cuba. The arrival of U.S. President Barack Obama in January 2009, along with a Democratic Party-controlled Congress, could set this process in motion. In addition, pressure from the U.S. business sector (which has sold $2 billion worth of food and agricultural produce to Cuba in recent years), combined with significant changes in the Cuban exile community in Miami (most of whose members are now keen for dialogue with Havana), has led to a new awareness in Washington that the United States has suffered an embarrassing defeat in its efforts to isolate Cuba and that it is time to adopt a new strategy. It is also significant that Cuba is the elected leader of the 118-nation Non-Aligned Movement, that it was elected to the new United Nations Human Rights Council with the support of 135 countries – 5 more than Canada – and that its motion at the UN General Assembly to condemn the U.S. embargo in October 2008 was supported by 185 countries. Clearly, the only country isolated in this context has been the United States, whose international political credibility reached new lows under the Bush administration.

Whatever might happen against the dramatic background of international politics, in terms of contemporary Canada-Cuba relations, there is little chance that the Harper government will move to melt the bilateral ice in Canadian-Cuban relations. What will most likely happen is that ministerial visits will be scaled back, and one should not expect any significant increase in Canada's development-assistance program for Cuba. Nor is it likely – even with Obama in the White House – that the government will undertake any serious efforts to have Cuba reintegrated into the inter-American fold. And no one should be under the illusion that Raúl Castro will be getting an invitation to visit Canada any time soon. In short, the prospect of a thaw in Canada-Cuba relations under Stephen Harper is not likely to make it onto the Conservative government's radar screen.

The most likely probability in the short term, then, is a Cuba policy more along the lines of maintaining the status quo of continued engagement at a reduced level of activity. At the same time, Prime Minister Harper needs to be mindful of the fact that Canadians – more than 650,000 of whom travel annually to Cuba on vacation – overwhelmingly support a Cuba policy that is based on dialogue and interaction. Moreover, Canadians in general were averse to the previous U.S. administration's foreign policy, not only towards Cuba but also to the rest of the international community,[54] and they are undoubtedly hoping for a change of course under Obama and the Democrats. Finally, Harper must know well the fate that befell Brian Mulroney when his policies resembled excessively those made in Washington – the prime minister was rudely turfed from office.

Even though there was a change of political leadership in Canada in 2006, the fundamental 'pull' and 'push' factors underscoring Canadian-Cuban relations remain the same as always. Stephen Harper's government will not alter this inescapable reality; instead, he will have to craft his own Cuba policy within these same policy constraints and determinants. The fact of the matter is that the minority status of his government – and his own inexperience in foreign policy matters – has essentially allowed Canada-Cuba relations to drift aimlessly since his coming to power. That does not mean that a Stephen Harper-led government, like those before him, will not seek to put its own stamp on Canada's relations with Cuba. But it does mean that he cannot radically change the policy without obviating one or more of the relationship's key determinants – and thus suffering the possible political, economic, and electoral fallout from doing so.

For electoral reasons, then, Harper probably knows that he cannot tinker with the current policy in any fundamental way without somehow negatively affecting public opinion in Canada.[55] As he no doubt fully understands, the safest approach within the strictures of a minority government would be to do and say as little as possible of a substantive nature about Cuba – and hope that Canadians will not ask or notice. But this Cuba policy of sustained indifference, while manageable in the short term, cannot be maintained over a longer period of time, especially as the succession process continues in Cuba (Raúl Castro, at age seventy-eight, will likely not remain in power for long), as U.S. economic interests continue to position themselves for a larger share of the Cuban marketplace, and as the Obama administration puts in place a more outward-looking and less unilateralist foreign policy towards the Americas. At some point, perhaps if he secures a majority government, Harper is going to have to show his true colours and unveil exactly what it is that constitutes his own policy on things Canadian-Cuban. That said, if the likely trend in Canadian politics of producing minority parliaments continues, Canada's Cuba policy will largely remain a 'muddling through' affair.

## Understanding Canada-Cuba Relations

Although relations today between Havana and Ottawa are somewhat strained at the political and diplomatic level (largely over issues of human rights), the bilateral relationship continues to function well in other areas.[56] In fact, diplomatic ties have not been broken, commercial relations have not been interrupted (with even a noticeable increase in two-way trade over the last few years),[57] and Canada's aid program (estimated at almost $10 million annually) continues to fund important projects in Cuba. Moreover, there is significant 'people-to-people' contact across a wide spectrum of civil society. Canadian businesses and NGOs remain the model to emulate for all foreign interests in Cuba. In terms of tourism – now one of the key pillars of Cuba's economy – Canada continues to be the major source of vacationers.

Granted, the overall relationship has cooled under prime ministers Paul Martin and Stephen Harper, and some of the heretofore friendliness and cordiality has dissipated, but the core of the bilateral relationship proceeds on a normal basis.[58] Stated differently, the fundamental underpinnings or driving forces of Canadian-Cuban relations are still very much in place – notwithstanding a clearly frostier bilateral milieu at the governmental level. For instance, Canada's CIDA sponsored a' successful February 2007 meeting between Canadian experts and Cuban officials 'on such issues as trade negotiations, commercial diplomacy and how to structure bilateral and multilateral agreements.'[59]

Even during the most difficult periods in bilateral relations, Ottawa has kept its sights squarely on the monetary and commercial side of the relationship.[60] Trade between Canada and Cuba reached record levels in 2007 – surpassing one billion dollars (up considerably from $630 million in 2003).[61] This, it must be remembered, was at a point when the relationship was badly strained. At the time of writing, the business community in Canada, much like its U.S. counterpart, continues to support a policy of dialogue and exchange with the Cuban government and people. It is increasingly aware of the fact, especially since large U.S. agri-businesses are making inroads into the Cuban marketplace and are positioning themselves for the eventual lifting of the economic embargo, that Canadian companies currently have a distinct advantage in terms of supplying Cuba with high-tech equipment, spare parts and machinery, and consumer and tourism-related durables; indeed, there is a growing body of evidence to show that U.S. producers are 'dumping' produce at extremely low prices, precisely to corner the future Cuban export market and thereby force out competitors, including Canadians. The Canadian business community also knows that closer political relations, or at least ones that are not completely dysfunctional, hold the key to opening up future (or perhaps even maintaining existing) trade and investment opportunities in Cuba.

The rationale for Canada's Cuba policy, however, cannot be explained solely in terms of commercial or investment considerations. It is necessary to take into account other important historical, external, and even domestic political variables as well. Though it is true that the overall policy is heavily influenced by trade factors, one should not discount the significance of past developments and the rich history that the two countries have shared. In light of that history, Canada's policy is more a function of what it has always been in previous decades: namely, one of recognizing the Cuban government (which clearly enjoys popular support), maintaining trade and diplomatic ties, cultivating Cuban connections, and looking to foster meaningful change from within by engaging the Cubans at every opportunity. While every Canadian government since 1959 has sought to add on to this policy its own unique bricks and mortar (and Stephen Harper will not be any different), the pre-existing historical foundation has always remained intact.

In one sense, Canada's Cuba policy has invariably reflected a desire on the part of successive Canadian governments, irrespective of political stripe, to carve out an independent and made-in-Canada role regarding revolutionary Cuba. This has, in part, manifested itself in a policy preference since the late 1980s to engage more fully in hemispheric affairs: first by joining the OAS in 1990, followed by the negotiation of the North American Free Trade Agreement (NAFTA) in 1993, and then by deepening Canada's involvement in the Summit of the Americas process. Solidifying Canada's relations with the wider Latin America/ Caribbean community has often been regarded as inextricably connected to stronger Canada-Cuba relations. By courting the Cubans, it was argued, Canada would not only send a potent message to a host of Latin American countries (which were often nervous about Canada repeatedly making common cause with its giant southern neighbour or acting as a gentle stalking horse for Washington), but it would also deliver a pointed signal to the U.S. government.

This is particularly important in light of the dramatic improvement of Cuba's contemporary relations with Latin America and the Caribbean. With socialist governments in Bolivia and Venezuela, and nationalist presidents elected in Ecuador, Paraguay, Argentina, Uruguay, Nicaragua, and Brazil, Cuba's continued resistance to U.S. pressure is widely appreciated. In Mexico, too, the continentalist approach of former president Vicente Fox has been widely criticized, while the Caribbean Community (Caricom) (and most Central American) nations remain firm backers of Cuba. Since Ottawa is moving increasingly towards the development of stronger relations with Latin America, this groundswell of regional respect for Cuba is an extremely important point for Canadian officials to consider.

Not surprisingly, Canadian governments in the past have not hesitated to invoke the so-called Cuba card in the larger context of Canada-U.S.-Cuba relations.[62] Political leaders in Ottawa have rarely missed an opportunity to exploit the contrast between Canada's engagement policy towards Cuba and the isolationist and hostile tendencies of successive U.S. administrations since 1959. By identifying and periodically highlighting this sharp difference in policy approaches towards Cuba, Canadian governments can maintain that Canada does indeed have a truly independent foreign policy, and not one simply formulated by officials in Washington. If he does not already know it, Stephen Harper would be wise to recall that Ottawa's symbolically significant made-in-Canada Cuba policy, especially when it serves to tweak the nose of Washington officialdom on certain occasions, not only reassures anxious Canadians about their political sovereignty and independence but also plays to their sense of pride and national identity.[63]

As the previous discussion clearly illustrated, Canada's long-standing policy of constructive engagement on many fronts has palpable domestic political import. Symbolically speaking, of course, it makes Canadians feel less dependent upon, and dominated by, the hyper-power to the south and enables them to differentiate themselves from their U.S. neighbours. This was especially true during the controversial Bush years, when Canadians were left feeling more and more anxious about finding themselves caught in a one-dimensional 'you're either with us or against us' global chessboard. Put simply, Bush's unabashed chauvinism, along with his boasts as a self-declared 'war president,' did not sit well with many Canadians. It remains to be seen how all of this might change under a more soft-power-oriented Obama administration. Still, public-opinion surveys have repeatedly demonstrated that Canada's continued relationship with revolutionary Cuba – as experienced political hands in Ottawa surely know – remains politically popular among a large segment of Canadians.

For any Canadian government even considering downgrading or severing relations with the Castro government, this political or electoral reality cannot be easily discounted. Indeed, while Canada's approach to Cuba is not based entirely on electoral considerations, the realization that a cordial relationship with Havana is politically popular at home has not been lost on successive Canadian governments – especially those clinging perilously to minority status. No government can lose sight of the fact that, of the large number of Canadians who travel every year to Cuba, many of them have established close friendships with ordinary Cubans.[64] Simply put, it is hard to imagine any Canadian government viewing the possibility of adopting a tougher line towards Cuba as a political winner – despite any siren-like calls from Washington to do so.

When one considers the motivations of the Cuban government, the explanatory factors are similar in some respects and noticeably differ-

ent in others. It is worth emphasizing, however, that the bilateral relationship is clearly a win-win situation for the Cubans – with almost no
risks or significant costs involved. Not surprisingly, the Cuban government is keenly interested in strengthening commercial relations with a
major Western, industrialized country like Canada (already one of its
largest foreign trading partners). While the Caribbean island country
has not completely turned the corner economically, two-way trade with
Canada has been particularly important during the Special Period. Furthermore, Canada has become not only a key supplier of high-tech and
consumer durables – which have been in short supply – but also a crucial source of much-needed foreign investment and commercial expertise (particularly in oil and mining exploration and tourism).

Of course, Cuba's relations with Canada provide the Cuban government with a host of political, diplomatic, and symbolic benefits. For
example, it is undoubtedly valuable for Havana to be in a position to
showcase its relationship with a long-standing member of the G-8 to the
rest of the international community, particularly one that is U.S.-friend-
ly and prepared to work cooperatively with the Cuban government.
The high-profile manner in which former prime minister Chrétien and
senior members of his cabinet were received, with widespread media
coverage and much fanfare, reflected the symbolic importance that the
Cubans attach to their bilateral relations with Canada (to say nothing
of the positive message that this sends to the wider community of nations). In an international community where the United States stands
out as the sole 'indispensable power,' and makes no effort to hide its intense disdain for the Cuban government, it does not hurt Cuba to have
a friend in Canada. Profitable relations with Canada, then, codify a certain degree of international credibility and respectability, which can be
repackaged by Havana for both domestic and external consumption.
Chrétien's 1998 official visit, for instance, was a major propaganda coup
for Fidel Castro, since it confirmed his legitimacy and underscored the
absurd and archaic nature of U.S. policy towards Cuba.

Needless to say, Cuban authorities are most interested in deepening the political and economic relationship with Canada for pragmatic
reasons of national interest. Clearly, Canada is important from an investment standpoint and in terms of valuable development assistance
and technical expertise from the Canadian International Development
Agency. And, with respect to the controversial Helms-Burton law, the
Cuban government has also been the beneficiary of Canada's unstint-

ing opposition to this anti-Cuba measure. It certainly does not hurt that Canada's leading role within the OAS might prove useful to Cuba not only in terms of its future reintegration in that organization (however unlikely that may seem today) but also in helping to develop a more globalized and export-oriented trade/development strategy for the island.

Overall, close relations with Canada offer a significant number of benefits for the Cubans – and without any onerous pre-conditions being attached. Cuban officials know full well that the Canadians are not out to do Washington's bidding, to destabilize the Cuban government, or to punish unduly the Cuban people; they know that Canada wants to work constructively and pragmatically with Havana. The government of Cuba might well disagree occasionally with the intent and the approach employed by the Canadian government, but it clearly views Canadian policy differently from the one-dimensional policy of U.S. administrations from Dwight Eisenhower to George W. Bush. All this, of course, could change if Obama does move to normalize relations with Cuba. But that is a big 'if' as of this writing. And that is why the Cubans are cognizant of the fact that a healthy and vibrant relationship with Ottawa could be utilized by Havana for a variety of purposes – not the least of which is to highlight the absurdity of the U.S. economic embargo and to help normalize (or to better mediate) relations with a more sensible U.S. government in the future.

## Conclusion

Despite the current cool nature of the Canada-Cuba relationship, it can probably best be described as correct, mostly cordial, and certainly commercial-oriented during the ongoing Special Period. The economic crisis in Cuba following the demise of the Soviet Union actually produced new opportunities, and some urgency perhaps, for both countries – along with continuing political difficulties rooted in past policy differences. And now the current succession process in Cuba after the illness of Fidel Castro and Raúl's ascension to the presidency has brought a new layer of uncertainty into the relationship and arguably inaugurated a temporary 'wait-and-see' approach. Still, the underlying adherence to a policy of 'constructive engagement,' with its emphasis on dialogue, commercial exchange, and bridge building, continues to be the primary organizing policy principle for Canada-Cuba relations.

While the past few years have had their share of diplomatic ups and downs, the central driving forces of the relationship – political symbolism and domestic politics, economic/investment considerations, and the cultural-tourism dimension – have largely remained unaltered in a period of diplomatic flux. It is also important to stress that Canada, unlike Cuba, has had to balance its policy towards revolutionary Cuba within the larger framework of the infinitely more important Canada-U.S. dynamic. When this is combined with specific measures initiated by the Cuban government, such as suppressing domestic dissent or making ill-considered comments about Canadian politicians, it goes some way towards explaining the erratic or muddling-through approach adopted by Ottawa. But in the absence of some significant domestic events in both countries, or some dramatic external developments in the international arena, the Canada-Cuba relationship will continue along the lines of its past levels of friendliness, engagement, and shared aims.

Canadian officials will undoubtedly persist, as they did throughout the Special Period, in expressing their concerns about the human rights situation in Cuba.[65] But they will likely refrain from taking a heavy-handed approach or hectoring the Cubans about their lack of political freedom (although the Harper government – or even a new Liberal government – might be tempted to do otherwise), the need for respect for civil and political rights, and the status of various political prisoners. As has been the case over the last decade or so, the Cuban government will maintain a dialogue with the Canadians on a variety of issues – including human rights and political liberalization – without making any firm or ground-breaking commitments. Both sides have essentially agreed that this is a sensitive area, that they share extremely different interpretations about these concepts, and that neither should operate under the assumption that fundamental political changes are going to take place in Cuba overnight. They have each resigned themselves, especially since the early 1990s, to the fact that long-term goals should not take precedence over the short-term benefits that each country derives from their bilateral interactions.

It is instructive to note that Canada and Cuba actually drew closer together over the past decade or more, partly because of economic pressures in Cuba and also because of a desire in Canadian political circles to put some much-needed distance between Ottawa and Washington via relations with Havana. People-to-people contacts (including business people, academics and students, and hordes of Canadian tourists) during this time also increased, and should not be dismissed as a key political/electoral factor in strengthening the relationship between the two countries. For Canada, the benefits resulting from this arrangement are not confined to trade and investment; the Canada-Cuba relationship has bolstered Canadian sovereignty and independence in foreign policy making, differentiated Canada from the United States, and reassured nervous Canadians about Ottawa's willingness to stand up to, periodically at least, pressures from Washington. Moreover, Canada's relationship with Cuba has also helped burnish Ottawa's international image and reputation – particularly in the mainly Cuba-friendly Americas.

Under Stephen Harper's tenure, not much is likely to change in terms of the pattern of relations firmly established during the Special Period. The key factor is that nothing dramatic is going to happen as long as the Harper government remains constrained by its minority status– unless, that is, the new Obama administration forces a change in course. For the moment, government officials are now reluctant to speak on the record about Canadian-Cuban relations, are somewhat mystified by the lack of political direction from above, and are effectively left scratching their heads and resorting to the refrain that Canada is in a 'let's wait-and-see' mode.[66] What we do know thus far is that neither Harper nor his current foreign affairs minister, Lawrence Cannon, has had any life-long or personal interest in things Canadian-Cuban. Moreover, neither does Harper nor Cannon appear to be seized or preoccupied with the Canada-Cuba file. Finally, there is no evidence as of yet that the Conservative government has even asked for a detailed or comprehensive review of Canada's current Cuba policy.

For these reasons, Harper's Cuba policy, such as it is, could very well be shaped by new foreign policy approaches south of the border and, on the domestic front, by the performance of the revitalized Liberal Party under the leadership of Michael Ignatieff and the delicate and often tricky nature of managing a minority government. More than likely, Stephen Harper's Cuba policy will resemble the muddling-through approach perfected by Jean Chrétien and Paul Martin, his Liberal Party predecessors and long-time political rivals. And, as Harper's July 2007 visit to the region indicated, the focus, such as it is, will continue to be on human rights and democratic development in Cuba.

Indeed, there is no compelling reason to think that Harper's policy towards Cuba – particularly in the short to mid-term – will significantly change from what it has been over the last decade or more.[67] Since the fundamental determinants of the bilateral relationship are still in place, the overall direction of Canadian-Cuban relations should remain intact. All bets are off, however, if the Obama administration leaves current U.S. policy on Cuba untouched and Harper then secures a majority government, which will have the ability, if it so wishes, to bring Canada into even closer alignment with the U.S. approach. Should that happen, nearly fifty years of relatively cordial Canadian-Cuban relations could be immediately turned on their head. In all probability, this is unlikely – the changing dynamics of U.S. politics will work against it, as will the continuing trend towards minority governments in Canada. Just as important is the strong people-to-people relationship between Canada and Cuba (which would lead to much popular discontent if Ottawa were to move against Cuba), and of course the nature of Canadian politics illustrates the need for a foreign policy independent of Washington. Should there be yet another minority government following the next election, the policy-making dispositions of both Canadian and Cuban officials for muddling through is likely to remain the order of the day. We may well have to wait for a majority government in Ottawa before any imagination or innovation is injected into the bilateral relationship.

NOTES

1  See John M. Kirk and Peter McKenna, *Canada-Cuba Relations: The Other Good Neighbor Policy* (Gainesville: University Press of Florida, 1997).
2  See Peter McKenna and John M. Kirk, 'Canadian-Cuban Relations: Is the Honeymoon Over?' *Canadian Foreign Policy*, 9, no. 3 (2002): 49–63.
3  In its Throne Speech of early February 2004, the Paul Martin government made references to Canada playing an influential role in world affairs and meeting its international responsibilities. In addition, it announced a comprehensive review of Canadian foreign policy to inform Ottawa's new international focus. Also see Martin's speech to the Canadian Newspapers Association, 'Transcript: Canada's Role in a Complex Role,' 30 April 2003, 1–9.
4  After the collapse of the Soviet Union in the early 1990s, and the fragmentation of the Eastern European bloc of countries, Cuba found itself suddenly cut off from a market that received 87 per cent of its exports. In

the absence of this economic arrangement, to say little of the $3–4 billion annually in Soviet subsidies and barter agreements, the tiny Caribbean country found its economy in a major tailspin. Not only did its economic capacity contract by some 50 per cent, but food rationing, periodic power outages, and widespread shortages of consumer durables became commonplace. See Gary Prevost, 'Cuba,' in Harry E. Vanden and Gary Prevost, eds., *Politics of Latin America* (New York: Oxford University Press, 2002), 325–55, and Thomas E. Skidmore and Peter H. Smith, *Modern Latin America* (New York: Oxford University Press, 1997), 263–93.

5 See Peter McKenna and John M. Kirk, 'Canada, Cuba and "Constructive Engagement" in the 1990s,' in Heather H. Nicol, ed., *Canada, the US, and Cuba: Helms-Burton and Its Aftermath* (Kingston, Ont.: Centre for International Relations, 1999), 57–76.

6 While there was undoubtedly lively debate about its precise impact on the Cuban government, some people recognized that the policy followed by the last ten U.S. presidents had precious little to show for it.

7 See Government of Canada, 'Notes for an Address by the Honourable Christine Stewart, Secretary of State (Latin America and Africa), to the 24th General Assembly of the Organization of American States,' 7 June 1994, 4.

8 Ibid.

9 See Michel Hogue, 'A Canadian Approach?: Canada's Official Development Assistance and Foreign Policy towards Cuba,' unpublished paper, March 1998, 1–17.

10 'Cuba's Absence at America's Summit Skirts Formal Agenda,' *Cuba INFO* 6, no. 16 (1996): 3.

11 Ibid.

12 Department of Foreign Affairs and International Trade (DFAIT), 'Robaina Visit to Mark 50 Years of Diplomatic Ties between Canada and Cuba,' News Release no. 56 (17 March 1995), 1.

13 DFAIT, 'Notes for an Address by the Honourable Christine Stewart, Secretary of State (Latin America and Africa), to the 25th General Assembly of the Organization of American States,' *Statement* (6 June 1995), 3.

14 Quoted in Mimi Whitefield, 'Saying "the Cold War Is Over," Canada Restores Aid to Cuba,' Miami *Herald*, 21 June 1994, A9.

15 Lloyd Axworthy, *Navigating a New World* (Toronto: Vintage Canada, 2004), 69.

16 For a more critical assessment, see Julia Sagebien, 'And the Mambo Kings Will Live On: Cuba after Fidel,' *Policy Options*, 27, no. 8 (2006): 70–4, and Yvon Grenier, 'Our Dictatorship: Canada's Trilateral Relations with

Castro's Cuba,' in Maureen Appel Molot and Fen Osler Hampson, eds., *Canada among Nations: Vanishing Borders* (Ottawa: Oxford University Press, 2000), 247–73.

17  See 'Canada's Gift to Mr. Castro,' *Globe and Mail*, 24 January 1997, A20.

18  See Drew Fagan, 'Our Man in Havana Wakes up Washington,' *Globe and Mail*, 25 January 1997, D1.

19  Laura Eggerston and Paul Knox, 'Cuba Law Swaying Canada, U.S. Says,' *Globe and Mail*, 22 January 1997, A1.

20  'Cuba Visit Likened to Appeasing Hitler,' *Globe and Mail*, 24 January 1997, A8.

21  Ibid.

22  See Robert Russo, 'PM Rebukes Cuba-Bashers,' Halifax *Chronicle-Herald*, 9 April 1997, 1.

23  See Janice Tibbets, 'Chrétien to Visit Cuba," Halifax *Sunday Herald*, 19 April 1998, A19. For an insider's account of Chrétien's visit, see James Bartleman, *Rollercoaster: My Hectic Years as Jean Chrétien's Diplomatic Advisor 1994–1998* (Toronto: Douglas Gibson Books, 2005), 272–302.

24  See Heather Scoffield, 'Summit Maps Path to Free Trade,' *Globe and Mail*, 20 April 1998, A1.

25  Canada, Office of the Prime Minister, 'Statement by the Prime Minister,' 15 March 1999.

26  See Joel-Denis Bellavance, 'PM Orders Review of Cuban Relations after Critics Jailed,' *National Post*, 16 March 1999, A1. Foreign Affairs Minister Axworthy was particularly perturbed by the maximum sentences meted out by the Cuban authorities, the failure of the Cuban government to grant Canadian officials observer status at the trials, and a subsequent toughening of Cuba's criminal code. In addition, Axworthy was unusually blunt about the question of Cuba's reintegration into the OAS, explaining that such a move meant 'accepting rules, accepting the rule of law, and clearly the sentencing of the dissidents indicates there's not much willingness there.' The minister then went on to warn: 'We've indicated that if you're going to be a member of the hemispheric community, you have to play by those rules.' Cited in Allan Thompson, 'Canada's Diplomatic Aid for Cuba Put on Hold,' Toronto *Star*, 17 March 1999, A2.

27  Confidential interview with Canadian official in DFAIT, 8 June 2000.

28  See Robert Fife, 'Castro Calls Canada "Enemy Territory," Talks Pan Am "Filth,"' *National Post*, 28 July 1999, A10.

29  See Joel-Denis Bellavance and Campbell Clark, 'Cuban Envoy Flies Home after Ending Hunger Strike,' *National Post*, 3 March 2000, A10.

30  Confidential interview with a senior Canadian official in DFAIT, 2 March 2000.

31  Quoted in Ian Jack, 'Ottawa Shifts Policy on Cuba, Supports Bush,' *National Post*, 16 March 2001, A11.

32  See Peter McKenna, 'Manley Courting Bush with His Cold Shoulder to Cuba,' Hamilton *Spectator*, 29 March 2001, A9.

33  See Sheldon Alberts, 'Why Cuba Was Not Invited,' *National Post*, 16 April 2001, D2.

34  See Jeff Sallot, 'Canada's Trade Mission to Cuba Signals Thaw,' *Globe and Mail*, 2 November 2002, A6, and Peter McKenna and John M. Kirk, 'It's Time to Make up with Cuba,' *Globe and Mail*, 6 November 2002, A12.

35  DFAIT, *Canada-Cuba Relations Fact Sheet*, October 2003, 1.

36  See Paul Knox, 'Graham Protests against Cuban Trials,' *Globe and Mail*, 8 April 2003, A8.

37  'OAS to Debate Resolution Condemning Cuba on Rights,' Washington *Post*, 22 April 2003, A9, and Pablo Bachelet, 'U.S. Fails to Pass anti-Cuba resolution at OAS,' Washington *Post*, 23 April 2003, A13.

38  However, Ottawa did not adopt an overly critical public posture towards the Cubans over the 2003 crackdown – unlike the Europeans. For the most part, Canada continued to engage the Cubans through joint efforts in health care, community participation, and cultural exhibits. Ottawa also sought to 'brand' Canada in Cuba by contributing to a public-affairs program (supporting academic talks in Cuba), efforts at economic modernization, and civil society assistance. Additionally, more than two million Cubans participated in the March 2007 Terry Fox run to raise money for cancer research – a substantial increase from the 260,000 in 2003.

39  At the mid-January 2004 special Summit of the Americas in Monterrey, Mexico, Martin replied to a reporter's question with the curt comment: 'Bien, écoutez bien, le Sommet des Amériques, c'est pour des pays démocratiques.' Translation: 'Well, listen carefully, the Summit of the Americas, is for countries that are democratic.' Transcript from the Prime Minister's Office, 11 January 2004.

40  See the transcript of closing comments at the special Summit of the Americas, 13 January 2004.

41  See Peter McKenna and John M. Kirk, 'Canadian-Cuban Relations: Old Wine in New Bottles?' in Michele Zebich-Knos and Heather N. Nicol, eds., *Foreign Policy toward Cuba: Isolation or Engagement?* (New York: Lexington Books, 2005), 67–86. Having said that, Canada's minister of agriculture, Andy Mitchell, did meet with his Cuban counterpart in Havana in late

March 2005, and Cuba's foreign minister, Felipe Pérez Roque, also met with senior Canadian government officials during a four-day visit to Canada in October 2005. But it is important to note that the Martin government deliberately downplayed the Roque visit so as to not upset Washington unduly. Confidential interview with an official in DFAIT, 31 July 2006.

42  Canadian Broadcasting Corporation, 'U.S. Ambassador Rebukes Ottawa for Lack of Support,' CBC News Online, http://www.cbc.ca, 26 March 2003, 1.

43  See Peter McKenna, 'Cuba Headed to Deep Freeze?' London *Free Press*, 3 January 2004, F3.

44  See James Travers, 'Rift Grows between PM and Mandarins,' Toronto *Star*, 1 February 2007, A21; Jeffrey Simpson, 'Stephen Harper's Proactive Inactive Foreign Policy,' *Globe and Mail*, 16 January 2006, A15; Lawrence Martin, 'The Harperites' Foreign Affairs Show Is Strictly Amateur Hour,' *Globe and Mail*, 11 November 2006, A17; and John Ibbitson, 'Tories File Foreign Policy Statement in Blue Box,' *Globe and Mail*, 18 August 2006, A4.

45  See John Ibbitson, 'Harper Sticks Close to Traditional Allies,' *Globe and Mail*, 15 July 2006, A10. Also see Ibbitson, 'Australia's PM Has a Lot in Common with Harper,' *Globe and Mail*, 17 May 2006, A5.

46  In confidential interviews, Canadian officials in both Washington and Ottawa have indicated that the Harper government has given them virtually no instructions on how to proceed on the Cuba file – other than to stay the course and adopt a wait-and-see posture.

47  See Jennifer Ditchburn, 'Canada to Be Helpful for Cuba-U.S. Relations When Castro Dies, Says U.S. Official,' Charlottetown *Guardian*, 19 December 2006, A5.

48  See Mike Blanchfield, 'Cuba si, would-be Cuban refugees no,' Montreal *Gazette*, 22 January 2007, A10.

49  See Tim Harper, 'Wilson Pushes Cuba Connection,' Toronto *Star*, 17 February 2007, A9.

50  See Lee Berthiaume, 'Cuba Saga Shows Signs of Complication in Ottawa,' *Embassy Magazine*, 20 December 2006.

51  See Government of Canada, 'Prime Minister Harper Concludes Meetings with CARICOM Leaders,' News Release (Ottawa: Prime Minister's Office, 19 July 2007), 5.

52  See Bill Curry, 'Cohiba Habanos, Gucci and More Given to PM, Family,' *Globe and Mail*, 5 January 2009, A6.

53  Government of Canada, 'Minister Bernier Issues Statement in Recognition of Day of Solidarity with the Cuban People,' News Release no. 123 (Ottawa: Department of Foreign Affairs and International Trade, 21 May 2008).

54  Tu Thanh Ha, 'No Contest in Canada: Kerry by a Landslide,' *Globe and Mail*, 27 July 2004, A3.

55  One Canadian Foreign Affairs official suggested that Harper would face a public backlash if he was perceived as changing Canada's Cuba policy to make friends with the United States. Confidential interview with a senior Canadian official in DFAIT, 31 July 2006.

56  See 'Chronicle on Cuba: January-December 2003' (Ottawa: Canadian Foundation of the Americas, 2003).

57  In 2006 bilateral trade reached the $1-billion mark. For a detailed analysis of Canadian business prospects, see Denis Seguin, 'Viva la evolucion,' *Canadian Business*, 80, no. 4 (12 February 2007): 63–7.

58  See Romina Maurino, 'Canadians Remain Optimistic about Cuba without Castro,' *Calgary Herald*, 3 February 2007, F2. Also, confidential interview with a Canadian official in DFAIT, 31 July 2006.

59  See Deirdre McMurdy, 'Canadian Officials Aim to Thaw Foreign Relations with Winter Trips Abroad,' Ottawa *Citizen*, 18 January 2007, A5.

60  Canada is now Cuba's fourth-largest trading partner. In terms of foreign direct investment in Cuba, Canada ranks at, or near, the top of the list of contributing countries. According to one Canadian official, the Martin government needed to be mindful of the fact that Canada was facing a new commercial competitor – namely, the United States – which is currently Cuba's seventh-largest trading partner and looking to displace Canadian exporters. Confidential interview with a Canadian official in DFAIT, 31 July 2006.

61  Government of Canada, *Trade Data Online* (Ottawa: Industry Canada, 2005). It should be noted that several Canadian companies (of the forty or so that operate there) have experienced some difficulties in getting payment from Cuban state-run enterprises. Reuters, 'Cuba Owes Canadian Oil Firms $69 Million (U.S.),' *Globe and Mail*, 28 December 2006, B5.

62  See Peter McKenna and John M. Kirk, 'Sleeping with an Elephant: The Impact of the United States on Canada-Cuba Relations,' in Morris Morley and Chris McGillion, eds., *Cuba, the United States, and the Post Cold War World: The International Dimensions of the Washington-Havana Relationship* (Gainesville: University Press of Florida, 2005), 148–79.

63  Ibid.

64  For a sampling of these relationships, see Bernie Farber, 'Hava Nagila, Havana,' *Globe and Mail*, 6 January 2007, F8; Laura Wides-Munoz, 'Cuban Exiles Get Gifts Home via Canadian Website,' Halifax *Chronicle-Herald*, 13 December 2006, C7; and Canadian Press, 'Company Offers Rebate for Taking Goods to Cuba,' Montreal *Gazette*, 28 January 2007, A6.

65  See Isabel Vincent, 'How Castro Killed Freedom of Speech,' *National Post*, 9 July 2004, A1.
66  Confidential interviews and e-mail exchanges with Canadian officials in both Ottawa and Washington, July-August 2006.
67  There is a general sense in DFAIT that Ottawa has genuine interests and values that need to be both protected and advanced in Cuba. And the consensus seems to be that the best way of accomplishing this is through dialogue and exchange with Havana and the Cuban people. Confidential correspondence with a senior Canadian official in DFAIT, 31 July 2006. See also Jim Travers, 'Washington Should Resist a Post-Castro Reflex,' Halifax *Chronicle-Herald*, 17 January 2007, A4.

# 8 'Northern Ice': Jean Chrétien and the Failure of Constructive Engagement in Cuba

ROBERT WRIGHT

Canada's Cuba policy in the Castro era is commonly thought to have ranged between the poles of 'constructive engagement' and 'benign neglect.' The former is typically identified with Liberal governments of Pierre Trudeau and especially Jean Chrétien, whose ministers adopted the terms 'constructive engagement' and 'principled pragmatism' to describe their approach to Cuba.[1] Neglect is understood to have characterized the approach of Conservative governments from John Diefenbaker to Steven Harper, the adjective *benign* signifying, importantly, that even the most anti-Castro of Tories have refused to follow the American example and subject Cuba to punitive trade and diplomatic sanctions. In Canada, the distance between these policies is salient, as Diefenbaker indicated when he famously told Pierre Trudeau in the House of Commons, 'During my period of administration we had relations with Cuba and that is right. We traded in non-strategic materials but we did not cuddle up to Castro.'[2]

There is yet another common idea about Canada's relationship with the Castro regime, however, and it stands uneasily in relation to the first. As a Canadian parliamentary backgrounder put it in 1998, 'while they share the goal of the democratization of Cuba, Canada and the United States have long differed over how best to pursue it.'[3] This is a comforting claim, since it not only glosses over policy divisions within both Canada and the United States but posits a common set of core values shared by North America's liberal democracies. Disagreeing about means, according to this view, matters relatively little if Canada and the United States have the same ends in common – even if, from time to time, bilateral irritants like Helms-Burton carry an enormous symbolic weight on both sides of the 49th parallel.

What interests me about these commonly held ideas is not so much what they reveal as what they conceal. Introducing the second report of the Bush administration's Commission for Assistance to a Free Cuba in 2006, Secretary of State Condoleezza Rice told the Cuban people: 'We will stand with you through the process of transformation to a democratic future.'[4] Lloyd Axworthy, the Liberal minister who came to personify Canada's policy of constructive engagement, said in 1998: 'Our engagement is designed to provide Cuba with the assistance and support that will be needed if a peaceful transition is to occur with full respect for human rights, genuinely representative government institutions, and an open economy.'[5] Are these statements so different? Is it possible that the chronic failure of both U.S. and Canadian policies to produce human rights and democratic reforms in Cuba, decade after decade, is in fact derivative of their common view of revolutionary Cuba as a society perched on the cusp of a transformative political and economic overhaul in the Western image?

The purpose of this chapter is to open up some of these questions by revisiting Jean Chrétien's 1998 state visit to Havana, ostensibly a defining moment in Canada's assertion of an 'independent' (read: anti-American) Cuba policy. I want to argue that, despite their superficial differences, what Canadian and American Cuba policies shared in the Chrétien years was the premise that liberal democracies in North America (and elsewhere) *ought* to be prodding the Cubans forcefully in the direction of liberal reforms. It is a premise that affronted the Cuban government in general and Fidel Castro personally, irrespective of whether it was articulated by the 'engaging' Canadians or the 'isolating' Americans. Rightly or wrongly, Cubans do not accept – any more than Canadians or Americans would – the intrusion of foreigners into their domestic affairs, whether this intrusion takes the form of the iron fist or the velvet glove. This refusal explains why the Chrétien state visit was an almost unprecedented diplomatic disaster in the history of Canada's relations with revolutionary Cuba.

## Constructive Engagement

Jean Chrétien's political mentor, Pierre Trudeau, terminated Canadian International Development Agency (CIDA) aid to Cuba in 1978 as a gesture of protest against Castro's intervention in various African hot spots, Angola foremost among them. Brian Mulroney did nothing to reverse this prohibition, nor to mitigate the frosty attitude that lay behind it. Thus, when Chrétien became prime minister, in October 1993, he faced a stark choice. He could maintain the status quo and continue fifteen years of 'benign neglect,' or he could return to the 'engagement' policy of his mentor. He opted for the latter.

It must have seemed a low-risk choice. By 1993, little remained of the original rationale for the diplomatic isolation of Cuba. Castro had removed his troops from Angola in 1991, for one thing. For another, Cuba's Cold War alliance with the communist bloc had collapsed along with the Berlin Wall and later the Soviet Union itself, deflating much of the anxiety many North Americans had harboured about the presence of communism in the western hemisphere. In 1991 Castro introduced his *Período especial en tiempo de paz*, signalling not only that Cuba's economy was in shambles but that the island was almost completely isolated and no longer any threat to NATO or anyone else. The main issue weighing on Chrétien's decision to engage with Cuba, human rights, was a comparatively new one, the product of the 'human rights revolution' that President Jimmy Carter and others had pioneered in the late 1970s.[6] The prime minister thus calculated that a pragmatic re-engagement with Cuba along lines similar to Pierre Trudeau's policy would carry limited political liability if it was paired with a strong, explicit Canadian objection to Cuban human rights abuses. The upside of such a strategy, of course, was the potential trade advantage to Canada – a concern never far from Jean Chrétien's thoughts about Canadian diplomacy. As James Bartleman, Canada's ambassador to Cuba in the early 1980s and Chrétien's special envoy to Cuba in the 1990s, later put it, the Liberal government 'hoped that closer ties would prepare the ground for Canadian companies to take advantage of the trade and investment opportunities certain to follow when Cuba eventually adopted a market economy.'[7]

In March 1994 Chrétien's foreign minister, André Ouellet, put in motion the policy that would come to be known as constructive engagement. He instructed Canada's diplomats to take 'a more positive position in the development of relations with Cuba,' which meant increasing high-level exchanges between the two countries and publicly criticizing the U.S. embargo, on the one hand, as well as beefing up Canada's criticism of Cuban human rights abuses via the United Nations, on the other.[8] Four months later, Secretary of State Christine Stewart told a meeting of the Organization of American States (OAS) that Canada desired 'positive and orderly change in Cuba,' after which she visited Havana and announced that the Canadian development assistance to the island that Pierre Trudeau had terminated would be reinstated.[9] Cuban Foreign Minister Roberto Robaina visited Canada in 1995. The same year, the speaker of the House of Commons, Gilbert Parent, visited Havana, followed by various Canadian bankers and trade officials.

Characteristically, Jean Chrétien's decision to re-engage with Cuba was taken with one eye on Washington and, in particular, on President Bill Clinton's announcement in 1995 that his administration would begin taking 'calibrated steps' towards the establishment of full diplomatic relations with Cuba.[10] But there was also a second, unprecedented 'opening to Cuba' in the air in the mid-1990s, one that would colour the Liberals' re-engagement strategy at virtually every turn. It was the sensational news, first announced in early November 1996, that Pope John Paul II would visit Havana, conduct an open-air Mass, and press for church-related reforms on the island (including freedoms for Catholic schools, charities, and media outlets, and compensation for nationalized church property).[11] The pope's own 'Cuba policy' was widely seen as a variation on constructive engagement. John Paul had played a crucial role in challenging the hegemony of the Soviets in Eastern Europe in the 1980s, and he made no secret of his willingness to use his own charismatic leadership and moral authority to challenge Fidel Castro's.[12] It was no accident that Chrétien, devout Catholic that he is, timed his visit to follow the pontiff's by mere months. More significant still was the influence of Vatican planning, for the pope announced his plan to visit Cuba after the Brothers to the Rescue incident had soured Bill Clinton on dialogue with the Castro regime.[13]

Fidel Castro first met Jean Chrétien in New York in October 1995, during the UN's fiftieth-anniversary celebrations. It was there that *El Comandante* first invited the Canadian prime minister to Cuba. The invitation was reissued the following spring, when the president of the Cuban National Assembly, Ricardo Alarcón, met with Chrétien in Ottawa. The prime minister expressed interest in meeting with President Castro – no doubt reckoning that it would to some extent evoke the glory days of Pierre Trudeau's historic state visit – but he was also blunt in expressing his hopes for radical political change in Cuba. He told a nonplussed Alarcón that 'Canada looked forward to the day when there would be an end to human rights abuses and the installation of democracy in Cuba.'[14]

In August 1996 President Clinton announced the appointment of a special envoy to consult with U.S. allies on the future of Cuba. The same month, Chrétien despatched James Bartleman secretly to Havana to enquire 'if Castro would be willing to deepen Cuba's relations with Canada and begin a dialogue on market and democratic reforms and human rights.'[15] Bartleman discussed the matter privately with the Comandante, presenting him with a fourteen-point *bout de papier* that listed 'possible areas for future collaboration' with Canada, including human rights. (This draft document would, in fact, form the basis of the 1997 *Joint Declaration of the Ministers of Foreign Affairs of Canada and Cuba* [CCJD] signed by Lloyd Axworthy.) Bartleman's message to Fidel Castro was that 'the world had changed and that countries that did not open their borders to the free flow of people, ideas, and trade would become marginalized.'[16] Chrétien agreed. When Cuban Vice-President Carlos Lage ventured to Ottawa several weeks later to convey Castro's willingness to open a new dialogue on the basis of the fourteen-point plan, the prime minister told him point blank that 'he would like to see the people of Cuba elect their leaders as was done in Canada.'[17] Bartleman later credited the prime minister with being even more aggressive on human rights with Lage than he had himself been with Castro: 'Lage made no comment but might have wondered whether Canada's aim was to help Castro adapt to globalization or to ease him out of office.'[18] The Comandante would later draw the same conclusion.

When Pierre Trudeau had gone to Cuba in 1976, in the midst of the Cold War, his main goals were to drum up trade and promote détente. He went to Havana fully expecting to 'agree to disagree' with Field Castro and thus imposed few diplomatic preconditions on the visit. Not so Jean Chrétien. The political climate had changed dramatically since the 1970s, and both Chrétien and his critics knew it. The prime minister was not about to risk his own political capital in a photo-op visit to Havana that Fidel Castro could manipulate to his own advantage. Chrétien wanted assurances from the Cubans that any high-level exchange with his government would produce concrete results; and the Cubans understood that, without such assurances, the Canadian prime minister might well retract the offer to establish a new dialogue.

As part of this subtle diplomatic dance, the Cubans agreed to host a visit by the Canadian commissioner of human rights, Maxwell Yalden, in November 1996. Yalden was, from Ottawa's perspective, the canary in the Cuban coal mine. His mission was to draw the revolutionary government into a 'structured dialogue on human rights.'[19] To achieve this improbable goal, he carried with him to Havana both carrots and sticks. 'A joint consultative mechanism' on human rights, Yalden reportedly told Foreign Minister Robaina, 'was a key element of any plan for a joint Canada-Cuba assistance plan.'[20] In the end, although Yalden was 'impressed' by the Cubans' willingness to exchange ideas about what such a mechanism might look like, he was forced to concede that 'it was difficult to engage in dialogue with Cuba about a problem it didn't even recognize existed.'[21]

When it became clear that the Cubans were reluctant to commit to concrete reforms as a pre-condition of a high-level visit, Chrétien's advisers urged him to maintain the dialogue but not to go to Havana himself. James Bartleman was one of the voices counselling caution. The Cubans had proved willing to pursue various memoranda of understanding, he later recalled, but they had 'stalled' on human rights reforms. Bartleman would later write about Cuban intransigence with a jaded eye: 'They were happy enough to attend seminars in Canada as long as Canada paid their expenses, and were, when pushed, willing to accord a limited freedom of action on non-governmental organizations in Cuba. There was, however, no meeting of minds. The Cubans repeated the Cold War communist double-talk that the Party reflected the will of the people, and that democratic elections and liberties in the developed world were but smokescreens for the interests of capitalists.'[22] Chrétien took note, and decided the time was not right for a prime ministerial visit. Thus, it was Lloyd Axworthy who ended up going to Havana, in January 1997.

### Axworthy in Havana

Lloyd Axworthy's visit to Cuba was the first by a Canadian foreign affairs minister since Fidel Castro took power in 1959. According to one recent study of constructive engagement, 'Axworthy hoped to reform the Cuban economic and political institutions and to train young technocrats to prepare the country for the possible transition to democracy.'[23] But this is not how it appeared when he went to Havana. Axworthy would engage the Cubans – and Fidel Castro personally – with the diplomacy of the grand gesture, which meant, among other things, taking pains not to affront them publicly the way Jean Chrétien had done in private. His visit would warm up the Cuban-Canadian dialogue, as intended, but it would also undercut the diplomatic advantage Canada had enjoyed in quietly pressing for concrete political reforms from the Cubans. Henceforth, the caution with which the diplomats and the Prime Minister's Office (PMO) had ventured into the new dialogue would count for very little, as would Jean Chrétien's repeated insistence that engagement with Cuba be paired with tough language on human rights. In the subtle dance of Canadian-Cuban dialogue, the Cubans would now lead.

Lloyd Axworthy and Jean Chrétien personified two competing strains in the Liberal foreign policy tradition, both of which, oddly enough, were characterized by their conservative critics as 'Trudeauite.'[24] For the pragmatic Chrétien, who personally led seven so-called Team Canada missions abroad between 1994 and 2002, the main emphasis was always trade. Axworthy, on the other hand, drew far more heavily on Pearsonian internationalism, hoping, as he later put it in his book *Navigating a New World,* that Canada might 'take a special kind of leadership in helping manage a world dominated by the power and influence of our continental neighbour.'[25] Yet, as William Christian observed in 1998, the two emphases were never entirely at cross-purposes: 'Anything Axworthy does has to be seen as nestled into the context of Chrétien's primary focus and drive in foreign policy, which is to expand Canadian trade. Axworthy has a more moralistic and humanitarian agenda than Chrétien has. He can exercise it in minor ways that don't contradict the main thrust.'[26] Although both men expressed the hope that Cuba would improve its human rights record and move towards Western-styled democracy, they agreed that good trade relations with the island should not be contingent on such reforms. (Bill Clinton made the same case for China when he extended it most-favoured-nation status and explicitly 'delinked' human rights from trade.)[27] The day before Axworthy left for Havana, the CBC's Julie Van Dusen asked him, 'Do you plan to link trade with human rights?' He replied, 'No, I think what we want to do is to have a good, continuing engaged dialogue with the Cuban government, based upon mutual interest.'[28]

Axworthy spent two days in Havana, and much of this time in the private company of Fidel Castro. Like Trudeau before him, Axworthy made no secret of his admiration for the Cuban leader. Appearing at the Canadian ambassador's residence unexpectedly for lunch on the second day of the visit, Castro chatted with Axworthy for so long that he had to cancel a scheduled public appearance. Castro's long-winded talk, which ranged from gardening to Canadian politics, was a 'tour de force,' Axworthy later said. The Comandante had even cracked some jokes.[29] Meeting the Canadian press outside the ambassador's residence after their meeting, Castro was obviously pleased. 'Canada has a lot of prestige,' he said. 'What it says and what it thinks has great meaning for us.'[30] When asked whether Axworthy had broached the subject of human rights with him, Castro replied, 'We spoke of everything. Among friends you can speak of everything.'[31]

The big story coming out of Axworthy's Havana trip was the publication, finally, of the fourteen-point Joint Declaration that had been under discussion for months. Axworthy knew beforehand that the Cubans had agreed to sign off on the document, which helps to account for his confident, amicable rapport with Castro. By the terms of this communiqué, Canada and Cuba pledged collaboration in six key areas of political reform in Cuba, including exchanges of judges and parliamentarians, cooperation on strengthening a Cuban citizens' complaints commission, discussion of human rights, and support for the work of Canadian and Cuban non-governmental organizations (NGOs). Less contentious items in the CCJD included cooperation in the areas of economic policy, banking, foreign investment, narcotics interdiction, the prevention of international terrorism, health matters, and various cultural, athletic, and academic undertakings. What Axworthy could not know at the time, of course, and what continued to worry Prime Minister Chrétien and his advisers, was whether the Cubans would take concrete steps to honour the accord. The ink had not dried on the Joint Declaration before its North American critics were calling it vague and even naive. They noted in particular that, rather than holding the Cubans to specific goals or timetables, it promised only 'regular reviews.'

Prior to his departure for Havana, Axworthy had taken pains to place his historic visit in the context of Canada's long-standing bilateral relationship with Cuba. Taking a page from the Trudeau oeuvre, he had said: 'We look forward to this meeting to discuss areas of trade, investment, governance, rights – all of the matters we have discussed in the past. That doesn't mean to say we will always share universally all opinions. But as long as we are prepared to dialogue with a sense of respect and openness and frankness, that's the best way to conduct matters between countries.'[32] Even in the immediate aftermath of the visit, Axworthy acknowledged that the CCJD was meant only as 'an opening' to ongoing discussions about reform in Cuba.[33] 'It's a good beginning,' he said. 'It's a start. It's a work in progress. We've had in the last 24 hours very broad, very open very frank discussions with ministers, President Castro and others. The dialogue has been very important.'[34] But before long, like Trudeau before him, Axworthy let his enthusiasms get the better of him. Just a week after he had returned from Havana, he boasted that he had made more headway with Castro in five hours than the Americans 'have accomplished in the last 30 years.'[35]

These were, of course, fighting words. The Cuban-American community, which had protested the Axworthy visit with a billboard campaign urging Canadian tourists to boycott Cuba, was incensed. In Washington, there was talk of the Canadian foreign minister having deliberately provoked the Clinton White House. Said State Department spokesperson Nicholas Burns: 'It doesn't make sense to reward a dictator in our own hemisphere who's completely behind the times. You [Canadians] reward him by sending your foreign minister down to visit, by having business as usual, by trading, and we think that's wrong.'[36] (When Burns got a laudatory call from Senator Jesse Helms, he realized that he had overstated his case, contacting the Canadian embassy in Washington to soften his remarks.) Not surprisingly, Helms himself – co-author of the 1996 Cuban Liberty and Democratic Solidarity (*Libertad*) Act – was Axworthy's harshest critic. He publicly compared Axworthy's visit with British prime minister Neville Chamberlain's appeasement of Adolf Hitler prior to the Second World War. For his part, President Clinton kept to the middle ground. He said he was gratified that Axworthy had discussed human rights and domestic reforms with the Cubans. But he added: 'I'm skeptical, frankly, that ... the recent discussions between the Canadians and the Cubans will lead to advances. I believe that our policy is the proper one, but I'm glad that the Canadians are trying to make something good happen in Cuba.'[37]

In Canada, elite opinion polarized along predictable lines. Historian Michael Bliss wrote that Axworthy's 'apparent adulation of Castro is shameful. Canadians get cheap vacations, but Cubans are no more free. It's just more hypocrisy on our part.'[38] At least one veteran Canadian diplomat disagreed. 'It was,' said Gordon Ritchie of Axworthy's visit, 'a most impressive performance.'[39] (Ritchie added: 'The American stance has never been about noble principle. It is about corrupt congressional politics, wealthy Cuban expatriates, a rich and powerful sugar lobby and a rich and powerful tobacco lobby.') Asked to comment on American criticisms of the Axworthy visit, Jean Chrétien observed that the United States had only itself to blame for Castro's iron-fisted grip on power. 'Let them normalize the situation between Cuba and the United States,' said the prime minister, 'and I don't think that Mr. Castro will have it easier.'[40] Chrétien also praised the Joint Declaration. 'The accord we signed with Cuba yesterday means there will be an ombudsman for Cuba's national assembly and a dialogue between Canada and Cuba on human rights,' he said. 'This is considerable progress.'[41]

Axworthy's public posturing was risky, something he learned even before he left Havana. Cuban officials arrested three high-profile dissidents (journalists Tania Quintero and Juan Antonio Sanchez, and Marta Beatriz Roque, director of the Association of Independent Economists) just hours after Axworthy's talks with Fidel Castro, apparently because they had been trying to circulate independent analyses of the Cuban economy. Axworthy pressed the Cuban government on their detainment, taking credit for their release after only several hours in custody. 'We took the opportunity to make that case and were given assurances that they had been released,' he told the press while he was still in Cuba.[42] More ominous for constructive engagement, however, was Roberto Robaina's blunt appraisal of Canada's ability to influence the regime's policies on dissidents. 'We are not a case for Canada to check,' he said during the press conference to announce the CCJD. 'Canada is not for us a teacher that gives us orders or certifies or decertifies us.'[43]

Whether the Joint Declaration produced any short-term benefits for Cuban dissidents and other victims of human rights abuses is doubtful. As Yvon Grenier noted in his stinging 2000 critique of Canada's Cuba policy, 'Our Dictatorship,' Ottawa took credit for the release of Ismael Sambra and twelve other dissidents in 1997 and 1998; but Sambra himself credited PEN Canada for his release and, in any case, the others were nearing the end of their sentences.[44] In its 1997 annual report on Cuba, Human Rights Watch acknowledged that 'Canada's role as a leading foreign investor in Cuba provided it with important leverage for pressuring Cuba to make genuine human rights reforms during 1997.' But the same report criticized the Joint Declaration for its failure to provide a 'concrete agenda for improvements in Cuban human rights practices.' It then concluded: 'Unfortunately, the Cuban government, which detained several dissidents during the negotiations, showed little sign of taking the accord seriously.'[45] To judge from Human Rights Watch's description of Cuba's persecution of dissidents in 1997, the apparatus of state repression barely paused during the Axworthy visit.

When Pope John Paul II visited Cuba for five days in late January 1998, he engaged in much the same diplomatic dance with Fidel Castro as the Canadians had. In a scene that foreshadowed the Chrétien visit four months later, Castro welcomed the pontiff at José Martí airport with a vitriolic speech attacking what he called the U.S. 'genocide' against Cuba. ('It was an ambush,' a Vatican official later told *Newsweek*.)[46] The pope reacted graciously. He kept to prepared texts for the twelve speeches he gave on the island, emphasizing that his mission on behalf of the church was spiritual rather than political. Even so, the pontiff's visit to Cuba represented a watershed in the extension of basic freedoms for the Cuban people, especially concerning matters of faith. According to Human Rights Watch, 'the pope's calls for freedom of religion, conscience, and expression and the release of political prisoners created an unprecedented air of openness.'[47]

In response to John Paul II's call for an amnesty – a request made indirectly through his secretary of state, which impressed Fidel Castro – the Cubans claimed to have released 299 prisoners. Of these, roughly one hundred were 'politicals.' Nineteen were released on condition that they exile themselves to Canada, and ultimately fourteen did so. A February 1998 press release from the PMO announced that Canada was happy to welcome these 'prisoners of conscience.' Prime Minister Chrétien was quoted as saying: 'The decision to release these prisoners demonstrates the benefits of a policy of constructive engagement with Cuba on a broad range of issues, including sensitive political ones.'[48] Once the exiles had landed in Toronto, Sarah DeCosse of Human Rights Watch flew up from Washington to interview them. They informed her that conditions in Cuba's prisons had deteriorated recently, noting that some prisoners were now being kept in solitary confinement for up to five years. DeCosse told *Maclean's* magazine that Canada was doing too little to press the Cuban authorities on their treatment of dissidents. 'As a leading foreign investor in Cuba,' she said, 'Canada really could exercise more leverage.'[49] Her detailed findings were published the following year as *Cuba's Repressive Machinery: Human Rights Forty Years after the Revolution.*[50]

According to James Bartleman, who visited the Vatican in the wake of the pope's visit, Rome feared that Cuban dissidents would face a crackdown when Cuba was once again out of the international spotlight. It therefore urged the Canadian prime minister to visit Havana as a means of forestalling this possibility. And indeed, in the aftermath of the papal tour, according to Human Rights Watch, 'Cuba's stepped-up prosecutions and harassment of dissidents, along with its refusal to grant amnesty to hundreds of remaining political prisoners or reform its criminal code, marked a disheartening return to heavy-handed repression.'[51]

Bartleman returned to Havana in February 1998 to resume negotiating the terms of a possible prime ministerial visit. He recalled Fidel Castro being in a 'foul mood' when they met, because he had not appreciated the Canadians' insistence that that there would be conditions before Chrétien would agree to see him. 'I'm tired of visitors that come asking the impossible,' Castro said. 'They are no better than the foolish Don Quixote.'[52] Bartleman pressed Castro to release more high-profile prisoners and to sign the UN Covenant on Economic, Social and Cultural Rights. But ultimately, at the end of an all-night visit with the Comandante in his private residence, Castro told Bartleman that he was not prepared to make any such concessions in advance of a visit by the prime minister. 'Don't ask Cuba to do anything that would damage it,' Castro said, 'and Cuba will not ask Canada to do anything that would embarrass it.'[53] According to Bartleman, this news discouraged Chrétien but did not cool his interest in visiting Cuba. 'Following the submission of my report on returning to Ottawa,' Bartleman later wrote, 'the prime minister decided to proceed with a working visit on April 27 and 28. In so doing, he hoped to reinforce Canada's policy of constructive engagement, in particular our desire to advance the cause of human rights. He was by now under no illusion that Castro wanted our help to ease the transition of his country to a market economy or was really interested in lessening Cuba's isolation in the hemisphere at the cost of loosening his totalitarian control.'[54]

Seen in retrospect, Chrétien's decision to visit an intransigent Castro was a decisive fork in the road for his Cuba policy. Like Roberto Robaina and Carlos Lage before him, Fidel Castro had sent a clear message to the prime minister that he would brook no outside interference in Cuba's domestic affairs. He was plainly not interested in being engaged constructively.

### Chrétien in Havana

Word of Jean Chrétien's plan to visit Cuba leaked while he was at the Summit of the Americas conference in Santiago, Chile, on 19 April 1998. (Canadian officials later said that it was the American delegation who leaked the story.) The two-day conference – at which every country in the western hemisphere but Cuba was represented – was designed to promote free trade. But, according to one observer, when word of Chrétien's imminent visit to Cuba leaked, the matter of how best to deal with Castro in hemispheric relations 'eclipsed' all others.[55] Some leaders used the news as a pretext to openly criticize U.S. policy on Cuba; others suggested that it was yet another signal that Cuba's isolation in the hemisphere was ending. 'Everybody's going to Cuba, and it's good for inter-American relations,' said a spokesperson for Mexican president Ernesto Zedillo.[56] When asked how word of his plan to visit Cuba was received at the summit, Chrétien replied: 'Most of the leaders who learned about it talked to me very positively about this decision. They all said it was a good thing.'[57] Chrétien was cagey about whether his visit meant that he would be inviting Fidel Castro to the next Summit of the Americas, to be held in Canada two and a half years hence. 'To invite someone new,' he said, 'you have to have a consensus that does not exist right now.'[58] These words would prove to be prescient.

Two days after the leak, the PMO issued a short statement announcing the upcoming Chrétien visit. In addition to talks with Fidel Castro, it said, the prime minister would be meeting with representatives of the Catholic Church as well as members of Cuban NGOs. 'Canada has long practiced a policy of constructive engagement with Cuba,' the prime minister was quoted as saying. 'We believe the best way to promote our values is through dialogue, not isolation.'[59] Lloyd Axworthy went even further, suggesting that Canada might play a role in reuniting Cuba and the United States. President Clinton, said Axworthy, was trying to build new bridges to Cuba. 'Frankly, the Prime Minister's visit is in a very crucial timing to help build that bridge. I think it really can provide a significant step because we have good relations with the United States.'[60] Much was made in the press of Chrétien's apparent willingness to ruffle American feathers, but at least one perceptive observer acknowledged that it was in Washington's interests to have a trusted friend at Castro's dinner table. 'If anything it's good for the United States to have a close ally who the United States can consult with to go and talk with Castro,' said Philip Brenner of American University, 'to get a first hand sense is this man still healthy, is he still lucid, what is his agenda?'[61]

In the days leading up to the trip, Canadian officials adopted a guarded tone with the national media. More than one journalist noted, for example, that Chrétien's aides would not state explicitly what would have to happen during the visit to deem it a success. In stark contrast with Trudeau's 1976 visit – which was cited in just about every news report leading up to Chrétien's trip – they made it clear that the prime minister would not be speaking at any public rallies in Cuba. The phrase 'working visit' was deployed repeatedly, implying that diplomatic pomp would be kept to a minimum. There would be no 'Viva el Primer Ministro Fidel Castro!' from Jean Chrétien! The prime minister was keenly aware of the need to raise human rights with Fidel Castro. 'Of course we will raise the question of human rights and political rights,' the prime minister said before his departure.[62] His 'background briefing book' mentioned explicitly that 360 political prisoners were incarcerated in Cuba.[63] Yet his aides gave not so much as a hint that the prime minister might raise specific dissidents' cases with Castro, despite the fact that some Canadian activist groups had been vocal in urging him to do so.

Like many Canadians of his vintage, Chrétien harboured sentimental feelings for Castro, and they influenced his decision to go to Havana. He told reporters that he had been enamoured of Castro in the 1950s. 'He was a very popular person, a young man taking on the Batista regime,' said Chrétien. 'He had been in jail, he had risked his life, he wanted to change society. At that time, I was fighting the Duplessis regime, so, as a student, he was a star for a lot of us.'[64] Chrétien elaborated on his and Castro's contrasting political philosophies: 'He still wants to use communism. I don't believe in it, it's been proven it doesn't work … I'm a practical politician – that doesn't mean I don't have goals, that I don't want to have social justice. I'm just not doctrinaire on the means. My view is we have to have growth in the world so there will be more money for governments to give to people who are suffering in society. I'm not in politics to make the rich richer. Castro wants the same thing. He has a different technique.'[65]

The prime minister arrived in Havana on the evening of Sunday, 26 April, 1998. His itinerary began with the inauguration of the new Terminal Three at Havana's José Martí airport, a facility whose air-traffic infrastructure was designed by the Ottawa firm Intelcan Technosystems and whose construction was underwritten by a $40-million loan from the Canadian Export Development Corporation. Cuban media were on hand to televise both leaders' remarks at the ceremony, and thus, as he had done during the pope's visit, Fidel Castro used the occasion to blast the United States. 'No state should pretend to have the right to starve another people to death,' he said, 'or let it die from diseases. That is genocide. That is turning a nation into a ghetto and imposing on it a new version of the Holocaust; it's like using biological, chemical or nuclear weapons. Those who do such things should be taken before an international court of law to stand trial as war criminals.'[66] In the same speech the Comandante also dismissed international criticism of

Cuba's human rights record. 'Let's do away with the infamous manipulations and slanders against Cuba by the hegemonic power on the [UN] Human Rights Commission. The heroic people of Cuba have been, in this century, an unblemished example in the struggle for man's dignity within, and outside, our homeland.'[67]

Jean Chrétien would later be pilloried in the press for not so much as flinching at his host's vitriol. The prime minister later said of Castro's remarks: 'I was not very happy because the words were too strong. I told him that. It was a very tough speech. But I wasn't warned that he would use the occasion to make what, for Cuba, is a normal speech.'[68] Instead, Chrétien kept to the standard diplomatic script and gave a measured speech. He emphasized Canada's commitment to 'a more dynamic, more democratic, more prosperous hemisphere, and to achieving 'greater social, economic, and political justice throughout the region.'[69] Chrétien later said of his own remarks: 'I was satisfied that I was raising all the points I wanted to raise. What was important was to tell everybody there that change is coming and you'll have to adjust. He was in the past. I was in the present and the future.'[70] But he and his entourage knew that Castro had put him on the ropes, and that they now had to counterpunch with something equally forceful. Later that evening, a Canadian official announced that Chrétien would appeal directly to Castro for the release of four Cuban dissidents – Vladimiro Roca, Martha Beatriz Roque, Felix Bonne, and Rene Gomez Manzano – all of whom had been imprisoned without charge in July 1997 for belonging to the Internal Dissidence Working Group. 'We are making a general plea for the release of all political prisoners,' the official told the press, 'and we're specifically asking for those four to be freed.'[71]

Jean Chrétien and Fidel Castro spent their first morning together in formal talks at the Plaza of the Revolution. In contrast with Pierre Trudeau's high-profile state visit in 1976, Castro's stage-management of the Chrétien visit was almost unremarkable. There were no crowds at Revolution Square to greet the Canadian prime minister. One twenty-three-year-old Cuban woman told Reuters that people were not aware of the visit. 'I didn't know anything about the visit of the Canadian president,' she said. 'My television is broken. Even if the television had been working, I wouldn't have seen it, because speeches bore me.'[72]

During the official talks, Chrétien went on the offensive. At one point, he stopped Castro mid-sentence to discuss the Joint Declaration, and to ask specifically whether the new Civilian Complaints Commission could include human rights complaints among its other responsibilities. Then came the showstopper. Chrétien thrust a card with the names of the four dissidents in front of Castro and asked that they be released from prison. 'You're getting to the toughest issues first,' Chrétien later recalled Castro saying.[73] James Bartleman's recollection of Castro's reaction was even more pointed: 'I have never been so humiliated,' he said in a barely audible voice. He would have walked out the door, I believe, had he not been in his own office. The dialogue never recovered, although the leaders remained at the table for two hours and fifteen minutes. The president had been prepared to release three low-level prisoners as a sort of human gift but the prime minister had just raised the stakes. It was at this point that Castro probably decided that the policy of constructive engagement with Canada had reached the limits of its usefulness. The Canadians were taking human rights far too seriously.'[74]

Chrétien was later asked exactly what had happened when he presented Castro with the list. He replied: 'It was tough, the first 20 minutes. He was shocked. He does not accept the words "political prisoners." He says: "They are prisoners. Don't you have prisoners in Canada?" I had to say yes. But how many are political prisoners? He said they are condemned under the laws of the country. I said: "Yeah, but I have a good case on some of them because they have not been tried." He said: "Have you never had somebody in jail in Canada who has not had a trial for six months?" And I know that we have that once in a while. He told me the Pope gave him a list [of political prisoners] and a lot of the people on that list were not in jail any more and some were dead.'[75] Once word got out that Chrétien had asked Castro to release the dissidents, the state visit captured the attention of Cubans and Americans. Elena Roque, sister of the imprisoned Marta Beatriz Roque, tearfully told an American reporter: 'I have faith in God that this petition will be heard. We will be waiting anxiously for news.'[76]

After the morning meeting, the prime minister had lunch with Cardinal Jaime Lucas Ortega y Alamino, where he discussed some of the reforms the pope had sponsored. James Bartleman and Chrétien aide Michael Kergin spent the afternoon in meetings with Cuban human rights activists, including Elizardo Sanchez. Chrétien and Castro reunited Monday evening for what was scheduled to be a two-hour 'working dinner' at the Palace of the Revolution but turned into a four-and-a-half-hour affair that ended only in the early hours of Tuesday morning. Canadian officials later described the dinner conversation as 'freewheeling,' taking in environmental concerns, world affairs, globalization, and the situation of Canada's Native people. Said one Canadian official: 'Castro was very much interested in picking the PM's brains about the world that was out there that Cuba is not a part of.'[77]

Tuesday morning the prime minister met with representatives of three Cuban NGOs – the church-based charity organization Caritas, the cultural organization Feliz Varela Centre, and the Martin Luther King Centre, a community housing organization. Officials of Oxfam Canada also attended the meetings. Tuesday afternoon, Chrétien did a walking tour of Old Havana with his wife, Aline, and attended a reception at the home of Canadian ambassador Keith Christie. Chrétien and Castro signed bilateral agreements respecting health-care delivery, audio-visual co-productions, and athletic exchanges. They opened negotiations on a Foreign Investment Protection and Promotion Agreement (FIPA), designed to promote foreign investment. They also signed an agreement in principle resolving Confederation Life's long-standing claim against the Cuban government for nationalizing its Cuban assets at the beginning of the Revolution. Fidel Castro was in good spirits when he bade farewell to the Chrétiens later that afternoon, evidence that the tensions of the formal talks had been at least partly attenuated by the amicable atmosphere of the working dinner. Yet, as James Bartleman observed, 'the good will between the leaders stimulated by the vigorous, candid, and friendly discussions of the previous evening did not disguise the fact that the Canadian initiative to engage Cuba in a policy of constructive engagement had gone as far as it could, at least as long as Castro was alive.'[78]

## 'Northern Ice'

Most Canadian pundits who had been following Chrétien's visit pronounced it entirely predictable, with no diplomatic breakthrough expected and none achieved. 'Jean Chrétien came and went,' wrote Paul Knox of the *Globe and Mail*, 'and Fidel Castro stood firm.'[79] Asked whether he had really expected the Cuban leader to change or whether 'we are merely laying the groundwork for a post-Castro future,' Chrétien replied: 'I think he is changing. The fact that my [airport] speech was on the air is a big change; the fact that I met the Cardinal in public. But if people naively thought I would go there and train the leader of the opposition, it was too high an expectation. One step at a time.'[80] Fidel Castro was asked whether he intended to modify his policies in light of Chrétien's appeals for change. 'The Revolution is the biggest change in history,' he responded, 'and we aren't going to give it up.' When asked for his thoughts on Chrétien's request that he free four jailed dissidents, Castro replied coolly, 'What he and I talked about is between him and me.'[81]

The prime minister had never made a secret of his jaded view of Cuban-American politics in the United States. Interviewed on CNN the day after his return from Havana, an unusually feisty Jean Chrétien asserted that the embargo was having no positive effect in advancing political reform in Cuba, and it was plainly hurting the Cuban people. 'I am told that the dentists do not have the proper anesthesia to serve the people,' he exclaimed. 'Come on!' The prime minister's advice for Washington was to take the high road. 'When you are that powerful, that is the time to be benevolent, to be nice, not to show your muscle.'[82] Asked whether he would be inviting Fidel Castro to the next Summit of the Americas meeting in Canada, he said he did not yet know and would prefer to wait and see whether the regime made any advances on political reforms.

Predictably, some of Chrétien's strongest American critics went after him. Writing in the *Harvard International Review,* New Jersey Democrat and Cuban American Robert Menendez said: 'Chrétien's visit was something of an embarrassment for Canada. Castro's refusal to discuss human rights refuted Canada's claim that it could successfully press for change in Cuba by engaging Castro. Canada is now faced with a choice: either it must abandon its efforts to press for reforms in Cuba or it must tie future efforts to Canadian economic interests in Cuba. This incident has proven that so long as Castro can dictate the terms of engagement, engagement alone will not lead to change in Cuba.'[83]

Menendez turned out to be correct. On 15 March 1999 a closed Cuban court tried the four dissidents that Chrétien had appealed to Fidel Castro to free. All four were found guilty of sedition and sentenced to jail terms ranging from three and a half to five years. For the prime minister, the convictions came as a blunt acknowledgment that his interventions had had no impact on Fidel Castro. Whatever the Cuban leader thought he could accomplish by cracking down on internal dissent, he had no qualms about risking the good opinion of Canadians in the process. Chrétien moved immediately to take what was, by diplomatic standards at least, strong action. The day the dissidents were sentenced he ordered a review of Canada's relations with Cuba. 'Cuba sends an unfortunate signal to her friends in the international community when people are jailed for peaceful protest,' the prime minister said in a press release.[84] He cancelled ministerial visits already on the books and postponed a trip to Cuba by a Canadian trade delegation. He froze talks with Cuba to set up a joint medical program in Haiti (which Fidel Castro later said punished only Haitians). Perhaps most symbolically of all, he terminated a Canadian plan to provide computer technology to help modernize Cuba's courts, his aides later stating that it would not be appropriate for Canada to collaborate with the regime's repressive legal apparatus.[85] On 30 June, a plainly frustrated Chrétien told reporters that, although he was not prepared to abandon constructive engagement, 'we have to put some northern ice in the middle of it.'[86]

The prime minister's luck worsened. On 24 July 1999 Human Rights Watch published the scathing book-length report by Sarah DeCosse, *Cuba's Repressive Machinery*. It called Canada's policy of constructive engagement a failure, Jean Chrétien's approach to Cuba 'meek,' and his state visit the previous year 'a wasted opportunity to build on the momentum ... begun by the Pope.'[87] Two days later, on 26 July – the most important date on the Cuban patriotic calendar – Fidel Castro gave a four-hour speech in Cienfuegos in which he included Canada in his harangues against the United States. The Cuban leader accused both the United States and Canada of deliberately manoeuvring against Cuba during the Pan American Games in Winnipeg, and he singled out the local *Sun* newspaper for urging Cuban athletes to defect. 'We have never seen so many tricks, so much filth,' said Castro, 'in the Pan American Games.'[88] Canadian Citizenship and Immigration officials acknowledged in a brief press release that three athletes had indeed sought refugee status, but they were not identified by name or even by country. Rumours circulated in Winnipeg that Castro's main objection to the games was the presence of opportunistic sports agents on the lookout for new professional talent, especially among Cuban baseball players.

Castro's and Chrétien's increasingly icy exchanges in the two years after the state visit did not prevent them from meeting privately in Montreal in October 2000 after the funeral of Pierre Trudeau, nor from sharing amicably their memories of the late prime minister. But, as most observers had long expected, the moment of truth for Chrétien's Cuba policy arrived the following year, when a decision had to be made on whether to include Cuba at the Summit of the Americas conference in Quebec. By this time, Lloyd Axworthy had been replaced as foreign affairs minister by John Manley, a man with little invested in constructive engagement and for whom the restoration of good Canadian-American relations was a top priority. To the surprise of no one, Manley announced that Cuba would remain outside the inter-American family because of its 'lack of commitment to democratic principles.' Jean Chrétien fell in behind this decision, telling the press that he had spent 'hours and hours' trying to persuade an intransigent Fidel Castro to abide by international human rights covenants.[89]

Fidel Castro then did something most extraordinary. Infuriated by the suggestion that he had allowed the Canadian prime minister to browbeat him for 'hours and hours,' he went on Cuban television on 25 April 2001 and described in minute detail what, exactly, he and Jean Chrétien had discussed during the 1998 state visit. (The 5,500-word text of his remarks was reprinted in *Granma* the next day.) He began by noting that he was not especially surprised when Chrétien placed the dissidents' names in front of him, since this had become 'a tactic consistently used by the U.S. government to apply pressure in favor of its friends, taking advantage of any friendly visit to Cuba.' After reminding the Canadian prime minister of all of the 'misdeeds and crimes' committed by the United States against Cuba, Castro identified the four dissidents as 'mercenaries in the service of the United States ... who were trying to destroy the Revolution.' In contrast with Bartleman's account of the remainder of the meeting as fraught with tension, Castro recalled the atmosphere as 'warm and friendly at all times.' Of Chrétien, the Cuban leader recalled: 'I carefully observed the Canadian prime minister's character and personality. He is a pleasant conversationalist and has a good sense of humor, and one can strike up an interesting exchange with him on various subjects. He is concerned about certain problems in the world today ... He appeared to be sincerely patriotic. He is loyal to his country and proud of it. He is a fanatical believer in the capitalist mode of production, as if it were a monotheistic religion, and in the naive idea that it is the only solution for all of the world's countries, on every continent, in every era, in every clime or region.'

The same congenial tone prevailed over the entirety of the state visit, Castro recalled, and there was much enthusiasm on both sides for the bilateral projects that had been discussed. Yet after the visit, he continued, Chrétien appeared to lose interest in Cuba. Little was done in Ottawa to follow up on the collaborative projects. Then, on 4 March 1999, 'we received a genuinely surprising response' from the Canadians. Lloyd Axworthy sent a letter to Roberto Robaina, in which he stated, among other things, that in light of the 'forthcoming sentencing of the members of the Internal Dissidence Working Group,' he would be asking his officials 'refrain from undertaking new joint initiatives.' Said Castro of this communication: 'Although I do not want to offend anyone, not even the distinguished author of this letter, it is impossible to ignore the arrogant, overbearing, interfering and vindictive tone in which this letter was written.'

Castro concluded his treatise with a grand rhetorical gesture, invoking his old friend Pierre Trudeau as a true friend to Cuba. 'I am sure that Trudeau would never have said that he spent four hours giving advice to someone who had not asked for it; nor would he seek excuses for excluding an honorable country from a meeting that it did not ask to attend, or ask it to sign an agreement that it would never have signed. History will say who is right.'[90]

## Conclusion

In September 1998, six months after Jean Chrétien's state visit, senior Canadian diplomat Peter Boehm, then serving as ambassador to the OAS, was invited to Miami to address the annual meeting of the Cuban Committee for Democracy. The mostly Cuban émigré crowd had come to hear him speak about 'how Canada approaches both Cuba and the Cuban dilemma in this hemisphere,' and they welcomed him warmly ('until the Miami media found out,' as he later noted sardonically[91]). Boehm opened his talk with a precis of Canada's long record of commercial relations with Cuba – what he called the two countries' history of 'engagement.' He then described how 'Canada has chosen to go beyond this into what we call constructive engagement, as our policy with Cuba reflects the priority the Canadian government attaches to deepening its involvement in the Americas. It defines a determined attempt to engage Cuba and to support movement in that country in the direction of peaceful transition and eventual reintegration into the hemisphere. We firmly believe that this is a goal that everyone supports; the means to achieve it differ of course. In Canada's view, we should face the fact that the Cold War is over; it is time to get on with things and for the largest country in the Caribbean region to be part of the new order.'[92]

This is as compelling a definition of Canada's Cuba policy in the Chrétien era as exists anywhere in the public record – the more so for the crucial distinction it makes between 'engagement' and 'constructive engagement.' Critics of Canada's Cuba policy – especially the hardliners in the United States and their Canadian allies – tended to pillory the Liberals as if all aspects of Canadian engagement with Cuba were de facto 'constructive.' According to this view, the only real alternative to any policy of engagement was embargo. Prime Minister Chrétien and especially Foreign Affairs Minister Axworthy did little to temper this perception, in part because they understood the political advantages of playing to a nationalist constituency in Canada that identified strongly with Fidel Castro's anti-imperialist views. But the failure to differentiate between 'engagement' and 'constructive engagement' also attracted the perennial criticism that Canada's ostensibly altruistic Cuba policy was in fact little more than a 'fig leaf' designed to hide a profitable bilateral trading relationship.

Boehm's allusion to Cuba's 'peaceful transition and eventual reintegration into the hemisphere' highlights the essential but still underappreciated premise of 'constructive' engagement: *it was a hedging policy*. Constructive engagement may well have evinced the symbolic importance to Canada of maintaining 'the dialogue,' as Yvon Grenier has argued, especially in the case of Lloyd Axworthy.[93] But the critical assumption – the one that the Canadians found themselves sharing increasingly not only with Washington but with Miami – was the inevitability of Fidel Castro's passing and the commonsense view that the Revolution as Castro had defined it was doomed to pass as well. Here was hard evidence, one might say, of the pervasiveness of Francis Fukuyama's 1992 claim that, with the globe embracing liberal democracy, we had achieved 'the end of history.' For the Chrétien Liberals, the advantages of constructive engagement were often invoked in the present tense, as happened, for example, when Jean Chrétien observed after his state visit that he thought Castro was 'changing.' But the policy was always positioned to look mainly towards the future, that is, to a 'post-Castro' future of liberal political and economic reforms.

Viewed in this light, Chrétien's state visit has to be seen as a far more complex and contradictory sort of diplomatic manoeuvre than it appeared to be at the time. He went to Havana knowing fully well that Castro did not want to be scolded for his human rights practices or for resisting liberal economic and political reforms. He demanded the release of four high-profile dissidents partly because he genuinely believed in pressing the regime on human rights, but also because he understood the enormous symbolic advantage this gesture might bring him as he positioned himself – and Canada – vis-à-vis Cuba's future. James Bartleman captured this logic succinctly in his own post-mortem on the 1998 state visit:

Was then prime minister Chrétien's initiative in the latter part of the 1990s a failure? Castro did nothing to open up either his economy or his repressive political system. On the other hand the luncheon with the archbishop helped consolidate the gains for the Church registered by John Paul II and our meeting with the dissidents could only have encouraged them. In addition, our efforts, however tentative, to implement the Fourteen Point Declaration exposed hundreds of Cubans to another way of managing an economy and governing a state that will not be forgotten when the transition comes, as it inevitably will, some day after the passing of Castro. The prime minister had the courage to take a risk for a noble cause that positioned Canada on the moral high ground for a major role in post-Castro Cuba.[94]

Constructive engagement, in short, was a policy designed primarily to position Canada on the right side of history. In this sense, it was an affront to the Cuban people in general, and to Fidel Castro personally. When Castro invoked Pierre Trudeau in his critique of Jean Chrétien, he was not merely invoking the name of a great Canadian statesman. He was invoking an entirely different philosophical approach, one based on an appreciation of the Cuban Revolution's claims to legitimacy, and on the fundamental principle that sovereign states had no business meddling in the domestic affairs of others. What the Chrétien Liberals shared with their nominal American critics – but not with their own mentor, Pierre Trudeau – was the arrogant supposition, to quote the American political scientist Julia Sweig, that 'without Fidel's iron fist to keep Cubans in their place, the island would erupt into a collective demand for rapid change. The long-oppressed population would overthrow Fidel's revolutionary cronies and clamor for capital, expertise, and leadership from the north to transform Cuba into a market democracy with strong ties to the United States.'[95]

*Constructive engagement* has failed, it is true, but *engagement* has not. Canadian politicians, diplomats, business people, students, academics, artists, and tourists have for years been building the myriad relationships and networks upon which real influence with their Cuban confrères rests – the influence not of the hard sell or of the grand gesture but of the everyday. Throughout the 1990s, while Washington and Ottawa were boldly fashioning policies designed to 'one day end Cuba's isolation,' thousands of Canadians were quietly working, each in their own way, to actually do so. The Cubans know this. So do the thousands

of Canadians for whom Cuba is a place of warmth, respect, and friendship.


NOTES

I would like to thanks Peter Boehm, Alexandra Bugailiskis, and Ramanand
Kamineni, all of Foreign Affairs Canada, for their willingness to be interviewed for background on this study.

1  See John M. Kirk and Peter McKenna, *Canada-Cuba Relations: The Other
Good Neighbor Policy* (Gainesville: University Press of Florida, 1997).
2  John G. Diefenbaker, House of Commons, *Debates*, 3 February 1976,
10572.
3  'Cuba and Sanctions Legislation,' *Report of the Canadian Section of the
Canada-United States Inter-Parliamentary Group* (May 1998), http://www.
parl.gc.ca/information/InterParl/Associations/U_S/may98/page9-e.htm.
4  Condoleezza Rice, 'Statement by Secretary Rice and Secretary of Commerce Carlos Gutierrez,' 10 July 2006, http://www.state.gov/secretary/
rm/2006/68764.htm.
5  Lloyd Axworthy, cited in *The Soft Touch: Canada & the World Backgrounder*,
65, no.1 (Ottawa: September 1999): 1.
6  See Robert Wright, *Three Nights in Havana: Pierre Trudeau, Fidel Castro and
the Cold War World* (Toronto: HarperCollins, 2007), chapter 10.
7  James Bartleman. *Rollercoaster: My Hectic Years as Jean Chrétien's Diplomatic
Adviser 1994–1998* (Toronto: McClelland and Stewart, 2005), 277.
8  Michael Bell et al., 'Back to the Future? Canada's Experience with Constructive Engagement in Cuba,' ICCAS Occasional Paper Series (Ottawa:
September 2002), 15.
9  Christine Stewart, cited in Michele Zebich-Knos and Heather N. Nicol,
eds., *Foreign Policy towards Cuba: Isolation or Engagement?* (New York: Lexington, 2005), 69.
10  Carl Mollins, 'The Cuba Connection: Tough Talk in Washington May Hurt
Canadian Companies,' *Maclean's*, 108, no. 26 (26 June 1995): 20.
11  See Linda Robinson, 'Castro Seeks an Indulgence,' *U.S. News & World
Report*, 121, no. 19 (11 November 1996): 51.
12  See John Lewis Gaddis, *The Cold War: A New History* (New York: Penguin,
2005), 192–3.
13  See the Introduction to this volume.
14  Bartleman, *Rollercoaster*, 279.

15  Ibid., 281.
16  Ibid., 286.
17  Ibid., 287.
18  Ibid.
19  Bell, 'Back to the Future?' 18.
20  Ibid.
21  Ibid., 19.
22  Bartleman, *Rollercoaster*, 289.
23  Bell, 'Back to the Future?' 16.
24  Kelly Torrance, 'Manitoba – Capital of the New World Order? Lloyd Axworthy Is Apostle of Canadianism to "Lesser Breeds without the Law,"' *BC Report*, 9 (1 December 1997): 6.
25  Lloyd Axworthy, *Navigating a New World: Canada's Global Future* (Toronto: Knopf Canada, 2003), 6.
26  William Christian, cited in Torrance, 'Manitoba,' 6.
27  Bill Clinton, *My Life: The Presidential Years* (New York: Random House, 2005), 174.
28  'Canadian Trade in Cuba' The National (CBC Television broadcast, 21 January 1997).
29  John DeMont and Andrew Phillips, 'A New "Opening,"' *Maclean's*, 97, no. 110 (3 February 1997): 34.
30  'Castro Calls Canada Friend, Sidesteps Questions on Rights,' Canadian Press NewsWire, 22 January 1997.
31  Ibid.
32  Lloyd Axworthy, cited in 'U.S. Says It's Wrong to Reward Castro with Axworthy Visit,' Canadian Press NewsWire, 21 January 1997.
33  DeMont and Phillips, 'A New "Opening,"' 34.
34  Lloyd Axworthy, cited in 'Castro Calls Canada Friend.'
35  Lloyd Axworthy, cited in DeMont and Phillips, 'A New "Opening,"' 34.
36  Nicholas Burns, cited in ibid.
37  Bill Clinton, cited in 'Same Goal, Different Means Bring Disagreement over Cuba,' Canadian Press NewsWire, 23 January 1997.
38  Michael Bliss, cited in Shafer Parker, 'The Professor's Divisions,' *Report / Newsmagazine*, vol. 27, no.12 (23 October 2000): 15.
39  Gordon Ritchie, cited in DeMont and Phillips, 'A New "Opening,"' 34.
40  Jean Chrétien, cited in ibid.
41  Jean Chrétien, cited in 'Same Goal, Different Means.'
42  Lloyd Axworthy, cited in 'Castro Calls Canada Friend.'
43  Roberto Robaina, cited in ibid.
44  Yvon Grenier, 'Canada's Trilateral Relations with Castro's Cuba,' in Mau-

reen Appel Molot and Fen Osler Hampson, eds., *Vanishing Borders: Canada among Nations 2000* (Toronto: Oxford University Press, 2000), 268.

45  Human Rights Watch, 'Cuba' (1997), http://www.hrw.org/worldreport/Americas-03.htm#P448_89148.

46  Unnamed Vatican official, cited in Brook Larmer and Rod Nordland, 'Preaching to the Masses,' *Newsweek*, 131, no. 5 (2 February 1998): 54.

47  Human Rights Watch, 'Cuba' (1998), http://www.hrw.org/worldreport99/americas/cuba.html.

48  'Canada Accepts 19 Cuban Prisoners of Conscience,' Former Prime Minister's Newsroom Archive, 26 February 1998, http://www.pco-bcp.gc.ca/default.asp?Language=E&Page=archivechretien&Sub=NewsReleases&Doc=news_re19980226742_e.htm.

49  Andrew Phillips and Bruce Wallace, 'The Chances of Change: In Cuba and Washington, Attitudes Slowly Shift,' *Maclean's*, 111, no. 18 (4 May 1998): 32.

50  Human Rights Watch, *Cuba's Repressive Machinery: Human Rights Forty Years after the Revolution* (June 1999), www.hrw.org/reports/1999/cuba.

51  Human Rights Watch, 'Cuba' (1998).

52  Fidel Castro, cited in Bartleman, *Rollercoaster*, 292.

53  Fidel Castro, cited in ibid., 296.

54  Bartleman, *Rollercoaster*, 297.

55  Heather Scofield, 'Summit Maps Path to Free Trade,' *Globe and Mail*, 20 April 1998, A1, 9.

56  Unnamed Mexican official, cited in ibid., 1.

57  Jean Chrétien, cited in ibid.

58  Jean Chrétien, cited in ibid., 9.

59  'Prime Minister Chrétien to Visit Cuba,' Former Prime Minister's Newsroom Archive, 21 April 1998, http://www.pco-bcp.gc.ca/default.asp?Language=E&Page=archivechretien&Sub=newsreleases&Doc=news_re19980421764_e.htm.

60  Lloyd Axworthy, cited in 'The Opposition Wanted Assurances from Jean Chrétien That He Will Raise Human Rights Issues When He Goes to Cuba Next Week,' CTV National News, 21 April 1998.

61  Philip Brenner, cited in 'Prime Minister Chrétien's Trip to Cuba,' Sunday Report – CBC Television, 19 April 1998.

62  Jean Chrétien, cited in Jim Brown, 'Chrétien Begins Cuban Visit,' Canadian Press NewsWire, 26 April 1998.

63  Mike Trickey, 'Prime Minister Jean Chrétien Arrived in Cuba,' CanWest-Global News, 26 April 1998.

64  Jean Chrétien, cited in 'Jean and Fidel: How a Pragmatist Tried to Sway an Ideologue,' *Maclean's*, 111, no. 19 (11 May 1998): 28.

65  Jean Chrétien, cited in ibid.
66  Fidel Castro, cited in Trickey, 'Prime Minister Jean Chrétien.'
67  Fidel Castro, cited in ibid.
68  Jean Chrétien, cited in Bruce Wallace, '"I Think He Is Changing": Interview with Canadian Prime Minister Jean Chrétien on His Visit to Cuba,' *Maclean's*, 111, no. 19 (11 May 1998): 28.
69  Jean Chrétien, cited in Bartleman, *Rollercoaster*, 298.
70  Jean Chrétien, cited in Wallace, '"I Think He Is Changing,"' 28.
71  Unnamed Canadian official, cited in Randall Palmer, 'Canada's Chrétien to Urge Cuban Prisoner Releases,' Reuters, 27 April 1998.
72  Yamila Hernandez, cited in Randall Palmer, 'Canada's Chrétien Challenges Castro on Prisoners,' Reuters, 28 April 1998.
73  Jean Chrétien, cited in 'Jean and Fidel,' 28.
74  Bartleman, *Rollercoaster*, 299.
75  Jean Chrétien, cited in Wallace, '"I Think He Is Changing,"' 28.
76  Elena Roque, cited in Palmer, 'Canada's Chrétien.'
77  Unnamed Canadian official, cited in 'Jean and Fidel.'
78  Bartleman, *Rollercoaster*, 301.
79  Paul Knox, 'Castro Defines "Change" Differently,' *Globe and Mail*, 29 April 1998, A15.
80  Jean Chrétien, cited in Wallace, '"I Think He Is Changing,"' 28.
81  Fidel Castro, cited in Paul Knox, 'Castro Defines "Change" Differently.'
82  Jean Chrétien, cited in Jeff Sallot, 'Stop Bullying Cuba, Chrétien Says to U.S.,' *Globe and Mail*, 30 April 1998, A13.
83  Robert Menendez, 'Road to Democracy: The Impact of U.S. Sanctions on Cuba,' *Harvard International Review*, 20, no. 4 (1998): 30–1.
84  Jean Chrétien, cited in 'Canada Eyes Harder Cuba Line after Activists Jailed,' Reuters, 16 March 1999.
85  See 'The Soft Touch.'
86  Jean Chrétien, cited in Jeff Sallot, 'New Cuban Ambassador Gets Cool Official Reception in Ottawa,' *Globe and Mail*, 30 June 1999, A15.
87  Human Rights Watch, *Cuba's Repressive Machinery*.
88  Fidel Castro, cited in David Roberts and Beverly Smith, 'Canada Avoids War of Words with Castro,' *Globe and Mail*, 28 July 1999, A15.
89  John M. Kirk and Peter McKenna, 'No Cigar on Cuban Relations,' *Globe and Mail*, 4 June 2001, A12.
90  'Response by President Fidel Castro Ruz, to a Question Posed by the Moderator of a Round Table Discussion on a Statement Made by Canadian Prime Minister Jean Chrétien during the Summit of the Americas,' http://www.cuba.cu/gobierno/discursos/2001/ing/r250401i.html.

91  Personal interview, 4 October 2006.
92  Peter Boehm, 'Notes for a Speech to the Annual Meeting of the Cuban Committee for Democracy,' delivered in Miami, 12 September 1998.
93  See Grenier, 'Canada's Trilateral Relations with Castro's Cuba.'
94  Bartleman, *Rollercoaster*, 302.
95  Julia E. Sweig, 'Fidel's Final Victory,' *Foreign Affairs* (January/February 2007), http://www.foreignaffairs.org/20070101faessay86104/julia-e-sweig/fidel-s-final-victory.html.

# 9 Ambassador MD: The Role of Health and Biotechnology in Cuban Foreign Policy

LANA WYLIE

For a few months in 2002, Cuban biotechnology received considerable international attention. That year, John Bolton, U.S. under-secretary of state for non-proliferation, claimed that 'the United States believes that Cuba had at least a limited offensive biological warfare research and development effort.' The possibility that Cuba would bring its considerable biotech and medical knowledge to bear in the palpable tension across the Florida Straits was raised in Washington yet dismissed in Havana as unthinkable. It was also dismissed by individuals such as former president Jimmy Carter and eventually downplayed by the secretary of state, Colin Powell, and the White House press secretary, Ari Fleischer.

Yet the idea itself and the resulting media blitz brought attention to what was, until then, a relatively unpublicized fact in the United States – that Cuba has one of the most successful and innovative biomedical systems in the world even though its doctors and scientists work in an environment where scarcity, shortages, and blackouts are relatively common. Although both the health system and bioresearch sectors continue to struggle with the contradictions of operating within a communist state in a capitalist world, they have juggled their myriad responsibilities and managed both to serve the needs of the Cuban populace and to honour their international commitments. Cuban life expectancy and other health indicators meet or exceed the levels achieved in much wealthier states. Furthermore, Cuban scientists have developed a number of important pharmaceuticals that are not only used to treat Cuban patients but are exported worldwide. Cuba also has a significant medical-assistance program that sends medical personnel to treat patients and establish health-care facilities in some of the world's poorest countries.

This chapter argues that Cuba has used its success in the biomedical field as an effective foreign policy tool. Cuba's emphasis on health and biotechnology has played a significant role in Cuba's approach to the rest of the world, resulting in benefits for Cuba and its international partners. For example, Cuba has joint-venture agreements with European biotech companies, provides medical assistance to many of its Latin American and Caribbean neighbours, and has an important medical-services agreement with Venezuela that gives Cuba access to oil at preferred prices. Yet, despite the wide-ranging and extensive links between Cuban and Canadian economies, governments, and societies, there are relatively few connections between Canadians and Cubans in biotech and health. This is an area of the bilateral relationship that could be strengthened for the benefit of both countries. Canadian policy makers, companies, and scientific researchers need to appreciate more fully the potential for partnerships and reap the mutual benefits from a more balanced relationship in the health and biotech fields. Thus, the danger in Cuban biotechnological research arises less from the type of images created in the minds of the likes of Mary Shelley, H.G. Wells, or even John Bolton than from the risk that some countries, including Canada, will not avail themselves of the wealth of knowledge, ingenuity, and potential created by Cuba's unique approach to the delivery of medical care and biotechnological research.

## Overview: Health and Biotechnology in Cuba

*Achieving Health Care at a Fraction of the Cost*

The Cuban health-care system is the most celebrated success story of Cuban science and ingenuity. Cuba has achieved health indicators that surpass other countries with similar GNP and match levels attained by some of the richest countries in the world. For example, Cuban life expectancy at birth (2004) for men is seventy-five years and for women eighty years, which is extraordinary in comparison to neighbouring countries such as Dominican Republic (64/70), Trinidad and Tobago (67/73), and Nicaragua (67/71). In fact, life expectancy in Cuba matches life expectancy in the United States (75/80) and approaches Canadian levels (78/83). Likewise, maternal mortality is low in Cuba (33 per 100,000 live births) in comparison to many other countries in the region. For instance, the rate in the Bahamas is 60, in Jamaica 87, in Mexico 83, and in the Dominican Republic 150.[1]

To obtain these results, Cuba spends much less per capita per year on health care ($229) relative to both Canada ($3,173) and the United States ($6,096) and achieves universal coverage.[2] Furthermore, with a limited budget, Cuba has managed to create a sophisticated scientific infrastructure that is capable of world-class biomedical research and the development of drugs that are competitive internationally as well as treatments that are relevant and affordable for the poorest countries.

The Cuban health-care system is comprehensively organized around individual neighbourhoods of approximately 600–800 individuals. Each neighbourhood is served by a family physician and nurse who live in the service area. These medical providers are assisted by a health committee that works with them to distribute information about the system and health care in general as well as serve as a conduit communicating the health concerns and complaints about the system back to the health-care providers or system administrators.

According to the Pan American Health Organization (PAHO), Cuba ranks number one in health equity since 100 per cent of Cubans have access to free health care under the system.[3] PAHO officials assert, 'In Cuba, no deaths occur for lack of medical care. All patients are able to seek same-day care in a family physician's office.'[4] Almost all (95 per cent) Cubans have a family physician.[5] In Canada, by contrast, 3.6 million people cannot find a family physician, which is greater than one-third of the total population of Cuba.[6]

Preventative medicine is the heart of the Cuban health system. Taught that the health education of their patients is a central part of their job, the neighbourhood health workers emphasize the connections between lifestyle and health. Fidel Castro gave up smoking his beloved Cuban cigars in 1985 to set an example for the population. Similarly, all Cubans are encouraged to monitor their health closely and check in regularly with their clinics.

Family doctors are expected to keep an eye out for any problems in their neighbourhood that might negatively affect health. In conjunction with community leaders, they monitor everything from garbage pickup to community programs for the elderly. The health-care workers engage in active research and are encouraged to submit their findings to journals or at conferences. Cuban health workers are thus kept abreast of advances in medical research which they then put into practice in their neighbourhoods.

*Cuban Biotechnology*

Although scientific research benefited immensely from the emphasis put on the sector after the Revolution, Cuban science has a long and illustrious history. The first Cuban scientific paper was published in 1673.[7] The University of Havana was established in 1728 and Cuba's first scientific society was founded in 1793.[8] Early scientists include Carlos Finlay, who identified mosquitoes as the host for yellow fever (1881) and proposed controlling the mosquito population in order to prevent the spread of the disease. This was a radical theory in the nineteenth and early twentieth centuries and was widely dismissed by scientists elsewhere for twenty years.

The Revolution led by Fidel Castro fundamentally changed Cuban biomedical research and production. Cuba had a small pharmaceutical industry prior to the Revolution but it was largely foreign-owned. Of those companies that were solely Cuban, many were of dubious quality and produced 'medicines' that would not pass minimum standards elsewhere. By the end of 1960, the new Cuban government had nationalized the American-owned enterprises and soon thereafter had set up a state-controlled industry.[9] The pharmaceutical industry benefited from the priority accorded to health and education by the state. The link between biological science and general health is stressed in Cuba. For example, in the 1990s, Cuba's minister of education stated that 'we think the next century is the century of biology. Microbiology and biochemistry will be used to solve problems, achieve higher production, feed humans and improve health.'[10]

There are over 30,000 Cuban employed in biological scientific research and development in Cuba, most of them working in one of the country's many scientific institutes.[11] Although the Cuban state established scientific institutes soon after the Revolution, it was not until the early 1980s that biotechnology research reached critical mass in Cuba. In 1981 the government established the Biological Front, a policy organization designed to guarantee that the state's biological research and development efforts would have full support and necessary funding. At this time, Fidel Castro was keenly interested in the applicability of interferons (IFNs) to treat cancer, and in 1982 the Centro de Investigaciones Biologicos (CIB) was founded to conduct Cuba's IFN research.[12] IFNs were then a promising new field of research with applications in the treatment of cancer and viruses, particularly hepatitis C. The current market for interferon therapies for hepatitis C is well over $2 billion in the European Union and the United States alone.

The mainstay of Cuban biotech, the Centro de Ingeniería Genética y Biotechnologia (CIGB), was established in 1986. The state invested US$100 million in the CIGB to ensure that the scientists could engage in research at a world-class facility.[13] The CIGB has become internationally respected for its work on vaccines, therapeutics, bioinformatics, and proteomics.[14] Most of Cuba's biotech success stories have come from this institute, which has over one hundred products in its drug pipeline. Its most well-known product is a recombinant hepatitis B vaccine which many maintain is the best such vaccine available in the world.

In fact, Cuba is best known for its pioneering vaccine research. For example, Cuban researchers have developed an innovative vaccine that protects against Haemophilis influenzae B (Hib), which can cause flu and meningitis. Even though vaccines already exist for this organism, the Cuban version has advantages; since it is synthetic, it is cheaper and of a better quality than the vaccines currently available. Because of the high cost of the vaccine produced elsewhere, Hib remains a problem in poorer nations, whereas successful yet expensive vaccination programs in wealthier countries have dramatically reduced infections. The technology developed in Cuba has the potential to be applied to other scourges such as tuberculosis, AIDS, and malaria. According to John Robbins, an immunologist with the U.S. National Institute of Child Health and Human Development, this innovation in Cuba is 'a pivotal step' that 'is going to pave the way for a new generation of vaccines.'[15]

In addition to the CIGB, the Finlay Institute, named after the famous Cuban scientist Carlos Finlay, has developed many vaccines. The Finlay Institute's vaccine against bacterial meningitis has been licensed by GlaxoSmithKline for distribution to Western countries. At one point, it was the only vaccine that was available to control meningitis B and was expected to earn hundreds of millions of dollars. It is effective against the viruses in Latin America but not against the many strains present in the United Kingdom and other major markets.[16]

One of the most exciting areas in vaccine research is being conducted by the Centro de Immunología Molecular (CIM). Scientists at the CIM are engaged in pioneering cancer and immunology research, with the goal of mobilizing the power of the immune system to attack tumours. Since tumours are rogue cells and not foreign infections, the immune system does not recognize them as disease. The goal of cancer vaccine research is to provide a treatment that will target tumour cells but not harm normal cells. The CIM has developed a vaccine against Epidermal Growth Factor (EGF) that has shown promise in clinical trials. The vaccine inhibits tumour growth by starving the tumour of EGF.[17] In 2008 the CIM announced that it had developed a lung-cancer vaccine that extends the life of patients by four to five months.

Since Cuban scientists are deeply versed in vaccine research, Cuban children are very well vaccinated. They receive inoculations to protect them against thirteen diseases – polio, typhoid, tetanus, measles, mumps, diphtheria, pertussis, rubella, tuberculosis, hepatitis B, haemophilus influenza B, meningitis B, and meningitis C.[18]

Although vaccines have been the mainstay of Cuban success, Cuban scientists are actively engaged in other types of research. For instance, the Centro Nacional de Investigaciones Cientificas discovered a natural anti-cholesterol drug derived from sugarcane. This substance, policosanol, has been shown to lower cholesterol levels safely and effectively. It is being marketed as an affordable alternative to prescription cholesterol-lowering drugs.[19] In addition, advanced research in neurology is proceeding in Cuba. For example, the Centro de Neurociencias de Cuba has created equipment to detect hearing damage in infants.

Cuban scientists have also been successful in many others areas, resulting in considerable income for the country through joint-venture agreements and sales with numerous biotech and pharmaceutical companies. For example, Cuba's CIM and Biocon India are working together to manufacture biomedical products in India.[20] The German company Oncoscience AG of Wedel is conducting clinical trials of a Cuban anti-cancer therapy.[21] Beckpharma, a British biotech company, signed an agreement with Cuba's Centro Nacional de Sanidad Agropecuaria (CENSA) to market Cuban drugs in Europe.[22] These companies are all benefiting from Cuba's strong biotech research and development sector.

In 2005 Fidel Castro asserted that 'the health-care system has become the most important sector in the exchange of goods and services between our country and the rest of the world in economical terms.'[23] Certainly, the biotechnology and health sectors have earned Cuba considerable foreign exchange. According to some estimates, by 2003 the health and medical research sector was bringing in approximately US$250 million and had achieved a respectable sixth-highest place among Cuban export sectors. Of that, health tourism raised

US$40million and biotechnology over US$150 million.[24] It is estimated that worldwide medical tourism will grow to billions of dollars by 2010 and Cuba is poised to take advantage of a significant percentage of that potential revenue.[25]

## Explaining Cuban Success in Health and Biotechnology

Strength in human resources is the most significant factor explaining the success of Cuban scientific endeavours. As Fidel Castro has stated, 'we do not have much financial capital but we do have a great human capital.'[26] The early commitment by the Cuban state to education and health has resulted in a large knowledge base with the education level of the Cuban population being similar to the levels reached in Europe and North America. Following the Revolution, the number of Cuban schools and universities multiplied. In recent years, at any one time, as many as 50,000 students are registered in Cuban universities and similar higher-education facilities.[27] The government encourages students to focus their education in science and health-related fields. By the beginning of the 1990s, there were hundreds of students enrolled each year at the University of Havana in biology, biochemistry, and microbiology programs, and many of these students have gone on to further scientific study, especially in medicine and engineering.

Moreover, as a consequence of not always having access to the necessary equipment, reagents, or medicines, Cuban research and medical treatment tends to be both resourceful and innovative. In their daily lives, Cubans are accustomed to making do with less, refitting old technologies, and mixing older methods with new knowledge. In this vein, Cubans are known worldwide for their ability to keep old American cars running even though they do not have access to spare parts. Likewise, Cuban doctors have retrofitted recycled magnets from ballistic missiles for use in electromagnetic therapy.[28] For Cuban health workers, the scarcity created by the embargo and lack of foreign exchange has meant increasing the use of herbal medicines. Cuban physicians have educated themselves about alternative therapies and herbal remedies; some doctors even have their own herbal gardens.[29]

Another component of Cuban success is that priorities for biotech research in Cuba come from one source – the Council of State. Research is focused and coordinated much like research conducted by biotechnology companies in the capitalist world. Clearly, there are significant drawbacks to this model since individual interests or creativity are sacrificed to projects favoured by the state. However, this concentrated effort does pay off in significant progress in the targeted applied research. In addition, Cuban drug discoveries proceed more quickly through clinical trials because the related health and scientific communities are both centrally directed. Consequently, the biomedical scientific community is closely tied to the health-care system, which reduces the obstacles to testing promising pharmaceuticals. Thus, rather ironically, Cuban scientists face fewer bureaucratic hurdles at this stage than researchers in most other countries.[30]

The Cuban health and bioscience sectors also benefit from the strong commitment by the government. The revolutionary government made health care and science priorities in Cuba's economic development. A quote from Fidel Castro is prominently displayed at Havana's Medical Research Park: 'The future of our nation is necessarily the future of men of science.'[31] This focus is a guiding vision for economic investment and government policy. From its inception, the revolutionary government was determined to foster Cuban excellence in science and health.[32] Health science has always received support from the state but in 1990 Fidel Castro redoubled that commitment when he designated biotechnology as one of the government's priority sectors. This ensured that biotechnology, like agriculture and tourism, would continue to receive investment despite drastic cutbacks to other areas of the Cuban economy and society. As a result, the Cuban government continued to allocate 1.5 per cent of its GNP towards scientific research and development even during the 'Special Period' of unprecedented economic crisis in the early 1990s.[33]

## The International Dimension of Cuban Health Care and Scientific Research

Excellent human resources, a targeted research program, and steadfast government support have translated into significant scientific breakthroughs that are recognized internationally. For example, Michael Levin, a British scientist who is engaged in a joint venture with the Finlay Institute, notes that Cuba has 'excellent laboratories, and their doctors and scientists have maintained world-class standards.'[34] A Harvard professor of medical anthropology, Paul Farmer, praises Cuba's Instituto de Medicina Tropical 'Pedro Kouri' (IPK): 'With a comparatively tiny budget – less than that, say, of a single large research hospital at Harvard – IPK has conducted important basic science research, helped to develop novel vaccines, trained thousands of researchers from Cuba and from around the world.'[35]

In addition, the Cuban health-care system and its medical specialists are internationally respected. Cuban doctors have made advances in the treatment and prevention of a number of illnesses, and the country's health system has attracted attention from health administrators and some prominent medical schools looking to improve their preventative health education. For example, employees of the British Ministry of Health along with one hundred British doctors travelled to Cuba in 2000 to see what lessons they could learn for use in the British health system. Likewise, doctors from the Harvard medical school have visited Cuba to learn about the Cuban model. As Richard Cash, of Harvard's Department of Population and International Health, explains, 'to see what Cuba does with limited resources and to contrast it with our system and other systems is valuable. Everyone that has gone to Cuba has come away clearly educated by the process.'[36] An Emory University medical student sent to Cuba to learn about the Cuban health system remarked, 'Cuba's doing pretty well on its own. It's not like they have a shortage of doctors so they need medical students to go down there and pick up the slack ... Our goal was just to learn about the healthcare system.'[37] In fact, an American organization was created in 1997 to encourage cooperation between Cuban and U.S. medical communities. Medical Education Cooperation with Cuba (MEDICC) asserts that 'health care in the United States and developing countries alike – especially for underserved populations – can be informed by Cuba's singular and evolving health practices, research and policies.'[38]

Cuba has achieved considerable international respect for its medical and scientific accomplishments. Yet the international dimension of Cuba's health system goes beyond serving as an example for scientists or health officials from other countries. It also has important consequences for Cuban foreign policy.

## Medical Diplomacy and Foreign Policy

Cuban achievements in health and biotechnology are not only harnessed by the state to fulfil its domestic health goals but are also used effectively in Cuban foreign policy. Because Cuba has more physicians per capita than any other country in the Americas including Canada and the United States, it is able to send doctors abroad.[39] When natural disasters or emergencies occur abroad, the Cubans are often one of the first medical units to arrive on the scene. For instance, Cuban doctors were among the first group of foreigners to arrive in the Kashmir region of Pakistan after the October 2005 earthquake; the Cubans set up thirty field hospitals in the region. Pakistan's president, Pervez Musharraf, thanked Cuba for providing more disaster relief after the earthquake than any other country.[40] Likewise, when Bolivia was hit by massive flooding in January and February 2007, the Cuban government quickly sent one hundred doctors to aid in the flooded regions.[41] Havana's willingness to provide effective emergency medical aid results in considerable international goodwill.

Although it generates much publicity, emergency aid is only one small part of Cuba's medical diplomacy. Cuba also provides longer-term health assistance. Thousands of Cuban physicians and other medical personnel are treating patients and helping to establish health systems in neighbouring Caribbean and Latin American countries and farther afield. For example, under the Bolivarian Alternative for the Americas (ALBA), a regional social-welfare program, Cuba has agreed to provide free eye operations and to pay the related transportation and accommodation costs for over half a million Latin Americans and Caribbean citizens each year. Known as 'Operation Miracle,' the program, which was inaugurated in July 2004, provided 485,476 eye operations between 2004 and 2006. According to Cuban Public Health figures, one out of every 87 Venezuelans, one in every 213 Bolivians, and at least one in 60 citizens from Antigua and Barbuda had been treated by 2006. The same source indicates that the program had established thirteen ophthalmologic centres in Venezuela.[42]

Operation Miracle has been a success for Cuban foreign policy. When the program was extended to Panama, President Martin Torrijos came to Havana along with seventy-eight patients and said he was personally making the trip 'as a sign of my thanks for the opportunity being given to many humble Panamanians to recover their sight.'[43] According to the former high commissioner to the United Kingdom from Antigua and Barbuda, Ronald Sanders, 'what Caribbean governments and people appreciate is not just that Cuba has been a consistent friend in time of need, but Cuba has given assistance at great sacrifice to itself. It is the quality of the assistance, and the knowledge that it is given despite hardship within Cuba, that has left a lasting impression on Caribbean people and, increasingly now, people in Central America.'[44]

Cuba has also used its medical resources and related reputation to cement its relationship with Venezuela and secure access to oil at preferred prices. In 2000 and then again in 2005, Cuba and Venezuela signed trade agreements that allow Venezuela to receive medical services from Cuban doctors, medicines, and medical equipment in exchange for providing oil to Cuba. The Cuban medical personnel work in Venezuela through the Barrio Adentro (Inside the Neighborhood) program, which was initially contemplated in 1999 after severe flooding in some of the poorest regions of Venezuela. In response to the floods, Cuba sent 454 health-care personnel to Venezuela to work in these regions. The willingness of the Cuban doctors to work in impoverished areas generally eschewed by their Venezuelan counterparts and the success of an initial pilot program impressed President Hugo Chavez and led to discussions that culminated in the oil-for-doctors deals.[45] Thus, in 2000, the Venezuelans agreed to provide 53,000 barrels of oil per day at a subsidized price if Cuba would assist Venezuela with its shortfall in medical personnel.[46] Under the 2005 agreement, the Cubans have said they will train 45,000 medical workers in Venezuela and provide places for 10,000 additional Venezuelans in Cuban medical and nursing schools.[47] While estimates vary, there are reportedly as many as 20,000 Cuban health-care personnel in Venezuela at any one time treating patients, establishing medical centres, and educating Venezuelan health-care workers.

In addition to sending doctors overseas, Cuban medical schools train large numbers of foreign students. Students from many countries, but mainly from developing regions, receive a free medical education in Cuba. In the medical school in Las Tunas alone, there are students from over thirty countries training to become doctors. Although the majority of international students are from Latin America, students have come from as far away as Africa. For example, in July 2006, twenty-two South African doctors graduated after completing five years of study in Cuba.[48] Interestingly, a few economically disadvantaged American students have been among those who have received a free health-care education in Cuban universities.

As well as sending doctors abroad and educating foreign students, the Cuban state encourages its doctors to treat foreign patients in Cuba. Medical tourism is a booming business. Estimates show that this type of tourism raises approximately US$40 million each year for Cuba.[49] Patients from all over the world arrive in Cuba for operations for everything from neurosurgery to cosmetic surgery. Treatment is normally as good as or better than the therapy they would receive in their home countries and comes at a fraction of the cost. Cuban specialists are internationally respected. For instance, patients suffering from cancer of the eye come to Cuba to be cared for by a Cuban ophthalmologist who has pioneered a novel therapy to arrest the progress of the disease.[50] Cuban doctors are also recognized as experts in the treatment of night blindness and Parkinson's disease.[51]

Canadians are among Cuba's international patients. In fact, a Quebec company, Health Services International, specializes in setting up medical services for foreigners in Cuba. This organization advertises that 'Cuba has become a premier destination for patients seeking first class medical attention. Perhaps Canadians have grown tired of long waiting lists to see doctors in their home town, or maybe it is because of the stellar health care system in Cuba.'[52]

Though it is illegal under U.S. law, Americans are also among those who purchase medical care in Cuba, often because it is less expensive than the American alternative. For example, at the Cira Garcia Central Clinic in Havana, Americans can obtain treatment for roughly half of what they would pay in the United States (in 1999 rhinoplasty cost $1,710 at Cira Garcia compared with $3,100 in the United States).[53] Since it is becoming widely known that Cuban physicians offer excellent treatment, the country is well positioned to take advantage of the expected growth in health tourism in the coming decades.

Transforming Cuba into a world-renowned health-science leader was an important goal of Cuban foreign policy. Fidel Castro frequently compared Cuba's progress in these areas to other countries. For example, in 1995 he said: 'Can anyone doubt Cuba's accomplishments in science? Among all the Third World countries, Cuba is unquestionably first. Does any other country have a movement like the Science and Technology Movement, in which over 1 million people participate ... Has any other country developed the level of scientific research we have attained in our universities, particularly over the last few years, and in the midst of a special period? We could also ask: Has any other country demonstrated more solidarity, or sent more doctors, teachers, technicians, or soldiers to the Third World than Cuba? Let that country raise its hand.' He continued: 'I am fully convinced that our flag has never been so respected, and our country has never been so admired ... It has never had so much prestige, nor were more hopes ever cast on her.'[54] After asserting that 'Cuba's prestige is growing apace because our country is doing things that nobody else is doing,' he cited examples such as Cuba's international eye-surgery program, education, and health-care aid.[55]

Cuba has also attempted to use its medical reputation and prestige to gather international support in its political struggle with the United States. In a statement before the UN Human Rights Commission, the Cuban representative urged the members not to condemn a country that had provided much international assistance – including having 'graduated from its intermediate- and higher-level schools over 41,000 youths from 123 countries; a people that today has more than 15,000 doctors working in 65 nations of the Third World.'[56] Fidel Castro himself has stated: 'Parallel to the increase in prestige of Cuba, the world is becoming more and more convinced that the U.S. policy on Cuba is sheer madness. We see this at the United Nations, which cast 101 votes against the blockade.'[57] According to *Granma*, Castro said that international aid 'makes us stronger because it won't be easy for an empire to destroy a people who are giving back eyesight to millions of Latin Americans.'[58]

Medical diplomacy plays a large part in Cuban foreign policy, influencing other countries' opinions of the island nation and being effectively deployed to garner necessary support or material resources required by the state. Although the impact of Cuba's medical system has been the most influential on Cuba's relations with Latin American and Caribbean states, it has also influenced Cuba's bilateral relations with other countries.

Canada has a prominent place in Cuban foreign policy because of the importance of Canadian investment, trade, and tourism to the Cuban economy as well as the symbolic significance of the relationship vis-à-vis the designation of Cuban as an enemy of the United States. Canadian and Cubans also share a commitment to universal health care and a focus on nurturing scientific development. Yet there are relatively few connections between Canadians and Cubans in this sector.

### Health and Biotechnology in the Canadian-Cuban Relationship

Despite being Cuba's leading source of foreign trade, Canada is not realizing the full potential of the relationship in the health and medical-research sector. Many of the official connections in this sector are directed from Canada to Cuba in the form of aid dollars and advice. In 2008 the Canadian International Development Agency (CIDA) was engaged in five health-related aid projects in Cuba. All but one of these were multilateral projects wherein Cuba was only one of the recipient countries. The multilateral projects included an effort designed to reduce the impact of environmental health hazards, a program to improve the provision of vaccines to children in Latin American countries including Cuba, and an effort to fight HIV/AIDS in the region. Another project assists Cuba indirectly by supporting the work of the Pan American Health Organization.[59]

The one bilateral project focused on Cuba is run by Health Partners International of Canada. CIDA channelled over $2 million in aid to Cuba through this NGO between 2003 and 2008. In fact, most of the recent Canadian medical aid to Cuba has been delivered through Health Partners International. This NGO was established in 1995 after former prime minister Pierre Trudeau grew concerned about the lack of basic medicines available to Cubans as a result of the embargo and economic collapse following the end of the Soviet Union. On Trudeau's initiative and with the cooperation of the Canadian government, Health Partners International implemented a medical-aid program designed to deliver medicines in short supply in Cuba to the island. The NGO also arranged for Aventis Pasteur to donate $4.5 million worth of flu vaccine to Cubans through the program.[60] In the decade from 1995 to 2005, almost $15 million in medical aid was sent to Cuba via this program.[61]

The Canadian government also supports health assistance in Cuba through the International Development Research Centre (IDRC). Recent IDRC projects in Cuba include improving health in the inner-city neighbourhoods of Havana and research on dengue fever in the country as a whole. The dengue project fostered connections between researchers at the University of British Columbia (UBC) and the Instituto Nacional de Higiene, Epidemiología y Microbiología in Havana.[62] Other Canadian NGOs have also supported the Cuban health system. For example, Comité de Solidarité Tiers-Monde de Trois-Rivières has helped equip rural health clinics with solar electricity and promoted dengue fever and HIV/AIDS awareness programs on the island.

Scientific research connections between Canadians and Cubans are likewise largely asymmetrical and often occur through aid projects. CIDA funds programs to aid Cuba's biotechnology sector, including a project between the Universidad Central 'Marta Abreu' de las Villas (UCLV), Santa Clara, Cuba, and the Institute of Biomedical Engineering at the University of New Brunswick (UNB). The stated objective of this project was 'to establish a Biomedical Engineering Education Infrastructure in Cuba.'[63] CIDA later funded another project between the Institute of Biomedical Engineering at UNB and three Cuban universities – UCLV, Instituto Superior Politecnico José A. Echeveria (ISP-

JAE) in Havana, and Universidad de Oriente (UO) in Santiago de Cuba. This project, which began in 2003 and is to continue until 2010, also involves the Hospital for Sick Children in Toronto. UNB's Ed Biden, the project's principal investigator, said that it will 'transfer the skills and knowledge of Canadian experts in biomedical and clinical engineering' to their Cuban counterparts.[64] In addition, according to a UNB press release, 'the project will equip advanced laboratories in each of the three partner universities in Cuba.'[65] Since they are aid projects, all of these efforts focus on the transmission of Canadian funding and related knowledge to Cuba rather than on mutual learning.

## Canadian-Cuban Collaboration in Biotechnology and Health

Cuba has the capability to be a strong partner in biotech research and development and consequently could be a source of knowledge and innovation for Canadian researchers. In fact, some academic connections have developed into partnerships. The University of Ottawa and the University of Havana collaborated on a human vaccine for flu and meningitis which was jointly patented by the universities in 1999. This was the first human vaccine made with a synthetic antigen and prevents one of the causes of childhood meningitis and Haemophilus influenza B (Hib).[66] Professor René Roy of the University of Ottawa met Dr Vicente Verez Bencomo of the University of Havana at a scientific conference in Ottawa in 1994, and they began to work together after further discussion at a 1995 conference in Havana.[67] The opportunity for Canadian and Cuban scientists to meet relatively freely led to this successful collaboration. Certainly, Canadian academics, in comparison to their American counterparts, are well situated to engage in partnerships for the benefit of both national communities.

Some Canadian medical schools have expressed an interest in learning from their Cuban counterparts. According to Jerry Spiegel, director of Global Health at the Liu Institute for Global Issues, UBC medical students were sent to Cuba to learn about Cuban innovations in the field. He said: 'The elective gave students a better appreciation of the range of population health issues and showed them how much is possible with limited resources.'[68] One of the Canadian students, Arlene MacDougall, explained: 'I learned how impressive the Cuban medical system was both in organization and delivery. I realized that a high quality of care could be given in the absence of technology and resources.'[69] Spiegel noted that 'public health is a national priority in Cuba

and funding is maintained at all costs ... We Canadians have a lot to
learn from this model.'[70] Yet these visits, like the scientific collaboration
between Canadians and Cubans, remain ad hoc. Collaborative efforts
depend on the possibility that individuals will search for unconventional models and for solutions to problems outside 'normal' channels.

Similarly, collaborations between the commercial biotech sector in
Canada and Cuban researchers are minimal. However, one Canadian
company has begun to realize the potential in Cuban science. In 1995
a small Ontario company, YM Biosciences, collaborated with the Centro de Immunología in Havana to commercialize cancer vaccines being
developed by the CIM. This collaboration, which resulted in the development of a therapeutic antibody to an agent that promotes tumour
growth,[71] has been a very successful venture for YM Biosciences. Its
chief executive, David Allen, noted: 'Out of all our relationships, the
Cuba venture has definitely become priority No. 1.'[72]

Although Canadian scientists can benefit from collaborations with
Cuban researchers, there is a downside to business partnerships. As
David Allen explained, 'developing a product that originates in Cuba
is definitely a greater challenge than developing a product that originates elsewhere.'[73] Complications include having to raise equity in Europe and difficultly in obtaining approval from the American Food and
Drug Administration (FDA) to market the drug in the United States.[74]
Other concerns relate to the business culture in Cuba. Operating largely
outside the capitalist system for decades has disadvantaged those Cubans who are now attempting to do business with foreign companies.
This also leads to frustration within the companies. For example, the
lack of adherence by Cubans to some accepted business practices and
norms complicates doing business in the country. Despite these obstacles, the successful partnership between YM Biosciences and Cuba's
CIM expanded in 2004 to include the American company CancerVax.[75]
This is a historic arrangement, the first deal approved between a U.S.
biotech company and Cuba. If Cuban biotechnology continues to produce successful medical treatments and pharmaceuticals, the pressure
on American policy makers to end their isolationist policy is likely to
become even more intense, which would alleviate some of the difficulties of Canadian-Cuban collaboration.[76] Even now, the benefits of partnership appear to be worth the potential headaches.

Yet these cooperative ventures are few, especially given the tremendous possibilities and the current crisis in the Canadian medical
system.[77] Although the Cuban system does have major drawbacks, Ca-

nadians could learn a great deal about how to run an efficient health-care system from their Cuban counterparts. One of the most common complaints about the Canadian system is the shortage of doctors and nurses. In Canada, 14 per cent of people do not have a family doctor and many of the family doctors now in practice are refusing to treat maternity patients or deliver babies because of fears of malpractice and disadvantageous fee structures.[78] In Cuba, as indicated earlier, only 5 per cent of people do not have a family doctor and there are very few difficulties with finding maternity care.[79]

Although waiting lists are a source of irritation in both Canada and Cuba, Cuba has begun to implement measures to address this problem. Between 1998 and 1999, Cuban waiting lists were reduced by 45 per cent.[80] Furthermore, anyone who has waited hours in a busy emergency room in one of Canada's hospitals might appreciate the strides the Cuban system has made in emergency services.[81] According to a recent study published in *Social Science and Medicine*, 'the Cuban experience with decentralising emergency services in direct collaboration with the first line health services, could be useful for other countries seeking a strategy to alleviate the pressure on overcrowded hospital emergency services and to reinforce the first line health services.'[82] Considering the surge in Canadian health-care costs, it is clear that, from the standpoint of organization and deployment of limited resources, we could learn much from the administration of health care in Cuba.

### Conclusion

Achieving results that rival those in much wealthier countries, the Cuban health-care and bioscience sector now plays a significant role in Cuba's international relationships. Cuba has used its comparative advantage in this area to foster relationships, obtain goodwill, and secure access to crucial resources. Medical diplomacy has become a crucial part of Cuba's foreign policy towards its Latin American and Caribbean neighbours. Yet the health-care sector has had little influence in the relationship between Canada and Cuba. This chapter has argued that the health-care and biomedical-research aspects of the bilateral relationship should be strengthened for the mutual benefit of the two countries.

There are lessons to be learned from Cuban experiences in providing health care and performing scientific research with limited resources. Many of these lessons are directly applicable to the challenges Canada faces with spiralling health-care costs and our attempts to nourish high value-added industries such as biotechnology. It should give us pause that Cuba can achieve such high-quality health-care indicators on such a limited budget. One of the keys to this success may be the focus of family practitioners on prevention of disease and education of patients. There are successful precedents for Canada-Cuba scientific collaboration, such as the groundbreaking vaccine for flu and meningitis. The future for joint ventures is promising on both the health-system and medical-research fronts. Educating Canadians about Cuban success in these areas is the first step towards more productive interactions along the lines of the Hib collaboration and the YM Biosciences joint venture.

Perhaps the best reason for examining the Cuban health-care system is that such an examination may help to preserve a common value of our societies, namely, government-administered health care for all citizens. Canadian policy makers, companies, and scientific researchers need to appreciate more fully the potential for partnerships and reap the mutual benefits from a more balanced relationship in the health and biotech fields.

NOTES

I would like to thank Duane Hewitt for sharing his knowledge of biotechnology with me. I would also like to acknowledge the outstanding research assistance of Jacquelyn Cummings and the financial support of the Arts Research Board of McMaster University.

1  World Health Organization (WHO), 'Core Health Indicators,' http://www3.who.int/whosis/core/core_select_process.cfm (accessed 5 July 2006).
2  These are 2004 figures taken from WHO, 'Country Profile. United States,' http://www.who.int/countries/usa/en/; 'Country Profile. Canada,' http://www.who.int/countries/can/en/; 'Country Profile. Cuba,' http://www.who.int/countries/cub/en/ (accessed 22 September 2007).
3  Pan American Health Organization (PAHO), 'Cuba: Profile of the Health Services System,' 8 June 1999.
4  Ibid.
5  Pol De Vos, '"No One Left Abandoned": Cuba's National Health System since the 1959 Revolution,' *International Journal of Health Services*, 35, no. 1 (2005): 189–207.

6   WHO, 'Country Profile, Canada,' http://www.who.int/countries/can/
    en/; and Louise Gagnon, 'Stats Can: 14% of Canadians have no family doc-
    tor,' www.cmaj.ca/cgi/reprint/171/2/124.pdf (accessed 7 August 2007).

7   David Lipschultz and Peter Rojas, 'The Next Biotech Corridor: Cuba?
    A Trip behind Cuba's Iron Curtain Reveals the Country's Best-kept Secret:
    Biotechnology,' *Red Herring Magazine*, 12 April 2001, http://www.global
    exchange.org/countries/americas/cuba/sustainable/redHerring041201.
    html (accessed 19 July 2006).

8   'Present Status of Science in Cuba: Focus on Chemistry,' *Chemistry Interna-
    tional*, 21, no. 2 (1999).

9   Pol De Vos, '"No One Left Abandoned,"'194.

10  Quoted in Julie Margot Feinsilver, *Healing the Masses* (Berkley: University
    of California Press, 1993), 123.

11  Jose de la Fuente, 'Wine into Vinegar – The Fall of Cuba's Biotechnology,'
    *Nature Biotechnology*, 19 (October 2001): 905–7.

12  Ibid.

13  Ibid.

14  See Ernesto López et al., 'Development of Cuban Biotechnology,' *Journal of
    Commercial Biotechnology*, 9, no. 2 (2002). Over half of the scientific papers
    published by Cubans in international, peer-reviewed journals come from
    scientists at the CIGB. See Halla Thorsteinsdóttir et al., 'Cuba – Innovation
    through Synergy,' *Nature Biotechnology*, 22, DC19–DC24 (2004).

15  Jocelyn Kaiser, 'Synthetic Vaccine Is a Sweet Victory for Cuban Science,'
    *Science*, 305 (23 July 2004).

16  Ivano de Filippis and Ana Carolina Paulo Vicente, *Diagnostic Microbiology
    and Infectious Disease*, 53 (2005): 161–7.

17  Tania Crombet Ramos et al., 'Treatment of NSCLC Patients with an EGF-
    Based Cancer Vaccine,' *Cancer Biology and Therapy*, 5, no. 2 (2006).

18  Miguel A. Galindo, 'Immunization and Vaccine Research in Cuba: Cuba's
    National Immunization Program,' *Medicc Review*, http://www.medicc.org/
    medicc_review/1004/pages/spotlight.html (accessed 2 February 2009).

19  'Natural Anti-Cholesterol Dietary Supplement: Policosanol,' *Life Extension
    Magazine*, June 2001, http://www.lef.org/magazine/mag2001/june2001_
    cover_policosanol.html (accessed 31 July 2006).

20  Embassy of India, Havana, 'BIOCON and CIMAB Expand Cooperation
    to Fight Cancer,' http://www.indembassyhavana.cu/Biocon_Cimab_
    agreement.htm (accessed 7 January 2006).

21  Tom Fawthrop, 'Cuba Sells Its Medical Expertise,' BBC News, 21 Novem-
    ber 2003, http://news.bbc.co.uk/1/hi/business/3284995.stm (accessed 3
    January 2006).

22  'Beckpharma Acquires First Products from Cuban Biotech Institute,' 2 December 2005, http://www.bionity.com/news/e/50619/?defop=and &edate=10/26/2006&pw=a&sdate=01/01/1995&wild=yes (accessed 21 September 2007).

23  Speech delivered by President Fidel Castro Ruz at the foundation ceremony of the 'Henry Reeve' International Contingent of Doctors Specialized in Disaster Situations and Serious Epidemics, and the national graduation of students of medical sciences, in Havana's Sports City, on 19 September 2005.

24  Fawthrop, 'Cuba Sells Its Medical Expertise.'

25  More recently, other nations, notably India, Costa Rica, and Thailand, have become medical-tourist destinations.

26  'Speech Given by Dr. Fidel Castro Ruz, President of the Council of State of the Republic of Cuba to the Students Graduating from the Havana Higher Institute of Medical Sciences, at the Karl Marx Theater on August 9, 1999,' http://www.cubasolidarity.net/fidelmed.html (accessed 3 May 2007).

27  'Cuba Tripling University Grads,' *PERIÓDICO* 26 (1 June 2006), http://www.periodico26.cu/english/education/grads060106.htm (accessed 19 July 2006).

28  Chelsea Merz 'The Cuban Paradox,' *Harvard Public Health Review* (summer 2002), http://www.hsph.harvard.edu/review/review_summer_02/677cuba.html (accessed 19 July 2006).

29  Allison O. Adams, 'Paradox Island,' *Emory Magazine* (summer 2002), http://www.emory.edu/EMORY_MAGAZINE/summer2002/cuba.html (accessed 26 July 2006).

30  Julie Margot Feinsilver, *Healing the Masses: Cuban Health Politics at Home and Abroad* (Berkeley: University of California Press, 1993), 125.

31  Michael Kranish, 'Incubating Biotech: US Charges Highlight Castro's Efforts to Build Industry,' *Boston Globe*, 15 May 2002.

32  De la Fuente, 'Wine into Vinegar.'

33  Chen May Yee, 'Cutting-edge Biotech in Old-world Cuba,' *Christian Science Monitor*, 17 April 2003, http://www.csmonitor.com/2003/0417/p14s03-stct.html (accessed 21 September 2007).

34  Tom Fawthrop, 'Cuba Ailing? Not Its Biomedical Industry,' *Straits Times*, 26 January 2004. Reprinted in *YaleGlobal Online*, http://yaleglobal.yale.edu (accessed 8 December 2005).

35  Ibid.

36  Merz, 'The Cuban Paradox.'

37  Adams, 'Paradox Island.'

38  Medical Education Cooperation with Cuba, 'About Meddicc,' http://www.medicc.org/about-us.php (accessed 26 April 2007).

39  WHO, 'Core Health Indicators,' http://www3.who.int/whosis/core/
    core_select_process.cfm (accessed 5 July 2006).
40  Hernando Calvo Ospina, 'Cuba Exports Health,' *Le Monde diplomatique*,
    August 2006.
41  'Cuban Doctors Aid Bolivian Flood Victims,' *Granma International*, 21 Feb-
    ruary 2007.
42  See 'Cuban Eye Surgery Programme Benefits Nearly Half Million Patients,'
    Caribbean News Net, 21 November 2006, http://www.caribbeannetnews.
    com/cgi-script/csArticles/articles/000043/004350.htm (accessed 14
    September 2008); 'Cuba and Venezuela Sign Agreements for $1.5 Billion in
    Projects,' *Granma International*, 1 March 2007.
43  'Panama Welcomes Cuba Eye Surgery,' BBC News, 30 November 2005,
    http://news.bbc.co.uk/1/hi/world/americas/4486708.stm (accessed
    14 September 2008).
44  Ronald Sanders, 'Cuban Medical Diplomacy: A Winner,' 26 November
    2007, http://www.bbc.co.uk/caribbean/news/story/2007/11/071123_
    sanders14_nov.shtml (accessed 14 September 2008).
45  C. Muntaner et al., 'Venezuela's Barrio Adentro: An Alternative to Neo-
    liberalism in Health Care,' *International Journal of Health Services*, 36, no. 4
    (2006): 803–11.
46  The deals have received considerable press attention. See, for example,
    Larry Rohter, 'Venezuela Will Sell Cuba Low-Priced Oil,' New York *Times*,
    31 October 2000.
47  Jorge Díaz Polanco, 'Salud y hegemonía regional,' *De Foreign Affairs
    En Español*, 6, no. 4 (2006), http://www.foreignaffairs-esp.org/
    20061001faenespessay060412-p30/jorge-diaz-polanco/salud-y-
    hegemonia-regional.html (accessed 21 September 2008).
48  'Cuba Graduates S African Docs,' Prensa Latina, 12 July 2006, http://
    www.escambray.cu/Eng/Scie&Tec/Stecgraduates060712128.htm (ac-
    cessed 26 July 2006).
49  Fawthrop, 'Cuba Sells Its Medical Expertise.'
50  'Health Tourists Head for Cuba,' BBC News, 19 August 1999, reprinted by
    CubaNet, http://www.cubanet.org/CNews/y99/ago99/23e8.htm (ac-
    cessed 11 July 2006).
51  Fawthrop, 'Cuba Sells Its Medical Expertise.'
52  Health Services International, http://www.hsi-ssi.com/en/medical-
    tourism-cuba.php (accessed 21 September 2008).
53  'Foreigners Flock to Cuba for Medical Care,' *Western Journal of Medicine*,
    175, no. 2 ( 2001): 81.
54  Fidel Castro Ruz, 'Castro Gives Fifth FEU Congress Address, Havana Tele
    Rebelde and Cuba Vision Networks in Spanish 2200 GMT 26 Mar 95.'

55 'It Is a Fact That the Party Is Strengthening Itself Like Never Before, Affirms Fidel, Presenting the Conclusions of the 5th Plenary of the Central Committee of the Communist Party,' *Granma International*, 4 July 2006.

56 'Statement Delivered by H.E. Mr. Felipe Pérez Roque, Minister of Foreign Affairs of the Republic of Cuba, at the High-level Segment of the 60th Session of the Commission on Human Rights,' Geneva, 17 March 2004.

57 'Fidel Castro Speaks at FEU Congress, 25 Mar 1995,' Castro Speech database, http://lanic.utexas.edu/la/cb/cuba/castro.html, February 2007.

58 'It Is a Fact That the Party Is Strengthening Itself.'

59 List of projects provided to the author by Sophia Robineault, senior program officer and analyst, Cuba Programme, Canadian International Development Agency, 10 September 2008.

60 'Trudeau Legacy Produces $23 Million Medical Lifeline to Cuba,' Canada NewsWire, 8 March 2002.

61 'HPIC Marks 10th Anniversary of Medical Aid Program for Cubans – Trudeau's Legacy Includes Medical Aid for Cuba,' Canada NewsWire, 24 March 2005. For more information, see www.hpicanada.ca.

62 For more information, see IDRC, 'Projects in Cuba, Ecosystem Approach to the Sustainable Prevention and Control of Dengue (Cuba) – Phase II,' http://www.idrc.ca/en/ev-67578-201_101545-1-IDRC_ADM_INFO.html (accessed 16 September 2008).

63 Sandra Howland, 'Canada and UNBF Help Cuba Develop Biomedical Capacity,' 13 November 2002, http://www.unb.ca/news/view.cgi?id=94 (accessed 21 September 2007).

64 Sandra Howland, 'UNB Know-How Boosts Cuba's Biomedical Capability,' UNB Fredericton News Release: C891, 30 January 2004, http://www.unb.ca/news/view.cgi?id=442 (accessed 1 January 2005).

65 Ibid.

66 Thorsteinsdóttir et al., 'Cuba – Innovation through Synergy,' 19–24.

67 Susan Hurlich, 'The World's First Synthetic Vaccine for Children,' CubaNow.Net, http://www.cubanow.cult.cu/global/loader.php?secc=10&cont=culture/num10/8.htm (accessed 7 January 2006).

68 Hilary Thomson, 'UBC Med Students Impressed with Cuban Health-Care System,' *UBC Reports*, 48, no. 13 (2002), http://www.publicaffairs.ubc.ca/ubcreports/2002/02nov07/cuba.html (accessed 19 July 2006).

69 Ibid.

70 Ibid.

71 'YM Biosciences Reports Positive EGF-R Antibody, Pivotal Phase II Results, 90.6% Complete Responses Seen with No Evidence of Skin Toxicity,' *Center of Molecular Immunology*, 21 December 2004, http://www.cim.sld.cu/noticias/noticia_ing.asp?NumN=65 (accessed 28 July 2006).

72  Lipschultz and Rojas, 'The Next Biotech Corridor: Cuba?'
73  Leonard Zehr, 'Biotech Builds on Cuban Innovation,' Cubanet.org, 2 May 2001, http://www.cubanet.org/CNews?y01/may01?02e8.hm (accessed 8 December 2005).
74  Ibid.
75  Andrew Pollack, 'Technology: U.S. Permits 3 Cancer Drugs from Cuba,' New York *Times*, 15 July 2004, http://query.nytimes.com/gst/fullpage. html?sec=health&res=9A04E1D8173AF936A25754C0A9629C8B63.
76  Lana Wylie, 'Revolutionary Biology: Cuban Biotechnology and US-Cuban Relations.' Working paper.
77  See, for example, Patrick Sullivan, 'Canada's Public Health System Beset by Problems: Report,' *CMAJ*, 166, no. 10 (2002); Nick Busing, 'Managing Physician Shortages: We Are Not Doing Enough,' *CMAJ*, 176, no. 8 ( 2007); Health Council of Canada, 'Health Care Renewal in Canada: Measuring up? Annual report to Canadians' (Toronto: Health Council of Canada, 2007), www.healthcouncilcanada.ca/docs/rpts/2007/HCC_ MeasuringUp_2007ENG.pdf (accessed 7 May 2007).
78  The College of Family Physicians of Canada, 'News Release: New Poll: Canadians Say Family Doctors Most Important to Their Health Care,' 23 October 2004, hospitalhttp://www.cfpc.ca (accessed 28 July 2006); New Women's College Hospital, 'Women's Health Matters News: More Than 1 in 5 Canadian Babies Delivered by C-section,' 22 April 2004, http://www. womenshealthmatters.ca/news/news_show.cfm?number=336 (accessed 28 July 2006).
79  In fact, according to the WHO, 99.9 per cent of births in Cuba are attended by a skilled health-care worker. The figure in Canada is 98.3 per cent. See WHO, 'Proportion of Births Attended by Skilled Health Personnel, Estimates by Country – 2006,' April 2006, http://www.who.int/reproductive-health/global_monitoring/data.html (accessed 31 July 2006).
80  PAHO, 'Cuba: Profile of the Health Services System,' 8 June 1999.
81  Brian Hutchison et al., 'Patient Satisfaction and Quality of Care in Walk-in Clinics, Family Practices and Emergency Departments: The Ontario Walk-in Clinic Study,' *CMAJ*, 168, no. 8 (2003); Wayne Kondro, 'No "Simple Solutions" to Emergency Log-jam,' *CMAJ*, 175, no. 1 (2006).
82  Pol De Vos et al., 'Shifting the Demand for Emergency Care in Cuba's Health System,' *Social Science and Medicine*, 60, no. 3 (2005): 609–16.

# 10 Canadian-Cuban Economic Relations: Past, Present, and Prospective

ARCHIBALD R.M. RITTER

Canada and Cuba have maintained a mutually fruitful economic relationship through much of the colonial era, from independence to 1959, and during the regime of President Fidel Castro from 1959 to 2007. The relationship flourished with respect to trade in the 1970s and 1980s. During the first half of the 1990s, the economic relationship was especially important for Cuba as it underwent its disconnection from the former Soviet Bloc. Canadian participants were enthusiastic and optimistic about future economic relations. However, in the 2000s, this was replaced by greater realism and perhaps some scepticism concerning the possibilities for deepening economic interaction, partly because of Cuba's quick displacement of Canada as a major source of agricultural imports by the United States after 2002. Canadian-Cuban relations will be determined in future by Cuba's future economic performance, the policy environment within which Cuba conducts its international economic relations, and the process of normalizing Cuban-United States relations.

The objective of this chapter is to analyse and explain the principal features of the economic relationship between Canada and Cuba in the decades of the 1990s and the 2000s, and to explore the major determinants and possible character of this relationship in future. A number of factors that will help shape the economic relationship in future are studied. First, Cuban economic recovery and greater prosperity may provide an important 'expansionary impact' on economic ties between the two countries. The character of economic policy in Cuba will also be an important determinant. The third factor, normalization of U.S.-Cuban relations, will have a variety of impacts, some of which will be 'expansionary' in nature and some of which will have a more negative 'displacement impact' for Canadian-Cuban economic relations. It is unclear whether the 'expansionary effect' will overwhelm the 'displacement effect.' Any future economic liberalization and *apertura* will also have mixed impacts on the economic relationship with Canada.

In this chapter, a range of economic linkages are examined, including trade in goods and services (notably tourism), direct foreign investment (DFI), international migration, and development assistance. Following a brief review of the evolving relationship from the 1959 Revolution to 1990, the nature of the economic relationship between Canada and Cuba is analysed in more detail for the 1990–2007 era. The future economic relationship is then explored, focusing on Cuba's economic recovery and policy environment and the impacts of normalization with the United States.

## Canada-Cuba Trade Relations

Canadian-Cuban economic relations were relatively modest before 1959. Trade flows do not seem to have been that large, although, when adjusted for inflation and population change, they appear more significant (see Table 1). Canadian banks and insurance companies were prominent in Cuba's economic life, however.

Following 1959, trade and 'correct' diplomatic relations were maintained between the two countries, Canada and Mexico being the only two countries in the hemisphere that did not break relations with Cuba. Canadian enterprises along with all other foreign firms were nationalized in 1960–1. Compensation was paid but a full and final settlement was not reached until November 1980. Some modest development assistance was provided beginning in 1972, but this was terminated in 1978 when such assistance was deemed by Canada to be inappropriate in view of Cuba's large-scale military interventions in Africa.

As can be observed in Table 1, the overall trade relationship between Canada and Cuba has waxed and waned in the 1960–2005 period. This, of course, is not surprising in view of the major changes that the Cuban economy underwent in these years. From a slow start in the 1960s, Canadian exports to Cuba increased substantially after about 1964. They reached high levels between 1974 and 1986, peaking at $870.7 million in 1980 in inflation-adjusted 2004 Canadian dollars. On the other hand, Cuban exports to Canada in this period were generally a good deal lower than Canadian exports. Indeed, throughout the 1960–90 period, Canada usually had a major trade surplus with Cuba.

Table 1
Canadian trade with Cuba, 1958–2006

| | Canadian Exports to Cuba | | Canadian Imports from Cuba | |
|---|---|---|---|---|
| Year | Current Values $CDN Millions | Constant 2004 $CDN Millions | Current Values $CDN Millions | Constant 2004 $CDN Millions |
| 1958 | 16.9 | 109.8 | 18.9 | 122.7 |
| 1960 | 13.0 | 82.1 | 7.2 | 142.1 |
| 1962 | 10.9 | 67.1 | 2.8 | 17.3 |
| 1964 | 60.9 | 359.1 | 3.4 | 29.4 |
| 1966 | 61.4 | 334.5 | 5.6 | 30.7 |
| 1968 | 45.0 | 227.5 | 5.1 | 25.9 |
| 1970 | 58.9 | 271.9 | 9.5 | 43.9 |
| 1972 | 58.7 | 248.3 | 11.1 | 46.8 |
| 1974 | 149.6 | 508.1 | 76.3 | 359.2 |
| 1976 | 258.4 | 734.0 | 60.3 | 171.8 |
| 1978 | 217.8 | 550.8 | 60.6 | 153.3 |
| 1980 | 419.8 | 870.7 | 157.3 | 325.2 |
| 1981 | 452.4 | 850.5 | 193.4 | 363.7 |
| 1982 | 324.4 | 558.7 | 94.8 | 163.3 |
| 1983 | 360.6 | 591.9 | 56.3 | 92.1 |
| 1984 | 337.6 | 537.0 | 62.7 | 100.1 |
| 1985 | 328.5 | 523.5 | 44.5 | 70.8 |
| 1986 | 364.5 | 552.3 | 71.1 | 107.7 |
| 1987 | 272.9 | 394.6 | 51.6 | 74.6 |
| 1988 | 229.4 | 317.0 | 36.6 | 50,7 |
| 1989 | 164.0 | 216.3 | 40.7 | 53.7 |
| 1990 | 170.5 | 218.3 | 130.2 | 165.5 |
| 1991 | 130.9 | 163.1 | 153.7 | 191.6 |
| 1992 | 130.9 | 161.0 | 256.1 | 315.1 |
| 1993 | 140.3 | 170.7 | 171.5 | 208.5 |
| 1994 | 107.7 | 130.0 | 194.4 | 235.0 |
| 1995 | 260.0 | 306.4 | 320.9 | 378.2 |
| 1996 | 263.0 | 304.8 | 401.2 | 465.0 |
| 1997 | 319.1 | 369.2 | 353.1 | 408.5 |
| 1998 | 431.7 | 493.8 | 334.2 | 382.8 |
| 1999 | 355.3 | 400.0 | 305.8 | 349.8 |
| 2000 | 333.1 | 365.1 | 408.5 | 447.7 |
| 2001 | 394.3 | 421.6 | 361.3 | 386.3 |
| 2002 | 280.6 | 293.3 | 325.1 | 339,9 |
| 2003 | 273.8 | 278.6 | 371.2 | 377.8 |
| 2004 | 327.7 | 327.7 | 590.1 | 590.1 |
| 2005 | 448.0 | 438.4 | 552.9 | 590.1 |
| 2006 | 512.9 | 533.4 | 629.2 | 654.4 |

Note: Trade values in constant $CDN are calculated using the Canadian GDP deflator with the base year set at 2004.
Source: Statistics Canada, Exports by Country, 65–003, and Imports by Country, 65–006; Industry Canada, Trade Data Online (TDO), Trade by Product (HS Codes), http://strategis.ic.gc.ca/sc_mrkti/tdst/tdo/tdo.php (accessed June 2007); Department of Finance, Quarterly Economic Review, June 1991; and IMF, World Economic Outlook, May 2000 and April 2005 for GDP Deflator.

As Cuba's economic difficulties began to intensify after 1986, its imports from all countries, including Canada, declined precipitously. In 'real' or inflation-adjusted terms, Cuba's overall decline in imports was about 70 per cent from 1986 to 1991. The principal cause of this decline, of course, was the termination of the special trade relationship with the Soviet Union, which had provided above-world prices for Cuba's sugar and nickel exports and below-world prices for Cuban imports of petroleum, not to mention generous trade credits never repaid. The ending of this hidden subsidization precipitated the decline in Cuba's export earnings and imports and generated the sharp economic contraction of 1990–4, from which it had fully recovered only by about 2006.

In general terms, Canadian exports to Cuba declined from the mid-1980s to 1994 mainly as a result of the contraction of the Cuban economy and especially because of the decline in exports of cereals to Cuba. However, after 1994, Canadian exports to Cuba rose quickly. This was due to several factors, including the renewed expansion of the Cuban economy, the vigorous marketing efforts by Canadian enterprises, and the diversification of Cuba's sources of imports (and exports) following the collapse of the special trade arrangements with the former Soviet Union.

Following the beginning of Cuba's economic recuperation in 1994 and continuing more or less to 2007, Canadian trade with Cuba expanded and became relatively important for Cuba. By 1998, Cuba's exports to, and imports from, Canada accounted for 8.0 per cent and 10.6 per cent of its total exports and imports respectively. Canada was Cuba's third-ranking export market, after Russia and the Netherlands. On the other hand, Canadian exports to, and imports from Cuba, constituted less than 1 per cent of Canada's total exports in 1998.

Cuba's exports to Canada also expanded from 1990 to 2006, though with some fluctuations. The increase was due to the expansion of nickel-concentrate exports from zero in 1990 to CDN$317 million by 1996. Nickel accounted for approximately 77 per cent of Cuba's total exports to Canada from 1996 to 1999. High nickel prices contributed to the high values of Cuban exports to Canada in 1996, and lower prices then contributed to their decline from 1996 to 1999. Exceedingly high prices for nickel from 2004 to 2006 then led to record levels of Cuban exports to Canada, reaching almost CDN$630 million in 2006 (Table 1).

Canadian exports to Cuba have fared less well than Cuba's exports to Canada since 1994. After 1994, Canadian exports to Cuba began to recover from their low levels of 1990–4, again with fluctuations. After

2001, however, Canada's exports started to fall short of its imports from Cuba. This was due largely to nickel-export volumes and high nickel prices. Canada has not maintained its export share in the Cuban market. As can be seen in Table 2, Canadian exports to Cuba have more or less stagnated since 2000, while other countries, including the United States, Venezuela, China, Spain, Germany, Vietnam, Japan, and Brazil, all have increased their market shares considerably. Canada's share of Cuba's import market has declined from about 7.6 per cent in 1995 to 4.3 per cent in 2005. By 2005, Canada was the fifth-ranking exporter to Cuba following Venezuela, China, Spain, and the United States. In contrast, Canada continues as a major export market for Cuba, accounting for 22 per cent of Cuba's exports, second only to the Netherlands, which is also a major importer of Cuban nickel.

In terms of the detail of the Canadian-Cuban trading pattern before 1990, its most significant feature was the large volume of cereal exports from Canada to Cuba (see Table 3). Cereal exports, mainly wheat, exceeded CDN$299 million (in current dollars) annually for the 1979–87 period – peaking at CDN$333 million in 1980. They accounted for 66 to 81 per cent of total Canadian exports to Cuba.[1] Cereals imports were recorded in Cuban statistical documents as imports from the Soviet Union, not from Canada, perhaps because they were transported on Soviet ships.[2] Cubans generally were and still are unaware that virtually all their wheat imports in this period were from Canada.

Some other features of the trade relationship are illustrated in Tables 3 and 4. The first and perhaps the most obvious characteristic of Canadian exports to Cuba is their instability. All major product groups and most specific items varied significantly from year to year. Much of this variation was related to the contraction and expansion of the Cuban economy, but some occurred within expansionary and contractionary periods as well.

A second feature in the trade pattern was the decline of Canadian cereals exports from levels exceeding CDN$300 million in the 1980s to zero in 1994 and low levels for some years before a recuperation in the 2000s, reaching a high of CDN$33.7 million in 2005.[3] This reflected a general reduction in cereal imports to Cuba as a result of the country's economic contraction to 1994. A second explanatory factor, however, was the provision by France of generous trade credits, amounting to US$160–200 million annually from 1996 to 2000, which were used mainly for the purchase of French cereals imports.[4] Moreover, when the United States legalized exports of agricultural products and phar-

Table 2
Cuba's major trading partners, 1988–2005 (millions of Cuban pesos)

Cuba's Major Sources of Imports

| | 1988 | 1995 | 2000 | 2001 | 2002 | 2003 | 2004 | 2005 |
|---|---|---|---|---|---|---|---|---|
| TOTAL | 7580.0 | 2882.5 | 4798.6 | 4793.2 | 4140.8 | 4612.7 | 6662.0 | 7628.1 |
| Africa | 12.1 | | 24.6 | 20.0 | 10.2 | 85.6 | 69.9 | 147.7 |
| Asia | 294.6 | 303.5 | 783.9 | 887.4 | 822.4 | 922.0 | 1091.0 | 1591.0 |
| of which: | | | | | | | | |
| China | 175.9 | 170.8 | 443.7 | 548.5 | 516.9 | 501.6 | 583.0 | 885.3 |
| Japan | 88.6 | 24.3 | 83.1 | 80.7 | 68.2 | 110.7 | 159.0 | 246.7 |
| Viet Nam | 8.7 | 67.9 | 48.9 | 59.1 | 69.0 | 78.2 | 146.1 | 251.8 |
| Europe | 6911.9 | 1101.3 | 1819.1 | 1679.6 | 1437.5 | 1542.2 | 1631.5 | 1888.9 |
| of which: | | | | | | | | |
| France | 27.2 | 210.7 | 289.9 | 270.6 | 212.3 | 184.9 | 149.9 | 168.2 |
| Germany | 57.4 | 52.1 | 77.8 | 98.7 | 78.4 | 115.1 | 130.1 | 309.3 |
| Spain | n.a. | 353.0 | 743.2 | 693.7 | 564.9 | 581.3 | 633.0 | 653.3 |
| USSR/Russia | 5364.4 | 56.8 | 111.3 | 81.7 | 74.5 | 59.0 | 74.6 | 136.8 |
| Oceana | 0.7 | 9.6 | 4.5 | 61.2 | 58.6 | 49.2 | 64.5 | 69.7 |
| Western Hemisphere | 360.4 | 1441,3 | 2163.4 | 2145.0 | 1812.0 | 2013.4 | 2815.0 | 3830.7 |
| of which: | | | | | | | | |
| Brazil | n.a. | 33.8 | 130,1 | 156.5 | 110.4 | 107.5 | 176.5 | 312.4 |
| Canada | 28.6 | 220.3 | 311.1 | 364.1 | 240.1 | 231.6 | 254.8 | 327.9 |
| United States | 0 | 0 | 0 | 4.4 | 173.6 | 327.2 | 443.9 | 470.3 |
| Venezuela | 28.0 | 236.6 | 898.4 | 951.5 | 725.3 | 684.6 | 1142.7 | 1859.0 |

Cuba's Major Export Markets

| | 1988 | 1995 | 2000 | 2001 | 2002 | 2003 | 2004 | 2005 |
|---|---|---|---|---|---|---|---|---|
| TOTAL | 5518.3 | 1491.6 | 1675.3 | 1621.9 | 1421.7 | 1671.6 | 2188.0 | 1996.7 |
| Africa | 64.9 | 108.8 | 12.9 | 16.0 | 25.7 | 16.8 | 7.8 | 19.0 |
| Asia | 406.1 | 327.2 | 204.5 | 147.6 | 170.7 | 142.0 | 150.0 | 164.0 |
| of which: China | 226.2 | 188.9 | 80.5 | 73.7 | 74.6 | 77.3 | 80.1 | 99.6 |
| Europe | 4948.9 | 702.8 | 990.6 | 1077.0 | 864.2 | 924.6 | 1151.3 | 962.1 |
| of which: | | | | | | | | |
| Netherlands | 52.6 | 43,2 | 116.8 | 333.9 | 296.6 | 419.4 | 647.1 | 599.7 |
| Russia | 3683.1 | 194.5 | 324.6 | 404.7 | 278.4 | 132.1 | 120.8 | 57.6 |
| Spain | n.a. | 93.3 | 150.2 | 143.6 | 144.5 | 178.7 | 174.2 | 161.2 |
| Oceana | 0.3 | n.a. | 0.5 | 0.6 | 2.2 | 1.9 | 0.6 | 1.7 |
| Western Hemisphere | 98.1 | 351.1 | 466.7 | 380.8 | 368.8 | 587.3 | 876.5 | 852.0 |
| of which: | | | | | | | | |
| Canada | 38.5 | 230.8 | 277.9 | 228.3 | 203.2 | 266.7 | 486.8 | 437.9 |
| United States | 0 | 0 | 0 | 0 | 0 | 0 | 0 | 0 |
| Venezuela | 21.8 | n.a. | 14,0 | 21.9 | 19.4 | 175.8 | 225.4 | 241.0 |

Source: Oficina Nacional de Estadisticas, 2001 and 2005; Anuario Estadistico de Cuba.

Table 3
Canadian exports to Cuba, 1986–2006 (CDN$ thousands)

| Product Group and Major Exports | 1986 | 1988 | 1990 | 1991 | 1992 | 1993 | 1994 | 1995 | 1996 |
|---|---|---|---|---|---|---|---|---|---|
| Agriculture/Fishing Products, of which: | 291,103 | 185,504 | 113,364 | 89,192 | 63,648 | 64,073 | 41,732 | 98,807 | 108,918 |
| Cereals | 264,207 | 159,742 | 94,302 | 60,985 | 29,041 | 25,868 | 0 | 34,413 | 33,848 |
| Dairy Products & Poultry | 5,952 | 0 | 13 | 12,453 | 6,608 | 12,895 | 3,846 | 18,798 | 8,693 |
| Meat | 0 | 348 | 40 | 2,742 | 11,000 | 8,394 | 4,957 | 12,297 | 25,046 |
| Vegetables and Fruit | 18,890 | 16,315 | 7,466 | 2,148 | 7,396 | 5,889 | 25,299 | 16,181 | 37,621 |
| Fish | 250 | 2,514 | 0 | 2,411 | 937 | 1,455 | 954 | 1,533 | 331 |
| Chemical and Allied, of which: | 7,457 | 6,815 | 4,174 | 2,715 | 10,548 | 5,139 | 7,068 | 25,407 | 17,403 |
| Pharmaceutical | 0 | 1,617 | 420 | 861 | 1,294 | 461 | 504 | 159 | 822 |
| Fertilizers | 2,225 | 0 | 0 | 7 | 2,013 | 1,257 | 5,273 | 21,345 | 13,913 |
| Plastics, Rubber and Allied | 1,514 | 1,180 | 2,322 | 3,834 | 1,814 | 6,969 | 2,548 | 5,078 | 7,139 |
| Wood, Pulp and Paper, of which: | 11,217 | 8,300 | 3,750 | 5,567 | 2,749 | 7,045 | 4,377 | 21,395 | 7,875 |
| Wood | 3,130 | 365 | 9 | 92 | 357 | 1,970 | 370 | 2,487 | 1,644 |
| Paper | 7,742 | 7,935 | 3,741 | 4,893 | 2,003 | 4,950 | 3,196 | 13,212 | 5,096 |
| Minerals and Metals, of which: | 28,653 | 8,941 | 24,342 | 7,478 | 7,058 | 9,646 | 11,759 | 29,514 | 37,769 |
| Mineral Fuels | 9,836 | 81 | 2,527 | 2,864 | 145 | 4,497 | 1,284 | 2,500 | 957 |
| Iron and Steel and Products | 108 | 4,264 | 2,591 | 2,409 | 2,321 | 2,300 | 4,914 | 10,585 | 18,842 |
| Other Metals and Products | 18,709 | 4,596 | 19,224 | 2,205 | 4,592 | 2,849 | 5,561 | 4,872 | 4,135 |
| Machinery and Equipment, of which: | 14,867 | 11,289 | 17,569 | 17,353 | 23,305 | 38,904 | 29,146 | 51,210 | 62,489 |
| Machinery and Engines | 2,578 | 5,574 | 3,931 | 5,884 | 13,706 | 24,674 | 11,563 | 28,846 | 38,956 |
| Electrical Machinery & Equipment | 3,562 | 2,940 | 10,052 | 8,352 | 4,474 | 6,644 | 5,718 | 9,229 | 13,024 |
| Railway Equipment and Rolling Stock | 902 | 741 | 734 | 445 | 281 | 1,633 | 3,247 | 2,123 | 763 |
| Other Vehicles | 7 | 2,030 | 2,512 | 1,681 | 4,589 | 5,340 | 6,934 | 10,886 | 9,229 |
| Miscellaneous Manufactures, of which: | 10,737 | 3,840 | 4,963 | 3,975 | 3,966 | 8,485 | 10,794 | 12,003 | 16,155 |
| Optical, Photographic, Measurement | 0 | 1,713 | 604 | 950 | 841 | 485 | 1,565 | 1,715 | 1,843 |
| Furniture | 0 | 1,212 | 1,337 | 1,667 | 1,587 | 1,390 | 2,548 | 4,638 | 6,462 |
| TOTAL | 364,549 | 229,413 | 170,496 | 130,865 | 130,946 | 140,348 | 107,734 | 257,929 | 263,063 |

| Product Group and Major Exports | 1997 | 1998 | 1999 | 2000 | 2001 | 2002 | 2003 | 2004 | 2005 | 2006 |
|---|---|---|---|---|---|---|---|---|---|---|
| Agriculture/Fishing Products, of which: | 111,556 | 167,573 | 174,781 | | | | | | | |
| Cereals | 17,560 | 12,985 | 31,092 | 32,388 | 23,153 | 8,022 | 107 | 2,379 | 33,736 | 18,750 |
| Dairy Products & Poultry | 11,312 | 20,314 | 14,649 | 12,236 | 19,187 | 7,933 | 8990 | 7,113 | 9,552 | 3,957 |
| Meat | 30,290 | 50,959 | 36,996 | 33,216 | 46,167 | 25,465 | 14,768 | 13,617 | 13,606 | 15,366 |
| Vegetables and Fruit | 44,064 | 72,516 | 86,213 | 15,175 | 24,212 | 31,103 | 13,564 | 40,702 | 14,394 | 11,550 |
| Beverages | 2,220 | 1,103 | 400 | – | – | – | – | – | – | – |
| Chemical and Allied, of which: | 13,638 | 14,848 | 13,799 | 4,377 | 4,254 | 4,528 | 3,683 | 2,520 | 6,059 | 11.846 |
| Fertilizers | 8,164 | 3,200 | 8,637 | | | | | | | |
| Wood, Pulp and Paper, of which: | 17,102 | 20,155 | 15,671 | | 13,734 | – | – | – | – | – |
| Wood | 1,182 | 2,855 | 1,135 | – | 13,734 | – | 18,785 | 18,500 | 15,779 | 20,622 |
| Paper | 15,221 | 17,245 | 6,981 | 13,734 | | 15,744 | | | | |
| Minerals and Metals, of which: | 51,195 | 44,098 | 29,365 | | 12,704 | 9,744 | 8,626 | 15,629 | 17,941 | 28.857 |
| Iron and Steel and Products | 23,595 | 12,682 | 6,449 | 9,591 | 1,789 | – | – | 267 | 15,135 | 35,584 |
| Other Metals and Products | 6,498 | 12,482 | 5,615 | 179 | | | | | | |
| Machinery and Equipment, of which: | 86,059 | 124,591 | 84,559 | | 98,982 | 66,319 | 92,004 | 93,734 | 148,877 | 138,289 |
| Machinery and Engines | 39,387 | 66,156 | 37,805 | 66,957 | 30,095 | 18,636 | 21,203 | 21,822 | 37,180 | 49,817 |
| Electrical Machinery & Equipment | 17,060 | 37,110 | 19,772 | 22,030 | 22,700 | 15,188 | 14,754 | 17,445 | 26,440 | 35,584 |
| Other Vehicles | 28,372 | 19,973 | 20,111 | 25,819 | | | | | | |
| Miscellaneous Manufactures, of which: | 19,275 | 31,583 | 18,047 | | | | | | | |
| Optical, Photographic, Measurement | 5,159 | 9,448 | 4,705 | 5,757 | 8,599 | 5,514 | 6,351 | 6,079 | 7,738 | 12,348 |
| Furniture | 5,584 | 12,186 | 6,083 | 2,119 | 5,158 | 3,602 | 5,135 | 7,659 | 7,996 | 10,292 |
| TOTAL | 319,058 | 431,706 | 355,335 | 383,128 | 394,373 | 280,642 | 273,769 | 329,727 | 447,986 | 512,854 |

*Source:* Statistics Canada, *Exports by Country*, 65–003; and Industry Canada, Trade Data Online (TDO), Trade by Product (HS Codes), http://strategis.ic .gc.ca/sc_mrkti/tdst/tdo/tdo.php (accessed June 2007).

Table 4
Canadian imports from Cuba, 1989–2006 (CDN$ thousands)

| Product | 1989 | 1990 | 1991 | 1992 | 1993 | 1994 | 1995 | 1996 |
|---|---|---|---|---|---|---|---|---|
| Fish & Crustaceans | 11,538 | 11,021 | 10,476 | 10,235 | 12,724 | 23,018 | 14,374 | 12,298 |
| Sugar | 61,420 | 114,752 | 79,858 | 114,902 | 41,744 | 48,696 | 57,539 | 59,153 |
| Beverages & Spirits | 1,103 | 621 | 2,220 | 1,082 | 707 | 274 | 191 | 419 |
| Tobacco & Products | 842 | 1,263 | 938 | 1,106 | 932 | 1,627 | 2,629 | 3,385 |
| Nickel Concentrate | 0 | 0 | 54,242 | 123,355 | 108,850 | 112,325 | 237,873 | 316,754 |
| Precious Stones | 9,245 | 0 | 3,100 | 2,982 | 2,184 | 3,711 | 1,529 | 3,805 |
| Other | 4,160 | 2,497 | 2,939 | 2,482 | 4,360 | 4,766 | 6,779 | 5,346 |
| TOTAL | 88,308 | 130,154 | 153,773 | 256,144 | 171,501 | 194,417 | 320,914 | 401,163 |

| Product | 1997 | 1998 | 1999 | 2000 | 2001 | 2002 | 2003 | 2004 | 2005 | 2006 |
|---|---|---|---|---|---|---|---|---|---|---|
| Fish & Crustaceans | 18,087 | 1,580 | 9,126 | 13,110 | 11,830 | 11,499 | 6,173 | 8,096 | 4,604 | 3,719 |
| Sugar | 42,614 | 40,474 | 27,339 | 16,201 | 27,284 | 20,342 | 7,395 | 95 | 79 | – |
| Beverages & Spirits | 419 | 77 | 375 | 523 | 966 | 656 | 863 | 662 | 532 | 1,395 |
| Tobacco & Products | 7,553 | 834 | 7,700 | 5,678 | 5,732 | 5,573 | 5,663 | 4,992 | 4,812 | 5,295 |
| Nickel Concentrate | 273,743 | 264,102 | 242,455 | n.a. | n.a. | n.a. | n.a. | n.a. | n.a. | n.a. |
| Precious Stones | 27 | 9,374 | 5,450 | – | – | – | – | – | – | – |
| Other | 10,710 | 16,874 | 13,348 | 373,015 | 315,464 | 287,033 | 357,098 | 576,272 | 542,832 | 629,183 |
| TOTAL | 353,126 | 333,467 | 305,791 | 408,572 | 361,276 | 325,103 | 371,192 | 590,117 | 552,861 | 629,183 |

*Source:* Statistics Canada, *Imports by Country*, 65–006; and Industry Canada, Trade Data Online (TDO), Trade by Product (HS Codes), http://strategis.ic.gc.ca/sc_mrkti/tdst/tdo/tdo.php (accessed June 2007).

maceuticals in 2002, Cuba expanded its imports of U.S. foodstuffs immensely, in part at the expense of potential Canadian suppliers.

Third, Canada's exports to Cuba became steadily more diversified in the 1990s and 2000s. Although cereals exports declined, other food exports increased, as did machinery and equipment and some 'miscellaneous manufactures.' Canadian enterprises succeeded in winning part of the market potential resulting from the ending of the special relationship with the former Soviet Union.[5]

The composition of Cuba's exports to Canada changed drastically in the 1996–2006 period. Cuba's traditional exports either disappeared or shrunk while nickel exports came to totally dominate the export pattern (Table 4). Cuba's sugar exports to Canada all but disappeared, reflecting the collapse of levels of sugar production in Cuba. Fish and crustaceans exports declined sharply. Tobacco exports to Canada rose in the 1990s but have declined somewhat or remained relatively stagnant in the 2000s. On the other hand, Cuba's exports of nickel concentrates have expanded rapidly. Since 2000, it is difficult to know the proportion of nickel exports to Canada precisely; this information is not provided by Statistics Canada, presumably because of confidentiality reasons since there is only one enterprise involved in the trade – Sherritt International. However, there is no doubt that this trade is larger than in 1999, when it accounted for almost 80 per cent of exports to Canada. Indeed, because Cuba's traditional exports have almost all declined or are insignificant, the place of nickel exports has become even more predominant.

Tourism, of course, constitutes an important Cuban service export in general and to Canada in particular. Canada has been a principal source of tourists since 1979 and in many years the largest national source. By 2006, Canada was by far the largest source of tourists, with 604,300 arrivals or 27.2 per cent of the total (see Table 5). Indeed, Canada consistently has been the largest single national source of tourists from 1990 to 2005. For the year 2004, the last year for which total tourism earnings were available, the foreign exchange earned by Cuba from Canadian tourism was probably in the area of US$623.5 million or CDN$809 million (at the prevailing exchange rate of US$1.00 = CDN$1.299 for 2004).[6]

If one takes both Canadian tourism services plus Canadian merchandise imports from Cuba into consideration, Canada contributed about CDN$1,400 million (or US$1.077 million) in 2004. This is almost 20 per cent of the total value of Cuba's foreign-exchange earnings from exports of goods and services (and not including remittance payments,

Table 5
Canadian tourism in Cuba, 1990–2006 (thousands per year)

| Year | Total Tourist Arrivals, All Sources | Canadian Tourist Arrivals | |
|------|-------------------------------------|---------------------------|--------------------|
| | | Number | Percentage of Total |
| 1990 | 340.3 | 74.4 | 21.9 |
| 1991 | 424.0 | 81.1 | 19.1 |
| 1992 | 460.6 | 94.1 | 20.4 |
| 1993 | 46.0 | 114.8 | 21.0 |
| 1994 | 619.2 | 109.7 | 17.7 |
| 1995 | 745.5 | 143.5 | 19.2 |
| 1996 | 1,004.3 | 162.8 | 16.1 |
| 1997 | 1,170.1 | 169.7 | 14.5 |
| 1998 | 1,415.8 | 215.6 | 15.2 |
| 1999 | 1,602.8 | 276.3 | 16.2 |
| 2000 | 1,774.0 | 307.7 | 17.4 |
| 2001 | 1,774.5 | 350.4 | 19.8 |
| 2002 | 1,686.2 | 348.5 | 20.7 |
| 2003 | 1,905.7 | 452.4 | 23.7 |
| 2004 | 2,048.6 | 563.4 | 29.5 |
| 2005 | 2,319.3 | 602.4 | 26.0 |
| 2006 | 2,221.0 | 604.3 | 27.2 |

Source: ONE, 2001 and 2006, *Anuario Estadistico de Cuba*; Naciones Unidads; *Cuba: Evolucion Economica Durante 1999*, A.111.

development assistance, or possible direct foreign investment flows).[7] Canada is clearly an important trading partner for Cuba.

## Canadian Enterprises in Cuban Joint Ventures

There has been a major inflow of direct foreign investment to Cuba since 1991, when it opened itself to such investment in joint-venture arrangements with state firms. By 2000, foreign firms in 50 per cent ownership 'economic associations' with Cuban firms dominated a number of sectors, including mineral and petroleum exploration (100 per cent of total), international cigar marketing (100 per cent), telephone communications (100 per cent), international tourist hotels (10 per cent plus management contracts in about 40 per cent of hotels), and rum export (100 per cent).[8] Canadian enterprises have established a presence in Cuba in such economic associations. However, Sherritt International dwarfs the other Canadian firms.[9]

By the end of 1999, there were 72 joint ventures between Canadian firms and Cuban state enterprises, constituting about 19 per cent of the total and exceeded only by Spain, according to Cuban statistics.[10] In terms of the estimated values of foreign investment actually delivered or committed – rather than merely announced – Canadian firms accounted for US$600 million, or about 34 per cent of total foreign investment as of March 1999, a larger amount by far than any other country by that date.[11] A number of the joint ventures with Canadian participation are outlined briefly below.

*Sherritt International*

Sherritt International has a major stake in the Cuban economy that generates significant benefits for Cuba as well as for Sherritt. Some key performance indicators of its Cuban operations are summarized in Table 6. Sherritt International's connection with Cuba commenced in 1991 with purchases of Cuban nickel concentrate for its refinery in Fort Saskatchewan, Alberta (which had had insufficient volumes of concentrate for many years as well as an expiration of a refining contract with INCO in 1990). In 1994 Sherritt International and the Compania General de Niquel established a 50/50 per cent joint venture which now owns the Moa extraction, processing, and smelting operation, the Alberta metals refinery, and the international marketing enterprise. Currently, the Cuban government is a foreign investor in Canada as the part-owners of the nickel refinery, a fact not well known either in Cuba or Canada. In November 1995 the company underwent a reorganization in which the foreign activities, mainly in Cuba, were spun off in a separate enterprise, 'Sherritt International,' from the older fertilizer activities in Canada. A share issue designed to raise CDN$350 million accompanied the reorganization and was quickly subscribed. The president of the company, Ian Delaney, also negotiated an agreement with the Cuban government permitting Sherritt to enter other sectors of the economy, including energy, oil and gas, agriculture, tourism, transportation, communications, and real estate. By 2000, Sherritt had successfully diversified its activities into a number of these areas and had become a major conglomerate in Cuba.

The linking of the Moa nickel deposit and part of Cuba's processing capacity with the Alberta refinery and its access to attractive energy sources was a masterful move and has generated important benefits for Cuba and for Sherritt. Cuba thereby acquired a market for its nickel

Table 6
Sherritt International's Cuban operations in summary, 1996–2007

| Year | Metals | | | Petroleum and Gas | | Electric Power | |
|---|---|---|---|---|---|---|---|
| | Nickel (Millions of pounds) | Cobalt | Revenue ($CDN millions) | Sherritt's Share, Net Production (bpd) | Revenues ($CDN, millions) | Installed Capacity (MWh, thousands) | Revenues ($CDN millions) |
| 1996 | 24.4 | 2.3 | 199.2 | 3,920 | 53.0 | n.a. | n.a. |
| 1997 | 31.1 | 2.7 | 211.8 | 4,413 | 47.1 | n.a. | n.a. |
| 1998 | 29.8 | 2.8 | 177.6 | 7,781 | 59.4 | n.a. | n.a. |
| 1999 | 31.6 | 3.4 | 193.3 | 13,143 | 106.5 | n.a. | n.a. |
| 2000 | 29.5 | 3.1 | 299.0 | 17,424 | 165.2 | n.a. | n.a. |
| 2001 | 33.1 | 3.3 | 230.3 | 10,979 | 176.7 | n.a. | n.a. |
| 2002 | 33.8 | 3.4 | 252.9 | 13,963 | 218.8 | n.a. | n.a. |
| 2003 | 35.8 | 3.5 | 321.1 | 15,057 | 223.1 | 226 | 26.8 |
| 2004 | 34.9 | 3.7 | 462.9 | 19,389 | 200.9 | 311 | 104.0 |
| 2005 | 35.6 | 3.7 | 428.8 | 16,895 | 237.5 | 311 | 98.5 |
| 2006 | 24.3 | 2.7 | 543.4 | 15,859 | 272.1 | 311 | 105.7 |
| 2007 | 32.5 | 3.5 | 805.7 | | 303.5 | 375 | 117.7 |

Note:
1. Sherritt's revenue and production values reported here are based on the joint-venture agreements between Sherritt and agencies of the Cuban government.
2. Before 2000, oil production is defined as Sherritt's share according to production-sharing agreements. After 2000, the definition of oil production becomes 'Gross Working Interest Production', which is oil production after allocation to joint-venture partners but before allocation to agencies of the Cuban government.
3. MWh: Mega Watt hour; bpd: barrel per day.
Source: Sherritt International, various Annual Reports and Financial Statements, 1996–2007.

concentrate, earning a good deal of foreign exchange. It also gained access to improved production technologies relative to its older 1950s vintage U.S. technology and its 1960s vintage Soviet technology. This has generated gains in productivity, energy efficiency, environmental impacts, and health and safety. Cuba is now the joint owner of a vertically integrated nickel operation, from extraction through to refining and international marketing. Cuba also has obtained, through Sherritt, new technologies and managerial skills for oil and gas extraction and utilization and electricity generation, while Sherritt is able both to utilize more fully its Canadian refinery and to use its base in nickel to enter other sectors in Cuba. Its earnings from its Cuban operations are significant. The joint venture has been able to increase metal production and achieve high net operating earnings, which have been in the area of 40 to 50 per cent of gross revenues for most years depending on international nickel prices.[12]

Further increased capacity in nickel extraction, concentrating, and smelting was announced in 2005.[13] Capacity was slated to increase by around 36 per cent, to 59,000 tons per annum, which should generate important additional value-added and foreign-exchange earnings for Cuba as well as profits for Sherritt. In June 2007 Sherritt President Delaney announced plans for further investments of CDN$1.25 billion for both the metals and the energy sectors.[14]

Sherritt International's petroleum and exploration activities have been particularly successful. New sources of oil and gas have been discovered and extraction rates have increased dramatically through enhanced recovery techniques from 1996 to 2000 (see Table 6). Sherritt holds interests in eleven production-sharing contracts with the Cuban government covering 3.55 million acres. It has a 100 per cent interest in four contracts by which it 'provides services and technical assistance to enhance the production at specific wells, or to drill new wells in existing fields,' in exchange for a percentage of new oil production and accelerated cost-recovery provisions. The seven other contracts are for the development of new oil and gas fields.[15] Exploration and oil field development activities have increased Sherritt's share of proven and possible oil reserves significantly (see Table 6). Natural gas recovery has also been improved through the construction of two processing plants, a feeder pipeline network, and a 30-km pipeline to Havana.[16]

Sherritt International invested CDN$215 million for the construction of two integrated gas-processing and electrical-generation systems for the production of electrical power, in Boca de Jaruco and Varadero.

(This natural gas was previously flared and completely wasted.) Commissioned in mid-2002, these operations had a combined capacity of 226 megawatts and generated a significant proportion of Cuba's electricity. At the same time, they reduced sulfur emissions, a potential problem especially at the Varadero site, which is adjacent to the hotel zone. By 2007, installed electricity-generation capacity had been further increased to 376 megawatts, following an 85-MW expansion that came on stream in early 2006. Part of the CDN$1.25-billion investment announced in 2007 was earmarked for further increases in electricity generation from natural gas, bringing total installed generating capacity to 526 megawatts.

In February 1998 Sherritt International acquired a 37.5 per cent share of Cubacell, the cellular telephone operator in Cuba, for US$38 million, but this seems to have been resold. 'Sherritt Green,' a small agricultural branch of the company, entered market gardening, cultivating a variety of vegetables for the tourist market and conceivably for export to Canada.[17] Sherritt also purchased a 25 per cent share of the Las Americas Hotel and golf course in Varadero and a 12.5 per cent share of the Melia Habana Hotel, both of which are managed by the Sol Melia enterprise.[18] This holding also seems to have been divested.

In November 1996 Sherritt raised CDN$675 million, or about US$475 million, mainly for investment in Cuba over the 1997–2002 period.[19] Some of these funds were utilized for construction of the gas-processing and electrical-generation plants. Sherritt also made short-term loans to Cuba at 16 to 18 per cent interest for the finance of the sugar harvest of 1997.[20] However, in 1999, Sherritt redirected approximately CDN$360 million for use outside Cuba, a possible indication of the declining relative attractiveness of investing in Cuba vis-à-vis other countries at that time.

By 2007, Sherritt's Cuban operations were large and growing. Gross revenues reached CDN$954.7 in 2006, with operating earnings[21] for all operations at CDN$540 million. Capital expenditures for 2005 were recorded at CDN$237.2 million, including $37.2 million in nickel, $122.1 million in oil and gas, and $77.9 million in electrical generation. This was a strong indication of the optimism and confidence with which Sherritt viewed its future in Cuba, despite the various uncertainties.[22] Nickel and cobalt production were slated to increase. The new Santa Cruz oil and gas operation was to come on stream in 2006. Continuing oil exploration appraisal and development drilling amounting to CDN$140 million were under way.[23] New electrical-power generation had just become operative and major new expansions were being implemented.

*Other Joint Ventures*

A number of mineral-exploration companies had established joint ventures in Cuba by 1994 in association with Geominera S.A. Some 25 per cent of Cuba's territory had been leased for exploration by Canadian firms, or for the 'proving up' of some known ore bodies for mine development. Cuba was an ideal location for such exploration because much of the country had been covered by aero-magnetic and geological surveys in the Soviet era, and probable mineral occurrences could be surmised. As the vice-minister of basic industry, A. de los Reyes Bernardez, is quoted as saying, 'We have found the haystacks, we now want others to help find the needles.'[24]

A number of mining enterprises invested in exploration projects in joint ventures with Geominera. Some firms, such as Holmer Gold Mines, Joutel Resources, CaribGold Resources, Northern Orion, and MacDonald Mines, did locate or furthered the exploration of mineral occurrences. Unfortunately, the exploration undertaken from about 1992 to 2007 yielded disappointing results. For the 1992–2000 period, the uninspiring results appear to have been the result of a variety of factors, including lower mineral prices that reduced the incentive to invest heavily on mineral exploration anywhere, increasing production of a variety of minerals in other parts of the world, and perhaps the greater difficulty of raising exploration financing in Canada following the Bre-X scandal. However, in the 2000–7 period as well, few of the projects produced strong results, despite higher mineral prices. This would suggest that either the quality of the deposits was lower than that for other regions of the world or that the investment conditions, policy environment, and/or political risk were worse than elsewhere. The following are a few of the most notable developments in the mining sector from 1992 to 2007:

- Holmer Gold Mines appeared to be in the process of advancing the Loma Hierro silver property to production through a drilling program and an agreement to lease another nearby mine. However, Holmer merged with Lake Shore Gold Corporation on 31 December 2004. Subsequently, reference to the Cuban project disappeared from Lake Shore publicity.

- Despite some successful discoveries including a gold deposit, Mac-Donald Mines ceased its activities in Cuba because of low mineral prices and because it did not receive support from GeoMinera S.A. for an application for a three-year extension to July 2002 for its exploration licence.[25]
- Joutel, another major player in Cuba, raised CDN\$2.7 million for an extensive program of exploration of the La Zona Barita gold discovery in the Sierra Maestra concession near Santiago de Cuba and the El Cobre copper, gold, lead, silver, and zinc deposits. Its conclusion was that the results ranged from 'positive to less than encouraging,' and deferred a detailed feasibility study on its most promising prospect on account of low mineral prices. The successor enterprise to Joutel, Thundermin Resources, continued to maintain the properties in an exploratory status but without further development as of early 2007.
- The Cobre Mantua gold mine in Pinar del Rio, under a joint venture of Northern Orion, a subsidiary of Miramar Mining Corporation (CEO Walter Berukoff) and Geominera, appeared to be promising as of 1995. However, Northern Orion's ability to develop the copper phase of the mine depended on third-party financing that had not been forthcoming as of May 2007.[26] In consequence, the prospect remains dormant.
- CaribGold Resources, following a 5,600-metre diamond drilling program that was completed in late December 1998, reported an inferred geological resource of 430,000 ounces of gold, consisting of 2,300,000 tonnes grading 5.83 g Au/t on its joint venture Jacinto Project near Camaguey.[27] However, this prospect also remained dormant as of 2007.

An interesting joint venture was that between a specifically created component of York Securities and Cuba's Centre for Molecular Immunology. This venture, signed in 1995, was designed to undertake and finance the clinical trials and field testing of some of the centre's medical innovations and technologies for treatment of various cancers, in preparation for their licensing and subsequent marketing in major world markets. This project may lead to successful trials and subsequent penetration of international markets by some of Cuba's oncological innovations. It appeared that such trials had not yet been completed by early 2007.

A major real estate/tourism project was announced in October 1998 by an association between Cuba's luxury hotel chain, Gran Caribe, and Cuban Canadian Resorts International for a 2,000-unit set of four time-share condominiums with hotel and resort facilities in East Havana, Cayo Coco, Varadero, and Santa Lucia. This project was expected to cost a total of US$250 million.[28] It would have opened up an important new type of tourism for Cuba, with great long-term potential. However, in May 2000, the Ministerio para la Inversión Extranjera y la Colaboración Económica (MINVEC) announced a prohibition of foreign ownership of condominium units. Such a prohibition has effectively killed this and other such projects and damaged the credibility of Cuban public policies towards foreign investment.

Another project is that of Leisure Canada, owned mainly by Walter Berukoff, for the construction of some eleven hotels, two golf courses, and a marina, all in the context of a 'Village' concept for which Leisure Canada apparently has the exclusive rights in Canada.[29] Perseverance seems to have won out for this project. A legal opinion from the Cuban state legal enterprise, Consultoria Juridica International, confirmed access to the surface rights on a 34,000-square-metre ocean-front property for the Monte Barreto all-suite resort project in the Miramar section of Havana. This permitted the establishment of a joint-venture board and a shareholders meeting in early May 2007 to authorize the investment in the 238-room Phase One of the project at the end of 2007.[30]

There are a number of other joint ventures with Canadian firms. One example is the venture between Heath and Sherwood International and Geominera S.A. for a variety of exploration drilling services for minerals and petroleum. A Canadian enterprise, Intelcan Techno-systems of Ottawa, was involved in the construction of five airports in Cuba in the last few years, including Varadero and Havana International airports. These projects were externally financed and will be paid for ultimately by tourist traffic for the most part. The CDN$52-million investment in the Havana airport, for example, was financed by the Export Development Corporation (EDC) (33 per cent) and Intelcan itself (15 per cent).[31] The ultimate payment for the airports will come from passengers who have been paying US$25.00 (or now CUC25.00) as an airport tax on departure as of 2000.

*Difficulties Faced by Foreign Investors*

Canadian and foreign investors have faced a variety of restrictions, problems, and uncertainties which affect their operations negatively and reduce the general attractiveness of investing in Cuba. First of all, there is general uncertainty and doubt about the commitment of the Cuban government to the course adopted regarding foreign investment. Although official documents destined for international consumption welcome DFI, other statements from former president Fidel Castro and the media, often destined for domestic consumption, raise questions regarding its future role. For example, ex-president Castro waged an 'anti-globalization' campaign at annual international conferences from 1999 on, and often with himself as the principal personage at the podium. At these high-profile events, he presented himself as the champion against international capitalist imperialism in its 'globalization phase' and often dominated the proceedings. This type of publicity undoubtedly generated uncertainty among potential investors. Even Sherritt has not felt itself immune from the general uncertainties in Cuba: 'The Cuban Government's future policies relating to foreign investors and foreign exchange payments could be affected by the political and economic environment resulting from its limited access to foreign exchange. The Corporation is entitled to the benefit of certain assurances received from the Government of Cuba ... that protect it from adverse changes in law, although such changes remain beyond the control of the Corporation and the effect of any such changes cannot be accurately predicted.'[32]

Secondly, while the foreign investment law outlines 'rules of the game' for foreign investors, in fact, each possible foreign investment is determined on a case-by-case basis. Each potential project must be negotiated with the counterpart enterprise and the MINVEC. After delays and significant investments of time and money, foreign investors can be turned down for a variety of reasons. The prohibition of the time-share-condominium ownership model noted earlier did not inspire confidence among foreign analysts and observers in the stability of the basic policy environment.

A well-publicized case of what appeared to be discretionary decision making is that of FirstKey Project Technologies, which had been in negotiations for a US$450-million joint-venture project to upgrade the old Soviet-era electrical generation plants, thereby improving Cuba's electricity system. This project was apparently supported with a CDN$600,000 grant from the Canadian International Development Corporation (CIDA).[33] According to the chairman of the enterprise, the Cuban government reneged on the contract and then used the FirstKey engineering study as a guideline in discussions with enterprises in a number of European countries. There are a variety of other similar stories in circulation. The result of these is that the business community became somewhat more sceptical regarding investment potential in Cuba.

A third general limitation on foreign investment is that those activities oriented to domestic consumption in the peso economy are essentially closed to foreign investors. This is because earnings in domestic pesos (or *Moneda Nacional*), worth about US$0.04, cannot be repatriated at that rate but must accept a fictional rate of 1 Domestic Peso = US$ 0.90, which is the operational exchange rate for investment inflows and production costs for foreign investors. This makes sales in the domestic peso economy (with *Moneda Nacional*) unprofitable, since imported inputs bear the foreign-exchange cost but earn only domestic pesos. In effect, only those activities that earn foreign exchange directly through exportation of goods or services and some activities that service the tourist sector for hard currency are worth pursuing because profit repatriation cannot otherwise occur.

Fourthly, there are a number of aspects of business management which in theory are controlled by the state. The first of these is recruitment and selection of employees, which must be done through the Agencia de Contratación a Representaciones Comerciales (ACOREC), and not by the foreign firm. The wage system and salary scale are determined by the government as well. The foreign enterprises must pay wages and salaries in U.S. dollars (or Euros, after the U.S. dollar was withdrawn from use within Cuba at the exchange rate of 1 old peso *Moneda Nacional*) per US$1.11 while the workers are paid in 'old pesos' or *Moneda Nacional* (with the relevant exchange rate for Cuban citizens in recent years at 20 to 26 pesos per U.S. dollar). Workers in some activities also have received a U.S.$ or now a Convertible Peso salary supplement. With hiring and remuneration beyond their control, the effectiveness of the personnel management by foreign enterprises may be impaired.

A further potential problem that must produce unease for Canadian and other foreign enterprises operating in Cuba is the absence of basic labour rights. Cuban workers do not have the right to undertake independent collective bargaining or to strike. Unions are not independent organizations representing worker interests but are official government unions. Independent unions and attempts to establish them are illegal in Cuba. While this situation makes the labour force more docile in the short term, it may present problems for Canadian and other foreign enterprises in the future.

The basic United Nations declarations support freedom of association for labour. The International Labour Organization's Declaration on Fundamental Principles and Rights at Work includes, as the first fundamental right of labour, 'freedom of association and the effective recognition of the right to collective bargaining.'[34] This basic right, together with specific labour legislation ensuring effective implementation, is included in the North American Free Trade Agreement (NAFTA) side agreement on labour as well. Under this agreement, workers have the right to organize their own unions freely – independent of government-dominated unions. Cuban labour practice clearly violates international standards in this area. Business operation and profit making through collaboration in such an internationally unacceptable legal environment places Canadian and other foreign firms in a disreputable and extralegal situation.

Another issue regarding Canadian firms and Cuban labour is that the Cuban government acquires the largest part of the wage and salary expenditures of Canadian or other foreign firms, and pays the actual workers a small fraction – about 4 to 5 per cent – of what the foreign firms actually pay. In this view, foreign enterprises in joint ventures with Cuban state enterprises are providing direct financial support for the Cuban government in foreign exchange and as a quasi-tax. This view is often made by the U.S. supporters of the embargo or the Helms-Burton Bill.[35] However, the real value of the monthly wages and benefits actually received by the average worker is a good deal higher than the 'slave labour' claim, though less than the payments by the foreign firms. The real value would include the in-kind benefits of medical services, on-the-job meals, and perhaps education (which is free at all levels) as well as bonus payments and low-cost rationed products.

The rationale for the government's policy of receiving payments from foreign firms in U.S. dollars or now Convertible Pesos but paying Cuban labour in 'old' pesos in *Moneda Nacional* at a parity exchange rate is threefold. First, if workers were paid directly in Convertible Pesos, their incomes would be very high, more than twenty times the national average. Such income disparities are contrary to the objective of maintaining an equitable distribution of income. Secondly, workers receive high-quality health care and education for free. These are financed by general government revenues, of which the implicit taxes examined here are one part. Thirdly, the government uses the foreign exchange acquired in this way to purchase imports of food, medicines, and so on, which are then made available to the general population at low domestic prices (for which 1 peso acquired US$1.11 of imports in 2007).

Foreign enterprises therefore do provide foreign exchange and tax revenues for the government using this mechanism. Its effect is to make Cuban labour somewhat expensive for foreign firms relative to that in neighbouring countries, thereby impeding foreign investment in a diversified range of more labour-intensive activities of the sort that often locates in export-processing zones. But it also permits the government to share the foreign-exchange earnings in a fairer and more politically acceptable manner and to provide social services more effectively to Cuban citizens.

Finally, the Helms-Burton Bill (or the 'Cuban Liberty and Democracy Act,' as it is officially labelled) has generated uncertainties for foreign enterprises entering joint ventures with properties that might conceivably have been confiscated from U.S. citizens. Perhaps the only Canadian firm seriously affected by this is Sherritt, which is working the Moa mine and processing plant that were confiscated from Freeport Sulphur in 1960. The confiscation/compensation issues in general, and the Moa Bay Freeport Sulphur case in particular, are immensely complex, and it seems almost impossible to predict a final outcome for Cuba or for Sherritt.[36] However, other Canadian enterprises establishing in Cuba are well aware of the Helms-Burton Bill and seem to have avoided involvement with properties subject to possible litigation.

## Canadian Development Assistance

From June 1994, when Canadian development assistance to Cuba commenced, to 2006, the Canadian International Development Agency allocated approximately CDN$85 million to Cuba. Of this amount, CDN$38.2 million was bilateral assistance. Another CDN$44 million was channeled through CIDA's 'Partnership Program' with non-governmental organizations (NGOs), universities, and other organizations. About CDN$2.5 million was allocated through multilateral bodies. The detail of the assistance programming is summarized in Table 7.

About 36 per cent of Canada's assistance has been 'economic' in character, with about $21 million in a program area labelled 'modernization of the state.' Another CDN$10.8 million from 'CIDA INC' has been used to support the initiation of projects by Canadian enterprises with Cuban counterpart firms or to promote Canadian export activities, with an emphasis on the 1994–9 period, when about CDN$6 million was pro-

Table 7

Canadian development assistance to Cuba, 1994–2007 (with projections)

| Assistance Program and Partners | Years | Value $CDN, millions |
|---|---|---|
| I   Bilateral Development Assistance | | |
| A. Support for Economic Reform | 1996–2000 | $5.00 |
| Micro-Enterprise Taxation (Revenue Canada/ONAT) | | n.a. |
| Training in Monetary Policy (Bank of Canada/Cuban Central Bank) | | 2.00 |
| Economic Management Training (Dalhousie, U. Toronto/Ministry of Finance and Planning) | | n.a |
| Economic Policy Dialogue | | |
| B. Dialogue on Governance and Human Rights | | |
| Human Rights Fund Pilot Project | 1995–8 | 0.50 |
| Dialogue Fund (Multiple Canadian and Cuban Partners) | 1997–9 | 1.20 |
| C. Social Sector | | |
| Paper for School Notebooks and Textbooks | 1997–8 | 6.50 |
| Medicines | 1997–8 | 1.00 |
| Local Initiatives Fund | 1998 | 0.30 |
| Food Aid (Soya Oil) | 1998 | 5.00 |
| SUB-TOTAL | 1994–8 | 18.60 |
| II   Non-governmental Development Assistance | | |
| A. NGO Division | | |
| Numerous Projects, Canada-Cuba Inter-Agency Project (15 Canadian and 20 Cuban NGOs) | 1997–2002 | n.a. |
| B. Institutional Cooperation Division | 1996–2000 | 4.80 |
| Carleton University/University of Havana | 1997–2000 | 0.48 |
| University of New Brunswick/Cuban Universities, Bio-Medical Engineering | (Five Years) | 0.71 |
| University of New Brunswick/Cuban Universities, Marine Biology | (Five Years) | 0.75 |
| University of Sherbrooke/University of Havana, Cooperative Management | 1999–2004 | 0.75 |
| University of Manitoba/National Institute of Epidemiology and Microbiology, Environmental Health Risk Assessment | 1997–9 | 0.13 |
| McMaster University/ISPJAE, Information Management | 1996–8 | 0.74 |
| McGill University, Management in Tourism | 1995–7 | 0.75 |
| Simon Fraser University, Small Business Training | 1999–2004 | 0.75 |
| Dalhousie University/Three Cuban Universities, M.A. in Integrated Coastal Zone Management | | 0.57 |
| Canadian Urban Institute and Evergreen Foundation, Metropolitan Park Restoration | 1997–2000 | 0.35 |
| New Brunswick Community Colleges/Universidad de Cienfuegos, Support for Continuous Education Programs | 1997–2000 | n.a. |
| Collège de Maisonneuve, Health and Nutrition Training | | n.a. |
| C. Youth Programming | | |
| Canadian World Youth/Cuban Ministry of Education | | |
| Youth Exchange Programs | | |
| Your Internship Program: Assignment of 23 young graduates for work in Cuba | 1994–9 | ±6.00 |
| D. Industrial Cooperation Program | | |
| Thirty activities: feasibility studies, training, environmental and technology transfer | | |
| SUB-TOTAL | 1994–9 | ±11.60 |
| III   Multilateral Development Assistance | | |
| Contributions to Cuba through UNDP, UNICEF, FAO, World Food Program, PanAmerican Health Organization | 1994–9 | 3.80 |
| TOTAL | 1994–9 | ±34.34 |

| Assistance Programs and Partners | Years | Value $CDN millions |
|---|---|---|
| I | | |
| Bilateral Development Assistance | 1994–2006 | $38.50 |
| A. Modernization of the state | | |
| Tax Administration (Revenue Canada/Oficina Nacional de Administracion Tributaria) | 1996–2005 | $6.00 |
| Economic Management (Ministry of Economic Planning) | 1999–2005 | 6.90 |
| Capacity Building (Certification Standards/ Ministry of Basic Industry) | 2001–9 | 8.10 |
| B. Local Development Cuba | | |
| NGO Strengthening Project (Oxfam) | 2000–3 | 1.00 |
| Community-based Development Project | | 1.20 |
| Local Human development in Eastern Cuba (UNDP) | 2004–9 | 5.00 |
| C. Social Sector Development | | |
| Pharmaceutical Donations (Ministry of Health) | 1995–2006 | 14.80 |
| D. Environment and Climate Change | 2002–5 | |
| Forestry management | | 1.20 |
| Rio Almenderas Clean-Up project | | 0.23 |
| Three climate change projects | | 1.40 |
| II | | |
| Partnership Branch | 1994–2006 | 44.0 |
| NGOs | | |
| Social Service Access (CARE Canada) | 2003–4 | 0.70 |
| Health projects (Comite de Solidarite Tiers-Monde de Trois Riviers) | | 1.10 |
| Wildlife Management (World Wildlife Fund Canada) | 2003–7 | 2.10 |
| A. Universities and Colleges | | |
| Northern Alberta Institute of Technology | 2000–4 | 0.40 |
| University of New Brunswick, Biomedical Engineering and Marine Sciences | 1999–2005 | 1.50 |
| University of Sherbrooke, MA in Co-operative Management | 1998–2004 | 0.70 |
| Dalhousie University. MA inCoastal Zone Management | 1999–2004 | 0.70 |
| University of Guelph, Environmental Engineering | 2002–7 | 0.80 |
| University of Manitoba, Environmental Health Risk Assessment | 2002–5 | 0.50 |
| New Brunswick Community Colleges, various projects | 1999–2008 | 1.50 |
| Institut de Technologie Agro-alimentaire de la Pocatierre, Sustainable Agriculture | 2003–8 | 0.50 |
| B. Youth Programming | | |
| Canada World Youth Exchange Program | 2002–5 | 1.50 |
| C. Other Institutions: various projects | | 1.50 |
| D. Industrial Cooperation program | | |
| Support for Canadian firms in association with Cuban Counterparts (53 since 1994) | 1994–2006 | 10.80 |
| III | | |
| Multilateral Assistance | | |
| Canadian contributions to Cuba through United Nations Organizations (World Food Program, UNDP, UNICEF, UN Population Fund, and the Pan-American Health Organization) | 1996–2006 | 2.50 |
| TOTAL | 1994–2006 | $85.00 |

Source: CIDA, 'Programming Framework, Canadian Cooperation Program in Cuba,' 2006, http://www.acdicida.gc.ca/CIDAWEB/acdicida.nsf/En/NIC-223122217-NDJ.

vided for around thirty projects. Some of the main economic programs were micro-enterprise tax administration, economic management, support for technical training and computer acquisition at the Cuban Banco Nacional, a program to help strengthen administration and professional economics at the Ministerio de Economía y Planifación, and training/certification programs for tradesmen in some basic industrial areas. Various types of commodity assistance were provided as well, including CDN$5 million for food aid (soya), paper for school notebooks and texts, and pharmaceuticals (CDN$14 million). Much of the assistance provided by NGOs was also aimed at various types of economic activities at the community level.

A small amount of assistance, some CDN$1.7 million, was directed towards human rights and governance initiatives including a 'Human Rights Fund Pilot Project' and 'Dialogue Fund' with multiple Canadian and Cuban partners. In the 2000–6 period, substantial emphasis continued to be placed on economic areas under the 'Modernization of the State' rubric. However, CIDA also directed funding towards local development projects as well as an interesting range of social and environmental projects through the Partnership and the Bilateral Branches, with NGOs and the universities as executing agencies.

Canada's International Development Research Centre has provided about CDN$1.1 million for research projects relating to urban agriculture, electronic commerce and sustainable tourism, and an MA program in economics at the University of Havana (designed to support upgrading in economics teaching and research in Cuban universities).

Although difficult to quantify, there have probably been significant benefits for the Cuban people from CIDA's assistance programs. The commodity assistance was of obvious importance in view of the shortages of foodstuffs and basic teaching materials in the 1990s. In-kind contributions of pharmaceuticals have been of similar benefit. The project in support of tax administration for the micro-enterprise or self-employment sector has been vital for public-revenue generation. However, it has also permitted the imposition of taxation burdens which are particularly onerous and perhaps lethal for such enterprises.[37] The other projects in support of public administration, training in economics, and economic policy making will have important benefits in the long run, but the short-term impacts appear limited.

The government of Canada has supported the trade and investment relationship with credits from the Export Development Corporation and some funding from CIDA for potential exporters and investors.

Table 8
Cuban permanent residents in Canada, 1980–2006 (number per year)

| Year | Number | Year | Number | Year | Number |
|------|--------|------|--------|------|--------|
| 1980 | 306 | 1989 | 129 | 1998 | 525 |
| 1981 | 40 | 1990 | 73 | 1999 | 693 |
| 1982 | 93 | 1991 | 165 | 2000 | 854 |
| 1983 | 106 | 1992 | 237 | 2001 | 971 |
| 1984 | 110 | 1993 | 385 | 2002 | 899 |
| 1985 | 148 | 1994 | 372 | 2003 | 876 |
| 1986 | 133 | 1995 | 443 | 2004 | 858 |
| 1987 | 140 | 1996 | 12 | 2005 | 979 |
| 1988 | 83 | 1997 | 560 | 2006 | 1,045 |

Source: Citizenship and Immigration Canada, 2006, 1996, and other years,http://www. cic.gc.ca/english/resources/statistics/facts2006/permanent/15.asp.

The EDC, for example, provided hard-currency funds for the new José Martí international airport at Havana, as well as the airport at Varadero, both of which, in turn, paid for exports of high-technology Canadian airport equipment. These two installations have been valuable for the development of Cuban tourism.[38]

**International Migration**

An economic dimension of Canadian-Cuban relations of steadily increasing significance is migration from Cuba to Canada. As indicated in Table 8, Cuban migration to Canada rose from low levels in the hundreds from 1981 to 1990 to over 1,000 per year in 2006. (Emigration from Cuba was exceptionally large in 1980 because of the Mariel exodus.) This, of course, is small compared to the overall flow of immigrants to Canada, which was 262,236 in 2005, and also relative to Cuban emigration, which was 33,358 in 2005 according to Cuba's Oficina Nacional de Estadisticas.[39] It is likely that some of the Cuban immigrants to Canada moved on to the United States, especially Florida, reflecting the attraction of the large Cuban American population there and the weather relative to Canada. How many Cuban immigrants to Canada eventually move on to the United States is not known.

There appears to be virtually no migration from Canada to Cuba. However, one could foresee circumstances in which some Canadian citizens in the future might take up residence in Cuba for at least part of the year if such property arrangements as time-share condominiums were to become possible.

Emigration from Cuba to Canada has increased for a variety of reasons. The economic difficulties of the 1990s provided an important 'push' force. Higher incomes in Canada plus political motivation have also been significant 'pull' factors. The possibility of migration has steadily increased as contacts with Canadians have intensified. This has occurred mainly through tourism, and significant numbers of Cubans have left the country after meeting and marrying Canadians. Other contact with Canadians, leading to migration, has occurred through business and professional travel abroad by Cubans and through educational opportunities for Cubans in Canada.

Detailed sociological information on Cuban emigrants is not available. However, my impressions are that, generally speaking, Cuban immigrants to Canada are relatively well educated, industrious, self-activating, and entrepreneurial. Cuban migrants also seem to be relatively young, for the most part, many having recently finished their education and just starting out on their careers. Migration arising through family reunification and migration of children in families also occurs, of course. Many, though not all, Cuban immigrants to Canada seem to have done reasonably well and have found work in their professional areas, something that is not easy in a new society with a different culture and language.

There are economic gains and losses – not easily quantifiable – arising from Cuban migration to Canada. Immigrants gain as a result of higher incomes. There are major gains in terms of civil and political liberties that exist in Canada vis-à-vis Cuba. For most, there are significant real gains in terms of the personal mobility and freedom of movement domestically and internationally that comes with higher incomes in a convertible currency, plus a Canadian passport.

There are economic losses for Cuba arising from the emigration of its citizens to Canada but also some gains. Cuba loses 'human capital' and the investment that has gone into rearing, educating, and providing medical attention for citizens who then leave the country. On the other hand, emigrants to Canada provide financial support and send funds back to their families in Cuba, funds ultimately captured by the tax administration and the central bank.

For Canada, there are major gains arising from Cuban immigration. Canada acquires the 'human capital' that Cuba loses, receiving mature adults often starting their families, without investing in the upbringing, education, or medical care of the immigrants prior to their arrival. In other words, Canada receives the benefit of the work of Cuban immigrants as parents and workers, while Cuba has made the investment in the human capital of the migrants. Impressionistic evidence suggests also that Cuban immigrants fit readily into Canadian culture and way of life. It is hard to detect any social costs to Canada that may arise from immigration from Cuba.

## Prospective Canadian-Cuban Economic Relations

The future economic relationship between Canada and Cuba will be shaped mainly by three factors: the strength and durability of Cuba's economic recovery; the character of Cuba's economic policies affecting trade and foreign investment; and the process and timing of normalization of relations with the United States.

A sustained recovery of the Cuban economy would promote a deepened and broadened economic relationship with Canada. A growing Cuban economy would permit increases in imports from all trading partners, including Canada. Conversely, Cuban economic stagnation or a slow and reluctant recovery would limit the expansion of imports into Cuba. At the same time, a steady and sustained economic recovery in Cuba requires expansion of its exports of goods and services. It is unlikely that Cuba can continue to rely on increased inflows of foreign exchange from remittances sent to their relatives by Cubans abroad, since this type of inflow may be close to its limits. Export-led economic growth will involve increased exports to Canada and elsewhere, as well as increased tourism.

Is a sustained recuperation of the Cuban economy probable in the next decade or so? That is a difficult, speculative question which is well beyond the scope of this chapter. However, a few comments are in order here. First, the driving force for the Cuban economy, namely export earnings, has strengthened considerably since the mid-1990s because of tourism, medical services, and nickel exports, but not because of other merchandise exports, which have stagnated and indeed declined. The foreign-exchange situation has also benefited greatly from Venezuelan subsidization through favourable terms and conditions for petroleum imports, and through increased domestic production of petroleum and natural gas which reduces import requirements (largely owing to Sherritt International). Is this foreign-exchange situation sustainable? A quick estimate would be 'yes' with respect to nickel exports, tourism,

and increased oil production which may in time move into oil exportation. But it is doubtful that Venezuelan generosity will continue forever,
and médical-service exports may also be transitory. Little progress appears imminent regarding the expansion of other merchandise exports.
On balance, the picture remains mixed but with a probable expansionary trajectory.

Other elements of Cuba's development strategy have not changed
and are unlikely to change for some time after Fidel Castro leaves the
scene. The central elements of this strategy include:

- a continuing predominant major role for public ownership, and
  state planning albeit on a more decentralized basis;
- a minor and perhaps reduced role for the domestic private sector
  together with limited direct foreign investment;
- maintenance of social programs within the context of conservative
  monetary and fiscal policies; and
- acceptance of 'monetary dualism' for the time being with a future
  strengthening of the role of the peso.

This basic approach, in place more or less since 1995, has had reasonable results so far, achieving an average annual growth rate in per capita
terms of 3.4 per cent from 1994 to 2002 and more rapid rates from 2003
to 2007. These more positive results should continue for some time.
On the other hand, if petroleum exports were to become possible, the
picture might improve dramatically. The downside possibility is that
nickel prices decline, and that lower petroleum prices impair the ability
or the willingness of Venezuela to support Cuba financially.

Some continuing problems may prompt scepticism regarding Cuba's
economic prospects in the near future. Among the difficulties and uncertainties often cited are:

- a dual exchange-rate system with negative consequences for export
  diversification and expansion;
- a generalized blockage of people's initiatives, energies, and en-
  trepreneurship owing to the unwillingness to extend further the
  reform process, especially for micro and small enterprise; and
- continuing low levels of *net investment* and continuing deterioration
  of parts of the capital stock.

Is the optimistic or the pessimistic estimate of Cuba's economic future more probable? Perhaps both are at least partially appropriate. In any case, the deeper and more sustained the economic recovery of Cuba, the better for Canada's relations with Cuba in terms of mutually beneficial interaction through trade, tourism, and investment.

Cuba's general economic policies relating to trade, foreign investment, and tourism are unlikely to undergo dramatic change in the short to medium term. 'More of the same' would be an obvious prediction as long as Raúl Castro remains at the helm. A further liberalization of economic policy and strengthened *apertura* appears highly improbable and a major reversal of the 'semi-*apertura*' policy measures is unlikely to occur, because the cost to Cuba would be high. This implies that the basic Canadian-Cuban economic relationship should not be affected seriously by changed Cuban policies in the next few years. However, Cuba has also shifted its priority partnerships to China and Venezuela, which, with state-directed trade, have become its most important trading partners. This will likely continue, and is not intrinsically beneficial for Canada.

The normalization of U.S.-Cuban relations, when it occurs, will have a major effect on the economic relationship between Canada and Cuba. Although any analysis of the possible processes of normalization is also beyond the scope of this chapter, there can be no doubt that it will take place at some time. When full normalization is established, it will have important effects on Cuban trade patterns, direct foreign investment, tourism, financial flows, and the availability of credit from international financial institutions and commercial banks as well as on Cuban economic prosperity.

The most immediate impact of normalization would likely be an increase in U.S. tourism to Cuba. After almost half a century of the embargo, there is a huge pent-up demand on the part of Americans to visit Cuba, and one might predict an explosion of 'curiosity tourism.' Family-reunification tourism would increase rapidly as Cuban Americans visit relatives with greater ease, lower costs, and greater frequency than is now possible. Short-term convention tourism, weekend tourism, cruise-ship tourism, ecological tourism, sport tourism, medical tourism, and 'snowbird' tourism (by pensioners for some of the winter months) should all increase as well. The result would probably be higher prices in tourist facilities, a construction boom in hotels, time-share condominiums, and sea-side cabanas, and an expansion of all tourist-related activities. The likely impact of such an expansion of U.S. tourism to Cuba is that Canadian tourism, which is concentrated in the lower-cost beach areas, would be squeezed out in part by higher prices. On the other hand, Canadian exports would benefit from the greater prosperity which U.S. tourism would help to generate.

Normalization with the United States and the prosperity that this should help generate will lead to expanded exports of goods and services to Cuba from the United States and vice versa. This is due to geographic and transport factors, since proximity provides low-cost and rapid access to many of each other's markets. Indeed, normalization could even lead to a reconnection of U.S. and Cuban railway systems. More frequent freighter connections, high-speed hydrofoil-passenger-boat connections, and a proliferation of airline routes will result in a steady reintegration of the two economies. The diversified U.S. economy is obviously capable of providing a broad range of consumer and capital goods and services competitively with other countries, and with relatively advantageous transport costs and delivery times.

Canadian exporters to Cuba therefore will face a challenge after U.S.-Cuban normalization. This has already happened with Cuban imports of agricultural products from the United States, legalized in 2002. Canadian exporters of a diverse range of products have established a strong presence in Cuba. Some Cubans also emphasize that the goodwill built over almost fifty years would not soon be forgotten. However, it is now clear that the location and logistic advantages of U.S. exporters, plus the activism and advantages of the Cuban American business community, will outweigh any lingering 'goodwill effect' with Canada. This is borne out by the alacrity with which Cuba shifted from Canadian to U.S. suppliers of agricultural products as soon as this became possible in 2002. Overnight or next-day delivery of products ordered from the United States makes continuation of some types of exports from Canada difficult, since delivery from Canada currently may take up to two weeks on ships leaving Canada every nine or ten days on average.

On the other hand, some of Canada's current exports to Cuba are competitive with U.S. products and should increase in a post-embargo Cuban economic recovery.[40] Machinery and equipment exports will face U.S. competition after U.S.-Cuban normalization, although Canada is competitive in certain types of capital equipment and should do well when the Cuban economy recovers.[41] Among the lines that are promising for the future are minerals machinery and equipment, papermaking equipment, medium-size aircraft, railway rolling stock and equipment, urban-transit vehicles, telephone-communications equipment, electrical generation and distribution equipment, and some specialized vehicles. However, a large proportion of Canadian exports may be threatened by U.S. competition. Many agricultural and food products, chemical products, pharmaceuticals, plastics, and a variety of light consumer goods may be replaced by U.S. suppliers if they have not been already. Needless to add, those types of products now supplied principally by China will likely continue to be supplied by that country for some time.

In summary, the recovery of the Cuban economy and the increase in foreign- exchange receipts that U.S.-Cuban normalization in time should bring about will be of benefit for some Canadian exporters while others may be replaced by U.S. suppliers. Will the 'recovery effect' outweigh the costs of the 'displacement effect' for Canadian exporters? Perhaps, but this is not assured.

Normalization will also induce U.S. enterprises to invest in Cuba, most immediately in petroleum extraction. With no further changes to the foreign investment law and within the current policy environment, one can imagine some but not many U.S. firms entering joint ventures. With policy liberalization in a post-Castro situation, however, large numbers of U.S. enterprises as well as those of other countries will likely begin investing in Cuba. Cuban Americans would also enter Cuba to set up small businesses, to establish joint ventures, or to finance business ventures with their Cuban relatives or counterparts.

Most Canadian firms in existing joint-venture arrangements seem to have entered Cuba with a long-term time horizon and knowledge that normalization with the United States would eventually occur. They therefore appear to be ready to adjust to this eventuality, although some may face difficulties. Sherritt's joint venture with the Compañia General de Niquel at Moa may face property-rights complications. This potential claim does not appear to be of great concern to Sherritt and its president, on the grounds that the compensation-claim issue was strictly between the governments of Cuba and the United States. Yet it is not clear how the compensation issue will be handled. Restitution is improbable. Full compensation is improbable if not impossible for all of the claims against Cuba (amounting to US$14.4 billion in mid-1996). Cuba is also ready with its own claims against the United States, totalling much more than the U.S. claims against it. However, any property rights dispute between the U.S. and Cuba over Moa could produce major uncertainties for Sherritt.

In summary, there are future uncertainties and challenges regarding the Canadian-Cuban economic relationship. Sustained economic improvement in Cuba, a favourable policy environment, and normalization of relations with the United States are intrinsically ambiguous and uncertain. These factors will have mixed effects, but effects that on balance should be positive for both Canada and Cuba.

## Conclusion

Canada and Cuba have developed a close and mutually advantageous economic relationship during the 1990s and 2000s. Trade, tourism, foreign investment, development assistance, and migration all expanded significantly from 1994 to 2007, albeit with some 'ups and downs.' The Canadian economic connection has been especially valuable for Cuba. Canada has been the largest trading partner, source of tourists, and investor in terms of the value of investment. The Canadian connection has been responsible for a very large proportion of Cuba's foreign-exchange earnings generated by tourists, nickel exports, domestic oil and gas extraction, and electricity generation.

Canada's economic relations with Cuba are likely to change in a variety of ways in the next ten to fifteen years. First, the United States and Cuba will undoubtedly normalize their relations sooner or later. When this happens, the economic and human interaction between those countries will quickly overwhelm the Canada-Cuba interaction. The 'geo-economic' gravitational pull of the United States will be overpowering. Indeed, this is already in process with the rapid expansion of U.S. exports of food and medicines after 2002. Following U.S.-Cuba rapprochement, Canadian trade and investment as a proportion of total trade and investment will likely diminish even though both might increase in absolute terms. In sum, the 'displacement effect' will be strong. Will it outweigh the 'expansionary effects' on Canadian economic relations with Cuba that will result from the economic recovery that will be stimulated by U.S.-Cuban normalization?

NOTES

1 Statistics Canada, *Exports by Country*, 65–003, successive years.
2 Comite Estatal de Estadisticas, Anuario Estadistico, 1988, 476–9.
3 Agriculture and Agri-food Canada, *Exports to Cuba, Canada's Agri-food, 2004–2007*, www.ats.agr.gc.ca/stats/Cuba_x_e.pdf+exports+to+cuba:+ca

nada%27s+agri-food+2007&hl=en&ct=clnk&cd=1&gl=ca (accessed 5 June 2007).

4  U.S.-Cuba Trade and Economic Council, 'Economic Eye on Cuba,' 21–7 February 2000, www.cubatrade.org/eyeon.2000h (accessed 25 September 2007).

5  The marketing efforts of Canadian firms in this period are illustrated by the fact that 112 out of a total of 493 enterprises represented at the 1994 trade fair in Havana were Canadian (*Granma International*, English Edition, 15 June 1994).

6  Oficina Nacional de Estadisticas, *Anuario Estadistico de Cuba*, 2001, 2005, and 2006 (2005, Table II.21), http://www.one.cu/aec2005.htm (accessed June and September 2007); and Naciones Unidas, Cuba: Evolucion Economica Durante 1999, A.111ONE, Capitulo XIII.

7  Naciones Unidas, Balance Preliminar de las Economias de America Latina y el Caribe, Santiago, Chile, 2006, 120.

8  J. Perez-Lopez, 'Foreign Investment in Cuba,' in Archibald R.M. Ritter, *The Cuban Economy* (Pittsburgh: University of Pittsburgh Press, 2004), 155.

9  Sherritt is one of largest foreign investors in Cuba along with the Spanish/ French Alliance Tabac Distribution or Altadis, which purchased 50 per cent of Cuba's cigar- exporting enterprise for a reported US$500 million.

10  Perez Villanueva, 'La Evolucion Economica Reciente en Cuba: Una Valoracion,' unpublished essay, July 2000, 27.

11  U.S.-Cuba Trade and Economic Council, 'Foreign Investment in Cuba,' 1999, www.cubatrade.org/foreign (accessed 25 September 2007).

12  Sherritt International, *Annual Reports,* various issues, http://www.sherritt. com/Investor_Relations/Financial_Reports/Annual_Reports.html (accessed September 2007).

13  'Importante ampliacion de la produccion de niquel metalico y cobalto,' *Granma*, 4 March 2005.

14  '1.25 Billion Slated for Cuba,' Miami *Herald*, 7 June 2007.

15  Sherritt International, 1999 *Annual Report*, 11, http://www.sherritt.com/ Investor_Relations/Financial_Reports/Annual_Reports.html (accessed September 2007).

16  Sherritt International, 1997 *Annual Report*, 13, http://www.sherritt.com/ Investor_Relations/Financial_Reports/Annual_Reports.html (accessed September 2007).

17  *Granma International*, 'Fruit and Vegetables in Varadero's Back Yard,' 3 April 1996.

18  Sherritt International, *Annual Report*, 2001, 16, http://www.sherritt.com/

Investor_Relations/Financial_Reports/Annual_Reports.html (accessed September 2007).

19  Sherritt International, 1997 *Annual Report*, 38, http://www.sherritt.com/ Investor_Relations/Financial_Reports/Annual_Reports.html (accessed September 2007).

20  R. Siklos, 'Sherritt Buys Cuba T-Bills,' *Financial Post*, 24–6 May 1997, 1.

21  Operating Earnings are defined as EBITDA, that is, earnings before taxes, interest, depreciation, and amortization, a standard measure for earnings.

22  Sherritt International, 'Management's Discussion and Analysis and Financial Statements,' 2006, 19.

23  Sherritt International, *Annual Report*, 2006, 19, 22, and 24, http://www. sherritt.com/Investor_Relations/Financial_Reports/Annual_Reports.html (accessed September 2007).

24  K.R. Suthill, 'Cuba Turns to the Pragmatists,' *Engineering and Mining Journal*, May 1994, 28–39.

25  MacDonald Mines, Consolidated Financial Statements, 1998 and 1999.

26  Northern Orion Resources , 40-F for 12/31/05, SEC File 1–31927, 31 March 2006, http://www.secinfo.com/d12MGs.117g.htm (accessed September 2007).

27  Business Wire, 'Carib Gold Announces 430,000 Ounces of Gold Near Camaguey, Cuba,' 1 February 1999, http://findarticles.com/p/articles/ mi_m0EIN/is_1999_Feb_1/ai_53680222 (accessed September 2007).

28  Cuban Club Resorts, 2000, www.cubanclubresorts.com (accessed June 2001).

29  Leisure Canada, Press Release, 17 August 2000, reproduced at www. cubanet.org.

30  Leisure Canada, Press Release, 'Leisure Canada's Monte Barreto Project Moves Forward with Surface Rights,' 18 April 2007.

31  D. Israelson, 'Our Man in Havana,' Toronto *Star*, 26 April 1998, B1.

32  Sherritt International, *Annual Report*, 2000, 23, http://www.sherritt.com/ Investor_Relations/Financial_Reports/Annual_Reports.html (accessed September 2007).

33  J. De Cordoba and C. Vizthum, 'Canadian Woes with Cuba,' *Wall Street Journal*, 28 June 1999.

34  International Labour Organization, 'ILO Declaration on Fundamental Principles and Rights of Work,' http://www.ilo.org/public/english/10ilc/ ilc86/com-dtxt.htm.

35  Charles Lane, 'Too Friendly with Castro,' Montreal *Gazette*, 3 April 1998; and Arnold Beichman, 'Castro's Curious Canadian Comforters,' Washington *Times*, 22 March 1996.

36 See L. Pease, 'David Atlee Phillips, Clay Shaw and Freeport Sulphur,' in
   *Probe magazine*, 3, no. 3 (1996), for an exploration of the initial nationalization and the events surrounding it.
37 Archibald R.M. Ritter, 'The Tax Regime for Micro-Enterprise in Cuba,'
   *CEPAL Review*, no. 71, United Nations: Economic Commission for Latin
   America and the Caribbean, August 2000, 139–56.
38 The EDC ensured repayment of the loans by encouraging the earmarking
   of funds generated from an airport-exit tax paid in the main by tourists on
   their return flights from Cuba.
39 Citizenship and Immigration Canada, Immigration Overview: Permanent
   and Temporary Residents, Facts and Figures, *Canada – Permanent Residents
   from South and Central America and the United States by Top Source Countries*,
   2005, http://www.cic.gc.ca/ENGLISH/resources/statistics/facts2006/
   permanent/15.asp (accessed 2 February 2007); and Cuba, Oficina Nacional
   de Estadisticas, Anuario Estadistica, 2005 (Table II.21).
40 Among the Canadian exports that may increase with normalization, accompanied by economic recovery, are traditional ones such as fertilizers
   (potash), cereals, animal-feed stocks, wood and paper, and non-ferrous
   and fabricated metals.

# 11 Canada-Cuba Relations: A Multiple-Personality Foreign Policy

MARK ENTWISTLE

In a recent book on Cuban foreign policy, Michael Erisman wrote, 'Canada has always had an unusual relationship with Cuba.'[1] His brief and specific characterization is loaded with content: an *unusual* relationship that has *always* been that way.

The relationship between Canada and Cuba has indeed been one of the more unique in Canadian diplomacy, not necessarily because of the substance of the relationship itself at any given moment, but because of its broader contours and setting. It is a case study in foreign policy and international-relations analysis that operates at different levels and on multiple terrains. It is one of the most politicized of Canada's foreign relationships.

Beginning with the succinct historical scene set by the co-editors of this volume, Robert Wright and Lana Wylie, in their Introduction, the contributors have highlighted in different ways this complexity. In some cases, the focus has been temporal, such as Dennis Molinaro's treatment of the Diefenbaker period, Greg Donaghy and Mary Halloran's look at the Trudeau years, or John Kirk and Peter McKenna's overview of the so-called recent 'Special Period.' In other cases, it has been functional, such as Arch Ritter's thorough analysis of the commercial and economic relationship. Hal Klepak has reminded us of the larger Latin American context of Canada's relations with Cuba.

It is a sustained relationship over time, and across the tumultuous divide of the 1959 Cuban Revolution, which makes it a unique lens through which to measure the behaviour of Fidel Castro's government over his almost five decades in power in Cuba. Don Munton and David Vogt have provided a quite unprecedented insider look at how Canadian diplomats on the ground tried to make sense of what was happening as Fidel Castro came to power and what it meant for Canadian interests.

Canada was the only major Western democracy not to sever full diplomatic relations with Cuba in the wake of the Revolution. Along with Mexico, it was the only other country of the Americas to remain in Havana when other Latin American governments left. In this sense, Cuba also, therefore, represents a story of some grit in Canadian diplomatic history, one that shows Canada's determination to be somewhere outside the traditional comfort zone of friendly and likeminded allies. In the early revolutionary period, Canada found itself really quite alone in Havana among Cuba's newfound friends from the various communist and 'national liberation' worlds.

The Canada-Cuba relationship is, above all, a human encounter that is surprisingly adaptable. Canadians and Cubans have been dealing with each other for two hundred years. At first, they bought and sold sugar, fish, and rum. Later, Canadian bankers financed the sugar trade and other business. The Royal Bank of Canada opened its first branch in Havana in 1899, bought its first Cuban bank in Santiago de Cuba in 1903, and followed the next year with purchase of the Banco del Commercio de Havana, all before the bank even moved its headquarters in Canada from Halifax to Montreal. By the mid-1920s, it was the single largest bank in Cuba, with sixty-five offices across the island, owing to the collapse of the Cuban financial sector in 1921 in the wake of the sugar industry's greedy over-expansion. The Royal Bank was in fact one of only two solvent institutions left standing (the other was the National City Bank of New York).[2] When gunmen wanted to strike a bank in the climate of political *gangsterismo* that enveloped Cuba in the later 1940s, they chose to attack the Royal Bank of Canada main branch in Havana in 1948.

The Bank of Nova Scotia had a smaller but also significant presence, including a majestic headquarters building in the centre of Havana's financial district with the floral emblems of Canada's provinces embedded in the marble floor of the central lobby. In December 1960, when Fidel Castro nationalized the foreign banks, he treated the Canadian banks differently from all the rest, paying compensation in cash rather than the usual long-term and never-issued state bonds. It has been suggested, but not documented, that the Royal Bank, alone among banks, had been permitted to repatriate its capital as part of the nationalization process.

Sir William Van Horne, of Canadian Pacific Railway fame, was a key developer of the early Cuban national railway system, learning his lessons from the Canadian experience in founding the Cuba Company in 1900 and pushing all the limits to build the transnational Cuban railway from Havana to Santiago de Cuba. As early as 1906, financiers in Montreal controlled the Havana Electric Railway.

Maritimers have known Cubans in more recent times when the Cuban fishing fleet put into port while seeking protein on the Grand Banks. Farmers in Quebec knew Cubans when they came to Canada to buy beef cattle, breeding stock, and bull semen in the 1960s and 1970s. Still more recently, Canadian business people have engaged in various sectors, including the Cuban biotechnology industry, as Lana Wylie has pointed out in her detailed study in this volume of the health and biotech sector in Cuba.

It is estimated that over 800,000 Canadian tourists visited Cuba in 2008, many of them, as has always been the case, from French-speaking Quebec. Cuban tourism officials predict that that number could increase significantly as better attractions like golf courses are added to the tourism sector. Already Cuba is the second most popular foreign destination for Canadians after Mexico; for example, as travel to Mexico fell 14.5 per cent during the period January-March 2006, that decline was offset by a 33.9 per cent increase in Canadian tourists to Cuba in the same period.[3] Canadian tourists enter Cuba through modern airports at Havana, Varadero, or Holguin built by a Canadian company, and most meet Cubans in various ways.

Canadian oil and gas field engineers and workers commute back and forth regularly between Cuba and Alberta. Representatives of various religious bodies and non-governmental organizations (NGOs) have been in Cuba for many years. The personal housekeepers to the papal nuncio in Havana are traditionally lay sisters from a Quebec order.

Anecdotal descriptions of the varied character of the relationship could continue on at some length. But the point here is that the human dimension is more important to understanding the nature of the Canada-Cuba relationship than any statistics of import-export volumes. As we will see later, this relationship is also a case study in the effect of assumed values, perceptions, worldview, and other 'soft' factors on the analysis of foreign policy. Those impressions held by everyday Canadians, whether business people or tourists, inform government in a kind of feedback loop in the development of Canadian policy on Cuba.

The strongest impressions are formed by familiarity. Most Canadians are not fearful in any way of the cultural encounter with Cubans; they do it daily in many spheres of activity and despite the difference in language and culture. And they do this because they can. After the rupture of the U.S. relationship with Cuba following the Revolution and the imposition of the travel ban preventing U.S. citizens from visiting the island, that kind of familiarity has been lost for several subsequent generations of Americans. Interestingly, Cuba is the only country in the world to which Americans are prohibited from travelling without the express permission of their government: for North Korea, Iran, Syria, Iraq, Libya, Vietnam, there is no problem.

One could imagine that the unhindered travel of Americans to the island, breeding the familiarity that comes from contact, would act as a similar mitigating factor on U.S. policy over time as the same kind of feedback loop was put in place. It is a conventional wisdom, even in official American circles, that, if the travel ban were to be lifted, the entire architecture of the U.S. trade and investment embargo against Cuba would start to fall away. This is the real reason why the hard-line elements of the Cuban American community in south Florida and New Jersey oppose so strenuously attempts by several members of Congress to lift or loosen the travel ban. The latter believe it to be un-American and unconstitutional. While doubtless true that American tourism would go some way to supporting the structures of the Castro brothers' state, the most subversive idea for Cuban American interests is the dismantling of the embargo from the inside on the United States side of the equation. Such a travel scenario would engage 'mainstream' Americans and crystallize for the first time in a long time a counter-vailing domestic political voice to the traditional Cuban American hard-line elite.

In working to isolate the defining characteristics of the 'unusual' Canada-Cuba relationship, let us start by looking at what that relationship principally *is not*.

It is not at least two things.

Trade alone does not drive Canada's foreign policy on Cuba. Trade is one important component of a much more diversified encounter between Canadians and Cubans. In his look in this book inside the origins of Canada's Cuba policy under Prime Minister John Diefenbaker, Dennis Molinaro gives us tantalizing glimpses of the internal bureaucratic machinations to advance Canadian arms sales to Cuba. But, in the end, policy was made on much different grounds related to the Cold War environment and Canada-U.S. relations.

Over the years, it has been argued that the protection of Canadian trade and economic opportunities is the keystone explanation of Canadian actions and foreign policy on Cuba. A more cynical variant of the economic-determinism school suggests that Canada has wanted from the beginning to secure its trade advantage given the absence of American competition on the island. Most treatments of the relationship have contained *de rigueur* sections on the ebbing and flowing of the annual bilateral trade statistics.

The fact is that Canada has had a long historic trading relationship with Cuba. Much useful detail can be found in John Kirk and Peter McKenna's *Canada-Cuba Relations: The Other Good Neighbor Policy*, still the reigning primer on the relationship.[4] Trade grew steadily through to the 1930s, when it logically dropped in economic depression to the point where the annual figures at the start of the Second World War were about half what they were in the 1920s. With the signing of the General Agreement on Tariffs and Trade by both countries in 1947, the trading regime became more ordered and easier. The 1970s were a high period; trade increased 13.5 times, from $48 million in 1969 to $648 million in 1981. It was in the middle of this activity that Pierre Trudeau made his 1976 state visit to Cuba. By the mid-1980s, Canadian business was facing increasingly tough competition – from Europeans and Latin Americans, since it was not even in competition with the Soviet Bloc's trading system.[5] The last 'spike' of trade activity occurred in the mid-1990s, when annual bilateral trade more than doubled between 1994 and 1996 from $319 million to $691 million.[6]

But it is also true that our trade with Cuba is modest when placed in the global context of Canadian trading patterns with leading partners. Given that Canada does 83 per cent of its annual two-way trade with the United States, that it trades more with Japan than with all of Latin America and the Caribbean combined, and that Cuba is Canada's sixth-largest trade partner in Latin America, trade with Cuba hardly ranks on the global Canadian radar screen.

On the other side of the ledger, Canada might be Cuba's second-largest trading partner overall (driven by nickel-ore exports from Cuba to be processed in a jointly owned refinery in Canada), but it is fifth among import suppliers, behind China, Venezuela, Spain, and the United States.[7] China's place is secured by mass imports of pots and pans, simple kitchen stoves, and, most recently, buses and trains. Venezuela is, of course, tied to oil supplies. Spain is a traditional trading partner. But the United States currently has been selling more to Cuba than does Canada – even with a trade embargo in place and with an active diplomatic campaign around the world to discourage other countries from trading with Cuba.

Opening its embargo in the formal context of a humanitarian response to hurricane relief for Cuba, the United States has since 2001 sold approximately US$2.3 billion worth of largely food products to the Cuban government (for payment in cash only without the need to extend credit as do other suppliers). In 2005 American producers sold $338 million worth of American chicken, grains, rice, and other foodstuffs to Cuba. In the first quarter of 2006, the United States sold three times as much food to Cuba as Brazil, becoming at least temporarily Cuba's single largest supplier of food and agricultural products. U.S. newspapers detail many such cases, such as one where a small-time meat reseller from Montgomery, Alabama, exported nine million pounds of ham to Cuba over an eight-month period,[8] and dozens of U.S. companies again flocked under legal Treasury Department licence to Havana for the 2008 version of the annual agricultural trade show, feverishly seeking business.

Inherent in the logic of 'realists' who believe that protection of trade interests has historically driven Canada's Cuba policy should be the assumption that a government that makes decisions based on trade, and is preoccupied by trade, would undertake actions to facilitate that trade. The reality has been the opposite in practice and the track record uneven. It is business people and entrepreneurs themselves who drive the trade independently and who often operate far from any official government support that exists. Many complain, in fact, that the Canadian government does not support them and at times in the past has even attempted actively to dissuade them from doing business in Cuba.[9] As a result of relatively modest Cuban arrears, principal export-support mechanisms like the lines of credit and facilities of the Export Development Corporation (EDC) have been largely unavailable to Canadian exporters for many years. Some EDC coverage has been tentatively reinstated recently as the Cubans have made efforts to pay off some of the arrears.

After the April 1998 official visit to Cuba by former prime minister Jean Chrétien, the Canada-Cuba relationship actually went into an official deep freeze on both sides for several years, and Canadian business continued to do what it does with virtually no government support. The application of Canadian trade instruments has never been muscular, or as dynamic as one would expect from a government that has supposedly based its Cuba foreign policy on trade promotion. Canadian ministers of trade seldom visit Cuba. And, if the objective had been theoretically to protect advantage and seize ground while American competition was kept out by their unilateral trade embargo, this has not worked very well because, as we have seen above, Americans are already in Cuba in a significant way and taking business away from Canadians.

An unexpected consequence of the disproportionate attention to trade in analysing the Canada-Cuba relationship has been to feed the criticism of Canadian policy by hard-line Cuban American leaders, who see the relationship as exploitative of the Cuban people and based on crass material gain. Frank Calzon, executive director of the Center for a Free Cuba and the original architect of the Washington lobbying effort of the Cuban American National Foundation, provides a typical hard-line Cuban American assessment of Canadian business in Cuba. He describes Canadian business people in Cuba as 'a handful of fortune seekers' and the way Canadians do business as follows: 'It is how the old imperial powers dealt with the natives of Latin America and Africa.'[10] Perhaps only in the hard-line Cuban American community is Canada perceived as acting as an imperial and colonial power.

Canada-Cuba relations are also *not* purely bilateral, a theme that runs consistently through *Our Place in the Sun.* One can identify some narrowly and truly bilateral elements, such as quota allocations in fisheries relations, but almost every aspect of the encounter has an echo or shadow that plays out in the Canada-U.S. relationship. Since the U.S.-Cuba relationship is so hostile, almost anything Canada does in or with Cuba can be suspect south of the 49th parallel.

So it is rather a triangulated Canada-Cuba-United States relationship, in which the asymmetrically powerful mutual neighbour hovers in the background and affects the conduct of the Canada-Cuba side of the triangle in myriad and complex ways. In some ways, the relationship with Cuba is functionally a subset of the Canada-U.S. relationship. In the same way, in the practice of Cuban foreign policy, the relationship with Canada is best understood as being related to the relationship with the United States. In fact, at the Cuban Foreign Ministry in Havana, this approach is secured organizationally by combining geographic relations with both the United States and Canada as the only clients in a single North American Department.

The interplay with the United States on Cuba can be formal or informal, more or less political, tangible or less so, depending on circumstances at any given moment. Sometimes the effect derives from self-imposed deliberations by Canadian policy makers who must consider possible U.S. reactions in making decisions to safeguard the enormous Canadian interest in the Canada-U.S. relationship, often from domestic political calculations in Canada. Greg Donaghy and Mary Halloran inform us that the Canadian government briefed the U.S. government on Pierre Trudeau's plans to visit Cuba a good six months before he went, and then was warned off the visit shortly before it occurred. John Kirk, Peter McKenna, and Robert Wright note that it was, in fact, the Americans who 'leaked' news of Jean Chrétien's own visit to Havana since they had been briefed in advance. The views of the United States have long been sought on any Canadian review of its Cuba policy by the Department of Foreign Affairs and International Trade, dating to at least the late 1970s. Sometimes the U.S. government has expressly lobbied the government of Canada to sever its trade and investment ties with Cuba in order to isolate the Castro brothers.

Occasionally, in the psychology of Canada-U.S. relations, Canadians can slip paradigms and take on, if temporarily, the U.S. perspective and perception on the Cuba issue. A case in point was the decision by former prime minister Chrétien to make human rights the aggressive centre point of his agenda with Fidel Castro before and during his 1998 'working' visit to Cuba, beyond the pro forma submission of a list of names of specific political prisoners to be released. In his contribution to this volume, Robert Wright dissects the case study of the Chrétien visit, and the assumptions underlying it, in painstaking and illuminating detail.

If the objective of that visit had been to accomplish something concrete, it went badly and affected the entire relationship for many years afterward. Indeed, Fidel Castro was still bringing up the Chrétien visit years later – as recently as December 2007 in a discussion, published in the Cuban communist party newspaper *Granma,* of Cuba's adherence to international human rights treaties. The net result of this very rare and valuable official encounter between heads of government was to achieve practically nothing.

The Canadian side had misunderstood the realities and dynamics of Cuban internal politics, and miscalculated its range of manoeuvrability with Fidel Castro in saying one thing in public about engagement and dialogue but delivering another message in private. With Fidel Castro that margin is very slim. Former European Union foreign affairs commissioner Manuel Marin, a Spaniard, had made the exact same discovery in his tension-filled February 1996 visit to Havana. Marin's experience should have warned the Canadians what to expect.[11]

A Canadian prime minister must certainly have human rights on the agenda. But Chrétien had not played to the strengths of long-standing Canadian Cuba policy to consolidate progress on structural engagement. He seemed rather to have changed course in favour of an approach that sounded a lot like it could have been crafted at the U.S. State Department. Perhaps the prime minister was calculating what he thought needed to be done to offset expected American criticism of his visit, but no amount of human rights championing with the Cubans will satisfy political Washington because their objectives are different. As likely, he simply lost sight of the nature of Canadian policy and what that policy could do in real terms, and, therefore, slipped into the U.S. paradigm of dealing with Cuba.

Sometimes the shadow of the U.S. falls on the Cuban side of the equation, where the Canadian arm of the triangle serves Cuba's interests in its own complicated relationship with the United States. Prime Minister Chrétien's 1998 state visit to Cuba also provides an example here. In his welcoming remarks to the Canadian prime minister on the tarmac of José Martí international airport in Havana, Fidel Castro defended the revolutionary status quo and launched a fierce anti-American attack.[12] With a grim-faced Jean Chrétien at his side, the Cuban president took targeted, conscious, and tactical advantage of the presence of the leader of one of the Americans' best friends and allies to make his comments; the juxtaposition with the Canadian relationship added communications value beyond the usual Castro critique of his American opponent. It is impossible to divorce the bilateral from this bigger nexus.

So what are the defining characteristics of this *unusual* Canadian relationship with Cuba? The formal definition of Canada's objectives in Cuba, as articulated by the Canadian government, contains several elements: to encourage a peaceful transformation of Cuba to a society with representative political institutions, with respect for individual human rights and with an open economy.[13] But there are equally important and unspoken components of that policy: heightened sensitivity to sovereignty issues, willingness to engage in dialogue free of value judgments, and, most important, focus on the future of Cuban society regardless of whether Fidel Castro and his brother Raúl remain in power or not.

The approach is generally described in recent times as a policy of *constructive engagement,* using a term actually coined by U.S. President Jimmy Carter in the context of the struggle against apartheid in South Africa.[14]

The fundamental difference between this Canadian approach and that of the United States is that U.S. policy is designed to provoke regime change through isolation and active interventionist support of a political opposition (as loaded with unexpected consequences as that is), while Canada is wholly disinterested in provoking regime change and deals with the structure of Cuban society as it is. Canada employs a diplomatic mechanism for avoiding the delicate subject of regime change by generally recognizing states themselves rather than governments. This approach offers much flexibility and provided the framework for Canada to stay in Cuba after 1959.

There is another difference between Canadian and American approaches to Castro's Cuba that gets virtually no attention. Canada tends to see Cuba in the context of broader regional security, as Hal Klepak has reminded us in this book, and the danger that a collapse in Cuba would pose to hemispheric stability and cooperation. If a post-Fidel succession or transition ended in violence or chaos, the pressures and tensions in the hemisphere would mount in the face of a polarizing situation. For this reason, Canada is more prone to care about national reconciliation in Cuba and the formation of a successor generation to lead a post-Fidel Cuba towards a more open and prosperous place. The United States government has a different perspective. At least rhetorically, it demands an end to the Castro era regardless of the cost, oddly enough because of its own private fears of mass migration from a Cuba in crisis. Its policies are intended to work in that direction; it never speaks of national reconciliation between different parts of the Cuban family. The United States views Cuba as a stand-alone and long-standing bilateral irritant in its own backyard and assumes a hemispheric perspective only when viewing the so-called 'Bolivarian axis' of the Castros and Venezuela's Hugo Chavez.

The reasons for the differences between the manifestations of Canadian and American policies on Cuba lie in history, different domestic politics, and different political cultures, values, and self-identities. We will return to this point later. The differentiation is important because it has implications even for assessing the effectiveness of relative policies. Much of the rush to assess and compare the results of the respective policies ends up comparing apples and oranges and is, therefore, of dubious value. If the effectiveness of Canadian engagement is being judged against the criteria established by U.S. policy, it cannot but be seen as a failure because the Castro brothers are still in charge. But this is a dead end.

Those who criticize engagement as having not delivered political reform in Castro's Cuba, including many Canadians, are unclear about the reality of the situation. No outside foreign policy on Cuba – Canadian, American, European, Mexican, Venezuelan, Chinese, or that of the Vatican – is capable of delivering political change by leverage with members of the Cuban political leadership. This is because the latter are best understood as being nationalist survivalists rather than ideologues, largely impervious to outside influence, who counterbalance relationships with some considerable agility and go to the openings they require at any given point in search of alternative partners. They engage in a process of continual 'diversification of reliance.' When the United States, Canada, Europe, and others demanded too much, history provided with serendipity Hugo Chavez and the Bolivarian subsidy to replace the old Soviet subsidy and much of the direct foreign investment of the mid-1990s. If the pendulum were to swing back in future to the global financial markets, where the prospect of returns from Cuba as a frontier emerging market caused investors to take greater risks and lower demands, the current Venezuelan position could wane.

It is simply not in the power of Canadian 'constructive engagement' to affect political reform, improve human rights, or open the economy in Cuba. Many Canadian policy makers have succumbed to the illusion and most Canadian of myths that the so-called special relationship resulting from over sixty years of unbroken diplomatic relations with Cuba confers on Canada some special ability to leverage this presence to elicit change, or to secure special trade preference. This is not the case. Political change will take place only when the Cuban political leadership, in its calculation of its own domestic politics, deems it to be in its interest. Witness the intrusion of U.S. commercial competition into the traditional Canadian food and agricultural trade sector, with the explicit encouragement of the Cuban authorities. The latter will trade with whoever gives them the best deal or best meets the national interest.

Robert Wright has provided us with a quote from Roberto Robaina, the former foreign minister of Cuba, a native of Pinar del Rio who spoke so quickly that even Cubans had a hard time understanding him at times, that sums up the Cuban attitude in a nutshell. Here Robaina was not hard to understand: 'We are not a case for Canada to check. Canada is not for us a teacher that gives us orders or certifies or decertifies us.'

So why should Canada have a relationship with Cuba at all? What worth is there in the relationship beyond providing consular services to the hundreds of thousands of Canadian citizens who vacation on the island each year?

There is much value to the stability of Cuba's post-Fidel future in having a partnership with a North American democracy that is not hostile, in providing exposure to different experiences to talented Cuban managers, especially a younger generation in their formative period, and in providing reassurance that succession (or even transition) will be in the company of foreigners who have a long-term and continuous involvement with their nation. In the period of some limited economic reform in the mid-1990s, Cuban officials often declared that their long-term economic model for the future looked like Canada,[15] and the pendulum could swing back to this same managerial class. So there is a track record of influence through presence. This is the meaning and consequence of Canada's policy. Only in the future will it be possible to judge its effectiveness fairly.

In fact, the term *constructive engagement* itself is misleading and does not capture the realistic objectives and real value of Canadian policy on Cuba. Use of the word 'constructive' implies ability to influence current structures beyond what is possible and is imbued with the mistaken assumption that Cuba is an isolated country waiting for readmission into the global community (with Canada's friendly push). Cuba is not isolated and we have seen this assumption appear throughout this volume in various quotes from Canadian politicians and government officials. To borrow from Dennis Molinaro's title of his study of the Diefenbaker origins of Canada's Cuba policy, *calculated engagement* might be more apt.

Cuban interest in Canadian experience and models has indeed a historical lineage. In the late 1860s, as fledgling Cuban *criollo* nationalism was manifested in an autonomy movement, the model that liberal leaders of the Cuban community proposed to Spain was one copying the relationship between Canada and Britain, encapsulated in the British North America Act. What these early Cuban nationalists were seeking was really a Spanish North America Act. They wanted colonial self-government and responsible government without cutting ties with the metropolis. It never came, of course. Yet, after the subsequent devastation of the first war of independence (the so-called Ten Years' War of 1868–78), and the shift from support for independence back to autonomy in the 1880s, it was again the Canadian model presented to Madrid as the solution.[16]

Canada-Cuba relations are at least two other things. First, they are a political science case study in the role of values, perceptions, and national identities in international relations and the analysis of foreign policy. Lana Wylie has started to lay down some important markers in this direction in both her forthcoming book, based on her doctoral dissertation, and her article 'Perceptions and Foreign Policy: A Comparative Study of Canadian and American Policy toward Cuba.'[17] The contemporary discourse on Canadian foreign policy has arguably been too heavily loaded to values-substance and could do with a course correction back to more discussion of the national interest. But Cuba is one example where, to really understand the dynamics of the relationship, values and identity must be seen as a key part of the puzzle. If not, how else to explain the striking and curious affinity of Canadians for Cubans, and vice versa, a familiarity that has held over time, across culture and language? A northern people should logically and naturally have little in common with a Latino Caribbean people. But it is not so.

And, against the backdrop of the triangular Canada-Cuba-U.S. interplay, this approach also provides a fuller explanation of why Canadian and American policies on Cuba differ so profoundly. History has bequeathed two different sets of assumptions and perspectives on world affairs to Canada and the United States, even when they might agree on the substance of specific issues, like the fight against terrorism and so on. In its narrative of nation, the United States perceives itself as the beacon of freedom and democracy with an almost messianic destiny to spread its governmental model. Derivative from this assumption is its treatment of the hemisphere of the Americas, at least philosophically, as its own protectorate based on hub-and-spoke bilateralism, from the Monroe Doctrine to the present day. So Cuba as run by Fidel Castro flies in the face of American perception and self-identity on two counts, thereby fuelling hostility. The fact that Castro is still there after ten U.S. presidents have come and gone is especially grating because of the implication of American powerlessness to 'fix a problem' ninety miles offshore dating from the Bay of Pigs fiasco.

There is none of this in the case of Canada. Whether national myth or not, many Canadians perceive Canada as internationalist, an arbiter, and an example of effective democracy, but not *the* model. It is a country of the Americas, one among equals. So the continued presence in itself of the Castro brothers does not bother Canada. It is rather natural that the two Cuba policies diverge.

A further part of the package is the impact of the psychology of *exceptionalism* in the national identity. Americans in general are inculcated to believe that they are members of a special nation endowed with historic greatness and destiny. But a strong strain of exceptionalism also exists in Cuban intellectual history, where Cubans have thought themselves more advanced, more progressive, somehow better than other Latin Americans, whether it be in the number of television sets, telephones, or cars per capita in the 1950s or the global impact of Cuban music. This sense of special destiny is personified in its most heightened state by Fidel Castro, who has pushed Cuba by every means to punch above its weight in global affairs, sometimes spreading mischief, sometimes to considerable effect in the international system. It is conceivable that Fidel Castro sees himself as the inheritor of the vision and mission of a bigger Latin American nation, anointed with the memory of José Martí and even Simon Bolivar. One of the reasons for the particularly jarring and conflictive relationship between the United States and Cuba, beyond domestic presidential electoral politics and the issue of confiscated property (which will inevitably be negotiated), lies in the meeting of an exceptionalist United States and an exceptionalist Cuban president. Canada might be morally sanctimonious, but it is not exceptionalist in its national narrative. So, in an opposite reflection of the Cuba-U.S. relationship, Canada does not provoke the tension of exceptionalist-on-exceptionalist politics.

One additional answer to the riddle of Canadians' and Cubans' mutual affinity is to observe that both Canada and Cuba are elusive nations, to borrow the characterization of Cuban nationalism offered by Damian Fernandez, director of the Cuban Research Institute of Florida International University.[18] The nationalism of both countries is a piece of unfinished business, still evolving and adapting, with different constituent parts promoting their own distinct narratives, making the distillation of nation rather flimsy at times. In Canada, to this day there has been no better imagery produced than the 'two solitudes' of life in French and English Canada (and this does not even reflect the added ingredients of the New Canada of immigration and aboriginal identity). This is analogous to the two solitudes of Cuban life – African and Spanish ancestry (which does not even reflect the hybrid 'brown' identity of the majority mulatto population).

In search of a modern unifying narrative for identity, Canadians invented internationalism and peacekeeping. In their parallel search, Cubans in the Castro era invented the rhetoric of global social justice and national liberation. But, most important, a large part of the self-identity of both nations is derived from simply *not being American* – historically, psychologically, and politically. It is a nationalism largely of not being, rather than being. It is a nationalism that produces a hypersensitivity to issues of national sovereignty, a vapour that both Canadians and Cubans inhale to the same degree and in the same way.

In his book *On Becoming Cuban,* historian Louis A. Pérez describes the interaction of Cuban nationalism with the dominant American presence in Cuba over one hundred years from the mid-nineteenth to midtwentieth centuries in ways that would be very familiar to and resonate with Canadians.[19] Cubans and Canadians understand each other on a deeper, at times subconscious, psychological plane that transcends language and culture. Arguably, the northern Canadian and the Latino Caribbean Cuban know each other more intimately than the Cuban and the American, especially since the Americans have not been on the island for almost five decades and, even when they were dominant in every imaginable way, treated Cuba as an exotic Other.

It is in this context that the shadow of former prime minister Pierre Trudeau has defined Canada-Cuba relations since his historic state visit to the island over thirty years ago, the first by a NATO leader after the 1959 Revolution. Even when Trudeau later visited Havana towards the end of his life, his relationship with Fidel Castro was cast as two equals sleeping with the elephant (in fact, Trudeau was probably one of a literal handful of foreigners to whom Castro really paid attention). Castro, an aficionado of American politics himself, valued Trudeau's assessments of U.S. motivations and attitudes.[20] The intellectual intimacy of Trudeau's relationship with Castro was applied as a metaphor for the entire relationship. Former prime minister Chrétien, who had himself lived in the political shadow of Trudeau for decades in Canadian politics, was perhaps motivated to try to repeat the imagery of the Trudeau visit in 1998. But, as we have seen, he slipped paradigms. Instead of trying to help interpret possibilities to Fidel Castro, he tried to be like the Americans. Historian Robert Wright treats the Trudeau-Castro relationship with unprecedented analysis and detail in his recent book *Three Nights in Havana: Pierre Trudeau, Fidel Castro and the Cold War World.*[21]

Lastly, Canada-Cuba relations are a case study of the interplay between domestic politics and foreign policy. One of the interpretations of foreign policy behaviour involves bureaucratic rivalry. In other words, a foreign policy outcome is the result of internecine struggles between different state agencies, each with its own interests, in which a dominant view emerges. There certainly is an element of this internal bureaucratic rivalry in the Canada-Cuba relationship, where, for example, the civil-aviation authorities or narcotics-enforcement agents of the Royal Canadian Mounted Police have a different set of interests and perceptions in dealing with their Cuban counterparts than those charged with global advancement of human rights. In general, the more functional an agency, the more impressed its members are with the technical ability and professionalism of their Cuban counterparts, and the more open to relationships. The often stormy relationship between the former Department of External Affairs and the Canadian International Development Agency over Cuba policy is a perfect case in point, as described by Greg Donaghy and Mary Halloran in their study in this volume of the Trudeau-era relationship. That tension persists to this day. An identical situation applies in the Cuban-American relationship as well, where the institution probably the most open to cooperation with the Cuban government is the U.S. military.

However, a more useful and sophisticated model seems to be that postulated in 1988 by Robert Putnam in his article 'Diplomacy and Domestic Politics: The Logic of Two-level Games.'[22] Putnam starts with two basic observations: that 'domestic politics and international relations are often somehow entangled' and that any analysis of foreign policy 'must stress *politics*.' The Canada-Cuba relationship is all about those observations. Canada's foreign policy on Cuba is an intensely political exercise.

The interplay of domestic politics and foreign policy is complex. Sometimes it involves assessment of the impact of Cuba policy on the critical Canada-U.S. relationship, either as the result of overt American interventions or based on prophylactic assessment of how the U.S. *might* react. Sometimes it involves responding to domestic constituencies and interest groups, who have expectations of what Canada should be doing in Cuba. The expectations of different constituencies can themselves be contradictory; for example, church groups can be oriented either to 'solidarity' and humanitarian interest in Cuba or to promotion of human rights. The focus creates markedly different expectations.

Both Cynthia Wright and David Sheinin explore some of the nuanced dynamics of these very constituencies in their studies of the activities of progressive churches and the early solidarity movement (the Fair Play for Cuba Committees) respectively. Cynthia Wright highlights also the early impact of the Cuba question on Quebec sovereignty and nationalist politics. This phenomenon continued into the 1990s, when the Parti Québécois government's 'foreign ministry' maintained its own careful but activist relationship with Cuba under the watchful eye of the federal Canadian government. Sheinin describes how conservative politicians in Canada used Cuba to attempt to discredit political opponents.

Sometimes the politics involves the conscious deployment by the Canadian government of the Cuba relationship to demonstrate and prove the independence of Canadian foreign policy vis-à-vis the United States, when that is deemed useful or necessary. The Canada-Cuba relationship is an indispensable instrument in the sovereignty tool kit. As recently as 3 August 2006, responding to Fidel Castro's provisional transfer of presidential power to his brother Raúl and a junta-like leadership team while recovering from an operation, Canadian Foreign Affairs Minister Peter MacKay used a specific and targeted formulation: 'Canada has always taken a sovereign, independent position vis-à-vis our relations with Cuba, and we'll continue to do so.'[23] The Conservative government of former prime minister Brian Mulroney was broadly assumed in public perception to be among the most 'pro-American' of Canadian governments, yet it was Mulroney who first issued an antidote blocking order in 1992 under the Foreign Extraterritorial Measures Act to try to prevent attempts by the United States to restrict trade between Cuba and U.S.-owned subsidiaries based in Canada. The context was the U.S. Cuban Democracy Act ('Torricelli Bill'). A Liberal government later strengthened the blocking order in 1996 in response to the so-called Helms-Burton law. At that time, Foreign Affairs Minster André Ouellet declared: 'We have made it clear time and again to the U.S. Congress and Administration that Canada will not tolerate any interference in the sovereignty of Canadian laws.'[24]

In Robert Putnam's conceptualization, governments operate at two levels or at two tables simultaneously – negotiation with the foreign partner and negotiation with domestic constituencies who have an interest in the policy or its implications. The permutations and overlays are multiple, and governments act to maximize what he calls the 'win-set' on the domestic political side to shape its foreign policy. Canada's relationship with Cuba fits this model well. The Canadian government, in an effort to create and sustain the widest possible win-set, constantly trades off the interests of domestic constituencies and bureaucratic players against one another. That exercise has led for decades to the policy of engagement rather than isolation.

An example of the two-table process at work was the negotiation with the Cubans of the fourteen-point action plan to guide the Canada-Cuba relationship, which was signed in 1997 but negotiated painstakingly over months beforehand.[25] Canada's win-set needed to contain elements related to human rights and political liberalization to meet the expectations of domestic human rights constituencies and to mute any adverse impact on the Canada-U.S. relationship. The Cuban win-set needed to include humanitarian food relief and technical-economic cooperation. The result was a carefully balanced roadmap for the relationship that opened unprecedented new ground, such as public discussion in Cuba of human rights, legal reform, and transparency of parliamentary institutions. Business interests were also addressed. The process was anchored in the domestic politics of both countries.

Canada is not alone among countries where Cuba is, in essence, a domestic political issue. In the United States, the issue is related directly to presidential electoral politics. In Spain, Cuba policy can create crisis for governments against the background of historical colonial memory and a complicated contemporary relationship. In Mexico, and even France, there are echoes of the same phenomenon.

In conclusion, Canada-Cuba relations are many things. They sit at the nexus of domestic politics and foreign policy, they reflect the core of national identities, they navigate the often-conflicting expectations of multiple domestic constituencies, and they are a human encounter. The relationship is different things to different people, and much of it happens outside the purview of government. It is a quintessentially Canadian foreign policy that has shown durability and a sustained national self-confidence over time.

Of what value to the world community is the Canadian relationship with Cuba? Given the embedded hostility of the U.S.-Cuba relationship as the legacy of a history that goes well beyond fixation with Fidel Castro and that can lead to serious miscalculation, perhaps a dose of dull but sensible Canadian 'peace, order and good government' can in some small way contribute to stability in the Caribbean and the hemisphere. Such value can be obtained only if the government of Canada understands its historic role and its limitations.

NOTES

The author wishes to thank and acknowledge the assistance of the Canadian Defence and Foreign Affairs Institute (CDFAI) of which he is a Fellow.

1  Michael H. Erisman, *Cuba's Foreign Relations in a Post-Soviet World* (Gainesville: University Press of Florida, 2000).
2  Hugh Thomas, *Cuba, or the Pursuit of Freedom,* rev. ed. (New York: Da Capo Press, 1998 [1971]), 464–6, 548.

3  See http://www.statcan.ca/Daily/English/060829/d060829b.htm.
4  John M. Kirk and Peter McKenna, *Cuba-Canada Relations: The Other Good Neighbor Policy* (Gainesville: University Press of Florida, 1997).
5  Ibid., 17–19.
6  Gillian McGillivray, 'Trading with the "Enemy": Canadian-Cuban Relations in the 1990s,' Trinity University Occasional Papers, no. 15, December 1997 (Trinity University, Washington, D.C.), 4.
7  Agriculture and Agri-Food Canada, 'Past, Present and Future Reports: Cuba,' www.ats.agr.ca/latin/4055_e.htm.
8  Ian Katz, 'United States Has Become Island's Top Food Supplier,' South Florida *Sun Sentinel*, 18 June 2006.
9  Numerous conversations between the author and Canadian business people from 1993 to 2006.
10  See note from Frank Calzon under title 'Subject: Helms/Burton Law' distributed by CubaNet, http://www.cubanet.org/CNews/y96/jun96/27e1.html.
11  Michael Bell et al., 'Back to the Future? Canada's Experience with Constructive Engagement in Cuba,' Institute for Cuban and Cuban-American Studies Occasional Paper Series, September 2002 (ICCAS, University of Miami), 17.
12  Carlos Alberto Montaner, *Journey to the Heart of Cuba: Life as Fidel Castro* (New York: Algora Publishing, 2001), 183.
13  Bell et al., 'Back to the Future?' 4.
14  Peter McKenna and John Kirk, 'Canada, Cuba and "Constructive Engagement" in the 1990s,' in Heather Nicol, ed., *Canada, the US and Cuba: Helms-Burton and Its Aftermath*, Martello papers (Centre for International Relations, Queen's University, Kingston, Ont., 1999), 60.
15  Various personal conversations between the author and diverse Cuban officials in Cuba from 1993 to 1997.
16  Montaner, *Journey to the Heart of Cuba*, 29–31.
17  Lana L. Wylie, 'A Comparison of American and Canadian Foreign Policies: The Significance of Identities, Values and Perceptions on Policy toward Cuba,' PhD thesis, University of Massachusetts at Amherst, 2003; 'Perceptions and Foreign Policy: A Comparative Study of Canadian and American Foreign Policy,' *Canadian Foreign Policy*, 12, no. 1 (2004).
18  Damian Fernandez and Madeline Camara Betancourt, 'Interpretations of National Identity,' in Damian Fernandez and Madeline Camara Betancourt, eds., *Cuba, the Elusive Nation: Interpretations of National Identity* (Gainesville: University Press of Florida, 2000).

19 Louis A. Perez, Jr, *On Becoming Cuban: Identity, Nationality and Culture* (Chapel Hill: University of North Carolina Press, 1999).

20 Personal conversations between Trudeau and Castro respectively and the author, and dinner conversations between Trudeau and Castro in Havana as witnessed directly by the author from 1995 to 1996.

21 Robert Wright, *Three Nights in Havana: Pierre Trudeau, Fidel Castro and the Cold War World* (Toronto: HarperCollins Canada, 2007).

22 Robert D. Putnam, 'Diplomacy and Domestic Politics: The Logic of Two-Level Games,' *International Organization*, 42, no. 3 (1988): 427–60.

23 See Canadian Press, 'Canada Won't Follow U.S. on Cuba: MacKay,' 4 August 2006, www.ctv.ca.

24 See www.parl.gc.ca/37/1/parlbus/chambus/debates.

25 For a copy of the Canada-Cuba fourteen-point plan, negotiated in Havana in 1996 by the author, see Bell, 'Back to the Future?' appendix A, 29–30.

# Index